UNITED NATIONS CONFERENCE ON TRADE AND DEVELOPMENT
GENEVA

TRADE AND DEVELOPMENT REPORT, 2009

Report by the secretariat of the
United Nations Conference on Trade and Development

UNITED NATIONS
New York and Geneva, 2009

Note

- Symbols of United Nations documents are composed of capital letters combined with figures. Mention of such a symbol indicates a reference to a United Nations document.

- The designations employed and the presentation of the material in this publication do not imply the expression of any opinion whatsoever on the part of the Secretariat of the United Nations concerning the legal status of any country, territory, city or area, or of its authorities, or concerning the delimitation of its frontiers or boundaries.

- Material in this publication may be freely quoted or reprinted, but acknowledgement is requested, together with a reference to the document number. A copy of the publication containing the quotation or reprint should be sent to the UNCTAD secretariat.

UNCTAD/TDR/2009

UNITED NATIONS PUBLICATION
Sales No. E.09.II.D.16
ISBN 978-92-1-112776-8 ISSN 0255-4607

Contents

List of tables

List of charts

List of boxes

Classification by country or commodity group

The classification of countries in this *Report* has been adopted solely for the purposes of statistical or analytical convenience and does not necessarily imply any judgement concerning the stage of development of a particular country or area.

The major country groupings used in this *Report* follow the classification by the United Nations Statistical Office (UNSO). They are distinguished as:

» Developed or industrial(ized) countries: the countries members of the OECD (other than Mexico, the Republic of Korea and Turkey) plus the new EU member countries and Israel.

» Transition economies refers to South-East Europe and the Commonwealth of Independent States (CIS).

» Developing countries: all countries, territories or areas not specified above.

The terms "country" / "economy" refer, as appropriate, also to territories or areas.

References to "Latin America" in the text or tables include the Caribbean countries unless otherwise indicated.

References to "sub-Saharan Africa" in the text or tables include South Africa unless otherwise indicated.

For statistical purposes, regional groupings and classifications by commodity group used in this *Report* follow generally those employed in the *UNCTAD Handbook of Statistics 2008* (United Nations publication, sales no. E/F.08.II.D.18) unless otherwise stated. The data for China do not include those for Hong Kong Special Administrative Region (Hong Kong SAR), Macao Special Administrative Region (Macao SAR) and Taiwan Province of China.

Other notes

References in the text to *TDR* are to the *Trade and Development Report* (of a particular year). For example, *TDR 2008* refers to *Trade and Development Report, 2008* (United Nations publication, sales no. E.08.II.D.21).

The term "dollar" ($) refers to United States dollars, unless otherwise stated.

The term "billion" signifies 1,000 million.

The term "tons" refers to metric tons.

Annual rates of growth and change refer to compound rates.

Exports are valued FOB and imports CIF, unless otherwise specified.

Use of a dash (–) between dates representing years, e.g. 1988–1990, signifies the full period involved, including the initial and final years.

An oblique stroke (/) between two years, e.g. 2000/01, signifies a fiscal or crop year.

A dot (.) indicates that the item is not applicable.

Two dots (..) indicate that the data are not available, or are not separately reported.

A dash (-) or a zero (0) indicates that the amount is nil or negligible.

Decimals and percentages do not necessarily add up to totals because of rounding.

Abbreviations

BCBS	Basel Committee on Banking Supervision
BIS	Bank for International Settlements
c.i.f.	cost, insurance and freight
CDM	Clean Development Mechanism
CDO	collateralized debt obligation
CDS	credit default swap
CEA	Commodity Exchange Act
CER	certified emission reduction
CFTC	Commodity Futures Trading Commission (United States)
CIS	Commonwealth of Independent States
CME	Chicago Mercantile Exchange
CO_2	carbon dioxide
COP	Conference of the Parties
COT	Commitments of Traders
DJ-UBSCI	Dow Jones-UBS Commodity Index
ECB	European Central Bank
ECLAC	Economic Commission for Latin America and the Caribbean
EIU	Economist Intelligence Unit
EU	European Union
EU ETS	European Union Greenhouse Gas Emission Trading System
f.o.b.	free on board
FAO	Food and Agriculture Organization of the United Nations
FDI	foreign direct investment
FDIC	Federal Deposit Insurance Corporation (United States)
FSA	Financial Services Authority (United Kingdom)
FSB	Financial Stability Board
FSF	Financial Stability Forum
GDP	gross domestic product
GEF	Global Environment Facility
GFCF	gross fixed capital formation
GHG	greenhouse gas
GNI	gross national income
GNP	gross national product
HIPC	heavily indebted poor country (also HIPC Initiative of the IMF and World Bank)
ICAC	International Cotton Advisory Committee

ICC	International Chamber of Commerce
ICE	Intercontinental Exchange (London, United Kingdom)
IEA	International Energy Agency
IMF	International Monetary Fund
IPCC	Intergovernmental Panel on Climate Change
IPR	intellectual property right
LDC	least developed country
LME	London Metal Exchange
LTCM	Long Term Capital Management
MDG	Millennium Development Goal
NYMEX	New York Mercantile Exchange
ODA	official development assistance
OECD	Organisation for Economic Co-operation and Development
OPEC	Organization of the Petroleum Exporting Countries
OTC	over the counter
R&D	research and development
RER	real exchange rate
S&P GSCI	Standard & Poor's Goldman Sachs Commodity Index
SDR	Special Drawing Right
SNLT	sectoral no-lose target
SPV	special purpose vehicle
TARP	Troubled Assets Relief Program (United States)
TDR	Trade and Development Report
TRIPS	trade-related aspects of intellectual property rights (also WTO TRIPS Agreement)
UNCTAD	United Nations Conference on Trade and Development
UN/DESA	United Nations Department of Economic and Social Affairs
UNDP	United Nations Development Programme
UNEP	United Nations Environment Programme
UNFCCC	United Nations Framework Convention on Climate Change
UNWTO	World Tourism Organization
USDA	United States Department of Agriculture
WESP	World Economic Situation and Prospects
WFP	World Food Programme
WTO	World Trade Organization

OVERVIEW

Speculators may do no harm as bubbles on a steady stream of enterprise. But the position is serious when enterprise becomes the bubble on a whirlpool of speculation. When the capital development of a country becomes a by-product of the activities of a casino, the job is likely to be ill-done. The measure of success attained by Wall Street, regarded as an institution of which the proper social purpose is to direct new investment into the most profitable channels in terms of future yield, cannot be claimed as one of the outstanding triumphs of *laissez-faire* capitalism – which is not surprising, if I am right in thinking that the best brains of Wall Street have been in fact directed towards a different object.

J.M. Keynes, *The General Theory of Employment, Interest and Money* (1936: 159)

A gloomy global outlook

Even before the financial turmoil turned into a full-blown crisis in September 2008, growth of gross domestic product (GDP) had ground to a halt in most developed countries. Subsequently the slowdown turned into a fully-fledged recession, and in 2009 global GDP is expected to fall by more than 2.5 per cent. The crisis is unprecedented in depth and breadth, with virtually no economy left unscathed. Even economies that are expected to grow this year, such as those of China and India, are slowing down significantly compared to previous years.

Starting in the United States subprime mortgage market, the financial crisis spread quickly, infecting the entire United States financial system and, almost simultaneously, the financial markets of other developed countries. No market was spared, from the stock markets and real estate markets of a large number of developed and emerging-market economies, to currency markets and primary commodity markets. The credit crunch following the collapse or near collapse of major financial institutions affected activity in the real economy, which accelerated the fall in private demand, causing the greatest recession since the Great Depression. The crisis has affected most strongly companies, incomes and employment in the financial sector itself, but also in the construction, capital goods and durable consumer goods industries where demand depends largely on credit. In the first quarter of 2009 gross fixed capital formation and manufacturing output in most of the world's major economies fell at double digit rates. Meanwhile problems with solvency in the non-financial sector in many countries fed back into the financial system.

The likelihood of a recovery in the major developed countries that would be strong enough to bring the world economy back to its pre-crisis growth path in the coming years is quite low. This is because neither consumption nor investment growth can be expected to revive significantly due to very low capacity utilization and rising unemployment. In addition, banks need to be recapitalized and their balance sheets cleaned of toxic assets before they can be guided back to their traditional role as providers of credit to investors in fixed capital. Until this is achieved, and in order to halt the contraction of GDP, it will be necessary to maintain, or even further strengthen, the expansionary stance of monetary and fiscal policies. Against this background, global GDP growth may turn positive again in 2010, but it is unlikely to exceed 1.6 per cent.

The crisis has reached developing countries

Almost all developing countries have experienced a sharp slowdown of economic growth since mid-2000, and many have also slipped into recession. The channels through which the financial and economic crisis spread to developing countries have varied, depending on factors such as their initial current account and net foreign asset positions, degree of exposure to private international capital flows, composition and direction of international trade in manufactures and services, dependence on primary commodity exports and inflows of migrants' remittances.

Some developing and emerging-market economies that had managed to avoid large current-account deficits, or even posted surpluses, for several years before the current crisis erupted have proved less vulnerable than in previous crises. This is particularly true for several Asian and Latin American developing countries that were hit by financial and currency crises between 1997 and 2001. This time, due to better managed exchange-rate policies in the years leading up to the crisis, they were not only able to prevent substantial currency overvaluation, but also to accumulate foreign exchange reserves. This put them on a solid financial footing and helped them to prevent excessive exchange-rate depreciations when the crisis began. Their domestic banking systems have also remained resilient, because, in drawing lessons from previous financial crises, their financial policies sought to keep private sector indebtedness and the degree of leverage of the banking sector relatively low.

Other countries, including many in Eastern Europe, felt the impact of the crisis through the general loss of confidence of the financial markets in their ability to cope with their specific exposure to the crisis. This led to the unwinding of carry-trade positions and a flight of capital to safety. As a result, several currencies came under heavy depreciation pressure and many countries had serious difficulties in rolling over their short-term external debts.

In *Africa* output growth is expected to slow down sharply in 2009, particularly in sub-Saharan Africa, where per capita GDP will actually fall. This will render it virtually impossible to achieve the United Nations Millennium Development Goals. In *Latin America and the Caribbean*, GDP growth is likely to fall by around 2 per cent in 2009, with Mexico undergoing a particularly deep recession. Overall, the Caribbean countries will probably avoid negative GDP growth. Most Latin American countries were in a relatively strong macroeconomic position at the onset of the global crisis, which has given them greater resilience to withstand a balance of payments or banking crisis so far.

While GDP in *East* and *South Asia* should continue to grow at 3–4 per cent in 2009, it is expected to fall in *West Asia*, where several economies have been hurt by tumbling prices of financial assets, real estate and oil. A similar downturn is forecast for many economies in *South-East Asia,* which rely heavily on exports of manufactures. The countries that have resisted recessionary forces better than others are those where the domestic market plays a more important – and increasingly growing – role in total demand, such as China, India and Indonesia. Moreover, the rebound in China in the second quarter of 2009 proves the efficiency of government deficit spending if applied quickly and forcefully.

Green shoots, but spring is far away

The improvement of certain financial indicators from their lows reached in the first quarter of 2009 and falling interest rate spreads on emerging-market debt and corporate bonds, combined with the rebound of securities, commodity prices and the exchange rates of several emerging-market currencies by mid-2009, were quickly seen as "green shoots" of economic recovery. But the economic winter is far from over: tumbling profits in the real economy, previous overinvestment in real estate and rising unemployment will continue to constrain private consumption and investment for the foreseeable future. As the crisis is global, reliance on exports offers no easy way out, since trade is expected to decline by about 11 per cent in real terms and any new trade expansion requires a recovery of consumption and investment somewhere in the world.

Given the weakness in macroeconomic fundamentals, an upturn in financial indicators in the first half of 2009 is more likely to signal a temporary rebound from abnormally low levels of prices of financial assets and commodities following a downward overshooting that was as irrational as the previously bullish exuberance. They are not a reflection of strengthened macroeconomic fundamentals but of a restored "risk appetite" among financial agents. Consequently, they could be reversed at short notice, depending on the pace of recovery and financial market sentiment.

The crisis was predictable

The present economic crisis was not a bolt from the blue; it broke out following years of huge disequilibria within and among major national economies. The most visible evidence of imbalances were the large current-account deficits in the United States, the United Kingdom, Spain and several East European economies, on the one hand, and large and growing surpluses in China, Japan, Germany and the oil-exporting countries on the other. In the United States and the other booming economies, growth was driven to a large extent by debt-financed household consumption, made possible by reckless lending and growing bubbles in the housing and stock markets.

It was clear that such disequilibria could not continue indefinitely. A globally coordinated adjustment, whereby surplus countries would expand domestic demand to compensate for slower growth in the deficit countries, had been consistently advocated by many observers and institutions, including UNCTAD in several of its *Trade and Development Reports (TDRs)*. In 2004, for example, the *TDR* on its very first page stated: "Large disparities in the strength of domestic demand persist among the major industrial countries, and increasing trade imbalances between the major economic blocks could ... increase instability in currency and financial markets". However, policymakers failed to acknowledge the need for an internationally balanced macroeconomic management of demand, and in several cases greatly overestimated inflationary risk. A hard-landing scenario was thus predictable.

Policymakers also failed to draw lessons from the experiences of earlier financial crises. Like previous ones, the current crisis follows the classical sequence of expansion, euphoria, financial distress and panic. In the build-up to the present crisis, a large proportion of the credit expansion in the United States and other developed economies financed real estate acquisitions, fuelled asset price inflation and spurred debt-financed private consumption rather than investment in productive capacity that could have generated higher real income and employment in a sustainable manner. After 2000, household debt increased rapidly in many countries, particularly in those economies where current-account deficits had widened, leading to an accumulation of external liabilities. What makes this crisis exceptionally widespread and deep is the fact that financial deregulation, "innovation" of many opaque products and a total ineptitude of credit rating agencies raised credit leverage to unprecedented levels. Blind faith in the "efficiency" of deregulated financial markets led authorities to allow the emergence of a shadow financial system and several global "casinos" with little or no supervision and inadequate capital requirements.

Speculative forces predominate over fundamentals in determining market outcomes

In the course of the crisis, financial distress spread directly across stock and bond markets and primary commodity markets, and put pressure on the exchange rates of some emerging-market currencies. The uniform behaviour of so many different markets that are not linked by economic fundamentals can be attributed to one common factor: the strong speculative forces operating in all these markets.

As participants in financial markets often seek speculative gains by moving before others do, these markets are always "ready for take-off", and eventually interpret any "news" from this perspective. Indeed, they often tend to misread a situation as being driven by economic fundamentals when these are just mirages, such as perceived signs of economic recovery in certain economies or fears of forthcoming inflation. As long as prices are strongly influenced by speculative flows – with correlated positions moving in and out of risk – markets cannot function efficiently.

Recognizing the lack of economic logic of these markets is key to understanding the roots of the current crisis, and should be the basis for further policies and reforms aimed at stabilizing the financial system. However, so far an appropriate appraisal by policymakers has not been forthcoming. The policy approach to tackling the crisis is focused on better regulation of actors and markets at the national level, but does not address its impacts on currency and commodity markets and on the future of an open trading system.

Excessive "financialization" of primary commodity markets

The impact of the financial crisis on developing and transition economies through the slowdown of trade was amplified by the sharp fall in international prices for primary commodities in the second half of 2008. To a large extent this is a symptom of the financial crisis itself. Commodity prices, stock prices and the exchange rates of currencies affected by carry trade speculation moved in parallel during much of the period of the commodity price hike in 2005–2008, during the subsequent sharp correction in the second half of 2008 and again during the rebound phase in the second quarter of 2009.

It is true that deteriorating global economic prospects after September 2008 dampened demand for commodities; but the downturn in international commodity prices was first triggered by financial investors who started to unwind their relatively liquid positions in commodities when the value of other assets began to fall or became uncertain. And the herd behaviour of many market participants reinforced such impulses.

Financial investors in commodity futures exchanges have been treating commodities increasingly as an alternative asset class to optimize the risk-return profile of their portfolios. In doing so, they have paid little attention to fundamental supply and demand relationships in the markets for specific commodities. A particular concern with respect to this financialization of commodity trading is the growing influence of so-called index traders, who tend to take only long positions that exert upward pressure on prices. The average size of their positions has become so large that they can significantly influence prices and create speculative bubbles, with extremely detrimental effects on normal trading activities and market efficiency.

Under these conditions, hedging against commodity price risk becomes more complex, more expensive, and perhaps unaffordable for developing-country users. Moreover, the signals emanating from commodity exchanges are getting to be less reliable as a basis for investment decisions and for supply and demand management by producers and consumers.

In order to improve the functioning of commodity futures exchanges in the interests of producers and consumers, and to keep pace with the participation of new trader categories such as index funds, closer and stronger supervision and regulation of these markets is indispensable. The financialization of commodity futures trading also confronts the international community with the issue of how supply-side measures can address excessive commodity price volatility. This issue is of particular importance for food commodities, because, despite some recent improvements, current grain and oilseed inventories remain very low. This means that any sudden increase in demand or major shortfall in production, or both, will rapidly trigger significant price increases. Hence, physical stocks of food commodities need to be rebuilt urgently to a level adequate enough to be able to moderate temporary shortages and buffer sharp price movements.

In 2009, food emergencies persist in 31 countries, and it is estimated that between 109 million and 126 million people, most of them in sub-Saharan Africa and South Asia, may have fallen below the poverty line since 2006 due to higher food prices. Despite plummeting international food prices in the second half of

2008, domestic food prices generally have remained very high, and in some cases at record highs. It appears that while the pass-through of commodity prices on international exchanges to consumer prices was high in the phase of increasing prices, it was low during the subsequent months of falling prices, which proves that the markets are not functioning in an orderly manner. In addition, forecasts by specialized agencies expect food prices to remain high in the longer run, mainly as a result of continuously rising biofuel demand and structural factors related to population and income growth.

In the first half of 2009, commodity prices rose again, reflecting the return of financial speculators to commodity markets, which appears to have amplified the effects of small changes in market fundamentals. Also, demand from China for current consumption and stockpiling will continue to influence commodity prices. Given the growth dynamics of China and a number of other large emerging-market economies, commodity prices could rise further once a global recovery sets in. However, based on prospects for the evolution of market fundamentals, those prices are not expected to return to the peaks registered in the first half of 2008 any time soon.

The monetary policy response and financial rescue operations in developed countries

Most policymakers took a while to realize the full magnitude of the financial and economic crisis. United States authorities were the first to take measures to counter the effects of the crisis. This is mainly because the bursting of the real estate bubble, financial difficulties of large financial firms, as well as signs of a looming outright recession, all emerged first in the United States economy. When other governments joined in rescue operations, these were mostly in reaction to pressing problems rather than pre-emptive in nature. In some cases, their macroeconomic policies were even procyclical, repeating the policy mistakes that aggravated the crises in several Asian and Latin American countries in the late 1990s and early 2000s.

The symptoms of the financial crisis were first treated by the provision of additional liquidity to banks in the major financial markets. This was followed by cuts in interest rates to lower the cost of credit, again with the Federal Reserve taking the lead; other central banks followed with a considerable time lag. The European Central Bank (ECB) moved in the opposite direction to begin with, considering it appropriate to raise its policy rate as late as July 2008 to counter a wrongly perceived risk of inflation – a move that clearly reflected a lack of understanding of the gravity of the unfolding situation.

In the United States and other developed countries, it soon became clear that influencing the monetary and credit conditions and providing traditional financing to depository institutions would not be sufficient to restore confidence in the financial markets and a normal functioning of credit supply. Governments and central banks undertook rescue operations of systemically important companies, mainly in the financial sector, on an unprecedented scale. They injected capital, provided guarantees, and helped banks "clean" their balance sheets by transferring their so-called "toxic" assets to publicly sponsored "bad banks". However, policy intervention to rescue banks with large amounts of assets of uncertain value is not without problems, because it may imply subsidizing shareholders and provide a form of insurance for banks without appropriate recompense by the beneficiaries. Rigorous monetary easing and large bailout operations may have prevented a meltdown of the financial system, but they were insufficient to revive aggregate demand and halt rising unemployment.

Unprecedented fiscal stimulus packages

As the crisis spilled over into the real sector, governments in many developed countries reacted with debt-financed increases in public spending and tax cuts. These were intended to counter the increasingly dramatic downturn in final demand, output and employment. Fiscal stimuli were first introduced in early 2008, but more forcefully after the slowdown in the United States had turned into an outright recession in the third quarter of that year.

The public resources deployed in such "fiscal packages" represent an average of some 3.7 per cent of GDP in the developed countries. In most countries they are stretched over a period of two years. But it is not only the size of such fiscal programmes that matters; different forms of spending and revenue cuts have different effects on demand and income. For example, an increase in public investment typically has a stronger impact than tax abates, and measures aimed at raising the disposable income of low-income groups generates more demand than tax reductions on high incomes. Moreover, most of these interventions have distributional effects and lasting consequences, most notably when they include investment in infrastructure. Consequently, a fiscal stimulus plan should be designed to maximize its impact on the economy, while at the same time aiming at long-term structural objectives.

The policy response in developing and transition economies

In developing countries, the scope for easing monetary policy varied greatly, depending mainly on their initial current-account position and the degree of openness of their capital account. Many Asian countries, including China, India and the Republic of Korea, began to move towards a more expansionary monetary policy from September 2008 onwards. By contrast, in other countries whose currencies came under (sometimes intense) pressure in the third quarter of 2008, the monetary authorities were even induced to temporarily tighten their policy stance before shifting to monetary easing in the first months of 2009.

A number of developing and transition economies also launched sizeable fiscal stimulus packages. On average, their size was even larger than those of developed countries: 4.7 per cent of GDP in developing countries and 5.8 per cent in transition economies, extending over a period of one to three years. The authorities in China were quick to announce a particularly large fiscal stimulus plan, amounting to more than 13 per cent of GDP. A number of other countries in Asia and Latin America also responded to the crisis with very expansionary macroeconomic policies, using the greater fiscal flexibility and policy space available to them because of their healthy current accounts and reserves.

By contrast, some developing and transition economies have had to turn to the International Monetary Fund (IMF) for financial support to stabilize their exchange rates and prevent a collapse of their banking systems. IMF lending has surged since the outbreak of the current crisis, extending to nearly 50 countries by the end of May 2009. However, the scope for expansionary policies to counter the impact of the crisis on domestic demand and employment has been severely constrained by the conditionality attached to IMF lending.

The international policy dimension

The unfolding of the global crisis did not receive attention in international decision-making bodies until October 2008, when the central banks of the major economies engaged in coordinated monetary easing. A novelty was that the United States Federal Reserve, for the first time since the end of the Bretton Woods system, provided four emerging-market economies with bilateral swaps to help them defend their currencies. Since November 2008, the G-20 has taken the lead in launching and coordinating international action to address the financial and economic crisis, although the question has been raised as to whether it is sufficiently inclusive.

In April 2009, the G-20 acknowledged the need for coordination of the fiscal stimulus programmes of different countries in order to enhance their overall impact on global demand and reduce the risk of protectionist reflex actions against "free-riders". However, not all countries have the same fiscal space: many developing economies need international support for their countercyclical policies. This was acknowledged by the G-20 in adopting the Global Plan for Recovery and Reform. In particular it was decided to significantly increase the IMF's resources, to provide additional lending through multilateral development banks and to support trade finance. Some of the proposed measures were not entirely new, while others reflected intentions rather than being concrete pledges.

Moreover, the effectiveness of the announced international support could have been greatly increased if it had been linked to a reform of the IMF itself, including changes to its governance structure, the system of allocation of Special Drawing Rights (SDRs) and the principles underlying the conditionality of its lending. Several announcements were made to the effect that the IMF would recognize countercyclical policies and large fiscal stimulus packages as the most effective means to compensate for the fall in aggregate demand induced by debt deflation. However, in reality, the conditions attached to recent lending operations have remained quite similar to those of the past. Indeed, in almost all its recent lending arrangements, the Fund has continued to impose procyclical macroeconomic tightening, including the requirement for a reduction in public spending and an increase in interest rates.

The need for financial support to low-income countries

Current debt servicing and debt sustainability have become more problematic, not only for countries whose liabilities to commercial lenders have increased rapidly in recent years, but also for a number of low-income developing countries, including several heavily indebted poor countries (HIPCs) which depend on borrowing from official sources. Despite the debt relief provided to them, the sustainability of their external debt situation remains highly vulnerable to shocks, and the fallout of the global economic crisis is impairing their ability to service their external debt without compromising their imports.

Low-income countries with balance-of-payments problems and limited fiscal flexibility require additional support that can best be mobilized in a concerted multilateral effort. Increases in bilateral aid flows that are integrated into fiscal stimulus packages in an internationally coordinated manner would also have expansionary effects in donor countries. In addition, a temporary moratorium on official debt repayments would allow low-income countries to counter, to some extent, the impact of lower export earnings on their import capacity and government budgets. Such a moratorium would be in the spirit of the countercyclical policies undertaken in most developed and emerging-market economies. It would not only constitute an important element in efforts to attenuate the impact of the global crisis on growth, poverty alleviation and investment in the debtor countries, but it would also contribute to stabilizing global demand. Compared to the size of the stimulus packages for developed countries, the total amount of such a temporary debt moratorium would be modest, amounting to about $26 billion for 49 low-income countries for 2009 and 2010 combined.

The problem is not inflation, but deflation

Growing budget deficits as a consequence of fiscal stimulus packages have prompted concerns that governments will burden future generations if they do not raise tax rates as soon as the crisis is over. However, in a growing economy, government revenue will normally rise sufficiently at constant tax rates to reduce the deficit if government spending is not on a permanent growth path. If governments were to remain passive in a situation of severe crisis, relying exclusively on automatic stabilizers, the fiscal balance would deteriorate as a result of lower tax revenues. On the other hand, a discretionary increase in public spending, especially when it boosts investment, may enhance production capacity and job creation, which in turn will enlarge the future tax base and thereby improve public revenues at given tax rates. Nevertheless, the size of the domestic public debt does matter, since it may compromise budget flexibility in the future. This is why, in order to be truly countercyclical, an expansionary fiscal policy in a recession needs to be combined with fiscal consolidation when recovery sets in and output growth accelerates.

There are also widespread concerns that the large injections of central bank money and the sharply rising budget deficits in many countries will sooner or later lead to inflation if governments and central banks do not react early to contain that risk. This fear is based on the monetarist view that "too much money chasing too few goods" inevitably creates inflation. However, "too much money" needs a channel through which to inject the virus of inflation into an economy. There are only two channels for this to happen: if demand growth exceeds potential supply growth ("demand-pull inflation"), or if increases in the costs of production, particularly labour costs, exceed productivity growth ("cost-push inflation"). In the present situation, with capacity utilization at historic lows and unemployment rising at a dramatic rate, there is little danger of either overheating or wage inflation for several years to come. It is a matter of years, not months, before economies that are now in deep crisis can be restored to a level of capacity utilization where supply cannot keep up with demand, or to a level of employment that could trigger demand for higher wages. This will allow central banks to gradually withdraw excess liquidity by selling revalued assets and absorbing excess money supply.

Indeed, deflation – not inflation – is the real danger. Wage deflation is the imminent and most dangerous threat in many countries today, because governments will find it much more difficult to stabilize a tumbling economy when there is a large-scale fall in wages and consumption. However, deflation will not cure itself. Therefore, the most important task is to break the spiral of falling wages, prices and demand as early as possible, and to revive the financial sector's ability to provide credit for productive investment to stimulate real economic growth. Governments and central banks need to take rapid and strong proactive measures to boost demand and avert the risk of deflation.

Rethinking monetary and financial policies

In many countries, Governments and central banks have set new precedents for supporting ailing financial institutions that had ended up in trouble on account of mismanagement. The need for such rescue operations has revealed that the huge profits and incomes earned from the financial activities of some market participants and managers over the past few years have been disproportional to the macroeconomic and social usefulness of the financial sector. The heavy involvement of governments and central banks therefore justifies a thorough review of the functioning of the financial sector, and a redefinition of the role of central banks and public financial institutions in supporting real economic activity. Large segments of the financial sector cannot be left to function like giant casinos without doing great harm to the real sector of the economy. As a logical consequence of the various efforts to rescue individual financial institutions, and in the interests of greater stability and reliability of the financial system, the balance between private activity and State involvement in the financial sector beyond the crisis may need to be revised fundamentally.

The need for more stringent financial regulation

One aspect of financial policy reform is the generally accepted need for strengthening financial regulation and supervision. In order to draw the right lessons for improving financial regulation, it is important to recognize that the collapse of the subprime mortgage market in the United States, while sparking the crisis, was not its fundamental cause. The current crisis is due to the predominance of finance over those productive sectors of the economy where real wealth is created, a predominance that was made possible by the euphoria over the efficiency of free markets. This euphoria led to excessive deregulation, an underestimation of risk and excessive leveraging in the years before the crisis. The build-up of risk could have been avoided if policies concerning the financial sector had been guided less by ideology and more by pragmatism.

Many now blame greed for the crisis, but greed has always existed and will always exist. Greed should therefore have been taken into account when evaluating the risks of financial deregulation, because today's predicament is the result of financial innovation in an environment of insufficient regulation and supervision. In the United States, the share of the financial industry in GDP grew from 5 per cent to 8 per cent between 1983 and 2007, while its share in total corporate profits rose from 7.5 per cent to 40 per cent. Policymakers should have been wary of an industry that constantly aims at generating double-digit returns in an economy that is growing at a much slower rate, especially if that industry needs to be bailed out every decade or so. Since herd behaviour can cause much greater damage in financial markets than in goods markets, the former need to be subject to stricter regulations.

Developing a more sophisticated financial system should not be an objective per se; more finance and more financial products are not always better than less. Large parts of the financial markets have come to be entirely detached from real sector activities. Securitization and other financial "innovations" have broken the traditional relationship between lenders, particularly banks, and borrowers. They have weakened the capacity and willingness of financial institutions to manage risk, and favour the development of a non-transparent, poorly regulated and undercapitalized shadow financial system. The contribution of those financial markets to social welfare is highly questionable. Indeed, several innovative financial products have negative social returns. Therefore, financial regulation should aim at reducing the proliferation of such instruments.

There is a fundamental flaw with a regulatory apparatus that is based on the assumption that protecting individual institutions will automatically protect the entire system. Actions that are good and prudent for an individual financial institution can have negative implications for the system as a whole. It is thus necessary to develop a new regulatory system that systematically discriminates between financial services for productive investment and betting or gambling in zero sum games.

The crisis offers important lessons for developing countries that seek to limit possible negative effects of external financial shocks on their own financial systems. They should aim at avoiding excessive currency and maturity mismatches in their balance sheets and real exchange rate appreciation, if necessary by comprehensive and countercyclical capital-account management. The crisis also shows that deeper financial systems can bring substantial benefits, but they can also cause considerable harm. Therefore, the process of financial development needs to go hand in hand with better and broader financial regulation and supervision. As regulatory reforms cannot be implemented overnight, developing countries should proceed with caution and avoid "big-bang" processes of financial reform.

The imperative need for reform of the international monetary and financial system

Financial market participants act on the basis of centralized information that is quite different from the disparate sources of information on normal goods markets. The large majority react to the same set of "information" or "news" with very similar patterns of taking on or unwinding of their exposure to risk. Speculation of this kind leads to upward and downward overshooting of prices, or even to price movement in a direction that is not justified by fundamentals. This causes lasting damage to the real economy and to the international trading system.

The realization that in a globalized world "shocks" emanating in one segment of the financial sector of one country can be transmitted rapidly to other parts of the interconnected system raises some fundamental questions about the wisdom of global financial integration of developing countries in general. The experience with the current financial crisis calls into question the conventional wisdom that dismantling all obstacles to cross-border private capital flows is the best recipe for countries to advance their economic development. While it is agreed that global finance has caused the current crisis, surprisingly little attention is being given to the management of global finance, and in particular speculative capital flows. Debates about reform focus primarily on improving national prudential regulation and supervision of financial players of systemic importance. These are important issues. But the experience of this financial crisis also supports the case for a more fundamental rethinking of global financial governance with a view to stabilizing trade and financial relations by reducing the potential for gains from speculative capital flows.

Reducing vulnerability to external financial shocks at the country level

Promoting proactive capital-account management may be one element in a revised governance structure that could give countries sufficient flexibility to manage their domestic macroeconomic policies and improve their prospects for economic stability. Effective capital-account management not only helps prevent volatile private capital flows from causing exchange-rate volatility and misalignment, and thereby destabilizing the domestic financial system; it also helps improve the reliability of price signals in domestic markets and the conditions for efficient resource allocation and dynamic investment.

Assertions that capital controls are ineffective or harmful have been disproved by the actual experiences of emerging-market economies. These experiences show that different types of capital flows can be limited effectively by a variety of instruments. These instruments range from outright bans or minimum-stay requirements to tax-based instruments like mandatory reserve requirements or taxes on foreign loans that are designed to offset interest rate differentials. Several instruments can be combined and flexibly handled to match specific local requirements. In many cases, instruments directly targeting private capital flows may be appropriately combined with and complemented by prudential domestic financial regulations. The capital account can also be managed in a countercyclical manner, by restricting the build-up of excessive foreign liabilities in good times and restraining capital flight during crises. In any case, it would certainly be a step forward if surging capital inflows were no longer perceived as a sign of strength, but as a potential source of disequilibrium, with grave repercussions for macroeconomic stability and trade. Thus, in pursuing its surveillance function, the IMF should more actively encourage countries to use, whenever necessary, the introduction of capital controls as provided for in its Articles of Agreement.

The dollar-based reserve system is increasingly challenged

In the discussion about necessary reforms of the international monetary and financial system, the problem of the United States dollar serving as the main international reserve asset has received renewed attention. Central banks, motivated by the desire to reduce exchange-rate risk in a world of financial and currency instability, have been increasingly diversifying their reserve holdings into other currencies, in particular the euro. Against this background, a proposal first discussed in the late 1970s has recently resurfaced. It argues for facilitating reserve diversification away from dollars without the risk of a major dollar crisis by giving central banks the possibility to deposit dollar reserves in a special "substitution account" at the IMF denominated in SDRs. These SDRs could also be used to settle international payments. Since the SDR is valued as the weighted average of the major currencies, its value is more stable than that of each of the constituent currencies. However, the problem of exchange-rate determination of the currencies of member States would remain. The exchange-rate risk would, at least partly, be shifted to the IMF, as it would imply a currency mismatch between the Fund's assets and liabilities. The risk would have to be covered either through the generation of higher revenues by the IMF or by guarantees from member States.

An international reserve system that uses one or several national currencies as a reserve asset and as a means of international payments also has the disadvantage of being dependent on monetary policy decisions by the central banks issuing those currencies. However, their decisions are not taken in response to the needs of the international payments system and the world economy, but in response to national policy needs and preferences. Moreover, an economy whose currency is used as a reserve currency is not under the same obligation as others to make the necessary macroeconomic or exchange-rate adjustments for avoiding continuing current-account deficits. Thus, the dominance of the dollar as the main means of international payments also played an important role in the build-up of the global imbalances in the run-up to the financial crisis.

Another disadvantage of the current international reserve system is that it imposes a greater adjustment burden on deficit countries (except if it is a country issuing a reserve currency) than on surplus countries.

This is because the former are compelled to reduce imports when their ability to obtain external financing reaches its limits, whereas surplus countries are under no systemic obligation to raise their imports in order to balance their payments. Similarly, central banks can easily counter pressure on their currency to appreciate by buying foreign currency against their own, but their possibilities to counter pressure for currency depreciation is circumscribed by the amount of their foreign exchange reserves. The IMF supports this bias by imposing restrictive policies on deficit countries as part of its loan conditions, rather than pressing surplus countries for more expansionary policies as part of its surveillance activities. Thus, as long as there is no multilaterally agreed rule for countries to support each others' economies through coordinated demand management and symmetric intervention in the foreign exchange market, the system has a deflationary bias.

Strengthening the role of SDRs

There has also been a suggestion to reduce the need for reserve holdings as protection against the volatility of financial markets by strengthening the role of SDRs. Indeed, in response to the increased needs for international liquidity in the current financial and economic crisis, the G-20 at its London Summit in April 2009 announced its support for a new general SDR allocation, which would inject $250 billion into the world economy and increase global liquidity. This proposal was supported by the Commission of Experts of the President of the United Nations General Assembly on Reforms of the International Monetary and Financial System.

However, the new SDRs would be distributed according to member countries' quotas in the Fund. This would mean that the G-7 countries, which have no real need for SDRs because they themselves issue reserve currencies or have easy access to international capital markets, would receive more than 45 per cent of the newly allocated SDRs. Less than 37 per cent would be allocated to developing and transition economies and less than 8 per cent to low-income countries. Thus the countries most in need of international liquidity from official sources would receive the smallest shares. This raises the more general issue of the geographical and time dimensions of SDR allocation.

From the point of view of criteria for geographical distribution, it has been suggested that in order for the SDR to become the main form of international liquidity and means of reserve holding, new SDR allocations should be made according to the needs of countries. Appropriate criteria for determining those needs would have to be worked out, but there can be no doubt that an allocation according to the current structure of IMF quotas is entirely out of line with needs. One approach would be to allow all countries unconditional access to IMF resources by an amount necessary to stabilize their exchange rates at a multilaterally agreed level. Another approach could be to link the issuance of SDRs with the needs of developing economies for development finance by allowing the IMF to invest some of the funds made available through issuance of SDRs in the bonds of multilateral development banks. Such a proposal was made by an UNCTAD panel of experts in the 1960s, before international liberalization of financial markets began, and when access to capital market financing by developing-country borrowers was very limited.

With regard to the time dimension, the question of frequency and cyclicality arises. If the purpose of SDR allocation is to stabilize global output growth, it would be appropriate to issue additional SDRs when global growth is below potential or during crisis periods, and to issue smaller amounts or retire SDRs in periods of fast global output growth. One of the advantages of using SDRs in such a countercyclical manner is that it would, in principle, facilitate the task of preventing excessive currency depreciations for countries in crisis. However, the rules and conditions for access would need to be elaborated carefully, including a determination of the level of exchange rates that should be stabilized. Therefore neither a substitution account, nor a central role for the SDR in the provision of international liquidity would solve the main problem underlying the need for the accumulation of large reserves, i.e. exchange-rate instability and the possibility of currency attacks.

Whatever form an enhanced scheme of SDR allocation may take, it will only be acceptable to all countries if the terms on which SDRs can be used as international liquidity are absolutely clear-cut, particularly the parity of the SDR vis-à-vis all national currencies. The Bretton Woods system and the European Monetary System provide precedents for what could be an appropriate solution for determining exchange rates within a multilateral framework. In these systems the implicit rule was that the exchange rate of a national currency with the international currency was determined by the purchasing power of that currency expressed in all other currencies. This rule may be difficult to introduce at the time the system starts, because of the problem of determining the initial purchasing power parities of each currency, but it would be straightforward and simple once the system was on track. It may also be necessary to apply some additional criteria that reflect structural features related to the level of development of different countries.

In the current global monetary (non-)system many countries, in particular emerging-market economies with open capital accounts, are faced with serious problems of exchange-rate management. Economies with an open capital account cannot absorb external shocks efficiently by adopting either entirely flexible exchange rates or by their rigid fixing. Under a system of freely floating rates, introduced on the assumption that market forces will efficiently determine the correct exchange rate, there is scope for huge fluctuations, as currency speculation drives exchange rates systematically away from the fundamentals and tends to lead to overvaluation and current-account deficits. Hard pegs, like currency boards, undermine price-led adjustments of trade and provoke speculation against the peg if the anchoring country is unable to strictly abide by the inflationary regime that prevails in the anchor country. Again, real appreciation and loss of competitiveness due to higher inflation in the anchoring country – reflected in huge current-account deficits – invite speculation, as they tend to cause a loss of confidence by the markets that the regime can be sustained. A viable solution to the exchange-rate problem would be a system of managed flexible exchange rates targeting a rate that is consistent with a sustainable current-account position, which is preferable to any "corner solution". But since the exchange rate is a variable that involves more than one currency, there is a much better chance of achieving a stable pattern of exchange rates in a multilaterally agreed framework for exchange-rate management.

Multiple benefits of a reformed international exchange-rate system

Therefore, what kind of system would be appropriate for the future globalized economy and for countries in crisis?

An internationally agreed exchange-rate system based on the principle of constant and sustainable real exchange rates of all countries would go a long way towards reducing the scope for speculative capital flows that generate volatility in the international financial system and distort the pattern of exchange rates. Since the real exchange rate is defined as the nominal exchange rate adjusted by the inflation differentials between countries, a constant real exchange rate results from nominal exchange rates strictly following inflation differentials. A constant real exchange rate (RER) at a competitive level would achieve the following:

- Curb speculation, because the main trigger for currency speculation is the inflation and interest rate differential. Higher inflation and higher interest rates would be compensated by the devaluation of nominal exchange rates, thereby reducing the scope for gains from carry trade.

- Prevent currency crises, because the main incentive for speculating in currencies of high-inflation countries would disappear, and overvaluation, one of the main destabilizing factors for developing countries in the past 20 years, would not occur.

- Prevent fundamental and long-lasting global imbalances, because all countries with relatively diversified economies would maintain their level of competitiveness in global trade relations.

- Avoid debt traps for developing countries, because unsustainable current-account deficits triggered by a loss in international competitiveness cannot build up.

- Avoid procyclical conditionality in case of crisis, because, if the system were to have symmetric intervention obligations, the assistance needed for countries under pressure to depreciate their currencies would come automatically from the partners in the system whose currencies would appreciate correspondingly.

- Reduce the need to hold international reserves, because with symmetric intervention obligations under the "constant RER" rule, reserves would only be needed to compensate for volatility of export earnings but no longer to defend the exchange rate.

Such a multilateral system would tackle the problem of destabilizing capital flows at its source. It would remove a major incentive for speculation and ensure that monetary factors do not stand in the way of achieving a level playing field for international trade. It would also get rid of debt traps and counterproductive conditionality. The last point is perhaps the most important one: countries facing strong depreciation pressure would automatically receive the required assistance once a sustainable level of the exchange rate had been reached in the form of swap agreements or direct intervention by the counterparty.

Establishing such a system would take some time, not least because it requires international consensus and multilateral institution building. Meanwhile, at the national level proactive capital account management could provide protection against destabilizing capital flows, and at the regional level greater monetary and financial cooperation, including reserve pooling, regional payments clearance mechanisms that function without using the dollar, and regional exchange-rate systems could help countries in the region to avert financial and currency crises, or manage them better if they occurred.

* * *

While the ongoing global financial and economic crisis, its impact on developing countries and the policy responses to that crisis have been at the centre of economic concerns since mid-2008, another pressing preoccupation for peoples and governments around the world continues to be the threat of global warming that implies considerable risks for living conditions and developmental progress. Against this background, TDR 2009 is also addressing the question of how increased efforts aimed at climate change mitigation can be combined with forward-looking development strategies and rapid growth in developing countries.

Global warming requires global action for adaptation and mitigation

Most scientific research suggests that the consequences of unabated climate change could be dramatic. There is broad agreement that a sizeable reduction of greenhouse gas (GHG) emissions is needed to reduce global warming to more acceptable levels, which would also significantly improve the prospects for human and economic development and poverty reduction compared to a scenario of unabated climate change.

Even if global warming can be limited to a generally accepted tolerable level, it is still expected to have adverse consequences for many countries, for example in terms of rising global mean sea levels, increased intensity and frequency of extreme weather events and lower agricultural output. This will require adequate adaptation measures, especially in developing countries, which are feeling the negative effects of climate change the most. This necessitates the mobilization of substantial financial and technical support by the international community for the poorer countries affected. But limiting global warming to tolerable levels also requires a shift of production and consumption patterns towards the use of those primary commodities, means of production and consumer goods that place a lower burden on the earth's atmosphere than the current GHG-intensive ones.

The scale of emission reductions needed to achieve meaningful mitigation of climate change can only be achieved through global action, and there is general agreement that developed countries need to lead such action. They are responsible for the bulk of emissions that have led to the current level of GHG concentrations in the atmosphere as result of past economic activity, and their per capita GHG emissions continue to be higher than those of other countries. They also have greater economic, technological and administrative capacity to shift rapidly to a low-carbon economy. But in developing and transition economies, especially in the largest and fastest growing among them, GHG emissions are on a steeply rising trend. This trend will continue unless they too take vigorous actions to change the energy mix and modes of production and consumption.

In the debate on climate change mitigation, the question of costs has received a great deal of attention. However, it is virtually impossible to base any rational decision on estimates of costs and benefits, because of their considerable uncertainty and the highly subjective judgements involved. What seems to be clear, however, is that an increase of global temperatures above a certain level implies incalculable risks of a serious deterioration of the natural environment and living conditions for the world's population in general, and for the population of developing countries in particular. Global warming and climate change mitigation may therefore best be approached from a risk-management perspective. From this perspective, the shift to more climate-friendly modes of production and consumption becomes a new public preference. And the policy task is to guide economic activities by introducing appropriate incentives, disincentives and regulations that impose or prohibit certain forms of production in line with this public preference.

Climate change mitigation and structural change

Historically, growth has been associated with increasing emissions, which gives the impression that there is a trade-off between growth and development and climate change mitigation. However, this does not have to be the case. Experiences from both developed and developing countries show that many synergies are possible between GHG emission reductions and development objectives.

In order to make climate change mitigation compatible with growth, particularly in developing countries, emissions regulation and control have to be made more stringent. The wider dissemination of existing technologies and the development of new technologies and more climate-friendly modes of production and consumption cannot be left to market forces alone; they also require strong and internationally coordinated government action.

Climate change mitigation is best understood as a process of global structural change. In the course of this process, economic activity will shift from GHG-intensive modes of production and consumption to more climate-friendly ones, causing losses and adjustment costs for many economic agents at the microeconomic level, but also generating new income and gains for others. In this sense, climate change mitigation has much in common with other processes of structural change in which new economic opportunities arise in both developed and developing countries, especially as a result of the rapid growth of new markets. From this macroeconomic perspective, climate change mitigation may even have a growth stimulating effect in many countries.

Generating new growth opportunities through structural change

There is considerable scope for developing economies in the years and decades ahead to gain from the opportunities that will emerge from the structural change towards renewable sources of energy, climate-friendly technologies, low-carbon equipment and appliances, and more sustainable modes of consumption. Successful participation in the new markets could help developing and transition economies to combine climate change mitigation policies with faster growth. It requires industrial policies that foster the creation of capabilities to produce or participate in the production of such goods and their subsequent upgrading.

At present, the global market for what is sometimes called "environmental goods" is clearly dominated by developed countries, but several developing economies already account for an increasing share of this market. For some countries, climate change mitigation offers new possibilities to exploit natural comparative advantages, particularly in the production of low-carbon energy, which so far have been of minor economic importance; for others it may offer opportunities to build new dynamic comparative advantages.

One way developing countries could participate in the markets for "environmental goods" is by integrating into international production chains, as many of them have successfully done in other sectors of manufacturing industry. Furthermore, they themselves could contribute to innovation in climate protection processes and environmental goods adapted to specific local circumstances and comparative advantages. The development of "clean technologies" and early participation in the production of equipment embodying such technologies in the context of a rapidly expanding international market confers "first-mover advantages", given that other countries will eventually need to adopt these technologies as well.

Integrating climate change mitigation in industrial strategies

Seizing opportunities offered by fast growing new markets and strategic integration into such markets are not entirely new challenges. They have been key elements in the design of successful development strategies that have focused on diversification away from a reliance on only a few export commodities and towards building comparative advantages in other areas of economic activity. Each developing and transition economy will need to devise its own strategy for integrating into the emerging markets for new products that help achieve GHG abatement objectives. Those strategies will have to take into account both the local needs for specific "environmental goods" and the possibilities of producing such goods locally, including for regional and global markets.

Experience from developed countries and several emerging-market economies shows that a successful industrial policy may comprise, among other elements, public sector engagement in R&D, simplifying access to patents, fiscal and financial support for new production activities, information dissemination, and FDI policies that favour integration into international production chains. Government procurement and temporary protection of specific subsectors can also have an important impact. A proactive industrial policy with a special focus on using existing comparative advantages and creating new ones in the production of environmental goods is of particular relevance in the context of forward-looking development strategies, because the policy space for support measures in this area is less narrowly circumscribed by multilateral agreements than in other areas.

Structural change requires targeted public support measures

There appears to be a huge potential for greater energy efficiency that could be exploited by wider dissemination of already existing technologies in both developed and developing countries. However, the creation and application of new technologies and the development of alternative energy sources also need to be accelerated. Putting a price on emissions in the form of taxes or tradable emission permits, and thereby changing the incentive structure for producers and consumers, could help set in motion a process towards establishing low-carbon economies. But such measures need to be accompanied by intervention on the supply side of other sources of energy. Managing supply adjustments and price formation for different sources of energy is necessary in order to prevent prices of non-fossil, renewable energy from increasing – relative to the prices of the more carbon-intensive types of energy – as demand for them grows. Therefore, producers of different fuels need to be involved in the formulation and implementation of an international climate change mitigation policy.

In many respects, introducing technologies that support climate change mitigation is not particularly different from other innovation activities: in a dynamic economy, they emerge from entrepreneurial spirit and the search for competitive gains. But unlike many other areas, technological progress and innovation for more climate-friendly modes of production and consumption cannot be left to changes in the incentive structure based on the market mechanism alone. The important public-good nature of low-carbon technologies and the urgent need to reduce GHG emissions in light of the risks of unabated climate change for future generations call for direct government intervention through the introduction of emission performance standards and strict regulations for GHG reductions. Until today, there has been insufficient investment in public and private research for the development of alternative sources of energy and cleaner production methods, which has led to "carbon lock-in" in current modes of production and consumption. Proactive policies are therefore needed, including subsidies and public acquisition of patents, to advance technological progress and accelerate the process of catching up from past underinvestment. Moreover, experience shows that technological change often advances faster when it also benefits from R&D in public institutions, and when the public sector takes the lead in the practical application of new technologies.

Promoting climate change mitigation through appropriate international agreements

The international community can support industrial development in this direction by allowing developing countries sufficient policy space in the context of relevant international agreements on climate change, trade, FDI and intellectual property rights. Given the global public-good character of climate change mitigation, consideration could be given to interpreting the flexibilities of the WTO Agreement on Trade-related Aspects of Intellectual Property Rights (TRIPS Agreement) in a way that would allow compulsory licensing for the production of equipment and goods that embed climate-friendly technologies, and for related processes, similar to the exemptions accorded for medicines in support of public health.

In strengthening the international framework for a climate policy, there is scope for many of its existing elements to contribute to more effective global GHG abatement efforts, and for greater participation of developing countries in those efforts. These elements include, inter alia, the promotion of carbon trading, and the two project-based mechanisms of the Kyoto Protocol – the Clean Development Mechanism and Joint Implementation – as well as the prevention of deforestation. The imperative of climate change mitigation requires a commitment to GHG reductions not only by developed countries, but also by emerging-market economies, which in recent years have drastically increased their GHG emissions. A promising approach to reducing GHG emissions would be to extend the coverage of existing cap-and-trade systems and increase their effectiveness.

In order to achieve a new climate agreement, it will be necessary that the distribution of responsibilities be viewed by all parties as sufficiently fair and equitable. On the one hand, an international emissions trading scheme would need to take into account the responsibility of the industrialized countries for the bulk of existing GHG concentrations in the atmosphere; on the other hand, it would need to recognize that the contribution of developing countries to GHG abatement critically depends on their having the appropriate financial resources and access to clean technologies, and the ability to develop their own environmental goods industries. Depending on the initial allocation of emission permits, an emission trading scheme could allow developing countries to sell emission rights that they do not require to cover domestically produced emissions, thereby providing some of the financial resources they would need for technology imports. Such an emissions trading scheme could complement official development assistance aimed at building greener economies in developing countries, as well as FDI policies that support technological upgrading and structural change in developing countries.

The large fiscal stimulus packages launched in response to the financial and economic crisis offer an ideal opportunity to accelerate structural change towards a low-carbon economy through additional public investment in activities and infrastructure in support of climate change mitigation, and through the provision of subsidies for acquisition of climate-friendly capital goods and durable consumer goods.

Supachai Panitchpakdi
Secretary-General of UNCTAD

Chapter I

THE IMPACT OF THE GLOBAL CRISIS AND THE SHORT-TERM POLICY RESPONSE

A. Recent trends in the world economy

1. Global growth and international trade

The world economy is experiencing its first contraction since the Second World War. Even before the problems in financial markets turned into a full-blown crisis in September 2008, the growth of gross domestic product (GDP) had ground to a halt in most developed countries. The bursting of the housing bubble in a number of countries, the subprime financial crisis in the United States, rising commodity prices, and in several countries, restrictive monetary policies led the global economy to the "brink of recession" in the first half of 2008 (*TDR 2008*: 1). Whereas the exhaustion of credit-based demand growth brought these economies to a standstill, the collapse of credit supply and financial asset prices pushed it into a severe recession. After slowing down from 3.7 per cent in 2007 to 2 per cent in 2008, global GDP is expected to fall by more than 2.5 per cent in 2009 (table 1.1).

This crisis is unique, not only in terms of its depth but also in the extent of its global reach: virtually no economy has remained unaffected. Even economies that are expected to grow this year, such as those of China and India, are slowing down significantly from their previous years of rapid growth.

It shows to what extent national economies around the globe have become interdependent, which makes it difficult for them to "decouple" from the global economic slump, especially as the initial shock originated in the largest economy. The speed at which the crisis spread to different countries was also remarkable: many developing and transition economies that had enjoyed robust growth until the second or third quarter of 2008 experienced a fall in GDP already in the last quarter of the year.

In the highly integrated international system, the financial shock propagated extremely rapidly. It spread to the real economy mainly through those segments of aggregate demand that are largely financed with credit, such as fixed investments and the consumption of durable goods. This is why the crisis has been felt the most acutely in manufacturing and construction, while other sectors like non-financial services have been less affected. With increasing uncertainty about levels of disposable income and demand, acquisitions of durable and capital goods were deferred and producers of these goods reduced inventories, resulting in a sharp contraction of production within a very short period of time. Available data for the first quarter of 2009 indicate double-digit reductions in gross fixed capital formation (GFCF) and manufacturing output in most of the world's major economies.

Table 1.1

WORLD OUTPUT GROWTH, 1991–2009[a]

(Annual percentage change)

Region/country	1991–2002[b]	2003	2004	2005	2006	2007	2008[c]	2009[c]
World	**2.8**	**2.7**	**4.1**	**3.4**	**3.9**	**3.7**	**2.0**	**-2.7**
Developed countries	**2.5**	**1.9**	**3.0**	**2.4**	**2.8**	**2.5**	**0.7**	**-4.1**
of which:								
Japan	1.0	1.4	2.7	1.9	2.0	2.4	-0.6	-6.5
United States	3.3	2.5	3.6	2.9	2.8	2.0	1.1	-3.0
European Union	2.3	1.3	2.5	1.9	3.1	2.9	0.9	-4.6
of which:								
Euro area	2.2	0.8	2.1	1.7	2.9	2.6	0.8	-4.7
France	2.1	1.1	2.5	1.9	2.4	2.1	0.7	-3.0
Germany	1.8	-0.2	1.1	0.8	3.0	2.5	1.3	-6.1
Italy	1.6	0.0	1.4	0.7	1.9	1.5	-1.0	-5.5
United Kingdom	2.8	2.8	3.3	1.8	2.9	3.1	0.7	-4.3
EU-12[d]	2.5	4.2	5.6	4.8	6.4	6.0	3.9	-3.6
South-East Europe and CIS	..	**7.1**	**7.7**	**6.7**	**7.5**	**8.4**	**5.4**	**-6.2**
South-East Europe[e]	..	2.6	5.3	5.7	5.3	6.0	4.0	-2.2
Commonwealth of Independent States (CIS)	..	7.6	8.0	6.8	7.8	8.6	5.5	-6.6
of which:								
Russian Federation	..	7.3	7.1	6.4	6.7	8.1	5.6	-8.0
Developing countries	**4.7**	**5.4**	**7.2**	**6.6**	**7.2**	**7.3**	**5.4**	**1.3**
Africa	2.9	4.9	5.3	5.6	5.7	6.0	5.1	1.2
North Africa, excl. Sudan	3.3	5.5	4.9	5.3	5.7	5.7	5.7	3.0
Sub-Saharan Africa, excl. South Africa	2.8	5.4	6.1	6.4	5.9	6.7	5.4	1.0
South Africa	2.3	3.1	4.9	5.0	5.4	5.1	3.1	-1.8
Latin America and the Caribbean	2.8	2.2	6.2	4.9	5.8	5.8	4.2	-2.0
Caribbean	2.3	3.1	3.8	8.1	9.4	6.2	3.5	0.3
Central America, excl. Mexico	4.2	3.8	4.5	4.8	6.5	6.8	4.4	-1.1
Mexico	3.1	1.4	4.2	2.8	4.8	3.2	1.4	-7.0
South America	2.7	2.4	7.4	5.6	6.0	6.8	5.5	-0.3
of which:								
Brazil	2.6	1.2	5.7	3.2	4.0	5.7	5.1	-0.8
Asia	6.0	6.8	7.9	7.5	8.0	8.1	5.9	2.6
East Asia	7.6	7.1	8.3	7.9	8.8	9.2	6.3	3.7
of which:								
China	10.1	10.0	10.1	10.2	11.1	11.4	9.0	7.8
South Asia	5.1	7.8	7.5	8.0	8.5	8.3	6.8	4.2
of which:								
India	5.8	8.4	8.3	9.2	9.7	9.0	7.3	5.0
South-East Asia	4.6	5.5	6.6	5.8	6.2	6.4	4.1	-0.8
West Asia	3.4	6.0	8.2	6.6	5.8	5.0	4.5	-1.3

Source: UNCTAD secretariat calculations, based on United Nations, Department of Economic and Social Affairs (UN/DESA), *National Accounts Main Aggregates* database, and *World Economic Situation and Prospects (WESP) 2009: Update as of mid-2009;* OECD, 2009a; ECLAC, 2009a; and national sources.
a   Calculations for country aggregates are based on GDP at constant 2000 dollars.
b   Average.
c   Preliminary estimates for 2008 and forecasts for 2009.
d   New EU member States after 2004.
e   Albania, Bosnia and Herzegovina, Croatia, Montenegro, Serbia and The former Yugoslav Republic of Macedonia.

Table 1.2

EXPORT AND IMPORT VOLUMES OF GOODS, BY REGION AND ECONOMIC GROUPING, 2003–2008

(Annual percentage change)

Region/country	Volume of exports						Volume of imports					
	2003	2004	2005	2006	2007	2008	2003	2004	2005	2006	2007	2008
World	**6.1**	**11.2**	**6.3**	**8.9**	**5.5**	**4.3**	**7.1**	**11.7**	**7.4**	**8.2**	**6.4**	**4.0**
Developed countries	**3.4**	**8.5**	**5.4**	**8.3**	**3.7**	**3.2**	**5.2**	**9.0**	**6.1**	**7.1**	**3.6**	**0.7**
of which:												
Japan	9.2	13.4	5.1	11.8	6.8	4.8	5.9	6.3	2.0	4.3	0.8	-0.8
United States	2.9	8.7	7.4	10.5	6.8	5.5	5.5	10.8	5.6	5.7	0.8	-3.7
European Union	3.5	8.6	5.6	8.6	2.9	2.9	5.5	8.5	6.6	8.8	4.5	2.2
South-East Europe and CIS	**7.9**	**11.7**	**-0.2**	**5.4**	**7.1**	**18.6**	**17.6**	**18.7**	**12.4**	**21.1**	**26.4**	**22.5**
South-East Europe	19.3	22.6	6.1	16.9	18.2	12.1	16.4	16.2	-0.7	8.9	23.2	13.5
CIS	7.2	11.2	-0.4	4.8	6.5	19.3	17.9	19.2	15.2	23.5	26.9	23.9
Developing countries	**11.8**	**16.8**	**9.2**	**10.5**	**8.3**	**4.7**	**11.1**	**17.5**	**9.9**	**9.4**	**10.4**	**8.5**
Africa	3.7	7.6	4.2	0.8	6.9	1.5	5.5	12.5	13.0	9.6	10.0	18.6
Sub Saharan Africa	3.3	8.9	3.6	-0.6	6.8	2.1	14.7	9.9	13.3	12.4	8.6	8.6
Latin America and the Caribbean	3.8	9.5	6.3	5.7	2.3	-1.0	0.7	13.6	10.5	13.3	11.7	6.7
East Asia	21.1	23.4	17.8	18.5	15.1	8.3	18.4	18.8	6.6	10.3	10.4	4.5
of which:												
China	33.4	31.7	26.9	25.4	21.9	12.5	32.9	24.6	8.4	13.2	14.2	7.7
South Asia	8.9	11.1	9.3	7.9	7.1	7.2	13.4	15.9	16.7	8.4	8.0	13.4
of which:												
India	11.1	18.2	16.1	10.2	12.8	9.5	17.1	18.6	22.2	7.8	12.2	17.7
South-East Asia	7.8	19.9	6.4	10.0	6.9	6.4	6.5	18.4	10.0	7.3	7.1	11.1
West Asia	6.9	11.3	0.2	2.9	-1.4	4.2	13.2	23.4	16.8	4.8	16.1	11.5

Source: UNCTAD secretariat calculations, based on *UNCTAD Handbook of Statistics* database.

World trade slowed down in 2007 and 2008, and has been shrinking at a fast rate since November 2008, in both volume and value. Trade volume growth decelerated first in the United States and other developed countries. Indeed in 2008, import volume growth actually turned negative in the United States and Japan. Trade expansion was more resilient in developing and transition economies. In particular, countries that had benefited from terms-of-trade gains until mid 2008 (i.e. mainly countries in Africa, the Commonwealth of Independent States (CIS), Latin America and the Caribbean, and West Asia), were able to increase their imports significantly, although in some cases the volume of their exports slowed down or even declined (table 1.2).

In the final months of 2008, the contraction in investment and consumption of durable goods in many countries was reflected in lower private domestic and foreign demand, leading to a sharp reduction of trade in manufactures. Lower demand by producers for raw materials added to the unwinding of speculative positions by financial investors in primary commodity markets, causing a sharp correction of previously rallying prices in these markets (see section A.2). In 2009, world trade is thus set to shrink considerably, by 11 per cent in real terms and by more than 20 per cent in current dollars (UN/DESA, 2009a and b).

All the major developed economies are in recession.[1] In the *United States,* economic activity is likely to fall by some 3 per cent. The credit crunch and declining incomes and wealth in that country have adversely affected personal consumption, which has been on a downward trend since mid-2008. As the prices of real estate began to tumble from 2006 onwards, residential fixed investment dragged down growth. More recently there has also been a strong reduction in non-residential fixed investment, owing to falling corporate profits, credit cuts and depressed demand. Government spending continued to grow moderately during 2008, compensating only slightly for the plummeting private demand. Net exports made the only significant contribution to growth in the United States, as imports fell faster than exports. Extensive support to the financial sector and some industries, most notably car manufacturers, has helped contain the worsening of the crisis, and an unprecedented fiscal stimulus package (see section D.4) may eventually result in a turnaround in domestic demand.

In *Japan*, the crisis had a direct impact on the two main engines that had sustained economic growth until 2007: exports and private non-residential investment. In the first quarter of 2009, they were down from the previous year by 37 per cent and 21 per cent, respectively. To some extent, the steep fall in export demand was due to the appreciation of the yen as carry-trade operations unwound with the financial crisis; but it was mainly the result of the sharp drop in international demand for machinery, electronic goods and automobiles, which struck at the heart of Japan's industry. Household consumption also fell, owing to declining employment and personal incomes, as well as wealth losses resulting from plunging asset prices. Consequently, real GDP was 8.8 per cent lower in the first quarter of 2009 than the year before. Some improvements can be expected in the second half of the year, as depleting inventories in other Asian countries could cause a recovery in demand for Japanese manufactures. In addition, the large fiscal stimulus package will help boost domestic demand. Nevertheless, Japan is likely to register a drop in GDP of between 6 and 7 per cent – one of the strongest among countries of the Organisation for Economic Co-operation and Development (OECD).

Countries of the *European Union* (EU) had already slipped into recession in the third quarter of 2008, and when the financial crisis entered a more dramatic phase in September 2008, it exacerbated the economic slump. In 2008 as a whole, annual GDP growth was still positive. Since most of the slowdown in economic activity occurred in the last quarter of 2008 and the first quarter of 2009, the bulk of the setback in production will be reflected in the statistics for 2009. Output in the EU is expected to fall by at least 4 per cent from its 2008 level, even on the basis of an optimistic scenario that production will stabilize or recover slightly in the second half of 2009. The turmoil had a direct impact on economies in which the financial sector accounts for a large share of GDP, such as Ireland and the United Kingdom, but most other European economies also suffered from the credit crunch and falling asset prices. The crisis also revealed that, after several years of large net capital exports, the financial sector of many European countries was heavily exposed to risks generated in the United States and other deficit economies, as many banks had sought to make high profits by accumulating risky assets abroad. Credit shortages, negative wealth effects and mounting unemployment affected private consumption and investment, and particularly construction, in many European economies. Spain, a country that based much of its recent growth on the construction sector, was especially hard hit. The sharp drop in international trade, particularly in capital goods and durable consumer goods, greatly affected countries that rely on exports of manufactures, such as Germany.

In *Eastern Europe*, lower demand from the euro area has mainly affected industrial production and exports of manufactures. Many countries in this region had posted significant and growing trade deficits in previous years, due partly to high domestic investment and partly to currency overvaluation that led to a loss of competitiveness of domestic producers in international markets. As carry-trade operations unwound and capital began to flee to safer forms of investment, several currencies in the region came under heavy pressure to depreciate. Some countries had to turn to the International Monetary Fund (IMF) for financial support, in some instances complemented by EU loans. This financial support has served to smooth currency depreciation in countries such as Hungary, while in others, such as the Baltic States, it has helped to maintain the exchange-rate peg. External financial assistance in all these countries has also aimed at preventing the collapse of their banking systems. If these were to fold, it would have grave consequences for Western European creditor banks. As IMF support for these countries is linked with traditional conditionalities, including monetary and fiscal tightening, it has had the effect of further depressing domestic demand following the bursting of the real estate bubble and the reversal of business and consumption credit. As a result, Baltic countries are likely to post double-digit negative growth rates in 2009.

In the *CIS,* GDP may fall by more than 6 per cent in 2009, led by recession in Ukraine, the Russian Federation and Kazakhstan. Export value has been declining in most countries due to lower prices and, in general, also smaller volumes. As international investors and lenders turned away in the search for reduced risk exposure, capital outflows and currency depreciations in several countries revealed the vulnerability of their banking sector. Tightening credit and deteriorating employment conditions caused a fall in domestic investment and consumption just when foreign demand also receded. In the first few months of 2009, year-on-year industrial output dropped in the Russian Federation and Ukraine by about 20 and 30 per cent respectively. The recession in the largest economies greatly affected other CIS countries, as exports and remittance inflows fell. The Governments of the Russian Federation and Kazakhstan launched sizeable stimulus plans, using financial reserves accumulated from the high oil revenues of the past few years.

In *Africa,* after five consecutive years of real GDP growth of between 5 and 6 per cent, the rate is likely to slow down to close to only 1 per cent in 2009, which means a significant reduction in per capita GDP. So far, the global crisis has affected the continent mainly through trade. Exporters of oil, mining products and agricultural raw materials have been particularly hard hit by the sharp fall in the prices of primary commodities. This means that governments whose revenues are directly linked to primary exports will have to adjust their expenditure programmes. More diversified African economies that have a significant share of manufactures in their total exports have been affected mainly by a fall in export volumes. In the last months of 2008, some food and oil importers in sub-Saharan Africa partly reversed the losses they had incurred from unfavourable terms of trade in 2007 and the first half of 2008, but they have not been able to translate such gains into higher growth. Growth remains constrained on the demand side by lower remittances and a slump in global demand for goods and services, including tourism, and on the supply side by insufficient investment.

In *Latin America and the Caribbean*, GDP is likely to fall, on average, by around 2 per cent in 2009. Mexico has felt the impact of the crisis the most strongly, with a loss of GDP in the order of 7 per cent in 2009; together with several Central American and Caribbean countries, it has been more affected than others by the decline in external demand for manufactures and reduced tourism. The impact of the crisis is reflected in the lower volume of trade, fixed investment and manufacturing output. Most of these variables showed double-digit contraction in all major countries in late 2008 and early 2009. South American countries have been affected largely by the fall in primary commodity prices, which have lowered their export and fiscal revenues. In some countries, this has put a brake on public spending that had been growing rapidly in recent years. In other countries, governments have been able to provide a fiscal stimulus – in some cases by using funds accumulated through surpluses in recent years – in order to compensate for lower private domestic and foreign demand. Most countries in the region were in a relatively strong macroeconomic position at the onset of the global crisis. Consequently, no banking or balance-of-payments crisis has occurred so far. Many countries allowed the depreciation of their currencies, but were able to avoid overshooting. Governments in the region have largely avoided adopting the procyclical policies that had aggravated the earlier crises between 1995 and 2001. In the present crisis, Latin American countries enjoy wider room for manoeuvre than in other episodes of crisis, and have been taking advantage of this for countercyclical measures.

In 2009, GDP is set to fall in several economies in *East and South-East Asia* that strongly rely on exports of manufactures, particularly capital and durable consumer goods. The dense production network of industries in the region has caused a parallel fall in industrial production and international trade. The countries that have been better able to resist recessionary pressures are those where the domestic market plays a more important – and growing – role in total demand, such as China and Indonesia. Moreover, proactive countercyclical policies may attenuate the effects of the economic slump in several countries. The impact of higher public spending on infrastructure as well as credit expansion is already visible in China, where output growth is likely to exceed 7 per cent in 2009. By contrast, Taiwan Province of China, Hong Kong (Special Administrative Region of China) and Singapore are expected to experience a sharp downturn. Overall, East Asia should be able to maintain a positive growth rate, while GDP in South-East Asia will probably decline, albeit less than the average for the world economy.

Almost all the *South-Asian* economies should continue to grow in 2009, but at a slower pace. They are feeling the impact of the crisis through reduced capital inflows, lower migrants' remittances and falling external demand. But since domestic demand accounts for a large and increasing share of total demand, South Asia, particularly India, is expected to see continued growth in 2009.

In *West Asia* as a whole, GDP is expected to fall only slightly, although growth performance will differ significantly among countries within the region. Several countries have been directly affected by the turmoil in financial markets, with sharp falls in real estate and stock prices, and attendant negative effects on private wealth. In some cases, banks' balance sheets and credit supply have also been badly hit. The oil exporting countries, like many others, have been affected by lower export earnings, mainly due to tumbling prices. In addition, reduced quotas agreed by the Organization of the Petroleum Exporting Countries (OPEC) have meant cuts in oil production in real terms. Private consumption and investment are expected to fall. In some countries, especially Saudi Arabia, higher public spending will compensate, at least partially, for lower private spending. In non-oil- or gas-exporting countries, economic growth is likely to decline due to lower remittances, exports and tourism receipts. In Turkey, GDP plummeted in the last quarter of 2008 and the first quarter of 2009, dragged down by reduced private consumption, investments and exports. A strong increase in public expenditure was not sufficient to prevent overall economic contraction, which will be the most severe for Turkey out of all the countries in the subregion.

By mid-2009, prospects for an economic recovery remained very uncertain. In several developed countries, the contraction of economic activity decelerated, compared to the almost free fall of previous months. Financial indicators show a recovery from the lows reached in the first quarter of 2009. Interest rate spreads on emerging debt and corporate bonds decreased, and prices of stocks and many commodities, as well as exchange rates of emerging-market currencies, rebounded. These indications are being interpreted by some observers as the "green shoots" of an imminent economic revival. But the main factors behind the economic crisis still prevail: massive write-downs of financial assets and continuing deleveraging by financial agents are hindering the supply of credit by the financial system; asset depreciation and rising unemployment are further constraining private demand; and overinvestment in real estate and underutilized productive capacity, together with bleak prospects for final demand, will continue to weigh down investment demand for some time to come. Taking these factors into account, the rebound in the prices of financial assets and commodities is more likely to be just a correction of the preceding downward overshooting in 2008, which was as irrational as the bullish exuberance in previous years. Furthermore, there are strong indications that recent improvements in the financial markets are largely due to a recovery of "risk appetite" by financial agents, but this could be reversed at short notice depending on speculators' mood or possible changes in macroeconomic policy stances.

If governments of the largest economies maintain their expansionary policies (see section D), GDP contraction may recede by 2010 and growth could return, although at a slower pace. According to estimates by the United Nations Department of Economic and Social Affairs (UN/DESA), world output might grow at 1.6 per cent in 2010, compared to its average growth of 3.6 per cent between 2003 and 2007.

2. Recent trends in primary commodity markets

(a) Price developments

The commodity price boom, which had continued unabated since 2002, came to an end in mid-2008, and turned into a sharp decline during the second half of the year. In the first half of 2009, the prices of many primary commodities rebounded although market fundamentals remained weak (OPEC, 2009; IEA, 2009a; RGE *Monitor*, 2009). Much of the recent developments in commodity prices can be attributed to the greater presence of financial investors in the markets for primary commodities (see chapter II).

Prices of all commodity groups except tropical beverages reached historic highs in nominal terms in 2008. In real terms, however, when deflated by the export unit value of manufactured goods of developed countries, only the prices of the metals and minerals group and oil reached record levels. Nevertheless, real prices for the other groups were significantly higher than at the beginning of the decade and also higher than their long-term trend. The price increases during the boom years were impressive for practically all commodities (table 1.3). But equally exceptional was the sharp and widespread price decline thereafter (chart 1.1). The price swings were more moderate for tropical beverages and agricultural raw materials than for other commodities.

While the deterioration of global economic prospects in 2008 caused a fall in commodity demand, the downturn in commodity prices was first triggered by a reorientation of speculative influences in these markets. Despite the downward correction in the second half of 2008, prices for all commodity groups, except oil, remained above their average of the past 10 years. A large number of commodity prices seemed to have bottomed out by December 2008,[2] but at this point prices of most commodity groups had only retreated back to about the levels of 2007. Only oil and minerals and metals had fallen roughly to the levels of 2005. The prices of oil, minerals and metals, and agricultural raw materials were worse hit than others by the slowdown in demand resulting from the slump in industrial production in developed countries (chart 1.1B).[3] Although producers of minerals and metals significantly reduced production, weak demand outpaced these supply adjustments, resulting in a build-up of inventories during the second half of 2008 (Desjardins, 2009).

The revival in some mineral and metal prices in early 2009 appears to be related to stock replenishments by manufacturing companies around the world and also to increases in strategic reserves, notably in China (Ulrich, 2009).[4] This could mean that the upward swing in prices may be short-lived if stockpiling ends before real demand picks up significantly. On the other hand, the influence of the speculative forces that also caused a rise in financial asset prices and some exchange rates against the trend in fundamentals could well compensate for this effect. Moreover, precious metals, mainly gold, have recently benefited from high demand as investors seek traditional safe havens in uncertain times.

Developments in oil prices have been leading price movements in other commodity markets. Oil prices may affect prices of other commodities through their impact on the production of substitutes for cotton (synthetic fibres) and natural rubber (synthetic rubber), their contribution to production and transportation costs, and by influencing the demand for food commodities for biofuel production as an alternative source of energy.[5] The price of oil has exhibited the highest volatility of all in recent months. The monthly average oil price increased from $53.4 per barrel in January 2007 to $132.5 per barrel in July 2008, and then dropped to $41.5 per barrel in December 2008. It increased thereafter to reach $68.5 in June 2009 (UNCTAD, 2009a).[6]

As the global financial and economic crisis continued to unfold, oil demand fell during the first months of 2009. By June 2009, forecasts were for an overall decline of 2.9 per cent in 2009, mainly on account of lower demand by members of the Organisation of Economic Co-operation and Development (OECD) (chart 1.2). This would represent the sharpest fall in a single year since 1981 (IEA, 2009a and b). In view of the low prices, between September and December 2008 the Organization of the Petroleum Exporting Countries (OPEC) announced cuts in production quotas to a total of 4.2 million barrels per day, equivalent to 4.8 per cent of 2008 world supply. Non-OPEC supply has remained flat. Due partly to the high compliance with OPEC production cuts, and partly to speculation, oil prices rebounded in the first half of 2009. OPEC production quotas remained unchanged during this period, and the International Energy Agency (IEA, 2009b) revised its forecasts for oil demand upwards for the first time in about a year. However, only China and other Asian countries showed signs of rising real demand, while demand in OECD countries showed no signs of recovery owing to declining industrial production (chart 1.1B).[7]

As for agricultural commodities, short-term price developments are determined not so much by changes in demand; they are mainly linked to factors that affect supply, such as weather, pests and diseases, and crop cycles. In early 2009, prices of tropical beverages have been propped up by crop shortages in major producing areas due to adverse weather conditions. This is the case for coffee in Colombia, Central America and Brazil (where coffee is in a low production year of its biennial crop cycle), cocoa in Côte d'Ivoire and Ghana, and tea in India, Kenya and

Table 1.3

WORLD PRIMARY COMMODITY PRICES, 2002–2008

(Percentage change over previous year, unless otherwise indicated)

Commodity group	2003	2004	2005	2006	2007	2008	2002–2008[a]	Jan.–Dec. 2008[b]
All commodities[c]	**8.1**	**19.9**	**11.7**	**30.4**	**12.9**	**23.8**	**164.0**	**-22.5**
All commodities (in SDRs)[c]	**-0.2**	**13.5**	**12.1**	**30.7**	**8.5**	**19.4**	**115.0**	**-19.3**
All food	**4.1**	**13.2**	**6.3**	**16.3**	**13.3**	**39.2**	**129.8**	**-11.8**
Food and tropical beverages	**2.3**	**13.2**	**8.8**	**17.8**	**8.6**	**40.4**	**126.3**	**-5.2**
Tropical beverages	6.2	6.4	25.5	6.7	10.4	20.2	100.8	-8.3
Coffee	8.7	19.8	43.8	7.1	12.5	15.4	160.3	-15.8
Cocoa	-1.3	-11.8	-0.7	3.5	22.6	32.2	45.1	10.9
Tea	8.4	2.1	9.1	11.7	-12.3	27.2	50.4	-0.9
Food	1.9	13.9	7.2	19.0	8.5	42.5	128.8	-5.0
Sugar	2.9	1.1	37.9	49.4	-31.7	26.9	85.9	-1.8
Beef	0.4	17.8	4.1	-2.4	1.9	2.6	25.8	-8.3
Maize	6.5	5.0	-12.0	24.4	38.2	34.0	126.7	-25.4
Wheat	-0.7	6.8	-1.4	26.6	34.3	27.5	126.6	-38.7
Rice	4.1	23.1	17.1	5.5	9.5	110.7	265.3	40.2
Bananas	-28.7	39.9	9.9	18.5	-0.9	24.6	60.3	23.8
Vegetable oilseeds and oils	**17.4**	**13.2**	**-9.5**	**5.0**	**52.9**	**31.9**	**154.8**	**-45.4**
Soybeans	24.1	16.1	-10.4	-2.2	43.0	36.1	145.8	-33.5
Agricultural raw materials	**19.8**	**13.4**	**4.0**	**15.0**	**11.2**	**19.4**	**115.6**	**-25.6**
Hides and skins	-16.8	-1.7	-2.1	5.1	4.5	-11.3	-22.1	-44.6
Cotton	37.2	-3.3	-11.6	5.9	10.2	12.8	54.4	-24.3
Tobacco	-3.5	3.6	1.8	6.4	11.6	8.3	30.8	9.8
Rubber	41.7	20.3	15.2	40.4	8.6	14.3	242.2	-53.6
Tropical logs	20.1	19.2	0.3	-4.7	19.5	39.3	127.8	-1.4
Minerals, ores and metals	**12.4**	**40.7**	**26.2**	**60.3**	**12.8**	**6.2**	**283.0**	**-37.0**
Aluminium	6.0	19.8	10.6	35.4	2.7	-2.5	90.6	-39.0
Phosphate rock	-5.9	7.8	2.5	5.3	60.5	387.2	755.8	84.2
Iron ore	8.5	17.4	71.5	19.0	9.5	65.0	369.8	0.0
Tin	20.6	73.8	-13.2	18.9	65.6	27.3	356.0	-31.2
Copper	14.1	61.0	28.4	82.7	5.9	-2.3	346.1	-56.5
Nickel	42.2	43.6	6.6	64.5	53.5	-43.3	211.6	-65.0
Tungsten ore	18.0	22.9	120.7	36.2	-0.6	-0.3	332.4	-3.0
Lead	13.8	72.0	10.2	32.0	100.2	-19.0	361.6	-63.0
Zinc	6.3	26.5	31.9	137.0	-1.0	-42.2	140.7	-52.9
Gold	17.3	12.6	8.7	35.9	15.3	25.1	181.2	-8.2
Crude petroleum	**15.8**	**30.7**	**41.3**	**20.4**	**10.7**	**36.4**	**288.9**	**-54.3**
Memo item:								
Manufactures[d]	**9.2**	**8.3**	**2.5**	**3.2**	**7.5**	**4.3**	**40.6**	..

Source: UNCTAD secretariat calculations, based on UNCTAD, *Commodity Price Statistics Online*; and United Nations Statistics Division (UNSD), *Monthly Bulletin of Statistics*, various issues.

Note: In current dollars unless otherwise specified.
   a Percentage change between 2002 and 2008.
   b Percentage change between January 2008 and December 2008.
   c Excluding crude petroleum.
   d Export unit value of manufactured goods of developed countries.

Chart 1.1

MONTHLY EVOLUTION OF COMMODITY PRICES, EXCHANGE RATES AND INDUSTRIAL PRODUCTION IN OECD COUNTRIES, JANUARY 2000–MAY 2009

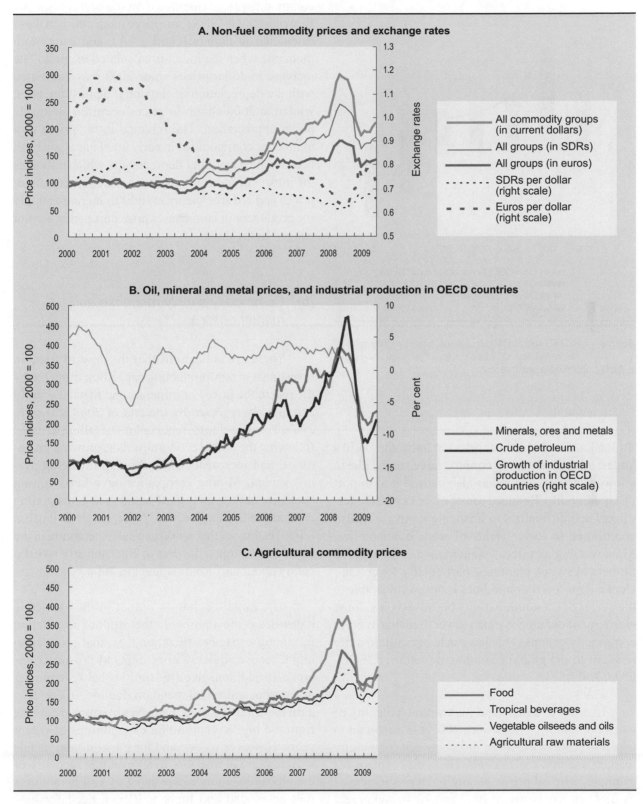

A. Non-fuel commodity prices and exchange rates

- All commodity groups (in current dollars)
- All groups (in SDRs)
- All groups (in euros)
- SDRs per dollar (right scale)
- Euros per dollar (right scale)

B. Oil, mineral and metal prices, and industrial production in OECD countries

- Minerals, ores and metals
- Crude petroleum
- Growth of industrial production in OECD countries (right scale)

C. Agricultural commodity prices

- Food
- Tropical beverages
- Vegetable oilseeds and oils
- Agricultural raw materials

Source: UNCTAD secretariat calculations, based on UNCTAD, *Commodity Price Statistics Online*, *UNCTAD Handbook of Statistics* database; and OECD, *Main Economic Indicators* database.

Note: Industrial production in OECD countries refers to year-on-year changes.

Chart 1.2

CHANGE IN OIL DEMAND, 2003–2009

(Million barrels per day)

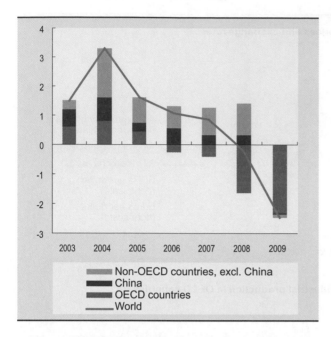

- Non-OECD countries, excl. China
- China
- OECD countries
- World

Source: UNCTAD secretariat calculations, based on International Energy Agency, *Oil Market Report* (various issues).
Note: 2009 data are forecasts.

Sri Lanka. Similarly, sugar prices in India, the world's largest sugar consuming country, have surged due to a lower harvest, which has also caused it to import this commodity. Reduced use of more expensive fertilizers and difficulties in financing inputs have also contributed to lower yields of some commodities. Moreover, higher prices for alternative crops have led farmers to switch plantings, particularly for cotton.[8] Demand for food commodities is not so vulnerable to the cycles of economic activity because their income elasticity of demand is much lower than that of other commodity groups. This has made agriculture more resilient to the global economic downturn (OECD-FAO, 2009).

In order to understand the extreme volatility of many commodity prices since 2007 it is important to take into account the closer links between commodity markets and financial markets. These may explain, for example, why oil prices in nominal terms increased by 289 per cent between 2002 and 2008, and in real terms (deflated by the United States consumer price index (CPI)) by 224 per cent, while the demand for oil rose by 10.4 per cent and oil supply by 12.5 per cent.[9] In addition, as commodity prices are typically denominated in dollars, the exchange rate of the dollar may have had an effect on price changes. Changes in commodity prices calculated on the basis of Special Drawing Rights (SDRs) are more moderate than those calculated in dollars (chart 1.1A), and even more moderate when the index is calculated in euros. The increase in dollar prices since 2002 was associated with the depreciation of the dollar against the euro, while the 2008 slump in prices occurred alongside dollar appreciation. The rebound in the prices of a number of commodities in early 2009 has again been accompanied by dollar depreciation, which mitigates the impact of increases in dollar prices on consumer prices and reduces the incentives to increase supply for producers in countries whose currencies are not pegged to the dollar.

(b) Commodity supply response and market outlook

There are indications that the upward trend in investment in new production capacities, triggered by the rise in the prices of minerals and metals, sharply and quickly reversed by the end of 2008 and early 2009. This was due to expectations of falling demand following the global economic crisis, growing inventories, and increasing difficulties in financing new investment. Mining companies have been cutting back production, laying off workers and postponing or abandoning exploration projects. BNP Paribas (2009) estimates that world capital expenditure in the metal and mining industries in 2009 and 2010 will be cut by about half from its level in 2008.[10]

The initial decline in output in the extractive industries is most probably the result of a reduction in mining capacity utilization,[11] so that production might recover quickly once demand prospects improve. In addition, given the time lag between mining investment and actual metal production, in the short term there may be some increases in supply resulting from the higher exploration expenditures of recent years. However, as demand for minerals and metals will rebound in response to an eventual recovery of the global economy, spare capacity and inventories will be eroded and there will be a need for new sources of supply. Thus, in the medium to long term, project delays and the current declines in exploration

Chart 1.3

GROWTH IN COMMODITY CONSUMPTION: CHINA AND REST OF THE WORLD, 2005–2009

(Per cent)

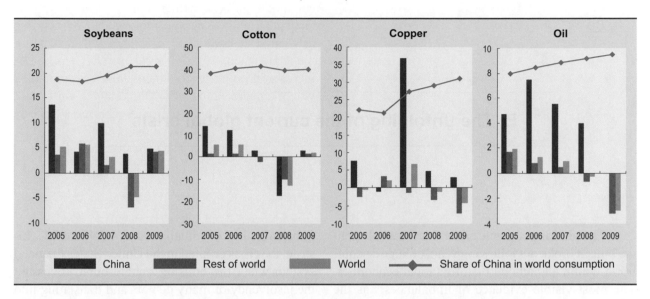

Source: UNCTAD secretariat calculations, based on USDA, *Oilseeds World Markets and Trade*, June, 2009; ICAC, *Cotton this week* (various issues); IEA, *Oil Market Report* (various issues); and Chilean Copper Commission (COCHILCO), *Copper Market Quarterly Review* (various issues).

Note: 2009 data are forecasts by USDA for soybeans, ICAC for cotton, COCHILCO for copper and IEA for oil.

expenditures may well lead to supply shortages (Ernst & Young, 2009). The situation is similar in the oil and gas sector, where investment also increased during the boom years, but investment budgets for 2009 fell by more than 20 per cent compared with 2008 as a result of lower prices and more difficult financing conditions (IEA, 2009c).[12]

In the agricultural sector, supply may react faster to changes in market conditions, particularly for commodities with crop cycles of around one year. On the other hand, the global food crisis has revealed the constraints that small farmers in developing countries face in increasing productivity (see also the annex to this chapter). As a result of the credit crunch, farmers have difficulty financing inputs, such as seeds and fertilizers, as well as new investments, forcing them to reduce plantings (von Braun, 2008; FAO, 2008). Reduced plantings worldwide, stemming also from lower agricultural prices and a slow downward adjustment of input prices, are expected to lead to lower harvests in the 2009/10 season.[13] In general, tighter credit conditions are a greater problem for farmers in developed and middle-income developing countries. However, the direct financial impact of the crisis most

probably has been proportionately lower for producers of agricultural commodities than for producers in the energy or mineral and metals sectors. This is because of the generally more conservative financing strategies in the agricultural sector (OECD-FAO, 2009). Over the medium to long term, however, any delayed investment for improving agricultural productivity will perpetuate existing supply constraints in developing countries.

Overall, demand from China continues to play a key role in world commodity market developments (chart 1.3), and has tended to have a stabilizing effect in the context of the current crisis. Given the continuing growth dynamics of China and a number of other large emerging-market economies, commodity prices could turn upwards again in response to signs of a global recovery. However, they may not return to the peaks registered in the first half of 2008 any time soon unless price movements caused by fundamental factors get amplified by speculative trading on commodity markets. The economic stimulus packages introduced in many countries can play an important role in boosting demand for commodities from its current low levels in the short term, because they have a strong infrastructure investment component. Prices are also likely to remain very volatile due to considerable uncertainty in the markets and to the intense financialization of commodity markets. From

a longer term perspective, however, there may be increasing pressure on natural resources, and commodity markets could tighten again in a few years' time.

B. The unfolding of the current global crisis

The present economic crisis was not a bolt from the blue; it broke out following years of huge disequilibria within and among major national economies. The most visible evidence of imbalances was the large current-account deficits in the United States, the United Kingdom, Spain and several East European economies, on the one hand, and large surpluses in China, Japan, Germany and the oil-exporting countries, on the other. These international imbalances were accompanied by mounting domestic tensions. In the United States, economic growth was dependent on debt-financed household consumption, made possible by reckless credit distribution and a growing bubble in the housing market. In China, growth based on exports and extremely high investment ratios accentuated economic, social and regional disequilibria, and prompted a policy reorientation aimed at promoting social expenditure and domestic consumption. In the euro area, tensions arose between member States as wage increases in Germany were kept below productivity gains, which undermined the competitiveness of producers in other countries.

Clearly, such disequilibria could not continue indefinitely. A globally coordinated adjustment whereby surplus countries would expand domestic demand was consistently advocated by many observers and institutions, including UNCTAD in several of its *Trade and Development Reports (TDRs)*.[14] However, policymakers failed to acknowledge the need for an internationally balanced macroeconomic management of demand, and, in several cases, greatly overestimated inflationary risk.[15] A hard-landing scenario was thus predictable. It could have occurred in international markets, if continuous current-account

imbalances had eventually led to a dollar crisis. Instead, the crisis erupted in the United States financial system when the housing bubble burst, revealing the insolvency of many debtors and translating into a full-blown financial crisis which rapidly spread throughout the international financial system.

The current financial crisis has much in common with previous crises: it followed the classical sequence of expansion, euphoria, financial distress and panic (Minsky, 1975; Kindleberger, 1978). During the expansionary phase, new profit opportunities attract investors and tend to increase asset prices; the resulting wealth-effect reinforces economic growth through higher demand. In the euphoria phase the process feeds on itself, since, unlike what typically happens in goods markets, rising prices of financial assets tend to increase demand for them, and this reinforces the belief of investors and speculators that the upward price trends will persist. This process can continue for quite a while, especially if investors can leverage their positions through credit, and thereby sustain the demand for financial assets. Indeed, the increasing market value of financial assets leads to an underestimation of risk by both borrowers and creditors, and facilitates access to ever more credit. The rising indebtedness of the non-financial sector and the growing leverage of financial institutions increase the vulnerability of the entire system to asset price changes.

In the build-up of the financial crisis, a large proportion of the credit expansion in the United States and other developed economies financed real estate acquisitions, fuelled asset price inflation and spurred debt-financed private consumption. After 2000, household debt increased rapidly in many countries (chart 1.4). The increase was particularly rapid in those economies where current-account deficits widened and, as a result, external liabilities were accumulated by what are sometimes referred to as Anglo-Saxon economies (Australia, Ireland, the United Kingdom and the United States) and by a number of Eastern European countries where household debt increased more than threefold, albeit from relatively low levels. This was similar to developments in Spain, where household debt had already started to rise in the mid-1990s. In other major developed economies, such as Germany and Japan – two of the main surplus economies – such debt rose more slowly, or even fell.

What makes this crisis exceptionally widespread and deep is the fact that financial deregulation and innovation raised credit leverage to unprecedented levels. Blind faith in the "efficiency" of deregulated financial markets led authorities to allow the expansion of a "shadow" financial system, in which investment banks, hedge funds and special investment vehicles were allowed to operate with little or no supervision and capital requirements (see chapter III). Moreover, the underestimation of risks, typical during financial booms, was aggravated by deficiencies in the operations of the rating agencies.

The euphoric phase came to an end when GDP growth in the United States began to slow down in mid-2006, the housing market there ceased to expand and the rise in asset prices – a vital condition for many debtors to remain solvent – levelled off. By that time it had become clear that economic growth led by debt-financed private consumption was unsustainable (*TDR 2006*, chap. I, section C.3).

The financial crisis rendered a soft landing impossible. Credit supply came to a sudden halt, as banks and other financial intermediaries ran out of liquidity and assets that had served as collateral for the debt of households and firms lost value at increasing speed. Asset depreciation led many debtors to insolvency and dramatically worsened the quality of financial institutions' portfolios.

The emergency provision of liquidity by central banks prevented large-scale bankruptcies, but it could not ensure the continuity of credit flows. Commercial banks had to be recapitalized, not only because they were suffering losses from non-performing loans, but

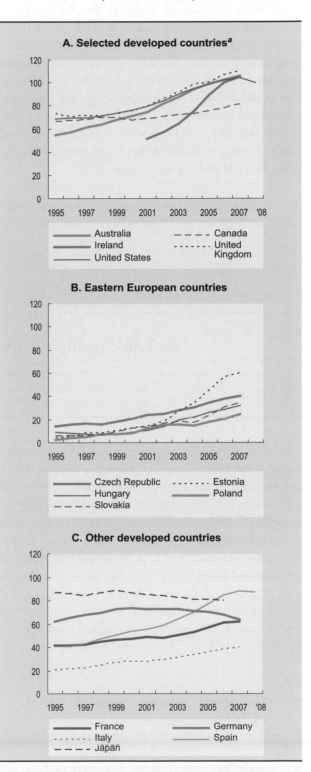

Chart 1.4

HOUSEHOLDS' LIABILITIES IN SELECTED COUNTRIES, 1995–2008

(Per cent of GDP)

A. Selected developed countries[a]

Australia — — — Canada
Ireland · · · · · · United
United States — — Kingdom

B. Eastern European countries

Czech Republic · · · · · · Estonia
Hungary — — Poland
— — — Slovakia

C. Other developed countries

France — — Germany
· · · · · · Italy — — Spain
— — — Japan

Source: UNCTAD secretariat calculations, based on OECD, *National Accounts* database; and national sources.
   a These comprise countries which are sometimes referred to as Anglo-Saxon countries, and Canada.

also because the remaining assets suddenly became more risky and – following the Basel II prudential criteria – required higher capital coverage. In order to comply with more stringent capital requirements, their provision of credit had to be cut back. Other financial institutions (e.g. investment banks, hedge funds and special investment vehicles), which relied heavily on short-term credit for covering long-term positions, were thus forced to sell part of their assets in order to meet short-term liabilities. The sudden contraction of credit supply exerted additional downward pressure on asset prices, causing a further deterioration in the solvency of borrowers and financial intermediaries alike,[16] and accelerating the process of debt-deflation (Fisher, 1933).

In this process, financial distress spread rapidly to the "real" sector of the economy. Overindebtedness

and insolvency, credit shortages and negative wealth effects due to losses in real estate and financial assets led to a contraction of final demand, especially for business and residential investment and durable consumer goods, all of which rely on credit finance.[17] As a result, year-on-year industrial production in the United States in the period January to April 2009 plunged by 12 per cent, and the volume of goods imports fell by 19.6 per cent. United States merchandise exports fell (by 15.9 per cent), as economic activity in its main trading partners also declined. Once the recession had set in, increasing unemployment led to a second round of falling demand. Between June 2008 and March 2009 unemployment grew further, from 5.6 to 8.5 per cent in the United States and from 7.4 per cent to 8.9 per cent in the euro area. Unemployment is expected to rise to double-digit levels in 2010.[18]

C. The ramifications of the spreading crisis

The world economy is experiencing a synchronized downturn: financial markets, capital flows, international trade and economic activity have been affected in all the regions of the world. The relative importance of the different channels of transmission between countries and markets has varied across countries, depending on factors such as initial current account and foreign asset or liability positions, exposure to private international capital flows, composition and direction of international trade in manufactures and services, dependence on primary commodity exports and inflows of migrants' remittances.

1. Financial contagion, speculation and adjustment

Since September 2008, financial markets for very different types of assets and in all major countries have been hit almost simultaneously by a financial shock of unprecedented magnitude. Financial distress

spread from one market to another, regardless of long-term "fundamentals". The financial shockwave submerged stock and bond markets in many countries, exchange rates of some emerging-market currencies and primary commodity markets all at the same time (chart 1.5).

The uniform reaction of so many different markets is often taken as an indication of the interdependence of these markets in a globalized economy. But there is more to it. The high correlation of the day-to-day price movements in many different markets that are not linked by economic fundamentals is largely due to the strong influence of speculative behaviour in all these markets (UNCTAD, 2009b).

According to the Bank for International Settlements (BIS, 2009), external bank assets, which had grown at an annual rate of 20 per cent between March 2002 and March 2008, declined by 14 per cent during the remainder of 2008. As net bank financing shrank, outstanding bank assets fell significantly, not only in

Chart 1.5

EVOLUTION OF PRICES IN SELECTED MARKETS AND COUNTRIES, JUNE 2008–JULY 2009

(Index numbers, 2 June 2008 = 100)

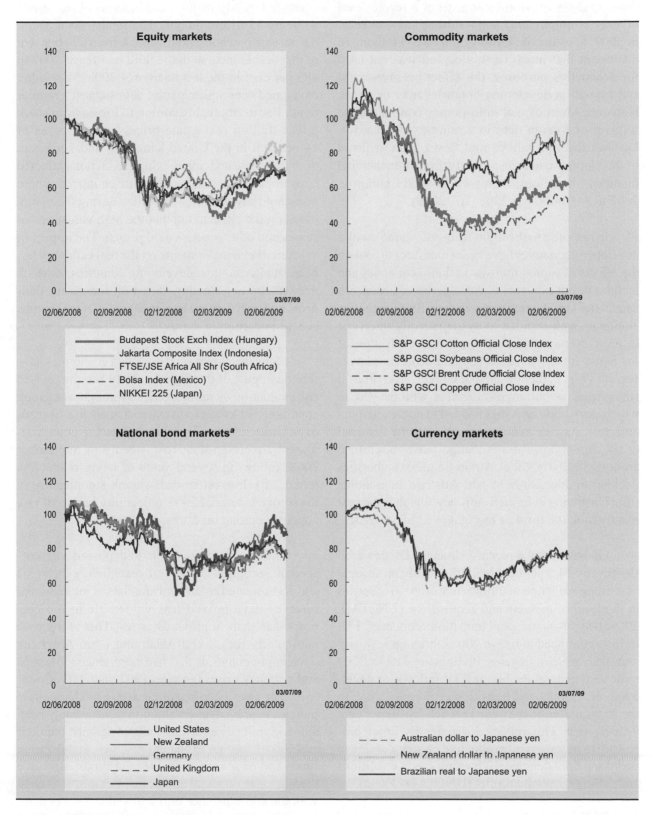

Equity markets
- Budapest Stock Exch Index (Hungary)
- Jakarta Composite Index (Indonesia)
- FTSE/JSE Africa All Shr (South Africa)
- Bolsa Index (Mexico)
- NIKKEI 225 (Japan)

Commodity markets
- S&P GSCI Cotton Official Close Index
- S&P GSCI Soybeans Official Close Index
- S&P GSCI Brent Crude Official Close Index
- S&P GSCI Copper Official Close Index

National bond markets[a]
- United States
- New Zealand
- Germany
- United Kingdom
- Japan

Currency markets
- Australian dollar to Japanese yen
- New Zealand dollar to Japanese yen
- Brazilian real to Japanese yen

Source: UNCTAD secretariat calculations, based on Bloomberg.
 a Yields on 10-year bonds.

developed countries but also in developing countries and offshore centres. Overall, private capital flows to emerging markets are expected to fall sharply. Preliminary data show a 50 per cent decline in such flows in 2008 to $466 billion, from a record level of $929 billion in 2007 and a further fall is forecast in 2009, to estimated flows of only $165 billion. To the extent that much of this capital was not used for productive purposes, the effect on investment and growth in developing countries may be small. However, lower capital inflows may complicate the rollover of foreign debt in a number of countries. Distinct from private capital flows, official flows to developing countries, mainly from international financial institutions, increased from $11 billion in 2007 to $41 billion in 2008 (IIF, 2009).

In response to the flight from risk, some smaller developed economies have taken measures to contain the effects of capital inflows on their economies and on their future exposure to the vagaries of liberalized capital markets. For example, in early 2009, the Swiss National Bank decided to systematically intervene in the currency market to limit the revaluation of the Swiss franc. This currency had depreciated over several years in the run-up to the financial crisis as it was one of the currencies, together with the yen, in which carry trade activities had led to massive capital outflows. As risk aversion grew with the financial crisis, capital flows and exchange-rate trends turned around. Similarly, the Austrian financial authorities decided in June 2009 to ban Austrian households from borrowing in foreign currency, which in the past mostly took the form of mortgages in Swiss francs.

Global foreign direct investment (FDI) flows fell sharply, by 14.5 per cent in 2008, mainly on account of a strong reduction in inflows to European countries in the form of mergers and acquisitions (UNCTAD, 2009c). In developing and transition economies, FDI inflows continued to rise in 2008, although at slower rates than in previous years. Preliminary data for 2009 indicate a general decline in FDI inflows, in developed, developing and transition economies alike. In the first quarter of the year FDI fell by 50 per cent year-on-year. This reflected a generally lower propensity to invest in real productive capacity, owing to shrinking final demand, tightening credit conditions and falling corporate profits (UNCTAD, 2009d).

Different kinds of financial shocks have had varying impacts on diverse economies. Losses in previously overvalued stock prices have reduced perceived household wealth more in developed countries than in developing countries. In the United States, household wealth in terms of outstanding financial assets fell by $10 trillion, and in terms of real estate value by $3 trillion in only 15 months. As a result, the net worth of households shrank from 629 per cent of disposable income in the third quarter of 2007 to 483 per cent in the last quarter of 2008.[19] For other developed economies, partial data suggest a similar trend. For example, in addition to losses from stock prices, falling real estate prices caused losses of 14 per cent in the United Kingdom, and 7 per cent each in France and Spain.[20] Such reductions affected consumption demand mainly in countries where household savings rates had fallen during the boom, based on the expectation that the high valuations of stocks and other assets would persist. The impact of stock market developments on the real economy has been smaller in most developing countries, as stock markets are not a major source of finance for their firms and only a small percentage of private savings is held in corporate shares.[21]

Many developing and transition economies have felt the impact of the flight to safety and the revised risk evaluation by rating agencies through worsening conditions for longer term external financing. Spreads over United States Treasury bonds for emerging-market sovereign debt rose steeply in September 2008, following several years of being rather low (chart 1.6). Interest spreads shrank significantly in the second quarter of 2009, reflecting a renewed "risk appetite" among investors.

Those economies that had posted current-account surpluses for several years before the crisis and accumulated significant amounts of international reserves have proved less vulnerable in the current crisis than in previous crises. This is the case particularly for several Asian and Latin American developing countries that had experienced financial and currency crises between 1997 and 2001. Countries that have been pursuing active exchange-rate policies to prevent overvaluation have not only been able to avoid large current-account deficits, but their cushion of foreign exchange reserves, stabilization funds and/or sovereign investment funds, also give them greater financial and policy flexibility to cope with the consequences of the global crisis. As these countries are not rigidly committed to either fixed or entirely flexible exchange rates, they accepted

Chart 1.6

YIELD SPREADS ON EMERGING-MARKET BONDS, JANUARY 2006–JULY 2009

(Basis points)

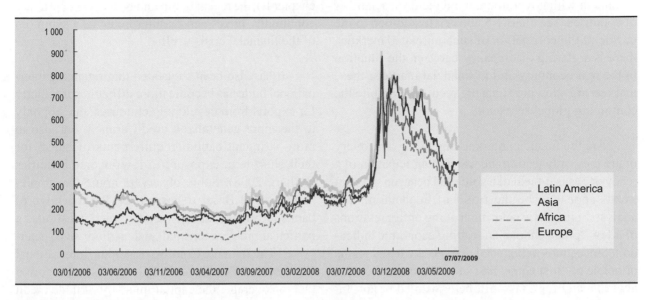

Source: Bloomberg.
Note: Data refer to JPMorgan Emerging Markets Bond Index, EMBI+.

a depreciation of their currencies in September–October 2008, instead of trying to stick to the peg by steeply raising their interest rates, as had frequently been the practice between 1997 and 2001. Their sale of international reserves and a moderate use of monetary tools in response to the pressures on their currencies have prevented excessive exchange-rate depreciations. The domestic banking systems have also remained resilient because, in drawing lessons from financial crises in the not-too-distant past, financial policies have been able to keep private sector indebtedness and the degree of leverage of the banking sector relatively low. Moreover, in these countries, deposits have been the basic counterpart of credit in banks' balance sheets. As a result, their banking systems were not hit by credit deleveraging when other sources of funding dried up.

The situation has been quite different in countries which have experienced huge losses in international competitiveness and rising current-account deficits over the past few years. This is particularly true for several emerging-market economies in Europe and the CIS. These countries had seen enormous gross and net inflows of capital, largely attracted by interest rate differentials. Such inflows led to substantial overvaluation of the local currencies with a concomitant loss of international competitiveness of their domestic producers. This resulted in extreme financial fragility, with mounting domestic and external indebtedness, and currency mismatches between debt and income. When the external shock from the subprime crisis hit the global economy the flight from risk stopped short-term private capital inflows and forced currency devaluation in a number of countries with huge current-account deficits and debt commitments, such as Hungary, Iceland and Ukraine. Other countries, such as the Baltic States and Pakistan, renewed their commitment to a fixed peg. The central banks of these countries were forced to use a large share of their international reserves to contain currency depreciation, but as the reserves were insufficient, they also had to turn to the IMF and the EU for financial support (see also section D.5).

In the second quarter of 2009, prices in most of the world's stock markets began to recover. Prices for several primary commodities followed a similar pattern, and several currencies that had suffered attacks in late 2008 also moved in parallel. These developments confirm the strong correlation between markets that are not fundamentally related to each other but are subject to the same kind of global portfolio management decisions. For example, the increase in the price of oil is closely correlated with the recovery of the Australian dollar and the Hungarian forint, the price of cotton rises in parallel with stocks in Malaysia, and the price of soybeans moves in tandem with government bond yields in a number of countries (see chart 1.5 above). In addition to the puzzle of the correlation of such unrelated markets, there is a glaring discrepancy between the situation in the real economy and in financial markets: these markets are showing signs of "recovery" despite the continuing global recession.

Are the financial markets signalling a recovery or are they only testing the water in anticipation of a recovery, as is typical of a so-called bear run? Recent trends appear to be the result of financial market analysts' simplistic and misleading interpretations of a few "green shoots" in leading economic indicators. Since gains in financial markets are based on the principle of "first come, first served", the markets are always ready for a take-off, be it justified or not. Indeed, they tend to interpret a situation as being driven by real factors even if the real factors are just mirages, such as perceived signs of economic recovery in certain economies or fears of forthcoming inflation. As long as financial prices are largely determined by speculative flows – with correlated positions moving in and out of risk – markets cannot deliver an efficient outcome. Speculative positions distort important prices instead of sending price signals that help improve the allocation of resources in the real sector of the economy. Recognizing the lack of economic logic of these markets is key to understanding the roots of the current crisis, and should be the basis for further policies and reforms aimed at stabilizing the financial system.

2. *International trade*

The evolution of international trade has mirrored that of economic activity. The volume of trade of developed countries levelled off in mid-2007, while GDP and trade in developing countries continued to expand in real terms until the third quarter of 2008. The worsening of the financial crisis in September 2008 radically changed economic conditions, leading to an abrupt downturn in production and trade across all the regions (chart 1.7). In the first quarter of 2009, the volume of world trade was 19 per cent below its level of the previous year. It was even

dramatically lower when measured in current dollar prices, as prices of most primary commodities fell sharply in the second half of 2008. Indeed, owing to the "financialization" of commodity markets (see chapter II), the recent boom and bust cycle of primary commodity prices can be interpreted as a symptom of the financial crisis itself.

It has also been suggested that financing international trade has become more difficult, particularly for exports from developing countries, due not only to the more generalized credit crunch, but also to more stringent capital requirements of banks for their short-term exposure to low-income countries (Caliari, 2008). Some observers argue that implementation of Basel II has eroded the incentive of banks to provide trade finance, which constitutes a particular problem for small and medium-sized enterprises. The Banking Commission of the International Chamber of Commerce (ICC, 2009) has reported that, on average, the capital intensity of trade credit under Basel II is four to five times higher than it was under Basel I. In the current situation, a tightening of trade financing conditions in the context of reforms in banking regulation is paradoxical, because trade credit involves financial instruments that are of the utmost importance for international trade activities. Moreover, historically these activities have involved very low risk, whereas the financial crisis was caused by a number of high-risk activities in the financial sector that have been almost entirely unrelated to activities in the real sector.

As the ICC explains, the lower availability of trade credit is not the result of an explicit recommendation for the treatment of credit in an effort to achieve a more appropriate capital adequacy ratio; rather it is due to the way in which a more general recommendation is implemented. While trade financing typically has a maturity of six months or less, the Basel II framework applies a one-year maturity floor for all lending facilities, which artificially inflates the capital costs of trade financing. It is therefore desirable for governments and international financial institutions to encourage national regulators to use the discretion they have to waive this floor for trade credits in order to prevent financial regulation reforms from having an unnecessary and procyclical impact on trade and production activities.

The simultaneous decline of exports and imports in all regions and subregions is another symptom of

Chart 1.7

WORLD TRADE BY VALUE AND VOLUME, JANUARY 2000–APRIL 2009

(Index numbers, 2000 = 100)

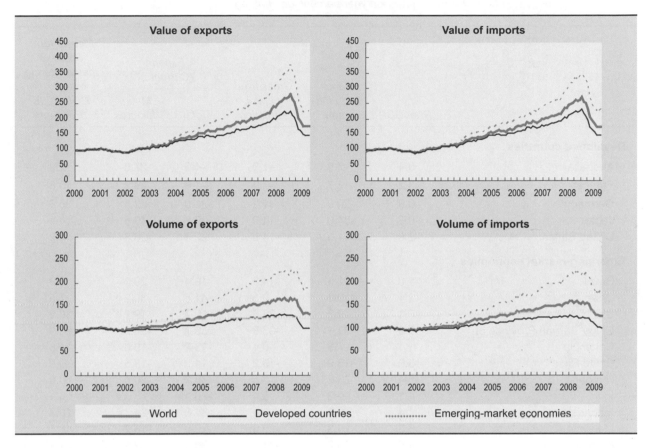

Source: UNCTAD secretariat calculations, based on the CPB Netherlands Bureau of Economic Policy Analysis, *World Trade* database.

the global nature of this crisis. In countries with a high share of manufactures in their export structure, and especially in countries that participate in international production networks, lower foreign demand leads to lower imports of raw materials and intermediate products. In primary commodity exporters, lower prices reduce the purchasing power of their exports. This effect of a parallel decline of exports and imports in most countries differs from that of more localized crises in the past, when the imports of the affected countries fell due to lower domestic demand, but their exports were much more resilient as demand in foreign markets continued to grow.

It is mainly the demand for investment and durable consumer goods that is falling. This is because the consumption of such goods can be more easily

deferred than that of food and basic services, but also because their acquisition partly relies on credit, which at present is more difficult and costly to obtain. As a result, countries that have a high share of investment and durable consumer goods in their total output have experienced a larger fall in industrial production and overall GDP growth than others. Among developed countries, Germany and Japan, for instance, have been worse affected by their declining exports of manufactures than other countries (table 1.4).

Several developing economies in Asia that are closely integrated into a dense production network for manufactures, and for which exports of manufactures represent a substantial share of GDP, such as Malaysia, the Republic of Korea, Singapore, Taiwan Province of China and Thailand, are also experiencing

Table 1.4

GDP, MANUFACTURING OUTPUT, GROSS FIXED CAPITAL FORMATION AND EXPORTS IN SELECTED COUNTRIES, FIRST QUARTER 2009

(Year-on-year percentage change)

	Real GDP	Manu-facturing output	Gross fixed capital formation	Exports (Current $) Total	Exports (Current $) Manu-factures	Memo item: Share of manufacturing exports in GDP, 2008 (Per cent)
Developed countries						
Australia	0.4	-7.9	-1.3	-4.5	-27.5	2.8
France[a]	-3.2	-18.7	-7.0	-21.6	-29.3	16.8
Germany[a]	-6.9	-20.9	-11.2	-21.0	-22.4	35.6
Japan	-8.8	-34.0	-14.9	-39.7	-40.6	14.1
United States	-2.6	-11.5	-14.5	-22.3	-20.8	6.9
Emerging-market economies						
Brazil	-1.8	-12.6	-14.0	-19.4	-29.1	5.9
Chile	-2.1	-9.1	-9.3	-41.5	-30.2	7.5
China	6.1	9.7	28.6	-19.7	-19.7	30.2
China, Taiwan Province of	-10.2	-33.1	-33.8	-36.7	-36.9	65.9
Colombia	-1.1	-7.6	-0.1	-13.2	-10.3	4.8
Costa Rica	-5.0	-16.9	-13.2	-14.9	-18.5	20.6
Hungary	-5.4	-23.2	-5.5	-38.7	-39.5	60.0
India	4.1	-0.2	6.4	-28.1	..	8.1
Indonesia	4.4	-3.7	-3.4	-31.8	-24.7	10.3
Malaysia	-6.2	-16.3	-10.8	-20.0	-18.2	48.5
Mexico	-8.6	-10.9	-11.8	-28.6	-22.8	21.1
Republic of Korea	-4.3	-16.8	-6.2	-24.9	-30.0	34.6
Russian Federation	-9.8	-19.6	-16.3	-47.7	-37.1	5.1
Singapore[b]	-10.1	-24.3	-14.8	-31.1	-26.1	67.4
South Africa	-1.3	-13.2	2.6	-31.3	..	15.0
Thailand	-7.1	-18.5	-15.8	-23.1	-21.9	45.9
Turkey	-13.8	-24.7	-29.7	-26.2	-32.7	14.1

Source: UNCTAD secretariat calculations, based on United Nations, *UN COMTRADE* database; OECD, *StatsExtracts* database; ECLAC, *CEPALSTAT* database; Economic Intelligence Unit (EIU); and national sources.

a Exports in euros.
b Exports exclude re-exports.

a strong contraction in economic activity, with GDP growth plunging between 4 and 10 per cent in the first quarter of 2009. In other Asian countries, such as China, India and Indonesia, declining exports of manufactures have had a less dramatic effect on industrial output and GDP owing to their large and still expanding domestic markets.

In Latin America, exports have fallen in all countries, but the impact of the crisis has been particularly strong in countries such as Mexico and Costa Rica, where GDP has been contracting rapidly since the last quarter of 2008. These economies rely heavily on exports of manufactures to the United States, and they have also been affected earlier and to a greater extent than other countries by lower income from tourism and workers' remittances. Although South American countries are also experiencing shrinking exports of manufactures, these exports contribute a lower share to total GDP: between 5 and 8 per cent in Brazil, Chile and Colombia, compared with more than 20 per cent in Costa Rica and Mexico and more than 30 per cent in many Asian economies (table 1.4). On the other hand, they are more vulnerable to the falling prices of primary commodities.

These declined sharply in the second half of 2008 (see above section A.2), with attendant consequences for the terms of trade. Like the preceding boom, the price slump associated with the global recession is affecting developing countries differently, according to their commodity trade structure. It has brought some relief to most energy- and food-importing countries, but in many cases this has been tempered by lower prices of other commodities that they export. The strongest negative impact of terms-of-trade changes are being felt in Africa and the least developed countries (LDCs), but also in many countries in Latin America, West Asia and the CIS that are highly dependent on oil. Lower export prices for commodities often have an impact on public finances, as many developing countries depend heavily on tax revenues from such exports, and translate into lower public consumption and investment. In some countries that had built financial cushions during the commodity boom, public expenditure could be maintained or even expanded. Nevertheless, in most oil or mining exporters in West Asia, North Africa and South America the losses from deteriorating terms of trade have contributed to a marked slowdown of GDP growth.

The global financial and economic crisis has also affected trade in services. The growth of world exports of transport, travel and other commercial services decelerated from 19 per cent in 2007 to 11 per cent in 2008. Based on available data, year-on-year global exports of commercial services in the fourth quarter of 2008 fell by 7–8 per cent (WTO, 2009). Maritime transport services reacted rapidly to the slowdown of global demand. Data on the deployment of both dry and liquid bulk, as well as on container ships, confirm an increasing withdrawal of vessels from service. Accordingly, the crisis has led to reduced port traffic. In addition, freight rates fell substantially during the final months of 2008. After reaching a peak in May 2008, the Baltic Dry Index plunged to its lowest level by the end of October (UNCTAD, 2009e).

Lower demand for travel services has also served to spread the economic crisis across countries. International tourist arrivals declined by 2 per cent in the second half of 2008, compared with an increase of 6 per cent in the first half of the year. Data for January and February 2009 indicate a roughly 8 per cent year-on-year fall. All regions have registered negative growth, with the exception of Africa, Central and South America.[22] West Asia, South Asia and Europe have been among the worst affected regions, with declines of 28.2, 14.6 and 8.4 per cent respectively. The World Tourism Organization (UNWTO) expects international tourism to stagnate or even decline by 2 per cent in 2009 (UNWTO, 2009).

3. *Migrants' remittances*

In recent years, migrants' remittances have become an important source of foreign exchange earnings for many developing and transition economies. At the microeconomic level they help sustain the living standards of many households, often lifting them out of poverty. They are also a source of financing for small enterprise and for residential investments. Statistical data on the evolution of migrants' remittances do not reflect the large proportion of remittances that are transferred through informal channels, which therefore are not recorded in balance-of-payments statistics. Although workers' remittances have frequently displayed countercyclical tendencies, as workers tend to send more money home when their home economies are experiencing adverse economic conditions, there is likely to have been only a small countercyclical effect, if any, in the current context, owing to the global reach of the crisis.

The strong rise in recorded remittances after 2000 was followed by a deceleration of flows to developing and transition economies in 2008 (chart 1.8). Over the year as a whole, remittances still rose by 8.8 per cent compared with 2007, to a total of $305 billion. Not counting the largest recipient, India – which benefited from a particularly strong rise in 2008 – the growth rate was only 6.1 per cent. In the second half of 2008, migrants' remittances began to decline, and in 2009 they are expected to fall by between 5 and 8 per cent (Ratha and Mohapatra, 2009), with reductions expected in all regions (table 1.5).

Chart 1.8

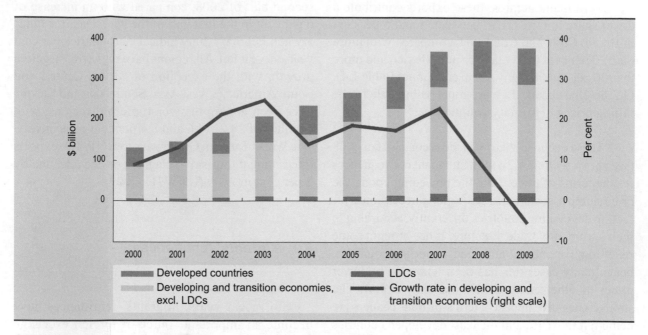

MIGRANTS' REMITTANCES, BY ECONOMIC GROUP, 2000–2009

Source: UNCTAD secretariat calculations, based on Ratha, 2009; and Ratha and Mohapatra, 2009.
Note: Migrant's remittances are workers' remittances, compensation of employees and migrants' capital transfers. Data for 2008 are preliminary estimates; data for 2009 are forecasts.

Table 1.5

GROWTH OF WORKERS' REMITTANCES TO DEVELOPING AND TRANSITION ECONOMIES, BY REGION,[a] 2000–2009

(Average annual percentage change)

	2000–2006	2007	2008[b]	2009[c]
Developing and transition economies	16.9	22.7	8.8	-5.0
of which:				
Europe and Central Asia	19.6	31.5	5.4	-10.1
Latin America and the Caribbean	19.0	6.6	0.2	-4.4
Middle-East and North Africa	10.9	21.6	7.6	-1.4
East Asia and the Pacific	19.6	23.2	7.2	-4.2
South Asia	15.2	31.5	26.7	-4.2
Sub-Saharan Africa	17.2	44.4	6.3	-4.4

Source: UNCTAD secretariat calculations, based on Ratha, 2009; and Ratha and Mohapatra, 2009.
  a Country groups as listed in the source.
  b Preliminary estimates.
  c Forecast.

Migrants' remittances are concentrated in a relatively small number of recipient countries: 10 countries account for more than half of total remittances, and the three largest recipients (India, China and Mexico) for more than one third. Whereas workers' remittances to India increased by more than a quarter in 2008, they already started to decline in Mexico (table 1.6). But remittances have a relatively large weight in many smaller – and mainly low-income – economies. In 2004, there were only two economies (Jordan and Lesotho), where remittance inflows amounted to 20 per cent of GDP or more, but by 2008 their number had quadrupled. In 16 developing and transition economies the share of inward remittance flows in GDP exceeded 10 per cent. Countries where such remittances account for a considerable share of GDP are particularly vulnerable to recession in the main immigration economies (i.e. countries of the European Union and the Gulf Cooperation Council, the Russian Federation and the United States), especially the sharp contraction in the construction and services sectors, which employ the largest number of foreign workers.

Table 1.6

MAJOR REMITTANCE-RECEIVING DEVELOPING AND TRANSITION ECONOMIES IN 2008

	Inflow of migrants' remittances	Annual change	Share of remittances in GDP
	($ million)	(Per cent)	
Ranked by volume			
India	45 000	27.6	3.7
China	34 490	5.0	0.8
Mexico	26 212	-3.4	2.4
Philippines	18 268	12.1	10.8
Nigeria	9 979	8.2	4.7
Egypt	9 476	23.8	5.8
Bangladesh	8 979	36.8	11.0
Pakistan	7 025	17.1	4.2
Morocco	6 730	0.0	7.8
Indonesia	6 500	5.3	1.3
Lebanon	6 000	4.0	20.7
Viet Nam	5 500	0.0	6.1
Ukraine	5 000	11.0	2.8
Colombia	4 523	0.0	1.9
Russian Federation	4 500	9.7	0.3
Ranked by share in GDP			
Tajikistan	1 750	3.5	34.1
Lesotho	443	0.0	27.4
Moldova, Republic of	1 550	3.5	25.3
Guyana	278	0.0	24.0
Lebanon	6 000	4.0	20.7
Honduras	2 801	6.7	19.6
Haiti	1 300	6.4	18.0
Nepal	2 254	30.0	17.8
Jordan	3 434	0.0	17.1
Jamaica	2 214	3.3	17.1
El Salvador	3 804	2.5	17.0
Kyrgyzstan	715	0.0	14.2
Nicaragua	771	4.2	11.5
Guatemala	4 440	4.4	11.2
Bangladesh	8 979	36.8	11.0

Source: UNCTAD secretariat calculations, based on Ratha, 2009; and *UNCTAD Handbook of Statistics* database.

Despite the crisis and the concomitant fall in migrants' remittances to developing countries, these remittances will nevertheless provide a larger foreign exchange inflow than official development assistance (ODA). However, the outlook for remittances, similar to that for exports of goods and services, depends on the effectiveness of economic stimulus packages, but also on possible changes in legislation pertaining to immigration of foreign workers in response to rising unemployment.

4. Developing-country debt and official development assistance

The financial crisis and the resultant global economic recession have undermined many of the fundamentals that had led to improvements in the debt situation of developing countries since 2002. The impact of the crisis on the debt positions has varied from country to country in terms of both timing and magnitude, depending on their initial economic conditions, the size and composition of their external debt, and the composition of their foreign exchange earnings. Unfavourable terms-of-trade changes, declining export demand, contraction in tourism and lower remittances resulting from the global economic crisis have reduced foreign exchange reserves and the ability of countries to service their external debt without compromising their imports.

Several transition economies in Eastern Europe and Central Asia had a large stock of foreign debt and current-account deficits even before the crisis, and their debt indicators are likely to become still worse in the context of stagnant or falling foreign exchange earnings. By contrast, due in part to its large accumulation of international reserves, Asia is better prepared than other regions to cope with the impacts of the global economic crisis. For the majority of countries in that region, it is unlikely that debt-to-GDP ratios will worsen significantly, despite a substantial deceleration of growth owing to their heavy reliance on exports. Most countries in Latin America had also increased their foreign exchange reserves, in addition to reducing their external debt, thanks to their current-account surpluses in 2005, 2006 and 2007. The ratio of external debt to GDP for Latin American countries fell, on average, from 42 per cent of GDP in 2003 to 19 per cent in 2008. In 2008, the region's current account went into deficit, which is expected to increase further in 2009 (to 2.3 per cent of GDP), despite the partial recovery in commodity prices (ECLAC, 2009a). Accordingly, debt indicators are likely to worsen for some Latin American countries, which will require additional official financing.

African countries have been the most seriously affected by the fall in primary commodity prices and the shortage of trade finance, but less so by reduced access to credit from private capital markets to which they have limited access even in normal times. Current debt servicing and debt sustainability has become more problematic, particularly in low-income countries, including several heavily indebted poor countries (HIPCs) that have passed the completion point under the HIPC debt relief initiative. In June 2008, 38 low-income countries, most of them in Africa, were estimated to have reserve holdings equivalent to less than three months of imports (IMF/IDA, 2008). In March 2009, the debt-to-GDP ratios of 28 low-income countries were reported to exceed 60 per cent – twice the value of the threshold level for debt sustainability for weak performers (IMF, 2009a).

The increasing difficulties of governments to honour their public debt servicing obligations are closely related to their deteriorating fiscal positions. About a quarter of low-income countries will face a fall in public revenue of more than 2 percentage points of GDP in 2009, and budget deficits in Africa are expected to rise, on average, by 4.7 percentage points of GDP (World Bank/IMF, 2009). To make matters worse, with the flight of international banks to safety after September 2008 exchange rates of many low-income countries depreciated, raising the domestic-currency equivalent of their debt servicing burden and their debt-to-GDP ratio. For instance, the dollar exchange rate of Zambia depreciated by 30 per cent, that of Ghana by 9 per cent and that of Uganda by 25 per cent.

A significant number of HIPCs that have passed completion point for debt relief will continue to remain at moderate or high risk of debt distress. As of June 2009 only 8 out of 24 HIPCs in this group could be considered as having low risk of debt distress, while four countries (Burkina Faso, Burundi, Gambia and Sao Tome and Principe) had a high risk of, or were already in, a situation of debt distress. On the whole, the debt sustainability of HIPCs that have passed completion point remains highly vulnerable to shocks. A worrying trend for the countries that are beyond completion point is that short-term debt is expected to rise considerably faster than more stable medium- to long-term debt. This gives rise to greater vulnerability to rollover difficulties and increases the risk of sovereign default (Detragiache and Spilimbergo, 2004). Against the background of the credit crunch, rolling over of short-term external debt has become more difficult and may imply considerably higher refinancing costs. Prospects are even bleaker for the countries that have not yet reached decision point under the HIPC Initiative, many of which are conflict or post-conflict countries. Under these conditions, a temporary moratorium on debt repayments could help prevent the emergence of a new, generalized external debt problem in developing countries (see section D.5 and box 1.2).

In 2008, total net ODA from members of the OECD Development Assistance Committee (DAC) rose by 10 per cent in real terms, to reach $119 billion (OECD, 2009b). While this is the highest dollar figure recorded to date, it represents only 0.30 per cent of members' combined gross national income (GNI) – a far cry from the 0.7 per cent target. Moreover, there are indications that, owing to the financial and economic crisis, aid budgets may shrink considerably (Roodman, 2008). Over the past 30 years, when donor countries have experienced economic or banking crises ODA has shrunk with a cumulative reduction of 4 per cent in the second year following the crisis, and 30 per cent in the fifth year.

ODA prospects for 2009 are uncertain, because aid budgets are increasingly being subjected to tighter budgetary pressure as donor governments implement large stabilization programmes. On the other hand, since ODA makes up only a small percentage of donor countries' budgets, its continued delivery is primarily a matter of political will. The United States, although at the epicentre of the current crisis, intends to increase its development assistance by 9 per cent in 2010, and Japan has already substantially increased its ODA disbursements; other donor countries may follow. This would not only help maintain the momentum of poverty reduction efforts in the beneficiary countries, but also add to the overall fiscal demand stimulus for the world economy as a whole (see section D.5).

D. Short-term policy responses to the global crisis

1. *A late awakening*

Most policymakers took a while to recognize the true nature and magnitude of the financial and economic crisis. Soaring global imbalances had long been identified by many observers as posing a severe threat to global stability,[23] but when the first signs of problems emerged at the centre of the global financial system around August 2007, governments were caught off guard and were generally slow to respond. As late as mid-2008, several monetary authorities, including the European Central Bank (ECB), still considered inflationary pressures to be the main risk to the global economy, and consequently tightened their monetary stances.

In all aspects of the policy response to the crisis, the United States led the action. This was largely because the bursting of the real estate bubble, balance-sheet difficulties of financial institutions, as well as signs of an outright recession first emerged in that country. When other governments joined in efforts to combat the crisis, it was mostly in reaction to pressing problems rather than pre-emptive. In some cases, macroeconomic policies have even been procyclical, repeating the policy mistakes that aggravated crises in several Asian and Latin American countries in the late 1990s and early 2000s.

The initial policy response consisted of liquidity provision to banks in the major financial markets to deal with the direct symptoms of the financial crisis. In addition, central banks cut interest rates to lower the cost of credit for both financial and non-financial agents. However, it soon became clear that traditional monetary policy measures would not be sufficient

to restore confidence in financial markets, and that unconventional measures would be required by central banks and fiscal authorities to contain the rapidly deteriorating asset positions of financial institutions. This led to unprecedented direct support by governments and efforts to rescue systemically important companies, primarily to strengthen the balance sheets of financial firms in the United States and several European countries.

The need for the United States authorities to provide State guarantees to large financial firms like Fannie Mae, Freddie Mac and Bear Stearns in the course of 2008, were early indications of the severity of the crisis. However, it was not until the collapse of a systemically important financial institution, the financial services firm Lehman Brothers, in September 2008 that the risk of a breakdown of the entire financial system was fully recognized. Subsequently, policymakers sought more systematic solutions for strengthening banks' balance sheets, and as the crisis spilled over into the real sector, governments of most developed countries reacted with fiscal stimulus packages.

Initial policy measures soon turned out to be insufficient and had to be broadened and deepened, leading to an unprecedented scale of government intervention in many developed countries. Governments in many developing and transition economies also embarked on expansionary monetary and fiscal policies, although their policy space for counter-cyclical action is often perceived as limited or has come to be circumscribed in the context of IMF-supported programmes. The following sections offer a review of the policy measures taken in various countries, along with international efforts to tackle the crisis.

2. Monetary policies

The pressing need for liquidity in the major financial markets was partly due to the high amounts of leveraged bank credit used by many operators in these markets in the build-up to the financial crisis. And it was also partly the result of new funding practices by most financial intermediaries. While traditional banking had relied on deposits for funding, in recent years investment banks, hedge funds, special investment vehicles and even commercial banks frequently issued short-term debt as a source of funding. As the institutions that provided them with liquidity (investment funds, insurance companies, pension funds, big firms and wealthy individuals) lost confidence in the quality of these assets, liquidity in money markets suddenly became scarce, and credit risk translated immediately into liquidity risk (Aglietta and Rigot, 2009). Governments responded to this liquidity crisis through gradual interest rate adjustments which are summarized in table 1.7.

In the United States, the Federal Reserve led the way to monetary easing with a first discount rate cut in mid-August 2007. The Bank of England started to ease its monetary policy stance in small steps only in December 2007. By that time, the ECB had already taken steps to boost liquidity in the banking system, as euro-area banks turned out to be heavily exposed to United States mortgage market risks. The ECB demonstrated much less flexibility than the Federal Reserve and the Bank of England in adjusting its interest rate to the changing macroeconomic situation. In July 2008 it actually raised the policy rate. One year after the outbreak of the market turmoil, and with the United States and the euro-area economies entering into recession, this move clearly reflected the ECB's lack of appreciation of the gravity of the situation. Had it grasped the true nature of the crisis, it would have eased monetary policy to help launch a quick recovery in member States and the world economy, rather than opting for monetary tightening to counter a wrongly perceived risk of inflation.

The sudden aggravation of the financial turmoil in September 2008 signalled to policymakers worldwide that policy action was urgently needed to prevent a financial meltdown and their economies from spiralling out of control. Major central banks around the world responded to the events of September by an unprecedented internationally coordinated policy easing in early October 2008 – a move that included the United States Federal Reserve, the ECB, the Bank of England, the Bank of Canada, and the central banks of Sweden and Switzerland. Many other central banks in both developed and emerging-market economies, including Australia, China, India, Japan and the Republic of Korea, embarked on easing their policy stance at about the same time. In other cases, though, the scope for immediate policy easing was more limited as a generalized "flight to quality" and carry trade unwinding exerted downward pressure on several emerging-market currencies.

Maintaining its momentum of monetary easing, the Federal Reserve reduced its Federal funds rate target to the historical low of 0.25 per cent by December 2008. It also undertook a number of "unconventional measures" to restore liquidity in the securitized money and credit markets. Given the predominance of markets and securitized instruments over banks in the United States financial system, these "credit easing" measures were seen as vital for reviving lending. In addition, the Federal Reserve has embarked on purchasing long-term Treasury and Agency securities with the aim of keeping longer term yields low, as short-term yields are near zero, a measure that would also seem appropriate in Europe.

The ECB was not only late but also relatively timid in easing its policy stance, as its key policy rate reached 1 per cent only in May 2009, down from 4.25 per cent in October 2008. In addition to extensive liquidity provisions to banks, which had begun in August 2007, the ECB announced in May 2009 that under its "enhanced credit support"[24] approach it would provide longer term refinancing than it did with its usual operations (three months). Accordingly, at the end of June 2009 it provided one-year financing of more than €440 billion to the euro-area banking system – the largest amount ever for a single ECB operation.

The Bank of Japan reduced its key policy rate from the already very low level of 0.5 per cent to 0.1 per cent in the fourth quarter of 2008, in addition to measures to facilitate corporate financing and outright purchases of longer term government securities.

Developing countries found themselves in very divergent situations regarding the scope for easing monetary policy, depending mainly on their initial

Table 1.7

INTEREST RATES IN SELECTED ECONOMIES, JULY 2007–MAY 2009

	Interest rates (Annualized in per cent)				Change in basis points		
	July 2007	July 2008	December 2008	May 2009	July 2007– July 2008	July 2008– Dec. 2008	Dec. 2008– May 2009
Argentina	9.34	8.98	11.12	10.82	-36	213	-30
Australia	6.25	7.25	4.25	3.00	100	-300	-125
Belarus	9.70	10.40	19.00	17.90	70	860	-110
Brazil	11.25	13.00	13.75	10.25	175	75	-350
Canada	4.50	3.00	1.50	0.25	-150	-150	-125
Chile	5.25	7.25	8.25	1.25	200	100	-700
China	3.33	4.14	2.79	2.79	81	-135	0
China, Hong Kong SAR	4.37	2.30	0.95	0.31	-207	-135	-64
Czech Republic	3.00	3.75	2.25	1.50	75	-150	-75
Euro area	4.00	4.25	2.50	1.00	25	-175	-150
Hungary	7.75	8.50	10.00	9.50	75	150	-50
Iceland	13.30	15.50	18.00	13.00	220	250	-500
India	6.00	6.00	5.00	3.25	0	-100	-175
Indonesia	8.25	8.75	9.25	7.25	50	50	-200
Japan	0.50	0.50	0.10	0.10	0	-40	0
Latvia	5.21	5.40	8.92	10.78	19	352	186
Malaysia	3.60	3.70	3.37	2.13	10	-33	-124
Mexico	7.25	8.00	8.25	5.25	75	25	-300
Norway	4.50	5.75	3.00	1.50	125	-275	-150
Pakistan	10.00	13.00	15.00	14.00	300	200	-100
Poland	4.50	6.00	5.00	3.75	150	-100	-125
Republic of Korea	4.75	5.00	3.00	2.00	25	-200	-100
Russian Federation	10.00	11.00	13.00	12.00	100	200	-100
Saudi Arabia	5.06	3.82	2.55	0.85	-124	-127	-170
Serbia	9.50	15.75	17.75	14.00	625	200	-375
Singapore	2.56	1.00	1.00	0.69	-156	0	-31
South Africa	9.50	12.00	11.50	7.50	250	-50	-400
Sweden	3.50	4.50	2.00	0.50	100	-250	-150
Switzerland	2.71	2.76	0.66	0.40	5	-210	-26
Thailand	3.25	3.50	2.75	1.25	25	-75	-150
Turkey	17.50	16.50	15.70	9.50	-100	-80	-620
Ukraine	9.00	15.90	14.80	17.20	690	-110	240
United Kingdom	5.75	5.00	2.00	0.50	-75	-300	-150
United States	5.25	2.00	0-0.25	0-0.25	-325	-175	0

Source: UNCTAD secretariat calculations, based on IMF, *International Financial Statistics* database; Bloomberg; and national sources.
Note: Data refer to key policy reference rates or target rates (end-of-period), except for Hong Kong (China), Latvia, Malaysia, Saudi Arabia, Singapore, Switzerland and Turkey (monthly average of 3-month interbank market rate); Argentina and Belarus (monthly average of 1-day interbank market rate); and Ukraine (weighted average rate of banks' refinancing of the National Bank of Ukraine).

current-account position and the degree of openness of their capital account. Some were even induced to temporarily tighten monetary policy as their currencies came under, sometimes intense, pressure. This was the case for Brazil, Chile, Mexico, Peru and the Russian Federation, where monetary policy was tightened in the third quarter of 2008, before initial steps for monetary easing were taken in the first months of 2009. Similarly, the South African Reserve Bank, confronted at the outset with a plunging rand and relatively high inflation, began easing its policy stance only in late 2008.

Asian economies in general moved earlier towards a more expansionary monetary policy. The People's Bank of China cut both its policy rates and minimum reserve requirements in several steps from September 2008 onwards, with money and credit aggregates recording rapid growth in the first quarter of 2009. Similarly, the Reserve Bank of India swiftly cut its key policy rates and banks' reserve requirements after mid-September 2008 (Subbarao, 2009). The central banks of Hong Kong (China), Indonesia, Malaysia, the Philippines, Saudi Arabia, Singapore, Taiwan Province of China, Thailand and Turkey reduced their interest rates, in most cases from already relatively low levels. Although it faced a sharp depreciation of its currency in the last quarter of 2008, the central bank of the Republic of Korea cut its key policy rates significantly.[25] By contrast, in Pakistan, where monetary policy is being operated under a 23-month IMF stand-by arrangement, interest rates remained high, as fighting inflation with a restrictive monetary policy has taken priority over countercyclical demand stimulation.

3. Support for ailing financial institutions

In September 2008 it also became clear that bank losses were much higher than initial estimates of losses from subprime mortgages had suggested. In the United States, the continuing decline in property prices and the ensuing credit crunch set in motion a wave of bankruptcies or near-bankruptcies of leading financial institutions. This changed the perception of the dimension of the crisis. Monetary authorities in developed countries began to intervene to an extent that went far beyond their role as lenders of last resort. They made available enormous amounts of liquidity, rescued financial institutions that were deemed systemically important, and adopted direct measures aimed at cleaning the balance sheets of financial intermediaries and restoring the availability of credit.

The virtual insolvency of two major government-sponsored institutions that played a central role in the mortgage market, Fannie Mae and Freddie Mac, was a decisive test as to how far the United States Government would go in supporting the financial system. It confirmed that the crisis in the market for subprime mortgages was only the tip of the iceberg, and that there was a risk of a general breakdown of the financial system. In early September, the two institutions were de facto nationalized, as the Government injected $100 billion into the capital of each institution, took over their control and opened an unrestricted credit line to keep them afloat.[26] Their effective nationalization was a logical step because of their status as government-sponsored enterprises. In addition, the government provided guarantees in support of the takeover of the investment bank Bear Stearns by JPMorgan Chase, which was an acknowledgment of the systemic importance of that bank.[27] However, similar support was not extended to Lehman Brothers, which had to file for bankruptcy in September 2008. In the aftermath of this event, money and credit markets seized up completely. By contrast, when the insurance giant, American International Group (AIG), hovered on the brink of bankruptcy as a result of its exposure to credit default swaps, the Federal Reserve rushed to its rescue with the provision of a credit facility of more than $180 billion. In exchange, the Federal Reserve obtained 80 per cent of the Group's capital – another case of nationalization.[28]

After dealing with these large institutions on a case-by-case basis, the Treasury launched the Troubled Assets Relief Program (TARP) that was approved by Congress as a part of the Emergency Economic Stabilization Act in October 2008. The objective of TARP is to allow the Treasury to buy or insure "troubled" (or "toxic") assets held by different types of institutions, for an amount of up to $700 billion. Under the original plan, financial institutions could sell their toxic assets to the government through a reverse auction mechanism. The original plan was soon replaced by one to inject capital into troubled institutions (TARP phase II). TARP funds would thus be used to buy preferred (non-voting) stocks and warrants in several large banks, which had to accept limits on the compensation schemes they offered their senior executives. In March 2009, the new Administration announced that most of the remaining TARP funds would be used to establish a public-private investment programme to acquire "toxic" assets. Under this arrangement, also known as the Geithner Plan, private investors can establish a 50-per-cent partnership with the Government in investment vehicles aimed at buying assets whose current market value is uncertain but which carry a high risk of non-performance in the future. Up to 85 per cent of the amount paid for the toxic assets purchased by such investment vehicles can be financed with non-recourse loans from the Federal Deposit Insurance Company (FDIC), and this could reach a total of $1,000 billion.[29]

In February 2009, "stress tests" were undertaken for the 19 largest banks in the United States to determine their chances of survival in case of a further deterioration of the macroeconomic situation.[30] Following their results, 10 of these banks were urged to raise $75 billion of capital in the course of the year; otherwise they would have to accept an injection of public capital that would considerably dilute existing private shares. The other nine banks were declared to be in a solid position and were allowed to return the TARP funds they had received earlier.[31]

Transferring "toxic" bank assets to the central bank or another publicly sponsored institution is a way of "cleaning up" the balance sheets of financial institutions. The idea behind this approach is that the restoration of banks' capacity and willingness to lend requires more time than they can afford in a crisis situation, since it implies a lengthy process of writing down the value of doubtful assets and a recapitalization from current profits. However, policy intervention in favour of banks with large amounts of such assets is not without problems, as it may imply subsidizing shareholders and a form of insurance for banks without appropriate recompense by the beneficiaries (see box 1.1).

The Government of the United Kingdom took similar action aimed at rescuing the British banking system. Under this programme, the Government has the authority to inject up to £50 billion of capital in several large banks in exchange for preferred shares. This enables banks to write down parts of their toxic assets. Accordingly, two leading mortgage lenders were nationalized. Banks also obtained access to up to £200 billion of short-term loans from the Bank of England and up to £250 billion worth of government guarantees for interbank loans. Banks that participated in the scheme had to agree to limit levels of employee compensation and dividend payments. In January 2009, the Government announced a second rescue package, which includes an insurance programme (the Asset Protection Scheme) aimed at protecting banks against losses arising from mortgage-backed securities and other asset-backed securities. It also contains a credit guarantee scheme that allows banks to issue bonds with a government guarantee. In exchange for this support, banks have to increase their lending.[32]

At the beginning of July 2009, the German Government also introduced a scheme that allows the transfer of toxic bank assets to newly created "bad" banks. Under this scheme, both privately and publicly owned financial institutions can transfer toxic assets into a "special purpose vehicle" (SPV) at 90 per cent of their book value. In exchange, these financial institutions receive bonds issued by the SPV that are guaranteed by a fund created in October 2008 for the stabilization of the financial system (SOFFIN). When the SPV is eventually liquidated, any profit will be paid back to the banks that transferred the assets. However, if the SPV makes a loss, the institutions that transferred the assets will not be able to pay out any profit to their shareholders until they reimburse SOFFIN for the losses incurred on its guarantees.

In Switzerland, in order to help UBS, the largest Swiss bank, to clean its balance sheet of toxic assets, the Government bought 6 billion Swiss francs (CHF) worth of new shares, and the Swiss National Bank granted UBS a loan of CHF 54 billion. UBS then used these newly raised funds to capitalize and fund a new "bad" bank to which it transferred toxic assets amounting to CHF 60 billion. This operation led to a considerable dilution of shares, in addition to which UBS shareholders will have to shoulder the first CHF 6 billion worth of losses on toxic assets and the Swiss Government will absorb the remaining losses, if any. Australia, Canada, Norway and Spain have also set up mechanisms for dealing with toxic assets (Khatiwada, 2009).

The "unconventional" interventions of the Federal Reserve, including the direct financing of private non-financial agents, led to an increase in the total of its balance sheet from $890 billion in early September 2008 to $2,055 billion in mid-June 2009. The composition of the Federal Reserve's assets also changed dramatically: in June 2007, 93 per cent of its outstanding credits was in the form of Treasury bonds; this share fell to 21 per cent in December 2008 and it was 31 per cent in June 2009.[33] The weight of risky assets grew correspondingly, including mortgage-backed securities, term-auction credit, credit extended to AIG and asset-backed commercial papers. These changes illustrate the extent to which the Federal Reserve felt obliged to replace the private financial system for the direct financing of economic activity. Thus the principle of independence of the central bank came to be set aside, and the distinction between fiscal and monetary policy became blurred: the Federal Reserve helped the Treasury in managing the crisis without having to wait for Congressional

Box 1.1

"TOXIC" ASSETS AND "BAD" BANKS

The financial crisis has led to a situation in which many banks are holding assets that have a market value well below their original book value, making the banks insolvent on a mark-to-market basis. Left to themselves these banks could be tempted to take too much risk ("gamble for resurrection") or take no risk at all and, by refraining from lending, stifle economic activity. There is thus a strong rationale for policy intervention.

If the remaining value of the bad assets is known, the solution is fairly simple: a government agency temporarily takes over the bank, helps recapitalize it and then sells it. This is what is routinely done by agencies like the United States Federal Deposit Insurance Corporation (FDIC) when banks are put under conservatorship or receivership. The situation is more complicated when the remaining value is unknown; this is when assets are considered as "toxic".

For illustration, one may consider the case of a bank which has assets with a book value of $1 billion and liabilities worth $900 million, so that the book value of its capital amounts to $100 million. Half of the bank's assets are safe, but the remaining half are toxic and are traded at 50 per cent of their book value. The bank is thus insolvent on a mark-to-market basis. If the private sector is not willing to recapitalize the bank, the government essentially has five options (which it can choose alone or in combination):

1. Buy the toxic assets (at a price somewhere between the assumed market price and their book value), and then liquidate them over a long period of time.

2. Give a subsidy to private investors interested in buying the toxic assets, and induce them to pay a price that can return the bank to solvency.

3. Inject public capital into the bank, but abstain from interfering with the management of the bank.

4. Take over the bank and guarantee all of its liabilities, and then use the good assets to create a new "good" bank (with a capital large enough to cover the bank's old liabilities); the good bank could eventually be re-privatized, and the bad assets put in a "bad" bank which will be slowly liquidated.

5. Convert some of the bank's liabilities into equity capital by imposing a debt-for-equity swap on the bank's unsecured creditors (as is often done in bankruptcies of non-financial firms), and create a new bank with fewer assets and liabilities.

The main problem with option 1 is the determination of the price of the toxic assets. In the above example, the minimum would be $400 million (the amount required to ensure the solvency of the bank), but banks may ask for more. This approach is similar to that of the original Troubled Assets Relief Program (TARP). It implies a subsidy for both shareholders and bondholders, but, since the real value of the toxic assets is unknown, it lacks transparency regarding the potential subsidy, and thus leaves considerable scope for lobbying to extract the largest possible subsidy. Option 2, which corresponds to the Geithner Plan, has been criticized for involving subsidies (again, for shareholders and bondholders) that are even more opaque (and possibly larger) than those involved in the original TARP, and even for inviting fraud (Johnson and Kwak, 2009; Krugman, 2009; Sachs, 2009; Young, 2009).[a] In option 3, which is similar to phase II of TARP, there is still a subsidy for unsecured debt holders and shareholders. This approach also appears to be problematic because the government supplies all the capital necessary to make the bank solvent without having any say in the bank's management. Bank nationalization, as in option 4, is similar to the approach Sweden adopted in response to the banking crisis that hit many Nordic countries in the early 1990s. It still generates a subsidy for the unsecured bondholders but does not subsidize shareholders.[b] The main complication with this approach is that the government or a government agency will need to manage the bank for a certain period of time. Option 5, similar to the practice with corporate bankruptcies, takes into account both the liability and asset side of the bank's balance sheet and assigns different rights to different types of liabilities.

A scheme suggested by Bulow and Klemperer (2009) is to create a "good" bank which holds the clean assets and the secured liabilities (including deposits), and a "bad" bank that holds the toxic assets and the unsecured debt and owns the equity of the good bank. From the taxpayer's point of view, this appears

Box 1.1 (concluded)

to be the cheapest and the fairest means to resolving the current situation because it does not imply any subsidy.[c] The main disadvantage of this approach is that the process of sorting out good and bad liabilities may end up being time-consuming and entail a substantial amount of litigation. Moreover, if the pool of unsecured creditors includes systemically important firms, the plan may amplify the crisis by imposing losses on them.

According to many observers, the last two options have the advantage of minimizing moral hazard and the fiscal cost of crisis resolution. They are variants of the approach which the IMF, with support of the United States, usually imposes on developing countries that are hit by a banking crisis. They are also similar to what the United States pressured Japan to do in the early 1990s. By contrast, as the current crisis is at home, the United States Administration considers the last two options as being too complex, given the large number of banks involved, and has adopted variants of the first, second and third options. This is somewhat surprising since the United States bureaucracy might have been expected to follow Sweden's example. Its choices may have been influenced by the desire to avoid what some observers might view as "excessive" intervention, and also by strong lobbying by the financial industry. Even conservative observers like James Baker, Lindsey Graham and Alan Greenspan have argued that temporary nationalization is preferable to the policies adopted by the current and previous Administrations.[d]

The presumption that the desire to protect the interests of Wall Street played a role in the management of the current crisis is consistent with the observation that, rather than giving banks a plain and visible – but politically unacceptable – subsidy, the subsidy was hidden and made as opaque as possible. Cynical observers argue that considerable effort was made to protect shareholders and limit the potential gains for public finances by adopting complex and opaque policies, probably on the assumption that policies that are both bad and complex tend to receive less opposition and scrutiny than policies that are both simple and bad (Snower, 2009). Financial markets reacted positively to the Government's support programme: bank shares initially dropped dramatically following the announcement of the stress-test programme in early February 2009, but they started to recover in early March, and by mid-June they had increased by 100 per cent from the trough and by 40 per cent compared with early February.

Those who are opposed to even a temporary nationalization of insolvent banks appear to forget that banks always have a public component, because the State is the ultimate guarantor of their liabilities. Several banks have positive equity value only because they enjoy implicit and explicit government guarantees. Seen in this light, the recent decision to allow banks that passed the stress test to return TARP funds (and thus no longer be subject to limits on executive compensation and dividend payments) seem paradoxical for at least two reasons. First, these banks received large subsidies when the government removed the enormous counterparty risk associated with credit default swaps issued by American International Group (AIG). Second, while market participants are fully aware that the adverse scenario used in the stress test was not as bad as what realistically should have been assumed, they remain confident that if a real adverse scenario were to happen, the Government would do whatever is necessary to save troubled financial institutions. In other words, all financial institutions have a call option on government resources. By allowing some institutions to return TARP funds and avoid tighter regulation, the Government is giving them this option without any charge.

---

[a]   For defence of the plan by an academic economist, see DeLong (2009).
[b]   In the Swedish case, insolvent banks were first asked to seek capital injections from their shareholders. The incentives for raising such capital were provided by the fact that if shareholders were not able (or willing) to provide new capital, the Government would force them to surrender control before providing public support (Jonung, 2009).
[c]   The bank will require new funds only if the secured liabilities (such as insured deposits) are greater than the assets. However, this is not a subsidy, but an insurance payment. Hall and Woodward (2009) describe how this was applied to Citigroup in the United States, and Buiter (2009) describes how it was applied to the Royal Bank of Scotland in the United Kingdom.
[d]   "How Washington can prevent 'zombie banks'" James Baker, *Financial Times*, 1 March 2009; "Greenspan backs bank nationalization" by Krishna Guha and Edward Luce, *Financial Times*, 18 February 2009; "Sen. Graham: Consider nationalizing banks", Charlotteobserver.com, 16 February 2009.

Table 1.8

FISCAL STIMULUS AND SUPPORT TO THE FINANCIAL SYSTEM IN SELECTED ECONOMIES
(Per cent of GDP)

	Fiscal stimulus[a]	Support for the financial sector[b]	Years to spend fiscal stimulus
Developed economies[c]	**3.7**	**48.5**	.
Australia	5.4	9.5	3
Austria	1.2	35.4	2
Belgium	1.4	31.0	2
Canada	4.1	24.8	3
France	1.5	19.1	2
Germany	3.6	22.2	2
Greece	0.8	11.6	1
Hungary	-7.7	9.1	2
Iceland	-7.3	263.0	2
Ireland	-8.3	266.4	3
Italy	0.3	3.3	2
Japan	4.7	22.3	3
Netherlands	2.5	46.5	2
Norway	1.2	17.8	1
Poland	1.2	3.2	2
Portugal	0.8	14.4	1
Spain	3.9	22.9	3
Sweden	3.3	70.2	2
Switzerland	0.5	12.0	2
United Kingdom	1.9	81.7	3
United States	5.5	81.1	3
Developing economies[c]	**4.7**	**2.9**	.
Argentina	6.4	0.9	1
Brazil	5.6	1.5	1
Chile	2.8	0.0	1
China	6.2	0.5	2
China, Hong Kong SAR	2.4	0.0	1
China, Taiwan Province of	2.1	0.0	1
India	1.8	6.4	3
Indonesia	2.0	0.1	2
Malaysia	2.8	6.3	2
Mexico	1.6	0.0	1
Peru	3.2	0.0	2
Philippines	3.1	0.0	1
Republic of Korea	6.2	20.5	3
Saudi Arabia	9.2	9.4	3
Singapore	8.0	0.0	1
South Africa	7.4	0.0	3
Thailand	3.4	0.0	1
Turkey	1.1	0.5	2
Transition economies[c]	**5.8**	**7.4**	.
Kazakhstan	11.1	0.0	2
Russian Federation	5.4	8.0	2
Total[c]	**4.0**	**36.1**	.

Source: UNCTAD secretariat calculations, based on UN/DESA, 2009b; IMF, 2009b and c; OECD, 2009a; Council of the European Union, 2009; ECLAC, 2009b; *UNCTAD Handbook of Statistics* database; and national sources.
　　a Corresponds to discretionary measures on public spending or revenues in response to the financial crisis, excluding the "automatic stabilizers".
　　b Comprises capital injection, purchases of assets, lending by government treasuries, central bank support provided with treasury backing, liquidity provision by central banks and guarantees, excluding deposit insurance provided by deposit insurance agencies. Liquidity provision by central banks only includes the new special facilities established to address the present crisis and excludes the operations of the regular liquidity facilities.
　　c Country grouping weights based on current dollars.

approval to commit funds (Aglietta and Rigot 2009, OECD, 2009a). Moreover, the Federal Reserve relies on the Treasury for guarantees to acquire massive amounts of risky assets, while the Treasury relies on Federal Reserve intervention to buy its long-term debt and prevent interest rates from soaring.

The sizeable bail-out operations and the provision of large amounts of liquidity by several central banks and governments (see also table 1.8) prevented a breakdown of the financial system. But these measures, even combined with sharp interest rate reductions, were not sufficient to return the financial system back to normal functioning and to fully restore credit availability to the non-financial sector. Similarly, while expansionary monetary policy is essential for keeping the financial and economic crisis under control, it is not sufficient on its own to bring about a recovery. Even with very low interest rates and healthy banks, credit will not recover as long as rising unemployment and falling incomes restrain demand, and faltering demand discourages investment. In order to stimulate demand, countercyclical fiscal policy measures that have a direct effect on aggregate demand are therefore indispensable.

4. Fiscal policies

As the financial crisis spilled over into the real sector, a wide consensus emerged that the effects of automatic stabilizers would not be sufficient to stop the downturn in aggregate demand. Consequently, governments in many developed and emerging-market economies reacted with discretionary fiscal stimulus and support measures, such as debt-financed increases in public spending and tax cuts, to counter the increasingly dramatic downturn in final demand, output and employment (table 1.8).

The United States Administration began introducing fiscal stimuli in early 2008, but adopted a more aggressive stance after the slowdown in that country had turned into an outright recession in the third quarter of that year. At the G-20 meeting in Washington in November 2008, the Managing Director of the IMF stated that a global fiscal stimulus in the order of 2 per cent of world GDP was essential to restore global growth (Strauss-Kahn, 2008). At their subsequent London Summit in April 2009, the

G-20 leaders reaffirmed their commitment "to deliver the scale of sustained fiscal effort necessary to restore growth".[34] Some months later, the IMF's First Deputy Managing Director, praised the fiscal stimulus for recent economic improvements and urged governments to spend the committed funds fully and in a timely manner, and to increase them if needed.[35] However, the spirit of these statements is not reflected in the conditions attached to the financial support that the IMF has been providing to several emerging-market economies. In most cases, procyclical fiscal tightening remains part of those conditions.

Indeed, ever since financial and macroeconomic crises affected developing or transition economies, the role of fiscal policy during crisis situations has been highly controversial (*TDR 2006*, chap. IV). In one view, an expansionary fiscal policy is necessary to support aggregate demand and help exit a crisis. In the opposite view, fiscal tightening[36] is indispensable to restore the confidence of financial markets, attract new capital inflows and "crowd in" private investment. This second view guided much of the conditionality set by the IMF in all the crises since the mid-1990s, but was criticized not only by various economists, but also by the IMF's Independent Evaluation Office (IMF-IEO, 2003). The criticism was directed at the procyclical nature of these policies and their unnecessary aggravation of the crises. It was also pointed out that contractionary fiscal policies cannot be effective in achieving their primary goal (i.e. the reduction of the fiscal deficits) because they push the affected economies deeper into recession and narrow the tax base.

This time, as the crisis has evolved, international support for a strong and active fiscal stimulus has increased, at least in developed countries, and even among institutions and actors that have traditionally been wary of State intervention. However, national fiscal policy responses and initial fiscal stabilization programmes, like the tax cut in the United States in early 2008, were a case of too little, too late. In the context of a major crisis with strong deleveraging pressures, tax reductions tend to be ineffective for reviving private consumption and investment, especially if they benefit mainly high-income segments of the population that have a relatively low marginal propensity to consume. Therefore, much stronger measures were needed after the collapse of Lehman Brothers in September 2008. Governments were compelled to increase public spending to compensate for falling private demand, or to subsidize certain types of private consumption and investment, assuming the role of what could be called "borrower and spender of last resort". Governments may also have found it difficult to resist pressures for demand stimulation after huge amounts of public money had been mobilized at an earlier stage for the rescue of banks and other financial institutions that were responsible for the crisis.

In the United States, the new Administration responded to the deepening recession in February 2009 with a fiscal stimulus package (American Recovery and Reinvestment Act) amounting to $787 billion to be used through 2009 and 2010. The increased Federal budget expenditures proposed by the Act included transfers to low-income workers and the unemployed, higher spending for health care and education, and investment in infrastructure, including renewable energy.[37] However, it is not clear how much *net* stimulus will remain after the contractionary effects of budget cuts at the local and state government levels are taken into account. Canada also launched a sizeable fiscal package that combines tax cuts and higher spending, including for infrastructure and housing investment, and transfers to vulnerable groups.

In November 2008, the European Commission had already launched the European Economic Recovery Plan which called for an immediate and coordinated effort by EU member States to boost demand. It suggests that member countries should provide a fiscal stimulus equivalent to 1.5 per cent of GDP, in addition to the stimulus resulting from automatic stabilizers and the support provided to the financial system (EC, 2009). National governments in the EU had varying priorities in the design of their respective policy responses. In the United Kingdom, a fiscal stimulus programme of 1.5 per cent of GDP was agreed for 2009, consisting mainly of a temporary cut in the value-added tax rate. In France, where the Government had already reduced taxes on high incomes in the course of 2007, a further stimulus was provided in the form of additional expenditure for major infrastructure projects and support to industries in difficulty and low-income households. In Germany, the main ingredients of the stimulus were tax abatements, subsidies on new car purchases and energy-saving home renovations, as well as additional infrastructure investments. In Spain, most of the stimulus takes the form of greater spending on public works and transfers to households and firms, in particular the automobile industry. The fiscal stimulus packages in Europe are generally smaller than the one being implemented in the United States. Policymakers have justified this on the grounds that Europe has relatively higher automatic stabilizers embedded in its welfare and tax regimes.

Japan was relatively late with a fiscal policy response to the crisis, but, including a recently announced new stimulus package, discretionary measures over the 2008–2010 period now amount to over 4 per cent of GDP. This package consists mainly of higher public spending for infrastructure investments in support of climate change mitigation, but also includes transfers to households, businesses and local communities. In China a fiscal stimulus package equivalent to more than 13 per cent of GDP was announced in late 2008. How much of this amount consists of new measures, not previously planned, is debatable. Nevertheless, even if one accepts the IMF's lower estimate of 6.2 per cent of GDP, it remains one of the largest fiscal stimulus packages in the world. Additional investment in transport and energy infrastructure, as well as in environmental protection, rural development, low-cost housing, education and healthcare, has already proved very effective in boosting domestic demand.

Like China, the Republic of Korea is implementing a fiscal stimulus programme that exceeds 6 per cent of GDP, but over a period of three years compared to two years in China. The largest fiscal package in Asia is probably that of Singapore, which amounts to 8 per cent of GDP, to be spent in a single year. Other Asian economies, such as Hong Kong (China), India, Indonesia, Malaysia, the Philippines, Saudi Arabia, Taiwan Province of China and Thailand, are also benefiting from sizeable fiscal packages, with particular emphasis on direct spending for infrastructure projects, but also including assistance to specific industries (Khatiwada, 2009). The fiscal stimulus is also significant in oil-exporting transition economies, such as Kazakhstan and the Russian Federation, where it is being financed with funds accumulated during the oil boom.

In Latin America and the Caribbean, the authorities of most countries have granted tax reductions and additional subsidies and/or expanded expenditure. In some countries, such as Argentina, Brazil, Chile, Mexico and Peru, public investment programmes are being accelerated or expanded substantially. Several

years of running fiscal primary surpluses has given these countries considerable room for manoeuvre. In addition, Chile and Peru will use resources accumulated in their stabilization funds, while Argentina has mobilized supplementary resources from the nationalization of its social security system. Other countries that were not able or willing to expand public expenditure sought to change its composition by shifting its uses to those activities that are more likely to have a strong impact on production and employment.

Several countries have also strengthened their social programmes with the aim of mitigating the social impact of the crisis, preserving employment and sustaining domestic demand. Governments in the countries mentioned above and in some other economies of the region, including Barbados, Belize, the Bolivarian Republic of Venezuela, Bolivia, Colombia, Costa Rica, El Salvador, Guatemala, Honduras and Jamaica, have taken measures to protect vulnerable groups of the population, such as raising minimum wages and pensions, and providing incentives to private firms to keep jobs or create new ones. These measures are also expected to stimulate private demand (ECLAC, 2009b).

The value of the fiscal packages aimed at stimulating demand in the countries for which data were available amounts to 3.7 per cent of GDP, on average, in the developed countries, 4.7 per cent in developing countries and 5.8 per cent in the transition economies (table 1.8). Direct comparisons between countries are difficult because the fiscal packages vary in terms of their time horizon: they extend over a period of between one and three years. However, Iceland and Ireland, and to lesser extent Hungary, are clearly distinct from all the other countries in the sample, as they have committed huge financial resources to rescue their financial sectors while at the same time adopting an extremely restrictive fiscal policy stance, including tax increases and cuts in public expenditure of more than 7 per cent of their GDP.

Developed countries, especially those that were directly hit by the bursting of speculative bubbles – Iceland, Ireland, the United Kingdom and the United States – are providing massive support to their financial systems. However, this support is of a different nature than current fiscal measures for demand stimulation. It represents contingent liabilities that may not involve actual fiscal expenditure. In the case of financial bail-outs and "bad bank" schemes, the final amount of subsidies will depend on many factors, including the revenues governments can obtain when they eventually sell the troubled assets or the restructured banks. In the case of fiscal stimuli, the fiscal burden as a result of lower tax revenues or higher expenditures should be assessed against the increase in government revenues that will result from the greater economic activity that would not have occurred in the absence of such stimuli.

Given the magnitude of the crisis, a substantial increase in budget deficits in most countries seems both unavoidable and justified. But the effectiveness of deficit spending and its medium-term impact on the public finances also depends on how the deficit is generated. Varying levels and composition of revenues and expenditures and different rates of GDP growth can yield similar levels of fiscal deficit. Moreover, not all fiscal deficits are expansionary. Higher public expenditure may provide an economic stimulus when it increases investment, consumption and employment, but not when it is used for the financing of a bank bail-out. Lower fiscal revenue, on the other hand, may encourage private spending resulting from tax reductions for low- and middle-income groups, but not when it results from reduced export earnings. Consequently, fiscal policies should not focus primarily or exclusively on fiscal balances, but rather on the level and composition of spending and revenues, in order to maximize their impact on the economy and contribute to long-term development objectives.

5. The international policy dimension

The unfolding of the global crisis did not receive attention in international decision-making bodies until October 2008, which was when central banks of major economies engaged in coordinated monetary easing.[38] A novelty was that also in October 2008, the United States Federal Reserve, for the first time since the end of the Bretton Woods system, provided four emerging-market economies (Brazil, Mexico, the Republic of Korea and Singapore) with a bilateral swap of $30 billion to help them defend their currencies.

Since November 2008 the G-20 has taken the lead in launching and coordinating international action[39] to address the financial and economic crisis, although its legitimacy has been called into question because the vast majority of developing countries are not represented.[40] At its London Summit in April 2009, the G-20 presented a Global Plan for Recovery and Reform that would "constitute the largest fiscal and monetary stimulus and the most comprehensive support programme for the financial sector in modern times".[41] It includes an increase in IMF resources by $500 billion (to $750 billion), a new allocation of $250 billion for Special Drawing Rights (SDRs), additional lending by multilateral development banks of $100 billion, and support for trade finance of $250 billion. However, a closer look at the programme (Giles, 2009) reveals that these figures relate in part to decisions that had already been taken long before the summit; others were more a reflection of intentions than concrete pledges. Only half of the additional resources for the IMF were made available immediately by some member States, while the financing of the other half remained unclear. Moreover, only part of the new SDR allocation will directly benefit those countries that are most in need of international liquidity: since the additional SDRs will be allocated to IMF members according to their quotas, only $80 billion will go to low- and middle-income developing countries.

Clearly, improving the potential for multilateral financial support in the current crisis can, in principle, help developing and transition economies counter the impact of the adverse external environment on their national economies. However, such support could have been made considerably more effective if it had been linked to a reform of the IMF itself, including a review of the principles that have guided the policy conditions attached to its lending. It was observed in past crises that those conditions mostly led the borrowing countries into even deeper crisis.

IMF lending has surged since the outbreak of the current crisis, extending to nearly 50 countries by the end of May 2009. The bulk of loans are in the form of either stand-by arrangements under the General Resources Account (SDR 48 billion) or the newly created lending facility – the Flexible Credit Line (SDR 52 billion) – which is available to countries with strong fundamentals, policies and track records of policy implementation. Close to 30 poorer developing countries receive support under either the Poverty Reduction and Growth Facility (SDR 1.7 billion) or the Exogenous Shocks Facility (SDR 0.4 billion)

(IMF, 2009d). Policy conditions attached to these IMF loans are fairly similar to those of the past, including a requirement that recipient countries reduce public spending and increase interest rates.

This is at odds with recent declarations by the IMF in which coordinated countercyclical policies and large fiscal stimulus packages have been recognized as the most effective means to compensate for the fall in aggregate demand induced by the debt deflation that followed the bursting of speculative bubbles in a number of financial markets.[42] This new position has not been applied to countries that are in real need of crisis lending; instead, the traditional stabilization and adjustment policy reforms are attached as binding loan conditions. Pakistan, for example, had to tighten both its fiscal and monetary policy, including drastically reducing its fiscal deficit from 7.4 per cent of GDP in 2008 to 4.2 per cent of GDP in 2009. In the stand-by agreement with Ukraine, approved in November 2008, the initial objective was to achieve a balanced budget, even though GDP was projected to fall by more than 10 per cent in 2009 and gross public debt was very low. However, in May 2009, the IMF was obliged to accept a loosening of fiscal policy and allow a fiscal deficit of 4 per cent of GDP in light of the continued weakening of economic activity, which could have been expected at the outset.[43] Belarus, Georgia, Hungary, Latvia and Serbia have all signed IMF agreements that require very restrictive fiscal policies, which could exacerbate these countries' economic downturns. Several studies that have examined fiscal and monetary targets in recent IMF loan programmes find that the Fund has also continued to impose procyclical macroeconomic tightening in almost all recent lending arrangements with developing countries (ActionAid and Bank Information Center, 2008; CEPR, 2009; TWN, 2009). For example, in the IMF programmes for Sao Tome and Principe, and Senegal the target is to bring fiscal deficits down to below 3 per cent of GDP, to be achieved through spending cuts where necessary. In Côte d'Ivoire and Ethiopia, the targets for 2009 are even more stringent, below 2 per cent of GDP. In Côte d'Ivoire, Malawi and the Congo, the IMF programmes aim to reduce inflation to below 5 per cent in the midst of the current crisis (Molina-Gallart, 2009).

Only Colombia, Mexico and Poland, the three countries that have been granted access to the IMF's new Flexible Credit Line (FCL), have been allowed to ease their monetary and fiscal policies. But in these countries the need for foreign financing is less severe than in others. Inflation and interest rates have been lower there than in some other crisis-stricken countries, so that they have attracted far fewer speculative inflows that could cause currency overvaluation, and which would undermine their international competitiveness.

The G-20 has not yet managed to lead the way for better international coordination of macroeconomic policies so far. Such coordination is important for three reasons. Firstly, economies with current-account surpluses (that had benefited from strong growth impulses from the deficit countries in recent years) would be able to make a greater contribution to global stabilization than countries that entered the crisis with large current-account deficits. At the same time, the distribution of global demand growth should be such as to reduce global imbalances rather than exacerbating them. If other countries, through their expansionary efforts, were to systematically fall behind the United States, there would be a strong likelihood of a resurgence of global imbalances. The slower the recovery and the wider the new imbalances, the greater will be the risk of increased protectionism.

Secondly, in order to make deficit spending viable in all countries, it would be essential to ensure that no country benefits unduly from unidirectional demand spillovers emanating from deficit-spending programmes of other countries without itself making a commensurate contribution to the global demand stimulus. Thirdly, low-income countries require additional support in the form of aid in order to help them in their ongoing efforts to achieve the Millennium Development Goals (MDGs). Such additional support can best be mobilized through a concerted multilateral effort. If a countercyclical increase in bilateral aid flows were to be integrated into fiscal stimulus packages in an internationally coordinated manner, it would also have an expansionary effect on demand in donor countries similar to a fiscal stimulus at home. By the same token, since it is highly likely that many indebted low-income countries hurt by the global crisis will encounter problems in maintaining external debt sustainability, a temporary moratorium on their debt repayments would be in the spirit of the countercyclical policies undertaken in most developed and emerging-market economies (box 1.2). It would not only be an important element in efforts to attenuate the impact of the global crisis on growth, poverty alleviation and investment in the

Box 1.2

A TEMPORARY MORATORIUM ON OFFICIAL DEBT

In 2005, countries devastated by the *tsunami* in the Indian Ocean were promptly offered a temporary debt moratorium by the creditors of the Paris Club. Though this was less visible than other emergency aid, the speedy and direct response of the creditors allowed those countries to allocate much of their financial resources to meeting their humanitarian and reconstruction needs. The current global economic crisis has all the characteristics of an economic tsunami.

Developing countries are innocent bystanders, yet most of them, including the poorest, are being hit by falling export earnings and workers' remittances. The collateral damage from the current crisis could well take the form of a debt crisis for some vulnerable economies. The debt sustainability of several low-income countries, including some of those that have reached the completion point for debt relief under the HIPC Initiative, is already seriously at risk. In this situation, timely crisis prevention is preferable to crisis management at a later date, because it avoids large costs in terms of lost output and human suffering. Debt service payments for the 49 low-income countries are estimated to total about $26 billion for 2009 and 2010, a small figure compared to the size of the fiscal stimulus packages launched in the countries that are also the main creditors to the low-income countries. The form of assistance could be similar to the ones provided after Hurricane Mitch in 1998 and the tsunami in 2005. For these two natural disasters, Paris Club creditors agreed not to expect any debt payments on eligible sovereign claims from the countries affected by these disasters for up to three years. The deferred amounts could be repaid over a period of several years in the future.

In the present situation, a temporary debt moratorium on all official debts could be offered to all low-income countries (with no discrimination), without imposing any conditionality or performance criteria, as a measure to counter the fallout of the global crisis. The temporary moratorium should automatically come to an end once the world economy is well on the road to recovery. At that point the situation and possible needs for further assistance of individual debtor countries could then be assessed on a case-by-case basis within the existing institutional framework. A debt moratorium could be implemented expeditiously, whereas a scaling up of ODA from bilateral or multilateral sources would require considerably more time and more complex decision-making and implementation processes.

Compared with the size of the stimulus packages for developed countries, the total amount of such a temporary debt moratorium would be minuscule. However, for the debtor countries, in particular for the low-income countries that rely on external financing from official sources, it would provide an important fiscal breathing space and compensate for shortfalls in foreign exchange earnings and fiscal revenue. It would function as a countercyclical measure which could contribute to the macroeconomic stability in these economies. This in turn will benefit the global economy as a whole. Indeed, in a deep recession like the present one, it is also in the interests of creditor countries to stabilize their exports to low-income countries, even though these exports represent only a small share of their total exports. Stabilizing any element of global demand is more conducive to recovery than maintaining high flows of official debt service.

debtor countries; it would also contribute to stabilizing global demand.

Another major shortcoming of the G-20 process, so far, has been that it has not launched serious reforms of the international monetary and financial system, including the design of new multilaterally agreed rules for exchange-rate management, cross-border financial flows and sovereign debt workouts, in addition to the creation of a new international reserve to replace the dollar. These issues are discussed in greater detail in chapter IV of this *Report*.

6. Outlook

Production, employment and income growth in the world economy in general, and in most economies individually, are unlikely to recover until banks are recapitalized, their balance sheets cleaned up of toxic assets and other major actors in financial markets have become more solid. In order to halt the contraction of GDP, it will be necessary to maintain or even further strengthen the expansionary stance of monetary and fiscal policies. Developing and transition economies remain highly vulnerable to depressed export markets. Since only a small number of them can replace falling external demand with faster domestic demand growth, they depend on recovery in the world's leading economies.

In many countries, Governments and central banks have set new precedents for supporting ailing financial institutions. This indicates that, beyond the crisis, the relationship between the State and the private sector, in particular private financial institutions, could be revised fundamentally in the interests of greater stability and reliability of the financial system. This would be the logical consequence of the various efforts to rescue individual financial institutions that ended up in trouble on account of mismanagement. The need for such rescue operations has revealed that the huge profits and incomes earned from the financial activities of some market participants and managers over the past few years have been disproportional to the macroeconomic and social usefulness of the financial sector. Thus it is clear that large segments of the financial sector cannot be left to function like a giant casino without doing great damage to the real sector of the economy. The recent heavy involvement of governments and central banks should therefore lead to a review of the existing modes of functioning of the financial sector. Such a review should not only look at the need for strengthening financial regulation and supervision (a topic discussed in greater depth in chapter III of this *Report*), but also at a redefinition of the role of central banks and public financial institutions in the economy.

The immediate objective of deficit spending is to avoid a further contraction in an economy, and possibly to foster a recovery of the productive sector. However, tax reductions or expenditure increase may also have longer term implications. For instance, they could influence income distribution in favour of social groups whose real disposable incomes have stagnated or fallen in recent years; or they could influence the pace of structural change, for example towards more climate-friendly modes of production and consumption (as discussed in chapter V of this *Report*). Well-conceived policies to overcome the crisis may therefore also help accelerate progress towards other strategic objectives.

Growing budget deficits as a consequence of fiscal stimulus packages have prompted concerns that governments will have to raise tax rates in order to be able to service the increasing public debt. Such concerns are unjustified, since, in a growing economy, government revenue will normally rise sufficiently at constant tax rates. By the same token, if governments were to remain passive in a situation of severe crisis, relying exclusively on automatic stabilizers, the fiscal balance will deteriorate as a result of lower tax revenues. Adjusting public spending to falling tax revenue might not lead to a lower fiscal deficit either, because the tax base will narrow further and more financial rescue operations might become necessary. By contrast, a discretionary increase in public spending, especially when it expands investment, enhances production capacity and job creation, and leads to higher GDP. This in turn enlarges the future tax base and thereby raises public revenues at given tax rates. This does not mean that the size of the domestic public debt is completely irrelevant; it may have undesirable effects on income distribution, and an increasing share of interest payments in the budget may compromise budget flexibility in the future. This is why, in order to be truly countercyclical, an expansionary fiscal policy in a recession needs to be combined with more restrictive fiscal policies when recovery has set in and output growth accelerates.

There are also widespread concerns that the huge injections of central bank money and the sharply rising budget deficits in many countries will sooner or later lead to inflation, and eventually to accelerating inflation if governments and central banks do not react early to contain this danger. This fear is based on the monetarist view that inflation is always a monetary phenomenon because it cannot be financed without additional money, and that "too much money chasing too few goods" will inevitably create inflation (Greenspan, 2009; Feldstein, 2009).

However, "too much money" needs a channel through which to inject the virus of inflation into an economy. There are only two channels for this to happen: if demand growth exceeds potential supply growth ("demand-pull inflation"), or if cost increases, particularly labour costs, exceed productivity growth ("cost-push inflation"). In the present situation, with capacity utilization at historic lows and unemployment rising with dramatic speed, neither overheating nor wage inflation is a realistic prospect for several years to come. It is a matter of years, not months, before economies that are now in deep crisis can be restored to a level of capacity utilization where supply cannot keep up with demand or to a level of employment that could trigger demand for higher wages. This will allow central banks to withdraw excess liquidity by selling revalued assets and absorbing excess money supply. Thus fears that "too much money" or rising government deficits could reignite inflation are unjustified in the current depressed state of the global economy.

Indeed, deflation – not inflation – is the real danger. Japan in the 1990s, following the bursting of the big bubble, provides an example of deflationary stagnation, which occurred despite huge injections of money and several attempts to reignite (albeit half-heartedly) a depressed economy (chart 1.9). The main problem is that with sharply rising unemployment the downward pressure on wages mounts. Wage deflation is the imminent and most dangerous threat in many countries today, because governments are finding it difficult to stabilize a tumbling economy when there is a large-scale fall in wages and consumption. However, deflation will not cure itself. Therefore,

Chart 1.9

UNIT LABOUR COSTS IN JAPAN, 1990–2008

(Index numbers, 1990 = 100)

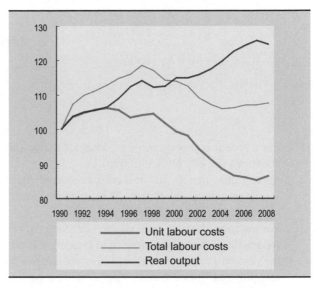

Source: OECD, *Main Economic Indicators* database.

the most important task is to break the spiral of falling wages, prices and demand as early as possible, and to revive the financial sector's ability to provide credit for productive investment to stimulate real economic growth. Governments and central banks need to take rapid and strong proactive measures to boost demand before the virus of deflation infects their economies.   ■

Notes

1 For a recent comprehensive outlook for the world economy, see UN/DESA (2009b).

2 As a group, metals and minerals registered their lowest price level in February 2009, and agricultural raw materials in March 2009.

3 For instance, the International Rubber Study Group reports that between September and December 2008, the year-on-year natural rubber consumption growth rate plunged from 2.1 to -3.4 per cent. This period registered a more abrupt fall in rubber consumption than that of the 2001–2002 global economic slow-down (IRSG, 2009). Cotton consumption declined by 13 per cent in 2008 (ICAC, 2009). The United States Department of Agriculture (USDA, 2008) considered this the worst global consumption contraction in 65 years.

4 This is the case not only for minerals and metals but also for other commodities. For instance, the re-building of cotton product pipeline inventories that shrank significantly during the economic downturn is also expected to provide a boost to consumption, with China accounting for more than half of this increase in 2009 (USDA, 2009a).

5 Oil price developments are also linked to those of other commodities through the mechanism of com-modity index investment (see chapter II).

6 Data refer to the average of Dubai, Brent and Texas.

7 Chinese oil imports reached a 12-month high in March 2009 as a result of strategic stockpiling by the Government and rising demand from refiners (Ulrich, 2009).

8 For cotton, see USDA, 2009a; for coffee, ICO, 2009a and b; for tea, EIU, 2009; and for sugar, USDA, 2009b. There are some indications that cocoa consumption may have been relatively more affected by the crisis (ICCO, 2009). In addition, shortages in cocoa supply are also related to structural problems in Côte d'Ivoire and a high incidence of plant disease.

9 UNCTAD secretariat calculations based on the IEA Oil Market Report (various issues), IMF International Financial Statistics and UNCTAD Commodity Prices online.

10 A survey by Fraser Institute (2009) indicates that the sector expects a dramatic fall in investment and exploration during the current economic downturn, with at least 30 per cent of exploration companies going out of business. Time magazine (2009) cites Merrill Lynch in estimating that mining investment will be 40 per cent lower in 2009–2010, and invest-ment in the oil sector will be 30 per cent lower in 2009 and 40 per cent lower in 2010 than expected before the crisis.

11 For instance, copper capacity utilization fell to around 78 per cent in the first two months of 2009, compared with an average of 87 per cent over the past five years (ICSG, 2009).

12 There is wide agreement throughout the energy sector on the possibility of a future energy supply crunch due to lower investment resulting from the global recession (see, for instance, CERA, 2008; and *The Economist*, 2009).

13 USDA (2009c) expects a 5 per cent reduction in wheat acreage and a 4 per cent reduction in cotton acreage in the United States. The planting area for corn will increase by 1 per cent from last year but this will still be 7 per cent lower than in 2007. The total area for principal crops is expected to shrink by approximately 1.2 per cent.

14 See, for instance, *TDRs 2006, 2007* and *2008*; WESP 2006, 2007 and 2008.

15 Some economic authorities dismissed the very ex-istence of a problem, believing that external imbal-ances could continue indefinitely, provided that the corresponding capital flows found productive uses (Economic Report of the President, 2006: 146). With respect to growing domestic indebtedness, there was added confidence that, since credit was essentially delivered to private agents, no crisis could occur, as the private sector would always be aware of the need to honour its debts. Such an idea was popularized at the end of the 1980s in Great Britain by then Chan-cellor of the Exchequer Nigel Lawson, and has been dubbed "Lawson's Law"; it ended in the pound ster-ling crisis of 1992 and severance from the European Exchange Rate Mechanism (O'Connell, 2006).

16   In the United States, delinquency rates in commercial banks climbed from 1.51 per cent of total loans in the first quarter of 2006 to 5.6 per cent in the first quarter of 2009. For real estate loans, delinquency rates were 1.36 per cent and 7.13 per cent in those periods (Federal Reserve, 2009a).

17   Gross private investment in the United States plunged by 23 per cent in the last quarter of 2008 and by 51.8 per cent in the first quarter of 2009 (at annual rates, seasonally adjusted); personal consumption of durable goods contracted by 14.8 and 22.1 per cent in the third and fourth quarters of 2008 respectively (also at annual rates, seasonally adjusted) (Bureau of Economic Analysis, 2009).

18   Actual figures are from Eurostat (epp.eurostat. ec.europa.eu) and the United States Bureau of Labor Statistics (www.bls.gov/news.release/empsit.toc. htm). The OECD forecasts that unemployment will rise in 2010 to 10.1 per cent in the United States and to 12.0 in the euro area (OECD, 2009a).

19   Between the third quarter of 2007 and the fourth quarter of 2008, outstanding financial assets of households and non-profit organizations decreased by almost 20 per cent, from $50.5 trillion to $40.8 trillion. Most of the losses were concentrated in corporate equities, mutual fund shares and pension fund reserves. In the same period, households' real estate value declined from $21.1 to $18.3 trillion (Federal Reserve, 2009b).

20   Price variations correspond to the first quarter of 2009 compared to the same period in 2008 (see *Monthly Digest of Statistics*, No. 761, May 2009 for the United Kingdom; *INSEE Conjoncture Informations Rapides* No. 147, 28 May 2009 for France; and *INE, Boletín Mensual de Estadística*, April 2009 for Spain).

21   A long-lasting stock market downturn will negatively affect future pension payments in countries where the majority of pension schemes are funded by private capital. In Chile, for example, retirement accounts lost almost one third of their value between December 2007 and December 2008 and in Argentina pension forecasts were so low that parliament voted a return to the previous public pay-as-you-go system (AIOS 2008).

22   In the case of Mexico, while UNWTO data for January and February 2009 still post positive growth of 13 per cent, this was before the outbreak of the A(H1N1) influenza virus. National data for January to April 2009 show a year-on-year decline in international arrivals of 5.9 per cent (SIIMT, 2009).

23   See for example, various issues of the *TDR* since 2005.

24   See "Supporting the financial system and the economy: key ECB policy actions in the crisis", speech by Jean-Claude Trichet, President of the ECB at a Conference organized by the Nueva Economía Fórum, and *The Wall Street Journal Europe*, Madrid, 22 June 2009; and "ECB looks to stimulus by stealth", *Financial Times* online, 24 June 2009, at: http://www.ft.com/cms/s/0/970be020-60f3-11de-aa12-00144feabdc0,dwp_uuid=70662e7c-3027-11da-ba9f-00000e2511c8.html?ftcamp=rss.

25   The Bank of Korea's (2009) response to the crisis also included a one-off interest payment on banks' required reserve deposits to support their recapitalization.

26   See *The Economist* online, 8 September 2008, at: http://www.economist.com/businessfinance/displayStory.cfm?story_id=12078933.

27   See "JPMorgan Chase and Bear Stearns Announce Amended Merger Agreement", JPMorgan Chase & Co, Press Releases, 24 March 2008, at: http://investor.shareholder.com/jpmorganchase/press/releasedetail.cfm?ReleaseID=301224&ReleaseType=Current.

28   See "US to take control of AIG", *Financial Times* online, at: http://www.ft.com/cms/s/0/271257f2-83-f1-11dd-bf00-000077b07658.html.

29   For investment vehicles, for the purchase of toxic assets for a total of $100 billion, both the private investor and the Government will need to contribute a minimum capital of $7.5 billion, and the FDIC will extend a non-recourse loan of $85 billion.

30   The adverse scenario of the stress test assumed an output contraction of 3.3 per cent in 2009 and no growth in 2010, a 22 per cent further decrease in home prices, and an unemployment rate of 10.3 per cent in 2010. Several observers have argued that the tests were designed to allow almost everybody to pass. Rather than setting extreme conditions, the assumptions of the "adverse" scenario were not too far from the expectations of private forecasters.

31   Banks requiring capital injection included Citigroup, Bank of America, Wells Fargo and GMAC. Banks that were allowed to return TARP funds included JPMorgan Chase, Goldman Sachs and Morgan Stanley.

32   See "BOE to make more capital available", *Financial Times*, 9 June 2009.

33   United States Treasury securities held by the Federal Reserve increased from $476 billion on 31 December 2008 to $633 billion on 17 June 2009, as it purchased long-term T-bonds as a way of maintaining long-term interest rates at relatively low levels.

34   G-20, The Global Plan for Recovery and Reform, 2 April 2009, at: http://www.g20.org/Documents/final-communique.pdf.

35   According to Lipsky (2009), "The spending measures already announced must be implemented if they are to support the incipient recovery. Moreover, if the signs of recovery turn out to be a false dawn, consideration may need to be given to providing additional stimulus". See also Freeman et al., 2009.

36   Required fiscal tightening concerns spending and revenue measures that affect global demand, but generally exclude the support of a troubled financial sector, even if it involves large fiscal costs.

37   The Congressional Budget Office provided a detailed breakdown of measures and a year-by-year estimate of the economic effects of the American Recovery and Reinvestment Act of 2009 in a letter to the Honorable Charles E. Grassley, a ranking member of the Committee on Finance of the United States Senate, available at: http://www.cbo.gov/ftpdocs/100xx/doc10008/03-02-Macro_Effects_of_ARRA.pdf.

38   On the same occasion, the Federal Reserve also authorized temporary bilateral swap lines to provide dollar liquidity to overseas markets through foreign central banks, with the ECB and the Swiss National Bank and later also with the central banks of Australia, Brazil, Canada, Denmark, Japan, Mexico, New Zealand, Norway, the Republic of Korea, Singapore, Sweden and the United Kingdom. In order to be able to offer liquidity in foreign currency to financial institutions in the United States, the Federal Reserve obtained swap lines with the Bank of England, the ECB, the Bank of Japan and the Swiss National Bank.

39   In November 2008, G-20 leaders declared a determination to "enhance our cooperation and work together to restore global growth and achieve needed reforms in the world's financial systems"

(G-20 Declaration from the Summit on Financial Markets and the World Economy, 15 November 2008, available at: http://www.fazenda.gov.br/portugues/documentos/2008/novembro/G20-SUMMIT-LEADERS-DECLARATION-2008-11-15.pdf).

40   See, for example, Hell (2008), as well as TWN Info Service on Finance and Development, "General Assembly thematic dialogue on economic crisis begins", Third World Network, 1 April 2009; and Archibugi D, "The G20 ought to be increased to 6 billion", at: http://www.opendemocracy.net/article/email/the-g20-ought-to-be-increased-to-6-billion.

41   G-20, Declaration on Delivering Resources Through the International Financial Institutions, London, 2 April 2009, available at: http://www.g20.org/Documents/Fin_Deps_IFI_Annex_Draft_02_04_09_-_1615_Clean.pdf.

42   For example, the IMF noted that "countercyclical monetary policy can help shorten recessions, but its effectiveness is limited in financial crises. By contrast, expansionary fiscal policy seems particularly effective in shortening recessions associated with financial crises and boosting recoveries" (IMF, 2009e).

43   For an explanation of the revision of the IMF stand-by agreement with Ukraine, see IMF Press Release 09/156, "IMF completes first review under stand-by arrangement with Ukraine and approves US$2.8 billion disbursement", Washington, DC, 8 May 2009.

References

ActionAid and Bank Information Center (2008). *Quick Fixes or Real Solutions? World Bank and IMF responses to the global food and fuel crises*. Brussels, December. Available at: http://www.eurodad.org/uploadedFiles/Whats_New/Reports/Quick%20Fixes%20or%20Real%20Solutions.pdf.

Aglietta M and Rigot S (2009). *Crise et rénovation de la finance*, Odile Jacob, Paris, March.

AIOS (2008). Asociación Internacional de Organismos de Supervisión de Fondos de Pensiones, *Boletín Estadístico* No. 20, December.

Bank of Korea (2009). *Monetary Policy Report*, March.

BIS (2009). Detailed tables on provisional and consolidated banking statistics at end-December 2008. Basle, April. Available at: www.bis.org/statistics/bankstats.htm.

BNP Paribas (2009). Is there a silver lining? The implications of the financial crisis for the non-ferrous metals industry. Presentation at ILZSG Industry Advisory Panel.

Buiter W (2009). Don't touch the unsecured creditors! Clobber the tax payer instead. Maverecon Blog, 13 March.

Bulow J and Klemperer P (2009). Reorganising the banks: Focus on the liabilities, not the assets. VOX EU, 21 March.

Bureau of Economic Analysis (2009). United States Department of Commerce, News Release, Gross Domestic Product: First Quarter (advance), 29 April.

Caliari A (2008). *Trade Issues Crucial for Dealing with the Global Financial Crisis.* Available at: http://www. networkideas.org/news/nov2008/print/prnt251108_ Trade_Issues.htm.

CEPR (2009). Empowering the IMF: Should Reform be a Requirement for Increasing the Fund's Resources? by Mark Weisbrot, Jose Cordero and Luis Sandoval, Center for Economic Policy and Research. Washington DC, April. Available at: http://www.cepr.net/ documents/publications/imf-reform-2009-04.pdf.

CERA (2008). "Recession Shock": The impact of the economic and financial crisis on the oil market. Cambridge Energy Research Associates, 15 December.

Cherny K and Ergungor E (2009). Sweden as a useful model of successful financial crisis resolution. VOX EU, 19 March.

Council of the European Union (2009). Report of the Task Force on reviewing the effectiveness of financial support measures, Brussels, 9 June. Available at: http://register.consilium.europa.eu/pdf/en/09/st10/ st10772-ad01.en09.pdf.

CPB Netherlands Bureau for Economic Policy Analysis (2009). World trade monitor, April.

Debelle G (2008). Market operations in the past year, Reserve Bank of Australia, 31 October. Available at: http:// www.rba.gov.au/Speeches/2008/sp_ag_311008.html.

DeLong B (2009). The Geithner Plan FAQ. Brad DeLong's Blog, 21 March.

Desjardins (2009). Commodity Trends. *Economic Studies,* May.

Detragiache E and Spilimbergo A (2004). Empirical models of short-term debt and crises: Do they test the creditor run hypothesis? *European Economic Review,* 48(2): 379–389.

EC (2009). Public Finances in EMU 2009, European Economy 5/2009 (provisional version). Commission of the European Communities.

ECLAC (2009a). Economic Survey of Latin America and the Caribbean 2008-2009. Economic Commission for Latin America and the Caribbean, Santiago de Chile, July.

ECLAC (2009b). La reacción de los gobiernos de las Américas frente a la crisis internacional: una presentación sintética de las medidas de política anunciadas hasta el 31 de mayo de 2009. Economic Commission for Latin America and the Caribbean, Santiago de Chile, 1 June.

Economic Report of the President (2006). Transmitted to the Congress in February 2006. United States Government Printing Office. Washington, DC.

EIU (2009). World Commodity Forecasts: food, feedstuffs and beverages. Economist Intelligence Unit, May.

Ernst & Young (2009). Mining and metals in adversity, May.

FAO (2008). Food Outlook. Rome, November.

Federal Reserve (2009a). Federal Reserve Statistical Release, Charge-off and delinquency rates on loans and leases at commercial banks, updated on 18 May. Available at: www.federalreserve.gov/releases/ chargeoff/delallsa.htm.

Federal Reserve (2009b). Flow of Funds Accounts of the United States, Flows and Outstanding, Fourth Quarter 2008, 12 March. Available at: www.federalreserve.gov/releases/z1/Current/z1.pdf.

Feldstein M (2009). The Fed must reassure markets on inflation. *Financial Times,* 29 June.

Financial Times (2008). US to take control of AIG, 16 September.

Financial Times (2009). Germany ready to help eurozone members,18 February.

Financial Times (2009). BOE to make more capital available, 9 June.

Financial Times (2009). ECB looks to stimulus by stealth, 24 June.

Fisher I (1933). The debt deflation theory of great depressions, *Econometrica 1,* October.

Fraser Institute (2009). Survey of Mining Companies 2008/2009.

Freeman C et al. (2009). The Case for Global Fiscal Stimulus, IMF Staff Position Note, 6 March.

G-20 (2009). The Global Plan for Recovery and Reform, 2 April. Available at: www.g20.org/Documents/ final-communique.pdf.

Giles C (2009). Large numbers hide big G20 divisions. *Financial Times,* 2 April.

Greenspan A (2009). Inflation is the biggest threat to a sustained recovery. *Financial Times,* 26 June.

Hall R and Woodward S (2009). The right way to create a good bank and a bad bank. VOX EU, 24 February.

Hell S (2008). The response of The United Nations to the global financial crisis. Fact sheet, Friedrich Ebert Stiftung. New York, December.

Henning R (2009). *The future of the Chiang Mai Initiative: An Asian Monetary Fund?* Peterson Institute for International Economics, PB09–5: 1–9.

ICAC (2009). Cotton this week. Changes in supply and demand estimates. International Cotton Advisory Committee, 2 June.

ICC (2009). *ICC Banking Commission Recommendations. Impact of Basel II on Trade Finance.* International Chamber of Commerce, 25 March. Available at: www.iccwbo.org/policy/banking/icccigde/index. html.

ICCO (2009). Cocoa Market Review. International Cocoa Organization, April.

ICO (2009a). The world economic crisis and the coffee sector, ED 2059/09. International Coffee Organization, 9 February. Available at: http://www.ico.org/ documents/ed-2059e-economic-crisis.pdf.

ICO (2009b). Coffee Market Report. International Coffee Organization, April.

ICSG (2009). Copper: Preliminary data for February 2009. International Copper Study Group Press Release. Lisbon, May.

IEA (2009a). Oil Market Report. International Energy Agency, May.

IEA (2009b). Oil Market Report. International Energy Agency, June.

IEA (2009c). The impact of the financial and economic crisis on global energy investment. International Energy Agency, May.

IIF (2009). Capital Flows to Emerging Market Economies. Institute of International Finance, January. Available at: www.iif.com/emr/article+204.php.

IMF (2009a). The implications of the global financial crisis for low-income countries. Washington, DC, March.

IMF (2009b). Update on Fiscal Stimulus and Financial Sector Measures, 26 April.

IMF (2009c). Fiscal Implications of the Global economic and Financial Crisis, IMF Staff Position Note, SPN/09/13, 9 June.

IMF (2009d). IMF Lending Arrangements as of May 31, 2009. Washington, DC.

IMF (2009e). *World Economic Outlook*: Crisis and Recovery. Washington, DC, April.

IMF/IDA (2008). Heavily Indebted Poor Countries (HIPC) Initiative and Multilateral Debt Relief Initiative (MDRI) – Status of Implementation. Washington, DC, September.

IMF-IEO (2003). Fiscal Adjustment in IMF-Supported Programs (Evaluation Report). International Monetary Fund - Independent Evaluation Office. Washington, DC.

INE (2009). *Boletín Mensual de Estadística*. Instituto Nacional de Estadística, April.

INSEE (2009). *Conjoncture Informations Rapides* No. 147. Institut National de la Statistique et des Etudes Economiques, 28 May.

IRSG (2009). Rubber industry report. International Rubber Study Group. Vol. 8, 7–9. January–March. Available at: http://www.rubberstudy.com/01_Introduction.pdf.

Johnson S (2009). The Quiet Coup. *The Atlantic*, May.

Johnson S and Kwak J (2009). Geithner's plan isn't money in the bank. *Los Angeles Times*, 24 March.

Jonung L (2009). The Swedish Model for Resolving the Banking crisis of 1991–93: Is it useful today? VOX EU, 14 March.

JPMorgan Chase & Co (2008). JPMorgan Chase and Bear Stearns Announce Amended Merger Agreement, Press Releases, 24 March.

Khatiwada S (2009). Stimulus Packages to Counter Global Economic Crisis: A review. *ILO Discussion Paper*, DP/196/2009.

Kindleberger C (1978). Manias, Panics and Crashes. A History of Financial Crises. The Macmillan Press Ltd., London and Basingtoke.

Kotlikoff L and Sachs J (2009). The Gasp is worse than you think. *Financial Times*, 7 April.

Krugman P (2009). Geithner Plan Arithmetic. *The Conscience of Liberal*, 23 March.

Lipsky J (2009). Fully Spend Stimulus Money to Back Crisis Recovery, Says IMF, *IMF Survey online*, 26 June.

Minsky H (1975). John Maynard Keynes, Columbia University Press - The Macmillan Press Ltd., London and Basingstoke, June.

Molina-Gallart N (2009). *Bail-out or blow-out? IMF policy advice and conditions for low-income countries at a time of crisis*. EURODAD, Brussels. Available at: http://www.eurodad.org/whatsnew/reports.aspx?id=3679.

O'Connell A (2006). Macroeconomic Policy in Developing Countries within the Current International Financial Architecture. Mimeo. Background paper prepared for UNCTAD's *Trade and Development Report 2006*.

OECD (2009a). Economic Outlook No 85, Preliminary Edition, June.

OECD (2009b). Development aid at its highest level ever in 2008. Press release. Available at: http://www.oecd.org/document/35/0,3343,en_2649_34487_42458595_1_1_1_1,00.html.

OECD-FAO (2009). Agricultural Outlook 2009–2018.

Office for National Statistics (2009). *Monthly Digest of Statistics*, No. 761, May.

OPEC (2009). Monthly Oil Market Report. Organization of Petroleum Exporting Countries, May.

Ratha D (2009). Remittances expected to fall by 5 to 8 per cent in 2009. Available at: http://blogs.worldbank.org/peoplemove/remittances-expected-to-fall-by-5-to-8-percent-in-2009.

Ratha D and Mohapatra S (2009). Revised Outlook for Remittance Flows 2009–2011: Remittances expected to fall by 5 to 8 per cent in 2009. *Migration and Development Brief 9*. Washington, DC, World Bank, 23 March.

Ratha D, Mohapatra S and Xu Zhimei (2008). Outlook for Remittance Flows 2008–2010: Growth expected to moderate significantly, but flows to remain resilient. *Migration and Development Brief 8*. Washington, DC, World Bank, 11 November.

RGE Monitor (2009). Are commodity prices getting ahead of fundamentals? RGE Analysts' EcoMonitor, 20 May.

Roodman D (2008). History says financial crisis will suppress aid. Centre for Global Development. Available at: http://blogs.cgdev.org/globaldevelopment/2008/10/history_says_financial_crisis.php.

Sachs J (2009). The Geithner-Summers Plan is Even Worse Than We Thought. VOX EU, 7 April.

SIIMT (2009). Síntesis. Sistema Integral de Información de Mercados Turísticos. Mexico DF, 19 June.

Snower D (2009). Redistribution through the Geithner plan. VOX EU, 20 May.

Strauss-Kahn D (2008). World Leaders Launch Action Plan to Combat Financial Crisis, IMF Survey online, 15 November.

Subbarao D (2009). Monetary Policy Statement 2009–10, *Reserve Bank of India Monthly Bulletin*, May.

The Economist (2008). Suffering a seizure, 8 September.

The Economist (2009). Bust and boom, 21 May.

Time Magazine (2009). What's driving the bull market in commodities? 25 April.

Trichet J-C (2009). Supporting the financial system and the economy: key ECB policy actions in the crisis, Speech at a Conference organised by the Nueva Economía Fórum and The Wall Street Journal Europe. Madrid, 22 June. Available at: www.ecb.int/press/key/date/2009/html/sp090622.en.html.

TWN (2009). The IMF's Financial Crisis Loans: No Change in Conditionalities. Third World Network, Penang, Malaysia, 11 March. Available at: www.twnside.org.sg.

Ulrich J (2009). China Inc's Renewed Buying Binge. JP Morgan's Hands-On China series, 15 April. Available at: http://www.lowyinterpreter.org/file.axd?file=Ulrich+-+China+Inc+Buying+-+April+15a.pdf.

UNCTAD (2009a). Commodity Price Statistics Online.

UNCTAD (2009b). The Global Economic Crisis: Systemic Failures and Multilateral Remedies. United Nations publication, sales no. E.09.II.D.4, New York and Geneva, April.

UNCTAD (2009c). Assessing the impact of the current financial and economic crisis on global FDI flows, UNCTAD/DIAE/IA/2009/3. Geneva, April.

UNCTAD (2009d). Global FDI flows halved in 1st quarter of 2009, UNCTAD data show; prospects remain low for rest of year, UNCTAD/PRESS/PR/2009/024. Geneva, 24 June.

UNCTAD (2009e). Global economic crisis: implications for trade and development, TD/B/C.I/CRP.1.7. Geneva, May.

UNCTAD (various issues). *Trade and Development Report*. United Nations publication, New York and Geneva.

UN/DESA (2009a). World Economic Situation and Prospects 2009, Update as of mid-2009.

UN/DESA (2009b). LINK Global Economic Outlook, June. Available at: http://www.un.org/esa/analysis/link/presentations09/geo200906.pdf.

UN/DESA/UNCTAD (various issues). *World Economic Situation and Prospects*, New York, United Nations.

UNWTO (2009). UNWTO World Tourism Barometer. Interim Update. Madrid, April.

USDA (2008). Cotton: World Markets and Trade. Worst Global Consumption Contraction in 65 Years. United States Department of Agriculture, December.

USDA (2009a). Cotton and Wool Outlook. United States Department of Agriculture, May.

USDA (2009b). Sugar: World Production, Supply and Distribution. United States Department of Agriculture, May.

USDA (2009c). Acreage. United States Department of Agriculture. National Agricultural Statistics Service, June.

USDA (2009d). USDA Agricultural Projections to 2018: United States Department of Agriculture.

von Braun J (2008). Food and agricultural crises: implications for agriculture and the poor. International Food Policy Research Institute, December.

Wall Street Journal (2008). Central banks cut rate worldwide, by Sudeep Ready and Joellen Perry, 8 October.

World Bank/IMF (2009). *Global Monitoring Report 2009*. Washington DC, March.

WTO (2009). World trade 2008, prospects for 2009. WTO sees 9 per cent global trade decline in 2009 as recession strikes. World Trade Organization Press release, Press/554. Geneva, 24 March.

Young P (2009). Why Geithner's plan is the taxpayers' curse. *Financial Times*, 1 April.

Annex to chapter I

THE GLOBAL RECESSION COMPOUNDS THE FOOD CRISIS

As is well known, the sharp increase in the prices of food commodities between April 2007 and May 2008 (chart 1.A1) had dramatic consequences for many developing countries. The greatest impact was on low-income countries, where poor households spend a large proportion of their income on food, and which are strongly dependent on food imports.[1] The prices of wheat, maize, rice and soybeans all peaked between March and July 2008, but then fell steeply until the end of the year. In early 2009, wheat and maize prices stabilized at their 2007 levels and rice prices at their early 2008 level. Food prices are still well above their longer term average. The factors that have caused the ongoing food crisis were discussed at greater length in *TDR 2008* (chap. II, section C). All these factors continue to influence the global markets for food commodities (Mittal, 2009). The features that have distinguished the current food crisis from previous episodes of rapidly increasing food prices include increasing demand for commodities for biofuel production and commodity speculation in financial markets (Peters, Langley and Westcot, 2009). Thus, apart from reflecting a major failure of development strategy (UNCTAD, 2008), the recent food crisis is closely linked to other global challenges, such as the financial and economic crisis, the energy crisis and efforts to address the problem of climate change.

According to estimates of the Food and Agriculture Organization of the United Nations (FAO), the combination of the high food prices and the global economic crisis has caused the number of hungry people in the world to soar by 100 million, resulting in more than one billion hungry people this year (FAO, 2009a). In 2009, food emergencies persist in 31 countries (FAO, 2009b), and between 109 million and 126 million people may have fallen below the poverty line since 2006 due to higher food prices.

Chart 1.A1

FOOD COMMODITY PRICES, JANUARY 2000–MAY 2009

(Index numbers, 2000 = 100)

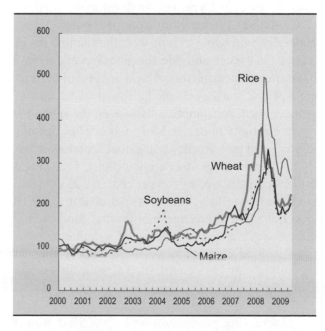

Source: UNCTAD, *Commodity Price Statistics Online.*

Sub-Saharan Africa and South Asia are identified as the most vulnerable regions (Purcell, 2009).

Following the surge in food prices, low-income food-deficit countries saw their food import bill double between 2005 and 2008. In 2009, it is expected to fall by 23 per cent as a result of lower prices, but it should remain much higher than the average of the past decade. For cereals, which are the most critical item for food security, the import bill in low-income food-deficit countries increased by 62 per cent in 2007/08. While lower prices are expected to knock down the size of that bill by 27 per cent in 2008/09, this is still 54 per cent higher than the average of the four previous seasons between 2003 and 2007 (FAO, 2009b and c).

The significant fall in international food prices in the second half of 2008 did not translate into substantially lower prices in developing countries. According to FAO (2009c), domestic prices have remained generally very high, and in some cases at record highs. It appears that while the pass-through between prices on international commodity markets and consumer prices was high in the phase of increasing prices, the reverse was not evident during the subsequent months of falling prices (Ghosh, 2009).

Lower food prices were the result of bumper harvests in 2008, mainly of cereals, due to increased plantings and favourable weather conditions. Cereal production rose by 13.2 per cent in developed countries, but by only 2.8 per cent in developing countries (FAO, 2009c). Producers in developed countries were generally better able to cope with the rising costs of inputs. On the demand side, the global recession may have affected demand for biofuels because of the lower oil prices, and the demand for feedstock because of reduced meat consumption. However, the relatively lower elasticity of demand for food implies that it is less affected by a slowdown in global economic activity than demand for other commodities. Total cereal utilization increased by 3.8 per cent in 2008/09, and is expected to rise again by 1.3 per cent in 2009/10 (FAO, 2009c). Moreover, non-market fundamental factors, such as the unwinding of speculative positions in food commodities and the appreciation of the dollar, may have contributed significantly to the sharp decline in international food prices.

Increasing production and somewhat slower demand growth eased market conditions and allowed

some replenishing of inventories, which had fallen to historically low levels in 2008.[2] In 2009, the stock-to-utilization ratio of grains and oilseeds is significantly higher than in 2008, but it is still about 16 per cent below the average for the decade 1996–2006, before prices surged.[3] Moreover, the situation seems to be reversing again in 2009. As a result of the lower prices, the prevailing high input prices, and the credit crunch, some farmers have been cutting back planting area (IRRI, 2008). Yields are also being affected by lower fertilizer use in order to reduce costs.

In addition, adverse weather conditions in different parts of the world are affecting crop prospects. World cereal production is forecast by FAO (2009b and c) to drop by 3 per cent in 2009/10 from the 2008/09 level, and to fall slightly short of use, so that stocks will partly be eroded. In the case of oilseeds (mainly soybeans), declining production in major producing countries, together with increasing demand, notably from China, may again reduce inventories to critically low levels in 2009. All this, together with the rebound in oil prices and the return of financial investors to commodity markets, is reflected in upward pressure on prices.

Thus, while the market balance has somewhat improved, any shock to food markets could exacerbate the food security situation. In addition, forecasts by specialized agencies expect food prices to remain high in the longer run, mainly as a result of continuously rising biofuel demand and structural factors related to population and income growth (OECD-FAO, 2009; FAPRI, 2009; USDA, 2009).[4]

The global recession has also had a negative impact on the food situation, notably in the poorest countries, where lower incomes resulting from declining employment and wages and falling remittances are limiting the capacity of poor households to buy food. In many countries, falling export revenues due to the low prices of their commodity exports and difficulties in obtaining trade finance have reduced import capacity and lower fiscal revenues have limited the scope for government action to address the symptoms of the food crisis. Moreover, in low-income food-deficit countries whose currencies depreciated since mid-2008 the fall in international food prices was not fully translated into lower domestic prices. The effects of the crisis are dramatically reflected in country case studies by the World Food Programme (WFP, 2009) for Armenia, Bangladesh,

Ghana, Nicaragua and Zambia, which confirm that poor households are eating fewer and less nutritious meals. Many are also cutting back on health care and children's schooling.[5]

The food crisis remains a vital concern; it requires a combination of short- and long-term actions. Short-term measures already being applied include increased emergency food assistance, cash transfers and improved safety nets to meet urgent food needs. A number of developing countries have also resorted to price controls and subsidies, and to various trade policy measures to protect their populations.[6] However, the latter have exacerbated the problem in world markets. Moreover, although these measures have sheltered consumers from exploding food prices, in some countries they have reduced incentives for farmers to increase production (Gandure, 2008). Some of these measures were relaxed with the easing of markets, which also may have contributed to lowering prices, but many of them remain in place. Moreover, several countries have acquired land overseas, particularly in Africa, with a view to securing food supplies. Such investments may bring some opportunities, but they also pose risks for the poor if their access to land is impaired. These investments should therefore be adequately regulated to ensure fair benefit-sharing (FAO, IFAD and IIED, 2009).[7]

Over the long term, food security will require more investment in agriculture to raise productivity. More remunerative prices for farmers would provide them with a greater incentive to boost production. Due to the lack of data, a systematic comparison of world market prices and farm-gate prices is not possible, but there are indications that many small farmers in developing countries, especially in low-income countries, have benefited only partially, if at all, from rising world market prices for their products. On the other hand, they have been affected by the higher world market prices for their inputs (Oxfam, 2008; Dawe, 2008).

The capacity to respond to price incentives would also require a more supportive institutional and financial framework. At the national level, this implies greater government support for agricultural research, development and infrastructure, purchase of inputs, provision of credit and extension services.

Such support was significantly reduced or even entirely abolished under structural adjustment programmes sponsored by the international financial institutions. At the international level, the removal of distortions in international agricultural markets, especially by dismantling agricultural support and protection in developed countries, could help increase agricultural incomes and production in developing countries. While the immediate effect might be an increase in food prices, in the medium term the benefits of the elimination of agricultural support in developed countries are likely to outweigh the adjustment costs of such a policy reform for developing countries, including net food importers (Herrmann, 2007).

Annual additional investments to ensure food and nutrition security, estimated at \$25 billion to \$40 billion (UN/DESA, 2008), are small compared to the fiscal stimulus and financial support packages that are now being implemented in developed countries in response to the financial and economic crisis. Official development assistance (ODA) for African agriculture would need to increase from the current \$1–2 billion to some \$8 billion by 2010 (MDG Africa Steering Group, 2008). The international response to the global food crisis has been rapid, notably with the establishment of the Comprehensive Framework for Action,[8] and has led to additional aid pledges for food and agricultural development. But so far, resources available to solve the food crisis have not increased sufficiently to meet all the priority needs, and disbursement of funds has been slow (FAO, 2009e; EC, 2009; Oxfam, 2009). Moreover, aid flows are threatened by the global recession (UNCTAD, 2009); the World Food Programme has already been obliged to scale down its food aid operations (*Financial Times*, 12 June 2009). Due to the continuing food emergency situation in many of the poorest countries, the international community should fulfil the pledges made to fight the global food crisis. Adequate compensatory financing should also be provided to developing countries to help them address balance-of-payments problems resulting from higher food prices. One such scheme is the Exogenous Shock Facility of the International Monetary Fund (IMF), which was modified in September 2008 in order to make it more effective. Since then it has provided financing to eight developing countries and one transition economy for a total of SDR 767 million (IMF, 2009).[9] ■

Notes

1   For a detailed discussion on the state of food insecurity in the world in connection with the high food prices, see FAO, 2008.

2   The stock-to-use ratio for aggregate global grains and oilseeds in 2008 reached its lowest level since 1970 (Trostle, 2008).

3   UNCTAD secretariat calculations based on USDA, *Production, Supply and Distribution* database.

4   According to FAO, to keep up with population and income growth, global food production needs to increase from average 2005–2007 levels by more than 40 per cent by 2030 and 70 per cent by 2050 (OECD-FAO, 2009).

5   Similar conclusions are also reached in a study by the Institute of Development Studies (IDS, 2009) for Bangladesh, Indonesia, Jamaica, Kenya and Zambia.

6   For a review of domestic policy responses to high food prices, see FAO, 2009d.

7   Similarly, the United Nations Special Rapporteur on the Right to Food has recently recommended some principles and measures, based on human rights, to discipline "land grabbing" (de Schutter, 2009).

8   The Comprehensive Framework for Action was established in 2008 by the United Nations Secretary-General's High-Level Task Force on the Global Food Security Crisis (see background information on the Task Force at http://www.un.org/issues/food/taskforce/). Other initiatives include the Initiative on Soaring Food Prices by FAO, the World Bank Global Food Response Programme, regional responses such as the African Food Crisis Response by the African Development Bank, the EU Food Facility and individual donors' aid pledges. In addition, there was a High-Level Conference on World Food Security: the Challenges of Climate Change and Bioenergy in Rome in June 2008, and a High-Level Meeting on Food Security for All in Madrid in January 2009. There has also been a proposal for the establishment of a Global Partnership for Agriculture and Food Security to include all agents involved: governments, the private sector, civil society, donors and international institutions. For more details on responses to the food crisis, see EC, 2009, and information on the food price crisis and the global food security challenge from the Global Donor Platform for Rural Development at: http://www.donorplatform.org/content/view/185/172.

9   See IMF Factsheet on the Exogenous Shock Facility at: http://www.imf.org/external/np/exr/facts/esf.htm.

References

Dawe D (2008). Have Recent Increases in International Cereal Prices Been Transmitted to Domestic Economies? The experience in seven large Asian countries, FAO. ESA Working Paper No. 08-03. Rome, April.

de Schutter O (2009). Large-scale land acquisitions and leases: A set of core principles and measures to address the human rights challenge. Special Rapporteur on the Right to Food, 11 June. Available at: http://www2.ohchr.org/english/issues/food/docs/Briefing-Notelandgrab.pdf.

EC (2009). Millennium Development Goals - Impact of the financial crisis on developing countries. Commission of the European Communities Staff Working Document. Brussels, April.

FAO (2008). The state of food insecurity in the world: High food prices and food security - threats and opportunities. Rome.

FAO (2009a). More people than ever are victims of hunger. Rome, June.

FAO (2009b). Crop Prospects and Food Situation. Rome, April.

FAO (2009c). Food Outlook. Rome, June.

FAO (2009d). Policy responses to higher food prices, CCP 09/8. Rome.

FAO (2009e). Responding to the food crisis: synthesis of medium-term measures proposed by inter-agency assessments. Rome.

FAO, IFAD and IIED (2009). Land grab or development opportunity? Agricultural investment and international land deals in Africa. Food and Agriculture Organization of the United Nations, International Fund for Agricultural Development and International Institute for Environment and Development, May.

FAPRI (2009). US and world agricultural outlook. Food and Agricultural Policy Research Institute. Ames, Iowa.

Financial Times (2009). Fund crunch threatens world food aid, 12 June.

Gandure S (2008). High food prices in the Eastern, Central and Southern Africa: Assessing impact and tracking progress towards meeting the CFA objectives. World Food Programme, December.

Ghosh J (2009). The unnatural coupling: Food and global finance: Paper presented at IDEAS Conference on "Re-regulating global finance in the light of global crisis". Beijing, April. Available at: http://www.networkideas.org/ideasact/feb09/Beijing_Conference_09/Jayati_Ghosh.pdf.

Herrmann M (2007). Agricultural support measures of advanced countries and food insecurity in developing countries: Economic linkages and policy responses. In: Guha-Khasnobis B, Acharya SS and Davis B, eds. *Food Security: Indicators, Measurement, and the Impact of Trade Openness*. Oxford, Oxford University Press.

IDS (2009). Account of crisis: Poor people´s experiences of the food, fuel and financial crises in five countries. Report on a pilot study in Bangladesh, Indonesia, Jamaica, Kenya and Zambia. Institute of Development Studies, Brighton, United Kingdom, January–March.

IMF (2009). IMF Lending at a glance online. Available at: http//www.imf.org/external/np/exr/map/lending/index.htm, accessed June 2009.

IRRI (2008). The financial crisis: Short and long-term impact on rice food security. International Rice Research Institute, December.

MDG Africa Steering Group (2008). Achieving the Millennium Development Goals in Africa. Sharm El-Sheikh, 1 July.

Mittal (2009). The 2008 food price crisis: Rethinking food security policies. G-24 Discussion Paper No. 56. New York and Geneva, UNCTAD, June.

OECD-FAO (2009). Agricultural Outlook 2009–2018.

Oxfam (2008). Double-edged prices: Lessons from the food price crisis: 10 actions developing countries should take. *Oxfam Briefing Paper*, Oxford.

Oxfam (2009). A billion hungry people: Governments and aid agencies must rise to the challenge. *Oxfam Briefing Paper*, Oxford.

Peters M, Langley S and Westcot P (2009). Agricultural commodity price spikes in the 1970s and 1990s: Valuable lessons for today. Amber Waves, Volume 7, Issue 1, March.

Purcell R (2009). The current food situation and the UN High Level Task Force on Food Security. Presentation at UNCTAD Multiyear Expert Meeting on Commodities and Development. Geneva, 6–7 April.

Trostle R (2008). Fluctuating food commodity prices. A complex issue with no easy answers. Amer Waves, November.

UNCTAD (2008). Addressing the global food crisis. Key trade, investment and commodity policies in ensuring sustainable food security and alleviating poverty. United Nations publication, New York and Geneva.

UNCTAD (2009). Keeping ODA afloat: no stone unturned. Policy Brief no. 7, (UNCTAD/PRESS/PB/2009/2), 7 March.

UN/DESA (2008). Don't forget the food crisis: New policy directions needed. Policy Brief No. 8. New York, October.

USDA (2009). USDA Agricultural Projections to 2018: United States Department of Agriculture.

WFP (2009). Financial crisis pushes poor families deeper into hunger. World Food Programme. Press release and case studies available at: http://www.wfp.org/stories/financial-crisis-pushes-poor-families-deeper-into-hunger. 11 June.

THE FINANCIALIZATION OF COMMODITY MARKETS

A. Introduction

The build-up and eruption of the current global financial crisis was paralleled by an unusually sharp increase and subsequent strong reversal in the prices of internationally traded primary commodities. Recent developments in commodity prices have been exceptional in many ways. The price boom between 2002 and mid-2008 was the most pronounced in several decades – in magnitude, duration and breadth. It placed a heavy burden on many developing countries that rely on food and energy imports, and contributed to food crises in a number of countries in 2007–2008 (*TDR 2008*, chap. II, section C). The price decline since mid-2008 stands out both for its sharpness and for the number of commodity groups affected. It was one of the main channels through which the dramatic slowdown of economic and financial activity in the major industrialized countries was transmitted to the developing world.

The strong and sustained increase in primary commodity prices between 2002 and mid-2008 was accompanied by the growing presence of financial investors on commodity futures exchanges. This financialization of commodity markets has caused concern that much of the recent commodity price developments – and especially the steep increase in 2007–2008 and the subsequent strong reversal – was largely driven by financial investors' use of commodities as an asset class.

Over the 78 months from early 2002 to mid-2008 the IMF's overall commodity price index rose steadily and nominal prices more than quadrupled. During the same period, UNCTAD's non-fuel commodity index tripled in nominal terms and increased by about 50 per cent in real terms. After peaking in July 2008, oil prices plunged by about 70 per cent within six months (which represents the largest percentage decline ever experienced over such a short period), while non-fuel prices fell by about 35 per cent from their peak in April 2008. Although considerable, this reversal corresponds to only about one seventh of the previous six-year increase, so that commodity prices have remained well above their levels of the first half of this decade. Although the timing differed from one commodity to another, both the surge in prices and their subsequent sharp correction occurred in all major commodity categories.

Much of the recent commodity price developments have been attributed to changes in fundamental supply and demand relationships (see chapter I, section A.2). However, the extreme scale of the recent changes in primary commodity prices, and the fact that prices increased and subsequently declined across all major categories of commodities, suggests that, beyond the specific functioning of commodity markets, broader macroeconomic and financial factors that operate across a large number of markets need to be considered to fully understand recent commodity price developments. The depreciation of the dollar was clearly one general, albeit minor, cause of the surge in commodity prices. But a major new element in commodity trading over the past few years is the greater presence on commodity futures exchanges of financial investors that treat commodities as an asset class. The fact that these market participants do not trade on the basis of fundamental supply and demand relationships, and that they hold, on average, very large positions in commodity markets, implies that they can exert considerable influence on commodity price developments.

This chapter aims at enhancing understanding of how the speculative activities of financial investors that are active in both financial and commodity markets can influence price movements to higher or lower levels than those dictated by market fundamentals. Section B shows how commodity futures trading has come to be increasingly influenced by the participation of financial investors that have no interest in the physical delivery of primary commodities. Section C discusses the determinants of financial investors' investment decisions, while sections D and E address the effects of their growing involvement on price developments, and the higher costs to commercial users of hedging against commodity price risk. Section F suggests the need for broadening and strengthening supervision and regulation of commodity markets so as to improve the informational value of commodity price developments for producers and consumers, and section G concludes.

B. The growing interdependence of financial and commodity markets

Commodity futures markets play an important role in price discovery and in the transfer of price risk from market participants that have an interest in the physical commodities (i.e. producers and consumers) to other agents that, driven by speculative motives, are prepared to assume the price risk. Traditionally, speculation relating to commodities has been based on information about demand and supply developments. The behaviour of market participants has been based on their perception of changes in these fundamental factors. However, in recent years an increasing number of financial investors have entered commodity futures markets. Motivated by portfolio diversification considerations that are largely unrelated to commodity market fundamentals, they regard commodities as an investment alternative to asset classes such as equities, bonds or real estate. They take positions in commodities as a group, based on their assessment of the risk-return properties of portfolios that contain a proportion of commodity futures relative to portfolios that contain only traditional asset classes.

> The behaviour of financial investors on commodity markets is motivated by considerations that are largely unrelated to commodity market fundamentals.

One way financial investors can gain exposure on commodity markets is through spot market activities (i.e. buying and accumulating physical commodities in inventories). This strategy has probably contributed to the price increases in the relatively small markets for precious metals such as gold and silver (Koh, 2007). However, it is more difficult to pursue this physical market strategy for other commodities, especially because of the greater storage costs they entail.

Chart 2.1

FINANCIAL INVESTMENT IN COMMODITIES

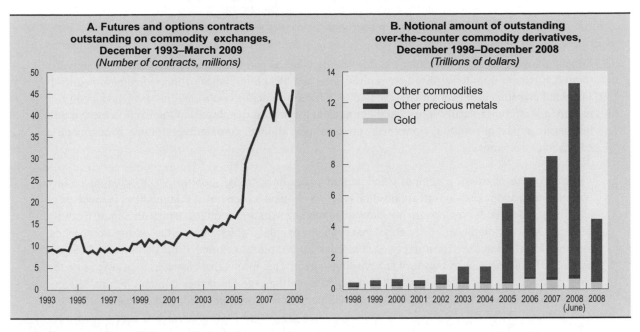

A. Futures and options contracts outstanding on commodity exchanges, December 1993–March 2009
(Number of contracts, millions)

B. Notional amount of outstanding over-the-counter commodity derivatives, December 1998–December 2008
(Trillions of dollars)

Other commodities
Other precious metals
Gold

Source: BIS, *Quarterly Review*, June 2009.

Another way investors gain exposure on commodity markets is by engaging in the markets for futures contracts or options. In futures contracts, the trader commits to buying or selling a commodity at a future date and at a pre-established price (the futures price). This contract may be traded later, so that the trader would not have to actually receive or deliver the commodity at the fixed time. Instead, the commitment would be transferred to other agents, who would then make a gain or loss depending on the changes in futures prices that may have occurred. When agents buy options, they gain the right (but not the obligation) to buy or sell a commodity at a future date and at a pre-established price, and they pay a premium to the agents who make the opposite commitment.

Trading volumes on commodity exchanges increased considerably during the recent period of substantial rises in commodity prices. The number of futures and options contracts outstanding on commodity exchanges worldwide rose more than threefold between 2002 and mid-2008 (chart 2.1A). During the same period, the notional value[1] of commodity-related contracts traded over the counter (OTC) (i.e. contracts traded bilaterally, and not

listed on any exchange) increased more than 14-fold, to $13 trillion (chart 2.1B).[2] However, financial investments in commodities fell sharply starting in mid-2008. Some observers have taken this parallel development of commodity prices and financial investments in commodities as *prima facie* evidence of the role of large-scale speculative activity in driving commodity prices first up and then down.

Most financial investors in commodities take positions related to a commodity index. Two common indexes are the Standard & Poor's Goldman Sachs Commodity Index (S&P GSCI) and the Dow Jones-Union Bank of Switzerland Commodity Index (DJ-UBSCI) (previously called the Dow Jones-American International Group Commodity Index (DJ-AIGCI)).[3] These indexes are composites of futures contracts on a broad range of commodities (including energy products, agricultural products and metals) traded on commodity exchanges.[4] Several variables determine the returns on investments in commodity indexes (see box 2.1).

Financial investors engage in commodity futures markets for portfolio reasons. This is based on the belief that adding commodity futures contracts to

Box 2.1

FINANCIAL INVESTMENT IN COMMODITY INDEXES AND
THE RELATIONSHIP BETWEEN FUTURES AND SPOT PRICES

Financial investment in commodity indexes is undertaken as part of a passive investment strategy (i.e. there is no attempt to distinguish between the good and bad performance of individual commodities). Financial investors gain exposure in commodity indexes by entering into a bilateral financial agreement, usually a swap, with a bank. They purchase parts in a commodity index from the bank, which in turn hedges its exposure resulting from the swap agreement through commodities futures contracts on a commodity exchange.

Financial investment in commodity indexes involves only "long" positions (i.e. pledges to buy commodities) and relates to forward positions (i.e. no physical ownership of commodities is involved at any time). Index funds buy forward positions often relating to futures contracts with a remaining maturity of about 75 working days (i.e. roughly three calendar months), which they sell as expiry approaches, at about 25 working days (or roughly one calendar month) prior to expiry of the contract, and use the proceeds from this sale to buy forward positions again. This means that investors that own, say, the November crude oil contract, will sell that contract and buy the December contract before delivery begins on the November contract. Then they will later "roll" from December into January, and so on. This process – known as "rolling" – is profitable when the prices of futures contracts are progressively lower in the distant delivery months (i.e. in a "backwardated" market) and negative when the prices of futures contracts with longer maturities are progressively higher (i.e. in a "contango" market).

Four variables determine the total return earned by financial investors in commodity indexes: spot return + roll yield + collateral return + recomposition yield, where the spot return reflects the spot price movements of the underlying commodities, the collateral return is the interest on the collateral[a] that the investors have to set aside as margin for investments in commodity futures positions, the recomposition yield arises from a periodic redefinition of the basket of commodities underlying a portfolio, and the roll yield is obtained from selling futures contracts that have an expiry date the month prior to the delivery month and using the proceeds to buy futures contracts with a longer maturity.

The roll yield is similar to the risk premium that speculators expect to earn by taking an opposite position to that of commodity producers that seek to hedge the price risk of their output. This risk premium corresponds to the difference between the current futures price and the expected future spot price at the time the position is taken. If the futures price is set below the expected future spot price, a purchaser of futures contracts (speculator) will generally earn the risk premium; by contrast, if the futures price is higher than the expected future spot price, a seller of futures contracts (hedger) will earn the premium. Assuming hedgers outnumber speculators, Keynes (1930) and Hicks (1939) – in their theory of "normal backwardation" – expected that, in general, the futures price would be lower than the expected future spot price, so that the risk premium would normally accrue to speculators.

The roll yield differs slightly from this kind of risk premium because index traders do not hold futures contracts until their expiry. When the price of futures contracts depreciates near the delivery date, the roll yield is negative. Roll returns were positive during much of the 1980s and 1990s, but since 2002 they have mostly been negative. However, given the large spot returns during the commodity price hikes between 2002 and mid-2008, the total return was nonetheless positive during most of this period (see chart).

The above implies that the total return on investment in commodity indexes partly depends on the intertemporal relationship between futures and spot prices on commodity exchanges. This relationship is known from financial markets, but the difference is that commodity futures markets trade contracts on assets that incur storage and interest costs – often called "cost of carry". This cost implies that in order to

Box 2.1 (continued)

SPOT AND ROLL RETURNS ON COMMODITY INDEX INVESTMENTS, JANUARY 1980–MAY 2009

(Per cent)

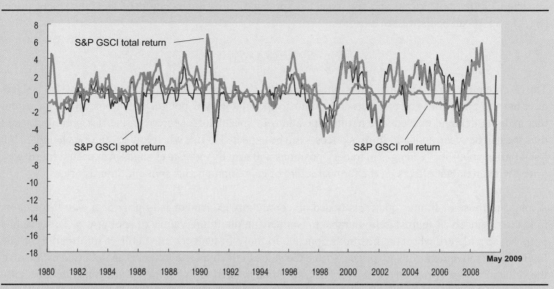

Source: UNCTAD secretariat calculations, based on Bloomberg.
Note: The roll return is the discount or premium obtained by "rolling" positions in futures contracts forward as they approach delivery. The numbers shown in the figure approximate the roll return (calculated as the difference between excess and spot returns of the S&P GSCI) and are expressed as six-month moving averages. The excess return reflects the return on commodity futures price movements, while the spot return reflects changes in spot prices.

induce storage, futures prices and expected future spot prices must increase more than the cost of carry to compensate inventory holders for the costs associated with storage. However, the cost of storage must be weighed against the so-called "convenience yield" (i.e. the *a priori* unmeasurable utility of physically owning a particular commodity or the premium when the inventory is sold). Inventory holders have the option to sell commodities on the spot markets when market conditions tighten, or to dispose of a secure supply of the commodity, thus insuring themselves against the costs associated with supply disruption. The convenience yield tends to be higher when inventories are lower, as tighter market conditions confer greater benefits for the physical ownership of a commodity. It will increase sharply when inventories fall below the level of short-term consumption requirements.

The above elements can be combined to determine the term structure of commodity prices. The difference between contemporaneous spot and futures prices – often called "basis" – depends on the relative size of the cost of carry and the convenience yield. The negative of the basis can be expressed as follows:

$$F_{t,T} - S_t = Int_t + w_t - c_t$$

where $F_{t,T}$ is the futures price at date t for delivery at time T, S_t is the spot price at time t, Int_t is the interest cost, w_t is the storage cost, and c_t is the convenience yield. An upward sloping futures curve, a phenomenon known as "contango", implies that inventory holders are rewarded for the cost of carrying inventories. A downward sloping futures curve, a phenomenon known as "backwardation", indicates that the convenience yield exceeds the cost of carry.

It should be noted that the notion of backwardation, which relates to the comparison of contemporaneous spot and futures prices, differs from the concept of "normal backwardation" (mentioned above), which

Box 2.1 (concluded)

compares futures prices with expected future spot prices. From the latter perspective, the basis is determined by a risk premium, $\pi_{t,T}$, which corresponds to the difference between futures prices and expected future spot prices, and the expected appreciation or depreciation of the future spot price, $[E_t(S_T) - S_t]$. It can be expressed as:

$$F_{t,T} - S_t = [E_t(S_T) - S_t] - \pi_{t,T}$$

The risk premium will be positive, thus attracting more speculators to the market, to the extent that hedgers have net short positions and offer a risk premium to speculators with net long positions, and to the extent that hedging demand exceeds the net long positions of speculators. Moreover, the risk premium – and thus the gap between spot and futures prices – can be expected to rise when low inventories heighten the risk of price volatility.[b] Changes in traders' positions will usually indicate changes in expected future spot prices with attendant effects on the term structure of contemporaneous spot and futures prices.

A major purpose of futures contracts traded on commodity exchanges is to provide a way for hedgers to insure themselves against unfavourable movements in the future values of spot prices. To serve this purpose, speculators who take positions opposite to those of hedgers must collect information on the likely future movements of spot prices, so that the value of the futures contract is an unbiased estimate of the value of the spot price on the delivery date specified in the futures contract. Policymakers, especially central bankers, commonly base part of their decisions on this feature, as they use the price of commodity futures contracts as a proxy for the market's expectations of future commodity spot prices (Svensson, 2005; Greenspan, 2004).

By contrast, the value of futures contracts will not serve this price discovery purpose (i) if those taking speculative positions base their activities on information unrelated to the underlying supply and demand fundamentals on commodity markets, or (ii) if the size of their position is substantially larger than that of hedgers so that the weight of their position determines prices. Empirical evidence generally indicates that futures prices are less accurate forecasts than simple alternative models such as a random walk without drift (i.e. expecting no change from current spot prices). Indeed, Bernanke (2008) has highlighted the difficulty in arriving at a reasonable estimate of future commodity price movements based on signals emanating from commodity futures markets. He therefore emphasizes the importance of finding alternative approaches to forecasting commodity market movements. Thus, empirical evidence indicates that mechanisms that would prevent prices from moving away from levels determined by fundamental supply and demand factors – the efficient absorption of commodity-related information and sufficiently strong price elasticity of supply and demand – may be relatively weak on commodity markets.

---

[a]   Collateral is a position set aside by traders to ensure that they are able to fulfil their contractual commitments. During the lifetime of a futures contract, the clearing house of the concerned commodity exchange issues margin calls to adjust the amount of collateral so as to reflect changes in the notional value of traders' contractual commitments.

[b]   Falling inventories signal the scarcity of the commodity for immediate delivery, which will cause spot prices to increase. Futures prices will also increase, but not by as much, because of expectations that inventories will be restored over time and spot prices will return to normal levels, and perhaps also because the risk premium rises. However, if inventories are slow to adjust, past demand and supply shocks will persist in current inventory levels.

their portfolio improves its overall risk-return characteristics: these contracts exhibit the same average return as investments in equities, but over the business cycle their return is negatively correlated with that on equities and bonds. Moreover, the returns on commodities are less volatile than those on equities or bonds, because the pairwise correlations between returns on futures contracts for various commodities (e.g. oil and copper, or oil and maize) traditionally have been relatively low (Gorton and Rouwenhorst, 2006).

Contrary to equities and bonds, commodity futures contracts also have good hedging properties against inflation (i.e. their return is positively correlated with inflation). This is because commodity futures contracts represent a bet on commodity prices, such as those of energy and food products that have a strong weight in the goods baskets used for measuring current price levels. Also,

> Financial investors invest in commodity markets with a view to broadening their portfolios in order to diversify risk.

futures prices reflect information about expected changes in commodity prices, so that they rise and fall in line with deviations from expected inflation. Furthermore, investing in commodity futures contracts tends to provide a hedge against changes in the exchange rate of the dollar. One reason for this may be the fact that most commodities are traded in dollars. Given that a depreciation of the dollar exchange rate reduces the purchasing power of commodity exports, exporters may attempt to increase commodity prices in dollar terms to compensate for any depreciation-related shortfalls in earnings. Commodity exporters may also diversify their reserve holdings by changing dollars into euros in order to reduce the exchange-rate risk associated with foreign-exchange reserves. This could explain why, between 2006 and 2008, the turning points in oil prices frequently mirrored those in the exchange rate of the dollar vis-à-vis the euro (Till, 2008: 33).

C. Problems with the financialization of commodity futures trading

Establishing a link between speculation and commodity price developments often meets with scepticism. This scepticism is based partly on the argument that financial investors only participate in futures and related derivative markets, and that they will affect spot prices only if they take delivery and hold the physical commodities in inventories. In relation to oil prices, for example, Krugman (2008) argues that speculative activity that drives prices above fundamental equilibrium prices will cause market imbalances and excess supply, which eventually must result in inventory accumulation. However, no inventory accumulation was observed during the

sharp increase in oil prices in 2007–2008, so that, according to this reasoning, speculation cannot have played a role in the oil price hike.

However, arbitrage forces may change spot prices following a change in futures prices, without a significant increase in actual transactions. Since the short-run price elasticity of commodity supply and demand is extremely low, only very sharp and lasting price changes can be expected to trigger significant supply and demand responses and related changes in inventories. Moreover, the financialization of commodity trading appears to have led to greater price

volatility (see below), which is known to increase precautionary demand. This in turn implies that an increase in spot prices should not necessarily be associated with a decline in market demand and a resulting accumulation of inven-
tories. Rather, the accumulation of inventories will occur only gradually and spot prices will overshoot during this process. This means that during peri-ods of increased precautionary demand "there is no reason to expect a positive contempora-neous correlation between in-ventories and the precautionary demand component of the spot price" (Alquist and Kilian, 2007: 37).

Arbitrage forces may change spot prices following a change in futures prices, without a significant increase in actual transactions.

Finally, as noted by the IMF (2008a: 89), "data on commodity inventories are poor and lack global coverage". Inventory data suffer from at least three shortcomings: (i) the absence of a common data-base that would include comprehensive data for all commodities; (ii) conceptual questions relating to the definition of relevant inventories, given that, currently, data are available only for inventories held at delivery points (e.g. for industrial metals, in warehouses at the London Metal Exchange (LME), and for oil, in Cushing, Oklahoma), while there are no data for inventories that are held off exchange but could be made available economically at the deliv-ery point at short notice; and (iii) information about inventories is often published with a time lag and sub-sequently revised (Gorton, Hayashi and Rouwenhorst (2007: 11). Overall, existing official inventory data are not reliable indicators in the debate on the relative impact of fundamentals and of financial investors on commodity prices.

Official inventory data are not reliable indicators in the debate on the impact of financial investors on commodity prices.

More fundamental scep-ticism with regard to the link between speculation and com-modity price developments is based on the "efficient mar-ket" hypothesis. According to this view, prices perfectly and instantaneously respond to all available information relevant to a freely operating market. Market participants continuously update their expec-tations from inflowing public and private informa-tion. This means that prices will move either when new information becomes publicly available (e.g. when harvest forecasts or changes in oil production are announced), or which private information is re-flected in prices through transactions.

There are at least two rea-sons why the efficient market hypothesis may fail in relation to commodity markets, at least in the short run. First, changes in market positions may occur in response to factors other than information about market fun-damentals. Second, individual market participants may take position changes that are so large relative to the size of the market that they move prices (the so-called "weight-of-money" effect).

To examine how different sorts of information may influence market positions, it is useful to group market participants into three categories based on dif-ferences in their rationale for position taking: informed traders, uninformed traders and noise traders.

Informed traders rely on information about cur-rent market fundamentals and on forecasts of future market conditions. However, making an informed market assessment faces two difficulties: (i) medium- and longer-term commodity supply and demand conditions are subject to considerable uncertainty (for example because of unknown depletion rates of non-renewable resources and unknown effects of climate change on agricultural production); and (ii) inventory data, which provide valuable signals for short-term price expectations, suffer from significant measurement errors, as already mentioned, and data on current global commodity supply and demand conditions are published with large time lags and are frequently revised. Therefore, informed traders must formulate price expectations on the basis of partial and uncertain data. This may lead them to focus on a small number of available signals, with the attendant risk of herding and copying the behaviour of others. Alterna-tively, it may cause traders to consider past price movements themselves as a good guide to future developments.

Noise traders trade for broader strategic reasons, and make position changes irrespective of prevailing conditions on commodity markets. On commodity markets, index traders behave like noise traders: they change their total positions in commodities based on information relating to other asset markets but which has no relevance for commodity markets. In addition, they tend to change the composition of their positions in commodities in response to different price changes for different commodities with a view to maintaining a specific commodity's predetermined weight in a commodity index. This makes it difficult for other traders to judge whether market prices are changing because of the position changes of the noise traders or as a response to new information about market fundamentals.

Uninformed traders, who glean information on future price developments from current and past price movements, are particularly exposed to such situations. They follow what may be called "momentum strategies" – buying commodities that have experienced rising prices and selling those that have underperformed. Uninformed traders observe price movements but are unable to identify whether price changes were caused by informed or noise trading. Hence, they risk misinterpreting a noise trader's position change as a genuine price signal and, by incorporating this signal into their trading strategy, perpetuate the "informational" value of this signal across the market. Given that uninformed traders often use similar trend identification techniques, they run the risk of collectively generating the trends that they then individually identify and follow. On commodity markets, money managers, such as pension funds, behave like momentum traders.

> Financialization of commodity trading appears to have increased price changes that are unrelated to market fundamentals.

One effect of momentum trading that uses statistical analysis tools is that the resulting changes in positions can be anticipated by other market participants. Thus, it provides continued arbitrage possibilities. Speculators will try to benefit from such profit opportunities. Traders working for financial institutions will do this in order to meet their institutions' short-term performance targets or reporting requirements, even if doing so implies going against signals from long-term fundamental supply and demand factors (de Long et al., 1990). This can lead to speculative bubbles. The same kind of snowball effect can be created by commodity trading by financial investors when they react to signals from other, non-commodity markets. This can occur if the price changes stemming from their position changes feed into momentum trading strategies. Momentum trading on commodity markets is not a new phenomenon. However, the trend towards greater financialization of commodity trading is likely to have increased the number and relative size of price changes that are unrelated to market fundamentals.

It is highly probable that these mechanisms, which lead to speculative bubbles, have been at work on commodity futures exchanges, given the correlation between the trading activities of index traders and those of momentum-trading money managers. Such a correlation during the period January 2005–August 2008 has been documented for agricultural markets such as cotton, maize, soybeans and wheat. On the other hand, the market presence of these trader categories in natural gas and crude oil markets has displayed an inverse relationship (Informa Economics, 2009).[5]

This difference between agricultural and energy markets also occurs with respect to the correlation between price volatility and the market presence of these two trader categories. For all the examined agricultural products, except soybeans, the trading activity of both these trader categories was observed to be positively correlated with price volatility, while the presence of index traders in the gas and oil markets was seen to be inversely correlated with price volatility. Given that price volatility was significantly higher in the oil and gas markets than in the agricultural markets (Informa Economics, 2009, Part 3: 5–12), and that these energy markets are generally much more liquid than agricultural markets, this finding suggests that on energy markets money managers could rely on a larger number of, and stronger, price signals, and were therefore less exposed to "wrong" signals coming from index traders. Hence, the impact of position taking by index traders on momentum trading has most likely been concentrated in agricultural markets.

A second reason why the efficient market hypothesis may fail on commodity markets relates to the fact that the number of counterparties (especially those with an interest in physical commodities) and the size of their positions are less than perfectly price elastic. Thus, large orders may face short-term liquidity constraints and cause significant price shifts. This implies the possibility of a temporary, or even persistent, "weight-of-money" effect, which is particularly high in commodity markets where the short-run price elasticity of both production and consumption is very low, and hence the physical adjustment mechanisms of markets are weak. As a result, in tight markets with minimum inventory levels, the relevance of expectations based on longer-term fundamental factors sharply declines, which makes it difficult to determine a market price solely on the basis of fundamentals. "This indeterminacy allows weight of the speculative money to determine the level of prices" (Gilbert, 2008a: 19).

The weight-of-money effect relates primarily to index-based investment. One reason for their relatively large size relates to the fact that index traders take positions across many commodities in proportions that depend only on the weighting formula of the particular index, independent of the specific market conditions for the individual commodities contained in the index. Hence, large positions taken by index traders implies a significant risk that the weight-of-money effect will exacerbate the price impact of trading in response to factors other than information about commodity market fundamentals.

The analytical distinction between informed, uninformed and noise traders (table 2.1) is difficult to apply in practice. The Commodity Futures Trading Commission (CFTC) – the institution mandated to regulate and oversee commodity futures trading in the United States – publishes trading positions in anonymous and summary form in its weekly *Commitments of Traders* (COT) reports. The CFTC classifies market participants as "commercial" if they are hedging an existing exposure, and as "non-commercial" if they are not.[6] However, it is widely perceived that, as a consequence of the growing diversity of futures market participants and the greater complexity of their activities, the COT data may fail to fully represent futures market activity (CFTC, 2006a). This is because those hedging, and therefore defined as

commercial market participants, have normally been considered entities involved in the production, processing or merchandising of commodities. However, many market participants who report positions as hedges, and who therefore fall under the "commercial" category, are in fact commodity swap dealers, such as commodity index traders, who have no interest in the physical commodities. If their underlying positions were held directly as commodity futures contracts (rather than being intermediated through OTC swap agreements), they would be categorized as "non-commercial".

Responding to these concerns, in 2007 the CFTC started to issue supplementary data on the positions of commodity index traders for 12 agricultural commodities (CFTC, 2006b).[7] The index trader positions include both pension funds, previously classified as non-commercial traders, and swap dealers, that had been classified as commercial traders. According to the CFTC (2009), commodity index traders generally replicate a commodity index, but may belong to either the commercial or non-commercial category.

A primary concern often expressed with respect to the financialization of commodity trading relates to the magnitude of index trader activity, combined with the fact that such traders tend to take only long positions. Table 2.2 provides evidence of the relative share of both long and short positions held by different trader categories in those agricultural markets for which the CFTC has been publishing disaggregated data for January 2006 onwards.[8] The data clearly show that index funds are present almost exclusively in long positions,[9] and that they account for a large portion of the open interest in some food commodity markets.[10] Indeed, over the period 2006–2008, the relative shares of index traders in total long positions in cotton, live cattle, feeder cattle, lean hogs and wheat were significantly larger than the positions of commercial traders in those commodities, while they were roughly of equal size for maize, soybeans and soybean oil.

While the number of index traders is relatively small, their average long position is very large (middle panel of table 2.2), sometimes more than 10 times the size of an average long position held by either

> The impact of index traders on momentum trading seems to have been concentrated in agricultural markets.

Table 2.1

COMMODITY FUTURES TRADING BEHAVIOUR: TRADITIONAL SPECULATORS, MANAGED FUNDS AND INDEX TRADERS

	Traditional speculators	*Managed funds*	*Index traders*
General market position	Active positions on both sides of the market; able to benefit in both rising and declining markets	Active, often large, positions on both sides of market; able to benefit in both rising and declining markets; relatively opaque positions	Passive, large and long-only positions in swap agreements with banks, which in turn hold futures contracts to offset their short positions; able to benefit only in rising or backwardated (spot price>forward price) markets; transparent positions
Position taking behaviour	React to changes in commodity market fundamentals (supply, demand, inventories); mostly trade in one or two commodities of which they have intimate knowledge; leveraged positions	Some (e.g. hedge funds) conduct research on commodity-market fundamentals and thus react to changes in those fundamentals. Others (e.g. commodity trading advisers) mostly use statistical analyses (trend identification and extrapolation, automatic computerized trading), which extract information from price movements. They thereby risk misinterpreting noise trader position taking for genuine price information, engaging in herd behaviour and causing snowball effects; leveraged positions	Not interested in fundamentals of specific commodity markets but may have views on commodities as a whole; relative size of positions in individual commodities determined by an index weighting formula; idiosyncratic position taking such as rolling at predetermined dates; position changes are relatively easy to predict; fully collateralized positions
Impact on liquidity	Improve liquidity	Active, large positions can improve liquidity and make hedging easier for large commercial users. In periods of rapid and sharp price changes, large positions are a "liquidity sponge", making it difficult for hedgers with commercial interests to place orders	Passive, large positions act as a "liquidity sponge"
Reaction to sharp price changes	May be taken by surprise if price changes are unrelated to fundamentals; can be forced out of the market if they lack liquidity to meet margin calls triggered by sharp price increases	Taking and closing positions are often automatically triggered by computer programs; risk of causing a snowball effect	Different price developments for individual commodities require recomposition of relative investment positions to preserve a predetermined index weight pattern; sharp price declines may cause disinvestment
Reaction to changes on other markets	Operate only in commodity markets; normally concentrate on one or a few commodities, and thus react little to developments in other markets	Operate across different asset classes. Commodities tend to have a fixed weight in managed fund portfolios, so that price movements in other markets can lead to position changes in commodity markets	Operate across different asset classes. Potentially strong links between commodity futures market activity and developments on equity and bond markets, in two ways: (i) risk-return combinations in other asset classes can become more attractive, causing a withdrawal from commodity markets; (ii) margin calls on other investments can trigger closing of positions in commodities and accelerate contagion across asset classes
Classification in CFTC Commitment of Traders Reports	Non-commercial user category	Mostly in non-commercial user category	Mostly in commercial user category

Source: UNCTAD secretariat.

Table 2.2

FUTURES AND OPTIONS MARKET POSITIONS, BY TRADER GROUP, SELECTED AGRICULTURAL COMMODITIES, JANUARY 2006–DECEMBER 2008

(Per cent and number of contracts)

Long positions

	Percentage share in total positions				Average position size			Speculative limits
Commodity	Non-commercial	Com-mercial	Index	Non-reporting	Non-commercial	Com-mercial	Index	
Maize	42.4	23.4	22.8	11.3	1 134	1 499	16 260	22 000
Soybeans	42.1	20.4	25.2	12.2	590	1 052	6 024	10 000
Soybean oil	38.0	28.4	23.8	9.8	790	1 719	4 418	6 500
Wheat, CBOT	39.0	12.3	41.1	7.5	553	964	8 326	6 500
Wheat, KCBOT	38.1	23.4	21.0	17.5	680	632	1 816	6 500
Cotton	41.0	20.1	30.7	8.3	363	1 010	4 095	5 000
Live cattle	39.3	12.0	39.7	9.0	580	409	4 743	5 150
Feeder cattle	42.5	15.7	24.6	17.2	258	162	469	1 000
Lean hogs	36.3	8.7	43.8	11.3	419	712	3 983	4 100

Short positions

	Percentage share in total positions				Average position size			Speculative limits
Commodity	Non-commercial	Com-mercial	Index	Non-reporting	Non-commercial	Com-mercial	Index	
Maize	34.7	47.2	1.2	16.9	618	2 469	1 579	22 000
Soybeans	36.4	44.6	1.2	17.8	365	1 696	736	10 000
Soybean oil	29.1	63.2	0.9	6.7	512	3 385	720	6 500
Wheat, CBOT	41.7	42.3	3.0	12.9	554	2 124	1 218	6 500
Wheat, KCBOT	20.4	56.0	0.5	23.1	378	1 123	221	6 500
Cotton	39.8	54.1	1.0	5.1	380	2 706	496	5 000
Live cattle	34.5	43.8	0.7	21.0	456	879	487	5 150
Feeder cattle	34.0	20.9	1.0	44.2	166	150	213	1 000
Lean hogs	38.3	43.1	0.8	17.9	405	1 952	353	4 100

Source: UNCTAD secretariat calculations, based on data from CFTC; speculative limits from Sanders, Irwin and Merrin (2008: 25).

Note: Following the methodology applied by Sanders, Irwin and Merrin (2008), spread positions were added to both long and short positions for the percentage shares in total positions. Average size of spread positions is not reported here.
CBOT = Chicago Board of Trade.
KCBOT = Kansas City Board of Trade.

commercial or non-commercial traders. Positions of this order are likely to have sufficiently strong financial power to influence prices (Capuano, 2006). As a result, speculative bubbles may form, and price changes can no longer be interpreted as reflecting fundamental supply and demand signals. All of this can have an extremely detrimental effect on normal trading activities and market efficiency, despite position limits that exist to contain speculation.[11]

During the period 2006–2008, index traders actually exceeded speculative position limits in wheat contracts on the Chicago Board of Trade (CBOT), and for other commodities they came much closer to these limits than did the other trader categories (right-hand panel of table 2.2). This is perfectly legal, as index traders are generally classified as commercial traders, and therefore are not subject to speculative position limits. But, as noted by Sanders, Irwin and Merrin

Chart 2.2

ESTIMATED INDEX TRADER POSITIONS AND COMMODITY PRICES, JANUARY 2006–MAY 2009

(Index numbers, January 2006 = 100)

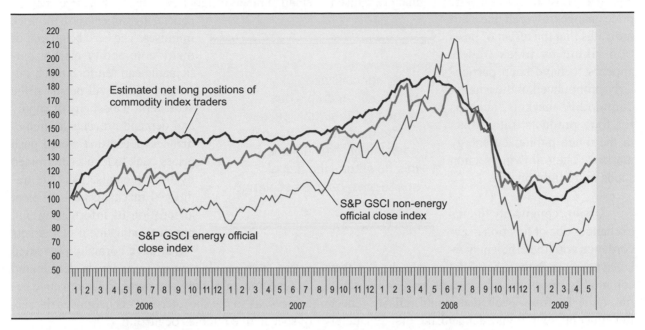

Source: UNCTAD secretariat calculations, based on Bloomberg; Goldman Sachs; and CFTC.

Note: The positions of commodity index traders are estimated based on the January 2006 weights of both the S&P GSCI and DJ-UBSCI, and index trader positions reported in the CFTC's Commodity Index Trader Supplement.

(2008: 8), "it does provide some indirect evidence that speculators or investors are able to use ... [existing] instruments and commercial hedge exemptions to surpass speculative limits".

While the COT reports cover only 12 agricultural commodities, the data which they provide can be used to gauge the importance of index trading more generally. One way of making such an estimation is to assume that: (i) all index traders follow the energy-heavy S&P GSCI and the agriculture-heavy DJ-UBSCI, with an imposed fixed market share of 50 per cent each in the S&P GSCI and the DJ-UBSCI; and (ii) the shares of the specific commodities within each of the two indexes have remained unchanged since January 2006 (i.e. when the COT data began to be collected).[12] To prevent different price movements for different commodities from unduly influencing the results, the estimation is based on data on the number of contracts, and is expressed as index numbers. It should be noted that it is a conservative estimate of the size of financial investments in commodities, because it only relates to index trading

but does not include positions taken by pension and hedge funds, investments in other vehicles (such as commodity mutual funds, exchange-traded funds and notes), equities of commodity companies and direct physical holdings. Neither does it include similar contracts that are traded over the counter, or trading activities outside the exchanges that are overseen by the CFTC.

The estimation suggests that the size of net long positions of index traders on commodity markets almost doubled between January 2006 and May 2008 (see chart 2.2). Index trader positions recorded sharp rises in the first quarter of 2006 and between the fourth quarter of 2007 and the second quarter of 2008, while they fell sharply in the third and fourth quarters of 2008. The chart also shows that the evolution of non-energy commodity prices is strongly correlated with that of index trader positions (the correlation coefficient being 0.93 for the period January 2006–June 2008), while the correlation between energy prices and index trader positions is somewhat weaker (the correlation coefficient being 0.84).

Correlation alone does not indicate causation. But there is little reason to believe that price changes caused position changes. On the contrary, given that index traders tend to follow a passive trading strategy, it is most likely that position changes caused price changes. Overall, the chart indicates that the effect of position taking by index traders appears to have been particularly pronounced in the smaller commodity markets, such as for food products, rather than in the much publicized energy markets. The following section sheds more light on this.

In sum, commodity futures exchanges do not function in accordance with the efficient market hypothesis. Rather, they function in such a way that commodity prices may deviate, at least in the short run, quite far from levels that would reliably reflect fundamental supply and demand factors. Financial investors that do not trade based on commodity market fundamentals have gained considerable weight in commodity markets. Given that commodity trading is based on partial and uncertain data on only a small number of signals, it is likely that large-scale financial investments provide price impulses. The herd behaviour of many commodity market participants can reinforce such impulses, which will persist if the short-term inelasticity of supply and demand prevents an immediate response that would push prices back to levels determined by fundamentals. Thus the traditional mechanisms – efficient absorption of information and physical adjustment of markets – that have normally prevented prices from moving away from levels determined by fundamental supply and demand factors have become weak in the short term. This heightens the risk of speculative bubbles occurring.

> The financialization of commodity markets has weakened their efficient use of information and physical adjustment mechanisms ... this heightens the risk of speculative bubbles occurring.

D. The impact of financialization on commodity price developments

1. Commodity prices, equity indexes and exchange rates

As already mentioned, financial investors in commodity markets aim to diversify their asset portfolios and/or hedge inflation risk. Their decisions to invest in commodities thus depend on broad-based portfolio considerations that also include the risk and return characteristics of other asset classes, including equities, bonds and exchange rates.

There is substantial historic evidence of the improved risk-return characteristics of portfolios that include commodity futures contracts in addition to equities and bonds. Gorton and Rouwenhorst (2006), for example, provide such evidence for the period 1959–2004. Investment in commodities appears to have been a particularly effective hedge against inflation and dollar depreciation since 2005, as the correlation between these two variables and commodity prices was much higher during the period 2005 to early 2009 than in previous years (chart 2.3A).

By contrast, there are indications that commodity prices, equity markets and the exchange rates of currencies affected by carry trade speculation[13] moved in tandem during much of the period of the commodity price hike in 2005–2008, and in particular during the subsequent sharp correction in the second

Chart 2.3

**CORRELATION BETWEEN MOVEMENTS IN COMMODITY PRICES AND
SELECTED FINANCIAL VARIABLES, JANUARY 2002–DECEMBER 2008**

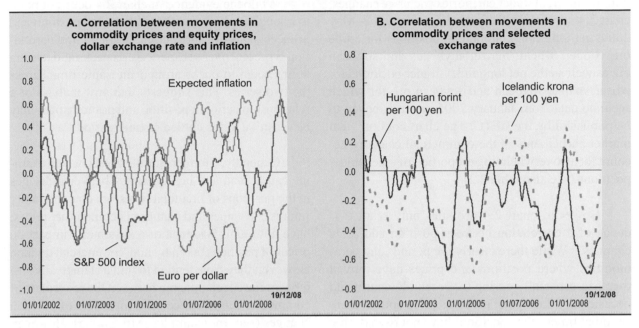

Source: UNCTAD secretariat calculations, based on Bloomberg.
Note: The data shown are six-month moving averages of 60-day rolling correlations between the S&P GSCI and the respective financial variable. Expected inflation is the difference between nominal and real United States 10-year bonds.

half of 2008. Commodity and equity prices were largely uncorrelated between 2002 and 2005, but were positively correlated during much of the period 2005–2008 (chart 2.3A). There has also been a strong correlation of commodity prices – particularly since 2004 – with the exchange rate of carry trade currencies such as the Icelandic krona and the Hungarian forint (chart 2.3B). This correlation was particularly strong during the unwinding of speculative positions in both currency and commodity markets during the second half of 2008 (UNCTAD, 2009: 28). Commodity index traders started unwinding their positions in commodities because their swap agreements with banks began to be exposed to significantly larger counterparty risks, while managed funds started unwinding their exposure in commodities when their leveraged positions faced refinancing difficulties.

> The close correlation between commodities and other asset classes during the second half of 2008 suggests that financial investors may have had a strong influence on commodity prices.

Taken together, this evidence for the past few years indicates that, relative to the historic importance of strategic diversification considerations, tactical reasoning may recently have played a greater role for financial investors in commodities. Indeed, the search for higher yields through commodities trading may have been based on the illusion of risk-free profit maximization, given the historic diversification and hedging characteristics of financial investment in commodities. Financial investors started to unwind their relatively liquid positions in commodities when their investments in other asset classes began experiencing increasing difficulties. This strong correlation between commodities and other asset classes during the second half of 2008 suggests that financial investors may have strongly influenced commodity price developments.

2. *Position taking and price developments*

To gauge the link between changes in the positions of different trader categories and price changes, chart 2.4 shows, for the period January 2002–May 2009, net long non-commercial positions for crude oil, copper, wheat, maize, soybeans and soybean oil, as well as the net long index-trader positions for wheat, maize, soybean and soybean oil, for which separate data from January 2006 onwards began to be published by the CFTC. The chart confirms that market participants in the commercial category account for an overwhelming proportion of index trader positions (see also table 2.2).

However, chart 2.4 provides only scant evidence of a correlation between position and price changes.[14] While there clearly are periods and commodities where positions and prices have moved together, especially during the recent downturn and occasionally during the previous price upturn, there are other times when positions have not risen during periods of rapid price appreciation. For example, in the wheat market there was no increase in either non-commercial positions or index trader positions during the steep price increase from mid-2007 to the end of the first quarter of 2008. By contrast, during the same period there appears to have been a positive correlation between market positions and prices in the maize and soybean markets, while the evidence is mixed for the soybean oil market.

For oil and copper, for which separate data on index trader positions are not available, non-commercial positions declined along with prices in the second half of 2008. On the other hand, evidence for the earlier price increase does not suggest a correlation between non-commercial positions and prices: non-commercial copper positions declined during the period of the sharpest price increases – roughly from the beginning of 2004 through mid-2006. For oil, non-commercial positions exhibited strong volatility, even as oil prices rose almost continuously from the beginning of 2007 through the second quarter of 2008, by which time net oil positions had dropped roughly to zero.

Since the beginning of 2009, there has been an increase in the net long positions of both index traders and non-commercial participants excluding index traders (chart. 2.4). This may indicate that after the strong decline in their positions during the second half of 2008, both these groups are once again taking large positions on commodity markets.

While the evidence in chart 2.4 does not point to a long-standing correlation between position and price changes, for most commodities some correlation is present over sub-periods, as peaks and turning points seem to occur around the same time across the two series. This suggests that any analysis of a relationship between position and price changes may be sensitive to the choice of time period.[15]

Generally, Granger causality tests, which examine causal lead and lag dynamics between changes in the positions of financial investors on commodity futures exchanges and changes in commodity prices, have not found evidence of a systematic impact on prices of positions taken by non-commercial traders. However, they have tended to find a statistically significant causal relationship between the movement of commodity futures prices and measures of position changes (see, for example, IMF, 2008b). However, the results of these studies suffer from a number of data problems. These include the aggregation of trader positions across maturities, the fact that weekly data cannot identify very short-term effects, even though intra-week trading activity may be significant (for example when index traders roll over their positions), and the fact that they usually concentrate on non-commercial positions thereby ignoring the positions of index traders.[16]

Using Granger causality tests to examine the effects of index-based investments on futures prices for grains on the Chicago Board of Trade, and CFTC's supplementary data reports in order to distinguish between positions held by index investors and those of other traders, Gilbert (2008a) found significant and persistent effects from index-based investments on the soybean market over the period February 2007–August 2008 (also apparent in chart 2.4), but failed to find such effects for maize, soybean oil or wheat futures. Investigating the same hypothesis in relation to the IMF food commodity price index using monthly data for the period April 2006–August 2008, Gilbert (2008b) found evidence that index investments in agricultural futures markets had raised food commodity prices. He explained this by the tendency of financial investors to look at the likely returns on commodities as an aggregate asset class, and not at likely returns on specific commodities.

Chart 2.4

FINANCIAL POSITIONS AND PRICES, SELECTED COMMODITIES, JANUARY 2002–MAY 2009

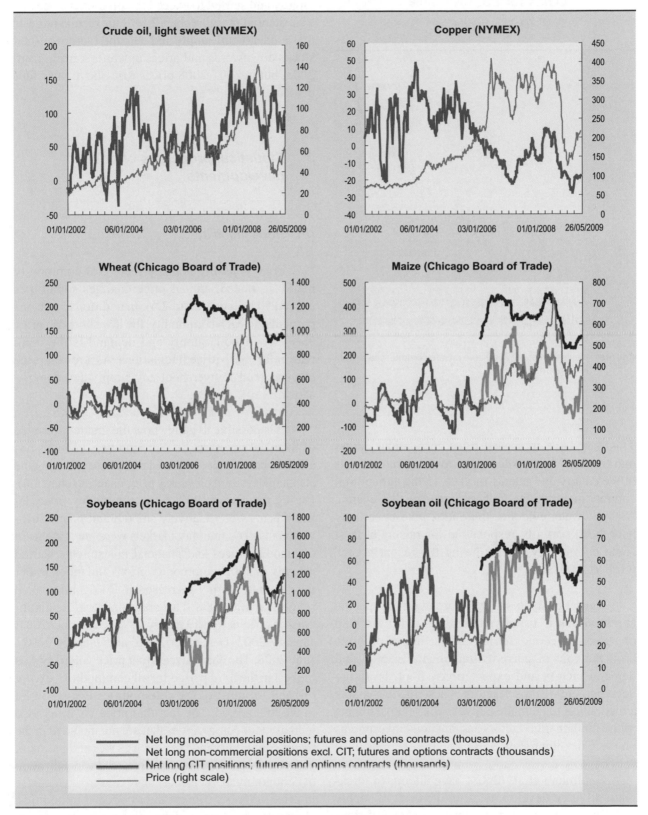

Net long non-commercial positions; futures and options contracts (thousands)
Net long non-commercial positions excl. CIT; futures and options contracts (thousands)
Net long CIT positions; futures and options contracts (thousands)
Price (right scale)

Source: UNCTAD secretariat calculations, based on Bloomberg; and CFTC.
Note: CIT = commodity index traders. Price refers to $/barrel for crude oil, cents/bushel for wheat, maize and soybeans, and cents/lb for copper and soybean oil.

Chart 2.5

ACTUAL AND PREDICTED CRUDE OIL PRICES, 1997–2008

(Dollars per barrel)

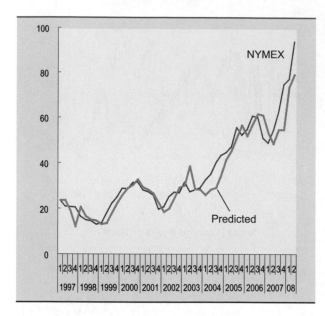

Source: Kaufmann et al., 2008; and private communication from RK Kaufmann.

This may have increased price correlations across markets and transmitted upward price movements in the energy and metals markets to the agricultural commodities markets. Gilbert concluded that, overall, "there is weak evidence that index investment may have been partially responsible for raising at least some commodity prices during the recent boom" (Gilbert, 2008a: 24).

Causal analysis of price formation for specific commodities is usually undertaken with the help of structural econometric models that incorporate both the role of current fundamental supply and demand factors and expectations about the future development of those factors. These models enable a distinction to be made between the relative impact of the fundamental factors and financial investments on price developments.

Kaufmann et al. (2008) have attempted to explain oil price developments on the basis of supply and demand levels, refinery capacity and expectations which provide an incentive for inventory storage that bolsters demand.[17] Crude oil prices predicted by the

model were fairly close to actual prices until about mid-2007, when the predicted prices began to grow rapidly but the actual prices increased even more rapidly and started to exceed the predicted prices by a substantial margin (chart 2.5). This result suggests that fundamental supply and demand factors pushed stocks downwards and prices upwards starting from 2003, but in 2007-2008 prices rose above their fundamental levels.[18]

3. Statistical properties of price developments

(a) Price volatility

Price volatility is a key feature of commodity markets; indeed, annual price changes sometimes exceed 50 per cent (chart 2.4). In addition to reasons particular to each commodity, the low short-run price elasticity of both supply and demand is the main reason for sharp price fluctuations. As a result, price changes tend to overshoot any supply and demand shock.

It is possible to gauge how the greater presence of financial investors on commodity exchanges has affected commodity price volatility by examining the standard deviation of weekly price changes (chart 2.6). During the period 1997–2001, commodity price developments were relatively smooth and financial investments in commodity markets were low. Booms in commodity prices and financial investments started roughly in 2002, commodity prices and index trader investments sharply increased in 2007 and peaked roughly in mid-2008. This analysis therefore distinguishes three periods: January 1997–December 2001, January 2002–December 2006, and January 2007–June 2008. The chart reveals that price volatility was highest in the third period for all commodities except oil, and for most of the commodities it was lowest in the first period. The fact that price volatility also increased for commodities that are not included in the major commodity indexes, such as rice and palm oil, may suggest that factors other than the financialization of commodity markets must have caused the increase in price volatility of exchange-traded commodities. However, there are clearly substitution effects between commodities of the two groups in terms of both production and consumption, as between wheat

Chart 2.6

COMMODITY PRICE VOLATILITY, SELECTED COMMODITIES AND PERIODS
(Per cent)

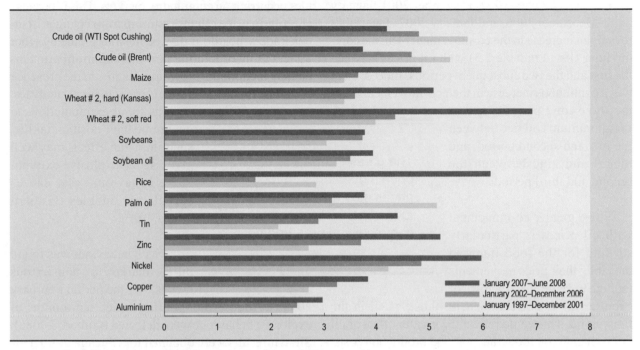

Source: UNCTAD secretariat calculations, based on Thomson Financial Datastream.
Note: Volatility is measured as the standard deviation of 12-month moving averages of weekly price changes.

and rice, and between palm oil on the one hand and soybean oil and crude oil on the other.

Time-series evidence based on daily price data for the period January 2005–August 2008 also shows that price volatility increased, except for crude oil (Informa Economics, 2009, part 3). What is more, this examination of non-public data indicates that positions taken by money managers, and in particular those taken by index traders, were positively correlated with price volatility in agricultural markets, as mentioned earlier. This speculative activity may well have been attracted by higher volatility. However, given that index traders generally follow a passive trading strategy, it is more likely that it was an increase in their activity that caused greater price volatility. Taken together, the evidence suggests that the growing participation of financial investors in commodity markets has increased price volatility.

> The evidence suggests that the greater involvement of financial investors in commodity markets has increased price volatility.

(b) Price co-movements

The financialization of commodity markets is likely to have caused a greater co-movement of prices across individual commodities, because financial investors generally lack commodity-specific knowledge and allocate funds to commodities by investing in a commodity index. Given that various commodities are included (according to some specified weights) in such indexes, the entire range of commodities is affected by changes in the prices of other asset classes. This triggers a change in the exposure of financial investors in commodities. Moreover, some commodity categories, such as energy and especially oil, often have a much greater weight in commodity indexes than, for example, food products. As a result, changes in energy markets based on actual or expected market conditions may be transmitted to other commodity markets, even though there may have been no change in the fundamentals of those other markets.

A further examination of the three sub-periods cited above (January 1997–December 2001, January 2002–December 2006, and January 2007–June 2008) reveals an increase in the co-movement of all the commodities (listed in table 2.3) with oil prices between the first and the two subsequent periods. Indeed, there was a continuous increase in their co-movements over the three time periods, except for aluminium and rice between the first and second period, and nickel and zinc between the second and third period.

The greater co-movement with oil prices is particularly striking for the food items in the table: their price movements tended to have a very low, or even negative, correlation with those of oil in the first period. This could reflect the greater effect of oil price changes on food transport and production costs. However, Mitchell (2008) estimates that the increase in energy and transport costs combined raised production costs in the United States agricultural sector by only 15–20 per cent. Part of the greater co-movement between oil and food prices may also be due to the diversion of food crops – particularly maize in the United States and oilseeds in Europe – into biofuel production. However, Gilbert (2008a: 15) examines the link between crude oil, biofuels and food prices and concludes that "there is as yet little econometric evidence that can substantiate the claim that the oil price and biofuel demand are driving food commodity prices". The co-movement between oil prices and the prices of other commodities was extremely high in the period July 2008–December 2008 (table 2.3, fourth panel), during which the strong price correction occurred. This may be partly due to the generally worsened economic outlook during that period. However, it is likely that most of this increased co-movement was caused by the withdrawal of index traders from commodity markets and the associated deleveraging of their energy-heavy futures positions across the different commodities. Moreover, the co-movement of prices of food items strongly declined (table 2.3). Taken together, this evidence suggests that the greater impact of oil price movements on food prices may have been due to the financialization of commodity futures trading.

> The greater impact of oil price movements on food prices may have been due to the financialization of commodity futures trading.

(c) Extrapolative behaviour and speculative bubbles

There is a strong probability of speculative bubbles occurring on commodity markets. This is because short-term price effects resulting from changes in index traders' positions may be misinterpreted by other traders as incorporating new market information, as already mentioned. More importantly, in the presence of uninformed traders that use statistical analyses, such as trend extrapolation, to determine their position taking, such short-run effects may well give rise to "explosive extrapolative behaviour" that causes speculative bubbles (Gilbert, 2008a, b).[19]

Such behaviour was found on the market for non-ferrous metals over the period February 2003 to August 2008, during which ten months of explosive behaviour were detected (Gilbert, 2008a). Similar results were obtained for Chicago grain markets in the period 2006–2008, including numerous instances of explosive behaviour of soybean oil prices (Gilbert, 2008b).[20] The finding of explosive behaviour of soybean and soybean oil prices is of particular importance because of the pivotal role of soybeans as substitutes for wheat and maize in production, of other vegetable oils and animal feedstuffs in consumption, and of crude oil in energy. Taken together, these results indicate that explosive extrapolative behaviour is widespread in commodity futures markets, and that this may have contributed to price volatility in recent years. The evidence also suggests "that the efficient markets view that uninformed speculation has no effect on market prices and volatility should be rejected" (Gilbert, 2008a: 21).

4. Conclusions

In sum, the above findings suggest that part of the commodity price boom between 2002 and mid-2008, as well as the subsequent sharp decline in commodity prices, were due to the financialization of commodity markets. Taken together, these findings support the view that financial investors have accelerated and amplified price movements

Table 2.3

CO-MOVEMENTS OF PRICE CHANGES, SELECTED COMMODITIES AND PERIODS

(Correlation coefficients, per cent)

	Alumini-um	Cop-per	Nickel	Zinc	Tin	Palm oil	Rice	Soy-bean oil	Soy-beans	Wheat, soft red	Maize	Crude oil (Brent)	Crude oil (WTI)
						*January 1997–December 2001*							
Aluminium	100.0												
Copper	60.5	100.0											
Nickel	43.4	47.7	100.0										
Zinc	48.9	41.2	36.5	100.0									
Tin	21.2	21.2	19.9	16.9	100.0								
Palm oil	-12.8	-3.5	-12.8	-7.2	-1.2	100.0							
Rice	12.3	6.1	3.2	3.8	7.9	-6.8	100.0						
Soybean oil	-0.1	14.6	3.3	-3.1	2.1	29.0	-2.5	100.0					
Soybeans	16.1	17.4	19.7	4.6	8.5	0.2	-7.6	55.2	100.0				
Wheat, soft red	2.7	4.6	6.5	1.5	7.0	1.6	-6.2	27.2	38.5	100.0			
Maize	-1.3	4.4	10.6	-1.8	4.2	2.5	-6.6	45.5	64.9	56.9	100.0		
Crude oil (Brent)	16.3	12.7	19.6	3.2	-1.1	-17.7	3.3	-4.6	-1.9	5.1	-3.0	100.0	
Crude oil (WTI)	16.7	13.7	19.4	5.9	-4.7	-17.1	2.8	-6.0	-1.9	3.5	-0.5	82.0	100.0
						*January 2002–December 2006*							
Aluminium	100.0												
Copper	65.4	100.0											
Nickel	43.2	50.3	100.0										
Zinc	58.3	69.7	45.8	100.0									
Tin	33.2	36.7	32.5	37.6	100.0								
Palm oil	6.0	9.4	2.3	7.0	10.6	100.0							
Rice	-2.4	6.0	-4.8	-3.7	7.1	8.4	100.0						
Soybean oil	8.8	11.5	2.8	13.2	12.7	43.4	3.5	100.0					
Soybeans	4.8	8.9	2.4	7.4	18.9	27.4	0.6	61.1	100.0				
Wheat, soft red	16.2	14.1	7.4	18.9	15.4	2.6	-8.1	24.3	26.9	100.0			
Maize	12.6	13.6	3.8	18.6	26.0	17.1	1.7	38.4	48.3	41.9	100.0		
Crude oil (Brent)	15.0	23.1	25.0	24.7	22.2	-4.6	-5.7	5.8	7.8	11.1	2.6	100.0	
Crude oil (WTI)	14.5	19.4	19.7	21.0	17.4	-0.7	-6.1	9.4	7.7	11.8	7.0	87.4	100.0
						*January 2007–June 2008*							
Aluminium	100.0												
Copper	62.1	100.0											
Nickel	48.3	42.4	100.0										
Zinc	56.0	67.1	43.4	100.0									
Tin	38.2	41.0	26.6	48.5	100.0								
Palm oil	36.9	31.1	33.9	32.7	10.7	100.0							
Rice	-14.9	-0.4	2.7	-6.3	-2.8	-7.5	100.0						
Soybean oil	41.4	20.3	26.5	17.8	16.3	61.5	-26.4	100.0					
Soybeans	34.3	15.3	26.3	9.9	12.4	51.6	-21.3	85.9	100.0				
Wheat, soft red	9.4	13.7	-10.1	3.2	6.4	4.7	-28.2	19.3	23.2	100.0			
Maize	13.8	2.2	10.8	8.8	11.2	18.5	7.1	22.0	35.5	23.8	100.0		
Crude oil (Brent)	28.9	26.1	6.0	5.6	19.2	15.7	0.7	31.5	22.8	13.9	9.7	100.0	
Crude oil (WTI)	18.9	21.4	-1.5	0.8	23.0	10.6	1.7	27.6	21.2	17.0	2.6	86.4	100.0
						*July 2008–December 2008*							
Aluminium	100.0												
Copper	48.9	100.0											
Nickel	43.9	55.3	100.0										
Zinc	52.4	71.4	63.6	100.0									
Tin	19.8	38.3	72.6	43.5	100.0								
Palm oil	22.2	49.0	10.2	33.2	-11.5	100.0							
Rice	29.7	22.3	-5.2	11.2	-13.1	-15.5	100.0						
Soybean oil	27.6	57.4	32.5	36.7	13.7	74.7	-2.7	100.0					
Soybeans	30.8	31.3	33.6	26.3	11.7	48.4	-3.5	79.2	100.0				
Wheat, soft red	13.4	11.1	-8.4	4.8	-29.2	37.3	-8.0	41.4	49.1	100.0			
Maize	27.6	31.9	26.5	17.2	-0.1	33.6	15.1	66.5	79.6	62.4	100.0		
Crude oil (Brent)	19.0	62.1	31.7	27.6	26.0	61.9	8.4	78.6	45.8	29.1	45.4	100.0	
Crude oil (WTI)	11.9	59.1	25.0	16.0	25.4	46.9	21.1	69.7	37.4	22.4	41.9	93.1	100.0

Source: UNCTAD secretariat calculations, based on Thomson Financial Datastream.
Note: Co-movement measured in relation to weekly price changes.

driven by fundamental supply and demand factors, at least in some periods of time. This acceleration and amplification of price movements can be traced for commodities as a group. Regarding the impact of financial investors on individual commodities, some effect can be observed in the oil market, but it appears that most of the impact occurred in the smaller

and less liquid markets for agricultural commodities, including food products. Some of these effects may have been substantial and some persistent. However, the non-transparency of existing data and the lack of a comprehensive breakdown of data by individual commodity and trader category preclude more detailed empirical analysis.

E. The implications of increased financial investor activities for commercial users of commodity futures exchanges

If the financialization of commodity trading causes futures market quotations to be driven more by the speculative activities of financial investors and less by fundamental supply and demand factors, hedging against commodity price risk will become more complex, and this may discourage long-term hedging by commercial users.

To the extent that financial investors increase price volatility, hedging becomes more expensive, and perhaps unaffordable for developing-country users, as they may no longer be able to finance margin calls. For example, during the period January 2003–December 2008, margin levels as a proportion of contract value increased by 142 per cent in maize, 79 per cent in wheat and 175 per cent in soybean on the Chicago Board of Trade (CME, 2008: 17–18). In early 2007, the LME raised its margin requirement by 500 per cent over the space of only a few months (Doyle, Hill and Jack, 2007). Larger, well-capitalized firms can afford these increases, but smaller participants may need to reduce the number of contracts they hold. This itself could reduce liquidity, add to volatility and discourage more conservative investors. Hedging

> To the extent that financial investors increase price volatility, hedging becomes more expensive, and perhaps unaffordable for developing-country users.

food commodity exposure may become particularly risky because of the typically long-term nature of such hedges, which correspond to harvest cycles. Indeed, evidence reported by the Kansas City Board of Trade (2008) pointed to a reduction in long-term hedging by commercial users at the beginning of 2008, caused by higher market volatility.

Moreover, since 2006, there have been numerous instances of a lack of price convergence between spot markets and futures contracts during delivery, for maize, soybean and wheat. The price of a futures contract that calls for delivery may differ from the current cash price of the underlying commodity, but these prices should very closely match when the futures contract expires. The difference between the futures and the cash price ("basis") tends to widen when storage facilities are scarce, and shrink when physical supply becomes tight. If, in an otherwise balanced market, prices diverge by more than the cost of storage and delivery, arbitrageurs usually act to make the prices converge eventually. Failure to do so would cause increased uncertainty about the reliability of signals emanating from the commodity exchanges with respect to making storage decisions and managing market position risks. This could eventually result in decreased hedging, as commercial users seek alternative mechanisms for transferring and managing price risk (Irwin et al., 2008). Commercial users might also decide to reduce their use of commodity exchanges because the non-convergence of futures and spot prices not only increases uncertainty but also the cost of hedging (Conceição and Marone, 2008: 56–57).

F. Policy implications

Price discovery and price risk management traditionally have been considered the main benefits that commodity futures exchanges can provide to developing-country users. Hedging on commodity futures exchanges, by reducing price risk, has also been viewed by some observers as an alternative to supply management under international commodity agreements. Meanwhile, commodity exchanges have begun to assume a broader developmental role, as they are increasingly seen to be useful to developing countries in terms of removing or reducing the high transaction costs faced by entities along commodity supply chains (UNCTAD, 2007). However, the financialization of commodity futures trading has made the functioning of commodity exchanges controversial. It has therefore become necessary to consider how their functioning could be improved so that they can continue to fulfil their role of providing reliable price signals to producers and consumers of primary commodities and contributing to a stable environment for development. This section seeks to address this issue by examining whether regulatory changes have been keeping pace with commodity market developments, in particular the participation of new trader categories such as index funds. The subsequent section addresses broader international policy measures.

> The functioning of commodity futures exchanges has to be improved so that they can provide reliable price signals to producers and consumers of primary commodities.

1. Regulation of commodity futures exchanges

Regulation of commodity exchanges has to find a reasonable compromise between imposing overly restrictive limits on speculative position holdings and having overly lax surveillance and regulation. Being overly restrictive could impair market liquidity and reduce the hedging and price discovery functions of commodity exchanges. On the other hand, overly lax surveillance and regulation would allow prices to move away from levels warranted by fundamental supply and demand conditions, and would thus equally impair the hedging and price discovery functions of the exchanges.

A substantial part of commodity futures trading is executed on exchanges located in the United States, which the CFTC is mandated to regulate. Abuse of futures trading by speculators is addressed by applying limits on "excessive speculation", defined as trading that results in "sudden or unreasonable fluctuations or unwarranted changes in the price" of commodities underlying futures transactions (section 4a of the Commodity Exchange Act (CEA)). In principle, speculative trading is contained by speculative position limits set by the CFTC (see section C above).

While it is often held that commodity exchanges have generally functioned well, the recent, very sizeable price changes occurring, sometimes within a single trading day, have raised growing questions about the appropriateness of existing regulations. These questions relate to both the adequacy of information that the CFTC is mandated to collect, and the extent of regulatory restrictions on financial investors relative to those imposed on participants with genuine commercial interests. The need for tighter regulations has been discussed under three headings: the "Enron loophole", the "London loophole" and the "swap dealer loophole".

The Commodity Futures Modernization Act (CFMA) of 2000 created the so-called "Enron Loophole" by exempting over-the-counter energy trading undertaken on electronic exchanges from CFTC oversight and regulation. The Enron loophole was addressed by legislation that entered into force on 18 June 2008. This legislation provides for the previously exempt electronic exchanges to become self-regulatory organizations. It also gives the CFTC greater authority to require data reporting on trading and on the positions of hedgers and speculators, and to suspend or revoke "the operations or regulatory status of an electronic trading facility that fails to comply with the core principles, fails to enforce its own rules, or violates applicable CFTC regulations" (Jickling, 2008: 5). However, some observers argue that this legislation has not gone far enough, because it covers only electronic trading but does not extend to bilateral swaps, and because it does not place energy commodities on the same regulatory footing as agricultural commodities that must be traded on the CFTC-regulated exchanges (Jickling, 2008; Greenberger, 2008).

The "London loophole" is closely related to the "Enron loophole", as only one of the active markets exempted from CFTC regulations handles a volume of energy trading similar to that handled by CFTC-regulated exchanges (CFTC, 2007). A large proportion of West Texas Intermediate crude oil contracts is traded on NYMEX, which is regulated by the CFTC. However, "look alike" contracts are traded in London on ICE Futures Europe (owned by Atlanta-based Intercontinental Exchange), which is regulated by the Financial Services Authority (FSA) of the United Kingdom. This means that traders can execute transactions in similar crude oil contracts on NYMEX and ICE, arbitraging between the two markets, yet the CFTC can oversee and regulate only the trading on NYMEX. The significance of this loophole may be illustrated by the fact that, in principle, under section 8a (9) of the CEA, the CFTC has the authority, "whenever it has reason to believe that an emergency exists", to take measures "including, but not limited to the setting of temporary emergency margin levels on any futures contract [and] the fixing of limits that may apply to a market position". However, the CFTC did not apply this mandate, for example, when on 6 June 2008 the price on oil futures contracts rose by about $11 per barrel in a single day. Greenberger (2008: 21) argues that the CFTC may not have done so because it had data only on contracts traded on NYMEX but not on similar contracts traded on ICE.

> Given the global nature of commodity futures trading, international collaboration among regulatory agencies is needed.

Proposed legislative action to close the London loophole was presented to the United States Congress on 12 June 2008 (Chilton, 2008), but so far it has not resulted in actual legislative changes. In the meantime, the CFTC introduced changes to the 'No-Action' letter issued in 1999 that granted the ICE permission to make its electronic trading screens available to trading in the United States. These changes provide for ICE trading and position data to be reported to the CFTC, and for the imposition of position limits (including related hedge exemption provisions) comparable to those applicable on the CFTC-regulated exchanges.

The "swap dealer loophole" has received considerable attention in the current debate on the changes needed in the CFTC's regulatory mandates. This is because swap agreements are concluded on OTC markets and thus escape the CFTC's supervisory and regulatory oversight.[21] Moreover, the greater involvement of financial investors in commodity futures trading has significantly increased the positions that swap dealers hold in commodity futures contracts. Swap dealers typically sell OTC swaps to their customers (such as pension funds that buy commodity index funds) and hedge their price exposures with long futures positions in commodities. Swap dealers are generally included in the category "commercial traders", as they use commodity exchanges for hedging purposes. This has allowed them to be exempted from regulation of speculative position limits. But contrary to traditional commercial traders, who hedge physical positions, swap dealers hedge financial positions. The combination of significant trading activity on OTC markets and the exemption of swap dealers from speculative limits on futures exchanges has severely constrained the ability of regulators to access sufficient information about positions. They would need such information in order to identify undue concentrations of positions, evaluate the overall composition of the market and assess its functioning.

Several proposals have been advanced on how to close the swap dealer loophole. For example, the Kansas City Board of Trade (2008) has proposed addressing the index fund hedge exemptions by limiting their total direct or indirect futures hedge positions to a maximum percentage in the contracts that have a remaining maturity of one or two months. This would create an additional incentive to spread the total position across several months and ease position concentration. It has also suggested changes to the definition of a bona fide hedger and a related distinction to be made in margin requirements between those that have true commercial hedge positions and those that hedge financial positions. In addition, it has proposed alleviating strains in financing margins by accepting commercial agricultural collateral (such as warehouse receipts). These last two changes, in particular, would tend to improve the functioning of commodity exchanges with respect to participants with truly commercial interests.

Given the global character of commodity futures trading, and the fact that through trading arbitrage some contracts involve the jurisdiction of regulatory authorities in more than one country, international collaboration among regulatory agencies is required. Such collaboration would involve not only the sharing and publishing of information, some of which is already in place, but also greater cooperation and harmonization of trading supervision.[22] It seems particularly urgent that exchanges whose legal base is London should be required to provide data on positions by trader categories similarly to those made

publicly available by the CFTC for some agricultural products through its COT supplementary reports. In addition, the product coverage of these supplementary reports needs to be enlarged. Product coverage has remained limited because for many commodities traded on United States exchanges, look-alike contracts can be traded in London. As a result, data on positions on United States exchanges provide only a partial picture of the total positions of traders that are active on both the United States and London exchanges. Moreover, in the absence of such data for energy products, legislation enacted in the United States to address the London loophole is probably unlikely to be effective unless similar data on positions taken on ICE are made available.

2. International policy measures

In addition to regulatory issues, the financialization of commodity futures trading confronts the international community with the issue of how supply-side measures can address excessive commodity price volatility. This issue is of particular importance for food commodities because, despite some recent improvement, grain and oilseed stocks remain very low so that any sudden increase in demand or a major shortfall in production, or both, will rapidly cause significant price increases (see annex to chapter I). Hence, physical stocks of food commodities need to be rebuilt urgently to an adequate level in order to moderate temporary shortages and buffer sharp price movements.

> Physical stocks of food commodities need to be rebuilt urgently, and should be sufficiently large to be able to moderate temporary shortages and buffer sharp price movements.

It has often been argued that it is difficult to finance and guarantee the accumulation of sufficiently high physical inventory stocks, especially of food commodities, so that they could function as physical buffer stocks. Moreover, holding large inventories around the world has often been judged economically inefficient, and it has been recommended that net food importing countries should rely on global markets rather than on building their own reserves. However, there can be little doubt that newly imposed trade restrictions (particularly for rice) played a role in exacerbating the spiralling increase in food prices in early 2008. This has added to anti-globalization sentiments and to more favourable assessments of the protection that national food reserves can provide.

Partly to counter such anti-globalization sentiments, and in particular as part of efforts to prevent humanitarian crises, von Braun and Torero (2008) – echoed by the G-8 summit in June 2008 – have proposed a new two-pronged global institutional arrangement: a minimum physical grain reserve for emergency responses and humanitarian assistance, and a virtual reserve and intervention mechanism. The latter would enable intervention in the futures markets if a "global intelligence unit" were to consider market prices as differing significantly from an estimated dynamic price band based on market fundamentals. However, adopting such a mechanism would commit a public agency to second-guess market developments. More importantly, in order to stem speculative price bubbles, the agency would

need to be prepared to sell large amounts of physical commodities. Given the certainty that any accumulated stocks will eventually be exhausted, there is considerable risk that speculators could mobilize significantly more financial funds than any public agency's capacity to provide physical commodities. Hence it is likely that the funds allocated to such an agency would be an easy target for speculators.

Even if a virtual reserve and intervention mechanism could be made to work satisfactorily, it would not make more physical commodities available on markets, except for emergency situations. Given that the historically low level of inventories was one determinant of the abrupt price hike in food commodities in early 2008, the question remains as to how incentives to increase production and productivity in developing countries, particularly of food commodities, could be fostered. Such incentives could include a reduction of trade barriers and domestic support measures in developed countries.

G. Conclusions and outlook

The financialization of commodity futures trading has made commodity markets even more prone to behavioural overshooting. There are an increasing number of market participants, sometimes with very large positions, that do not trade based on fundamental supply and demand relationships in commodity markets, but, who nonetheless, influence commodity price developments.

Due to the limited transparency of existing data, as well as the lack of a comprehensive breakdown of data by individual commodity and trader categories that would enable a determination of the position changes of different trader categories, it is difficult to conduct a detailed empirical analysis of the link between speculation and commodity price

developments. Nevertheless, various existing studies and new results provided in this chapter indicate that the activities of financial investors have accelerated and amplified commodity price movements. Moreover, these effects are likely to have been substantial, and in some cases persistent. The strongest evidence is found in the high correlation, particularly during the deleveraging process in the second half of 2008, between commodity prices and prices on other markets, such as equity and currency markets, which were particularly affected by carry-trade activities. In these markets, speculative activity played a major role.

These effects of the financialization of commodity futures trading have made the functioning of commodity exchanges increasingly contentious. They tend to reduce the participation of commercial users, including those from developing countries, because commodity price risk hedging becomes more complex and expensive. They also cause greater uncertainty about the reliability of signals emanating from the commodity exchanges with respect to making storage decisions and managing the price risk of market positions.

It is unclear whether financial investors will continue to consider commodities as an attractive asset class. The trading strategy of index investors has proved to be strongly dependent on specific conditions (i.e. rising or backwardated markets) to be profitable. Moreover, since their strategy is fairly predictable, other market participants may make sizeable profits by trading against index investors. Hence, financial investors are likely to move away from investing passively in indexes towards more active trading behaviour, either by adopting a more flexible approach in determining how and when to roll forward positions, or by concentrating on other investment vehicles such as commodity-exchange-traded funds.[23] This implies that the distinction between short-term oriented managed funds and other financial investors will become less clear. Its effect on commodity prices will largely depend on the extent to which such a shift in financial investors' trading strategy leads to a greater concentration on specific commodities, instead of commodities as an aggregate asset class. But such a potential shift in financial investors' trading behaviour is unlikely to reduce the relative size of their positions. Thus they will continue to be able to amplify price movements, at least for short periods of time, especially if they concentrate on individual commodities.

Data for the first few months of 2009 indicate that both index traders and money managers have started to rebuild their speculative positions in commodities. This makes a broadening and strengthening of the supervisory and regulatory powers of mandated commodity market regulators indispensable. The ability of any regulator to understand what is moving prices and to intervene effectively depends upon its ability to understand the market and to collect the required data. Such data are currently not available, particularly for off-exchange derivatives trading. Yet such trading and trading on regulated commodity exchanges have become increasingly interdependent. Hence, comprehensive trading data need to be reported to enable regulators to monitor information about sizeable transactions, including on similar contracts traded over the counter that could have an impact on regulated futures markets.

In addition to more comprehensive data, broader regulatory mandates are required. Supervision and regulation of commodity futures markets need to be enhanced, particularly with a view to closing the swap dealer loophole, in order to enable regulators to counter unwarranted impacts from OTC trading on commodity exchanges. At present, banks that hold futures contracts on commodity exchanges to offset their short positions in OTC swap agreements vis-à-vis index traders fall under the hedge exemption and thus are not subject to speculative position limits. Therefore, regulators are currently unable to intervene effectively, even though swap dealer positions frequently exceed such limits and may represent "excessive speculation".

Another key regulatory aspect concerns extending the product coverage of the CFTC's COT supplementary reports and requiring non-United States exchanges, particularly those based in London that trade look-alike contracts, to collect similar data. The availability of such data would provide regulators with early warning signals and allow them to recognize emerging commodity price bubbles. The resulting enhancement of regulatory authority would enable the regulators to prevent bubble-creating trading behaviour from having adverse effects on the functioning of commodity futures trading.

Developing-country commodity exchanges might want to consider taking similar measures, where relevant,[24] though their trading generally tends to be determined more by local commercial conditions than by any sizeable involvement of internationally operating financial investors. ∎

Notes

1   Notional amount refers to the value of the underlying commodity. However, traders in derivatives markets do not own or purchase the underlying commodity. Hence, notional value is merely a reference point based on underlying prices.

2   The Bank for International Settlements (BIS) is the only source that provides publicly available information about OTC commodity trading. However, commodity-specific disaggregation is not possible with these data.

3   In the DJ-UBSCI, weights primarily rely on the relative amount of trading activity of a particular commodity, and are limited to 15 per cent for individual commodities and to one third for entire sectors. In the S&P GSCI, on the other hand, weights depend on relative world production quantities, with energy products usually accounting for about two thirds of the total index.

4   A commodity exchange is a market in which multiple buyers and sellers trade commodity-linked contracts according to rules and procedures laid down by the exchange and/or a mandated supervisory and regulatory body. Such exchanges typically act as a platform for trade in futures contracts (i.e. standardized contracts for future delivery). For further details, see UNCTAD, 2006.

5   The study was done using daily data. Such data are not publicly available, but could be used by Informa Economics (2009) as their study was commissioned by a consortium of futures exchanges. The authors conclude that the positive correlation between the trading activities of index traders and those of momentum-trading money managers on agricultural markets may simply indicate that in this period, during most of which prices were rising strongly, money managers favoured the same "long" strategy that index traders routinely use.

6   More precisely, among the types of firms engaged in business activities that can be hedged and therefore classified as "commercial" by the CFTC are merchants, manufacturers, producers, and commodity swaps and derivative dealers. The CFTC classifies as "non-commercial" all other traders, such as hedge funds, floor brokers and traders, and non-reporting traders (i.e. those traders whose positions are below the reporting thresholds set by an exchange).

7   These 12 commodities are: feeder cattle, live cattle, cocoa, coffee, cotton, lean hogs, maize, soybeans, soybean oil, sugar, Chicago wheat and Kansas wheat.

8   Using data on bank participation in futures markets, Sanders, Irwin and Merrin (2008: 9) show that index trader activity in grain markets started in 2003, and that the most rapid increase in trader positions occurred between early 2004 and mid-2005. Given that the CFTC's index trader data start only in 2006, they cannot reflect these events.

9   A long position is a market position that obligates the holder to take delivery (i.e. to buy a commodity). This contrasts with a short position, which is a market position that obligates the holder to make delivery, (i.e. to sell a commodity). Net long positions are total long positions minus short positions.

10   Open interest is the total number of futures contracts – long or short – in a market, which have been entered into and not yet liquidated by an offsetting transaction or fulfilled by delivery.

11   Speculative position limits define the maximum position, either net long or net short, in one commodity futures (or options) contract, or in all futures (or options) contracts of one commodity combined, that may be held or controlled by one person other than a person eligible for a hedge exemption, as prescribed by an exchange and/or the CFTC.

12   The results do not materially change if commodity shares are based on 2009 weights.

13   For a discussion of carry trade speculation, see *TDR 2007,* chapter I.

14   The absence of any systematic difference in recent price developments between commodities that are traded on futures exchanges and those that are not is sometimes cited as further evidence for an absence of any significant impact of financial investors on price developments (ECB, 2008: 19). This evidence

is interpreted as supporting the view that commodity prices have been driven entirely by supply and demand fundamentals, and that futures exchanges have simply provided the mechanism through which information about fundamentals is reflected in market prices.

15 Informa Economics (2009) uses the concept of "price pressure" to investigate the effects that daily changes in position taking by different trader categories have on daily final prices. They consider price pressure that pushes prices towards their daily end level, which they call "true value", as beneficial, and price pressure that pushes prices away from that level as detrimental. For all the analysed agricultural products, except cotton, the study finds that commercial traders had the lowest ratio of beneficial to detrimental price pressure, while money managers and index traders had the highest such ratios. In other words, among all the trader categories, commercial traders, who supposedly trade on the basis of information on fundamental supply and demand conditions, exerted the least influence on daily price discovery, and financial investors exerted the most influence. Informa Economics (2009, part 4: 34) interprets this finding as indicating that commercial traders are only concerned about hedging their price risk, but do not care much about whether commodity prices reflect fundamental supply and demand conditions. But the finding could also be interpreted as meaning that the weight of financial investors in commodity futures trading is such that more often than not it moves prices away from levels that would have occurred on the basis of fundamental market conditions. The concept of price pressure applied to arrive at this finding nonetheless raises methodological issues. It assumes, for example, that all price changes result from position changes (i.e. based on private information), and that prices do not react to newly available public information. According to Grossman and Stiglitz (1980), this implies an assumption of complete information *inefficiency* of commodity markets.

16 Most existing studies that use Granger-causality tests have had to rely on publicly available weekly data on positions in commodity markets. However, a frequently quoted study by the Interagency Task Force on Commodity Markets conducted Granger causality tests for the oil market using non-public data on daily positions of both commercial and non-commercial traders, as well as those of various sub-groups of traders for the period January 2003–June 2008 (CFTC, 2008). This study also found no evidence that daily position changes by any of the trader sub-categories had systemically caused price changes in oil futures contracts over the full sample period. This means that, at least in the crude oil futures markets, results of Granger-causality tests appear to be largely unaffected by using either daily (instead of weekly) data or position changes for sub-groups of traders instead of aggregated data.

17 More precisely, Kaufmann et al. (2008) specify the near-month price of crude oil on the New York Mercantile Exchange (NYMEX) as a function of: (i) the equivalent of days of consumption of existing OECD crude oil stocks; (ii) a factor that reflects OPEC capacity utilization, OPEC's share of global oil production and the extent to which OPEC members cheat on their quota; (iii) United States refinery utilization rates, which may be subject to abrupt temporary disturbances during the hurricane season; and (iv) expectations as reflected by the difference between the price for the 4-month and the price for the 1-month futures contract for West Texas Intermediate on NYMEX. This difference indicates whether the market is in backwardation or contango, with contango providing an incentive to build and hold stocks, thereby bolstering demand and ultimately prices. On the basis of this relationship, price changes can be estimated with an error correction model, where first differences of the above variables as well as the forecasting errors of previous periods are taken as independent variables.

18 Prometeia (2008) adopts a similar approach in examining whether the strong increase in oil prices between mid-2007 and mid-2008 can be explained by rational pricing behaviour of market participants or whether it reflects a bubble. The tests cannot reject the presence of a bubble. Prometeia (2008) interprets the evidence as pointing to the role of financial investor activities on commodity futures markets in accelerating and amplifying price movements that in the medium and long run are driven by fundamentals. However, other structural models for the oil market ascribe much of the recent price developments to fundamental supply and demand factors. These models do not infer demand shocks from an econometric model, but treat repeated revisions of forecasts of real income growth in emerging and advanced economies as a series of exogenous demand shocks for the global crude oil market (e.g. Kilian and Hicks, 2009). However, it is hard to believe that informed oil traders would be repeatedly surprised by the impact on oil demand of buoyant growth in emerging economies. Moreover, any such calculation is extremely sensitive to assumptions about the short-run price elasticity of supply and demand.

19 More formally, tests for explosive extrapolative behaviour are based on the following equation: $\ln f_t = \alpha + \beta \ln f_{t-1} + \varepsilon_t$, where f_t and f_{t-1} are the current and past prices respectively, β is the autoregressive factor, and ε is an error term.

20 The number of these instances indicates that there is a higher probability of them being due to

explosive speculative behaviour than merely chance occurrences.

21 On 13 May 2009, the United States Government unveiled a plan designed to increase the transparency of OTC trading and tighten its oversight and regulation (see http://www.ustreas.gov/press/releases/tg129.htm). The centrepiece of the announced plan is to allow regulators to mandate the clearing of all standardized OTC derivatives through regulated central clearinghouses that would require traders to report their activities and hold a minimum level of capital to cover losses. While details of the proposed legislative changes still need to be determined, it appears from the plan that standardized derivatives would be traded on exchanges or through clearinghouses, while customized or individualized derivative products would not. This means that the plan would not cover swaps. Some commentators argue that this distinction between customized and other derivatives and the fact that swap-based transactions "would be reported privately to a 'trade repository', which apparently would make only limited aggregate data available to the public", is a serious shortcoming of the proposed plan (Partnoy, 2009).

22 The Financial Services Authority (FSA), which monitors commodity markets in the United Kingdom, considers commodity markets as specialized markets which are dominated by professional participants, and hence require less regulatory attention than equity and bond markets. It supervises firms that are active in commodity markets in order to ensure the financial stability of market participants so that contract settlements can take place on time and without default by any party. In addition, it mandates commodity exchanges to regulate their own markets with a view to providing clearly defined contract terms and ensuring against manipulation. In their advice on the European Commission's review of the commodity trading business, the Committee of European Securities Regulators (CESR) and the Committee of European Banking Supervisors (CEBS) pointed to potential problems relating to the low levels of transparency in OTC commodity derivatives trading and the current client categorization rules and transaction reporting requirements. However, they concluded that there was not much benefit to be gained by mandating through legislation greater pre- and post-trade transparency in commodity derivatives trading, and that the current practice of how regulated markets reported trading was sufficient (CESR, 2008).

23 Commodity exchange traded funds are listed securities backed by a physical commodity or a commodity futures contract.

24 To the extent that history is a guide for current events, developing countries would be ill-advised to close their commodity futures exchanges. For example, Jacks (2007) provides a historical account of the establishment and prohibition of commodity futures markets and shows that such markets have generally been associated with lower, rather than higher, price volatility.

References

Alquist R and Kilian L (2007). What do we learn from the price of crude oil futures? Discussion Paper No. 6548, Centre for Economic Policy Research, London.

Bernanke B (2008). Outstanding issues in the analysis of inflation. Speech delivered at the Federal Reserve Bank of Boston's 53rd Annual Economic Conference, Chatham, MA, 9 June.

Capuano C (2006). Strategic noise traders and liquidity pressure with a physically deliverable futures contract. *International Review of Economics and Finance*. 15(1): 1–14.

CESR (Committee of European Securities Regulators) (2008). CESR's/CEBS's technical advice to the European Commission on the review of commodities business. CESR/08-752; CEBS 2008 152 rev. Brussels.

CFTC (Commodities Futures Trading Commission) (2006a). Comprehensive review of the Commitments of Traders Reporting Program. *Federal Register*, 71(119): 35627–35632.

CFTC (2006b). Commodities Futures Trading Commission actions in response to the "Comprehensive Review of the Commitments of Traders Reporting Program",

5 December. Available at: http://www.docstoc. com/docs/873643/Comprehensive-Review-of-the-Commitments-of-Traders-Reporting-Program.

CFTC (2007). Report on the oversight of trading on regulated futures exchanges and exempt commercial markets. Available at: http://www.cftc.gov/stellent/ groups/public/@newsroom/documents/file/pr5403-07_ecmreport.pdf.

CFTC (2008). Interim report on crude oil. Interagency Task Force on Commodity Markets. Washington, DC, CFTC. Available at: http://www.cftc.gov/stellent/groups/public/@newsroom/documents/file/ itfinterimreportoncrudeoil0708.pdf.

CFTC (2009). About the Commitments of Traders Reports. Available at: http://www.cftc.gov/marketreports/ commitmentsoftraders/cot_about.html.

Chilton B (2008). Why the London loophole should be closed. *Financial Times*, 24 June.

CME (Chicago Mercantile Exchange Group) (2008). Fundamental factors affecting agricultural and other commodities. Available at: http://www.cmegroup. com/trading/commodities/files/Ag_Slides_12-31-08.pdf.

Conceição P and Maronc H (2008). Characterizing the 21st century first commodity boom: Drivers and impact. UNDP/ODS Working Paper. United Nations Development Programme, Office of Development Studies, New York, October.

de Long JB et al. (1990). Noise trader risk in financial markets. *Journal of Political Economy*, 98(4): 703–738.

Doyle E, Hill J and Jack I (2007). Growth in Commodity Investment: Risks and Challenges for Commodity Market Participants. London, Financial Services Authority, Markets Infrastructure Department.

European Central Bank (ECB) (2008). *Monthly Bulletin,* Frankfurt, European Central Bank, September.

Gilbert CL (2008a). Commodity speculation and commodity investment. Forthcoming in *Journal of Commodity Markets and Risk Management*.

Gilbert CL (2008b). How to understand high food prices. Unpublished. University of Trento, Italy.

Gorton G and Rouwenhorst KG (2006). Facts and fantasies about commodity futures. Working Paper No. 10595, National Bureau of Economic Research, Cambridge, MA, March.

Gorton G, Hayashi F and Rouwenhorst KG (2007). The fundamentals of commodity futures returns. Working Paper No. 13249, National Bureau of Economic Research, Cambridge, MA, July.

Greenberger M (2008). Testimony before the House Energy and Commerce Subcommittee on Oversight and Investigations Regarding Energy Speculation: Is Greater Regulation Necessary to Stop Price Manipulation? Part II, 23 June. Available at: http://www. michaelgreenberger.com/files/June_23_2008_testimony.pdf.

Greenspan A (2004). Oil. Remarks to the National Italian American Foundation, Washington, DC, 15 October. Available at: http://www.federalreserve.gov/boarddocs/speeches/2004/200410152/default.htm.

Grossman SJ and Stiglitz JE (1980). On the impossibility of informationally efficient markets. *American Economic Review*, 70(3): 393–408.

Hicks JR (1939). *Value and Capital*. Oxford, Oxford University Press.

IMF (2006). *World Economic Outlook*, Autumn. Washington, DC, International Monetary Fund.

IMF (2008a). *World Economic Outlook*, Autumn. Washington, DC, International Monetary Fund.

IMF (2008b). *Global Financial Stability Report*. Annex 1.2. Washington, DC, International Monetary Fund.

Informa Economics (2009). An evaluation of the influence of large reporting traders on futures markets performance. Available at: http://www.informaecon. com/TraderStudy/TraderStudy.htm.

Irwin SC et al. (2008). Recent convergence performance of CBOT corn, soybean, and wheat futures contracts. *Choices*, 23(2): 16–21.

Jacks DS (2007). Populists versus theorists: Futures markets and the volatility of prices. *Explorations in Economic History*, 44(2): 342–362.

Jickling M (2008). The Enron Loophole. Congressional Research Service Report for Congress. Order Code RS22912, 7 July. Available at: http://assets.opencrs. com/rpts/RS22912_20080707.pdf.

Kansas City Board of Trade (2008). Agricultural markets performance: Talking points April 2008. Available at: http://www.cftc.gov/stellent/groups/public/@ newsroom/documents/file/event042208_c026.pdf.

Kaufmann RK et al. (2008). Oil prices: the role of refinery utilization, futures markets and non-linearities. *Energy Economics*, 30(5): 2609–2622.

Keynes JM (1930). *A Treatise on Money,* Vol. 2. London, Macmillan.

Kilian L and Hicks B (2009). Did unexpectedly strong economic growth cause the oil price shock of 2003–2008? Discussion Paper No. 7265, Centre for Economic Policy Research, London, January.

Koh P (2007). Commodity markets: a drop in a puddle. *Euromoney*, 4 June: 146–149.

Krugman P (2008). The oil nonbubble. *New York Times*, 12 May.

Mitchell D (2008). A note on rising food prices. Working Paper No. 4682, World Bank, Washington, DC, July.

Partnoy F (2009). Danger in Wall Street's shadows. *New York Times*, 15 May. Available at: http://www.nytimes.com/2009/05/15/opinion/15partnoy.html.

Prometeia (2008). Analisi e previsioni - prezzi delle commodity. Bologna, October.

Sanders DR, Irwin SH and Merrin RP (2008). The adequacy of speculation in agricultural futures markets: Too much of a good thing? Marketing and Outlook Research Report 2008-02. Department of Agriculture and Consumer Economics. University of Illinois at Urbana-Champaign. Forthcoming in *Review of Agricultural Economics*

Svensson LEO (2005). Oil prices and ECB monetary policy. Princeton University. Unpublished. Available at: http://www.princeton.edu/svensson/papers/ ep501.pdf.

Till H (2008). The oil markets: Let the data speak for itself. In: Amenc N, Maffei B and Till H, eds., *Oil Prices: The True Role of Speculation*. Nice, École des Hautes Études Commerciales (EDHEC), Risk and Asset Management Research Centre.

UNCTAD (2006). Overview of the World's Commodity Exchanges. Document no. UNCTAD/DITC/ COM/2005/8, Geneva.

UNCTAD (2007). The development role of commodity exchanges. Document no. TD/B/COM.1/EM.33/2, Geneva.

UNCTAD (2009). The Global Economic Crisis: Systemic Failures and Multilateral Remedies. New York and Geneva, United Nations.

UNCTAD (various issues). *Trade and Development Report*. United Nations publication, New York and Geneva.

von Braun J and Torero M (2008). Physical and virtual global food reserves to protect the poor and prevent market failure. Policy Brief 4, International Food Policy Research Institute, Washington, DC, June.

Chapter III

LEARNING FROM THE CRISIS: POLICIES FOR SAFER AND SOUNDER FINANCIAL SYSTEMS

A. Introduction

The most serious financial crisis since the Great Depression, the de facto nationalization of a large segment of the United States financial system, and the deepest global recession since the Second World War are now casting doubts on assumptions made by a number of economists on the functioning of contemporary finance. Many economists and policymakers believed that securitization and the "originate and distribute" model would increase the resilience of the banking system, that credit default swaps would provide useful hedging opportunities by allocating risk to those that were better equipped to take it, and that technological innovation would increase the efficiency and stability of the financial system. And Alan Greenspan (2003), as Chairman of the Federal Reserve, once stated: "Although the benefits and costs of derivatives remain the subject of spirited debate, the performance of the economy and the financial system in recent years suggests that those benefits have materially exceeded the costs". Events of the past two years warrant a reappraisal of these assumptions.

> Excessive leverage in the years before the crisis could have been prevented if policymakers had been less ideological and more pragmatic.

As discussed in chapter I of this *Report*, a major cause of the financial crisis was the build-up of excessive risk in the financial system over many years, made possible by new financial instruments that obscured debtor-creditor relations. Many new financial instruments that were praised as enhancing financial efficiency were delinked from income generation in the real sector of the economy.

This could largely have been prevented if policymakers had been less ideological and more pragmatic. Policymakers should have been wary of an industry that constantly aims at generating double digit returns in an economy that is growing at a much slower rate (UNCTAD, 2007), especially if that industry needs to be bailed out every decade or so.[1] Because there is much more asymmetric information in financial markets than in goods markets, the former need to be subject to stricter regulations. Inappropriate risk assessment, based on inadequate models, has resulted in lax financial control and encouraged risky financial practices. This suggests that a greater degree of prudence and supervision is necessary, including more regulation – not deregulation as in the past.

The case for reviewing the system of financial governance now seems obvious, and has been made by many leading economists (e.g. Aglietta and

Rigot, 2009; Brunnermeier et al., 2009; Buiter, 2009; Goodhart and Persaud, 2008; Hutton, 2009; Subramanian and Williamson, 2009; and Stiglitz, 2009). It is therefore surprising that the G-20, the intergovernmental forum mandated to promote constructive discussion between industrial and emerging-market economies on key issues related to global economic stability, has paid very little attention so far to the necessary reforms of the financial system. Its recent communiqués highlight several problems with tax havens and offshore centres (which played a minor role, if any, in the build-up of the current crisis), but provide no proposals on how to redesign financial regulation.

Financial markets in several developed countries have come to resemble giant casinos in that a large segment of their activities is entirely detached from real sector activities. The crisis has made it abundantly clear that more finance and more financial products are not always better, and a more sophisticated financial system does not necessarily make a greater contribution to social welfare. On the contrary, several innovative financial products have had negative social returns. Thus, in order to reap the potential benefits of financial innovation, it is necessary to increase the clout and responsibilities of financial regulators.

This chapter seeks to draw lessons for financial regulation from the current financial crisis, which is the deepest and widest since the Great Depression. In addition, it discusses why and how the overall effectiveness of financial regulation will depend on the way in which measures for financial reform at the national level are combined with a reform of the international monetary and financial system – a topic examined in greater detail in chapter IV.

Section B of this chapter briefly discusses to what extent the nature and context of the current financial crisis differ from previous, milder ones. Section C reviews principles that could guide improved regulation and supervision of national financial systems, and examines various types of regulatory measures that could help prevent the occurrence of similar crises in the future. Section D focuses on lessons that developing-country policymakers may draw for their own financial policies from a crisis that originated in the world's financial centre.

B. The current crisis: some new facets, but mostly the same old story

There are certainly some elements that differentiate the current crisis from previous ones. The new elements – which, ironically, were intended to increase the resilience of the financial system – include the "originate and distribute" banking business model, financial derivatives (such as credit default swaps) and the creation of a "shadow" banking system.

However, there are also many elements that are not new. Any student of Kindleberger (1996) or Minsky (1982), would have recognized that, as in previous crises, the roots of the current turmoil lie in a self-reinforcing mechanism whereby high growth and low volatility lead to a decrease in risk aversion and an increase in leverage credit, which in turn leads to higher asset prices. This eventually feeds back into higher profits and growth and even higher risk-taking. The final outcome of this process is the build-up of debt, risk and large imbalances that at some point will unwind. The proximate cause of the crisis may then appear to be some idiosyncratic shock (in the current case, defaults on subprime mortgage loans), but the true cause of the crisis is the build-up of debt and risk during good times. Vulnerabilities linked to regulatory arbitrage, which are at the heart of the current crisis, were not unpredictable and indeed were anticipated by several economists.[2]

The recognition that the current crisis has many common elements with previous crises has important implications for financial regulation and it raises several questions. Why did policymakers make avoidable mistakes? Why did they forget that policymaking should be rooted in pragmatism and not ideology? Why did they disregard the well-known fact that market-based risk indicators (such has high yield spreads or implicit volatility measures) tend to be low at the peak of the credit cycle, precisely when risk is high? (Borio, 2008).

The standard interpretation is that these policy lapses where driven by policymakers' blind faith in market discipline. In that case, the current crisis might lead to a new generation of more pragmatic and less ideological policymakers. According to some commentators, however, the problem is deeper and relates to the fact that the financial industry managed to capture policymaking in a number of important countries, leading policymakers to assume that "what is good for Wall Street is good for the country" (Johnson, 2009).

Arguably, another group of observers who could have been more critical of the faith in free markets when guiding influential policymakers – whether captured by the financial industry or not – is the academic economists. In view of the vast literature and rich empirical evidence on financial markets' proneness to excesses and crises, it is surprising that there was so little challenging of the popular belief in the supposedly unchallengeable wisdom of unfettered market forces. Economic theory teaches that, especially in financial markets, the invisible hand may require guidance and restraint through proper regulation and supervision. And yet, by acting as uncritical cheerleaders, mainstream academic economists, too, have played an important role in propagating the free market faith. As Acemoglu (2008: 4–5) self-critically observes: "... we were in sync with policymakers ... lured by ideological notions derived from Ayn Rand novels rather than

economic theory. And we let their ... rhetoric set the agenda for our thinking and ... for our policy advice".

> Economists and institutions whose views do not fully conform with the orthodoxy are often marginalized, and their policy advice is not taken seriously.

This sobering admission raises a number of important questions concerning, for instance, incentive structures in academia, and mechanisms for selecting and channelling expert policy advice. Society may not be well served by incentive structures in academic research institutions (often sponsored by the tax-payer) which marginalize views that do not conform to the mainstream (Eichengreen, 2009). Furthermore, and as the current crisis also highlights, there are risks to society if policy advice is effectively monopolized by propagators of the mainstream view, and if policy-shaping debates take place in a sterile environment of convergent and homogeneous views. This has also been recognized by the United States Congressional Oversight Panel:

> Government, industry, Wall Street, and academia typically employ economists with similar training and backgrounds to create their forecast, leading to optimism and convergence of economic forecasts ... A Financial Risk Council composed of strong divergent voices should avoid overly optimistic consensus and conventional wisdom, keeping Congress appropriately concerned and energized about known and unknown risks in a complex, highly interactive environment.
>
> Congressional Oversight Panel, 2009: 47–48.

The importance of creating a forum comprising economists with different backgrounds and approaches cannot be overstated. For instance, the International Monetary Fund (IMF, 2009) argues that policymakers were not ready for the crisis because "warnings provided by official bodies before the crisis were too scattered and unspecific". It has proposed a joint IMF-Financial Stability Forum to provide "early warnings" (IMF, 2009). However, it is at least debatable as to whether such an arrangement would ensure a healthier and more objective debate than before, since past experience suggests that it would bring together only those economists that hold the mainstream view. Instead, in order to meet the challenge posed by the Congressional Oversight Panel cited above, a wiser step may be to entrust the role of vigilant observers that provide early warnings to a more diverse body. One such body would be the Commission of Experts of the President of the United Nations General Assembly on Reforms of the International Monetary and Financial System (often referred to as the Stiglitz Commission), which is composed of economists of far more diverse backgrounds and views.

C. How to deal with the fragility of the modern financial system

---

According to Christopher Cox, Chairman of the United States Securities and Exchange Commission, it has become "abundantly clear that voluntary regulation does not work".[3]

The financial sector acts like the central nervous system of modern market economies. In principle, its function is to mobilize the capital necessary to finance large investment projects, to allocate funds to the most dynamic sectors of the economy, and, through its payments system, to enable management of the complex web of economic relationships that are necessary for economies characterized by a high degree of division and specialization of labour. However, it does not always fulfil these functions properly.

An effective financial system is essential for economic development, but the presence of informational asymmetries, high leverage and maturity mismatches render financial systems unstable and prone to boom and bust cycles. Consequently, almost every country has detailed legislation aimed at regulating the domestic financial sector.

However, there are several problems with modern financial regulation. The most fundamental of these is the assumption that "markets know best" and that regulators should not try to second-guess them. As noted by Stiglitz (2009: 5), "If government appoints as regulators those who do not believe in regulation, one is not likely to get strong enforcement".

1. Defining and measuring efficiency

The ultimate objective of financial regulation should be the creation of a sound and efficient financial system. There are, however, several possible definitions of an efficient financial system (Tobin, 1984; Buiter, 2009), each of which has different welfare implications. Therefore, the design of a properly functioning regulatory system aimed at maximizing social welfare requires a clear understanding of these different definitions:

- *Information arbitrage efficiency* relates to the price formation process. In an information efficient market, prices reflect all available information. Without insider information, it is impossible to earn returns that constantly beat the market.

- *Fundamental valuation efficiency* refers to a situation in which the price of a financial asset is determined entirely by the expected present value of the future stream of payments generated by that asset. This definition of efficiency rules out bubbles or price volatility not justified by changes in fundamentals.

- *Full insurance efficiency* refers to market completeness. According to this definition, a market is efficient if it can produce insurance contracts that cover all possible events.

- *Transactional (or technical) efficiency* refers to the market's ability to process a large number of transactions at a low cost, and the ability to trade large amounts of a given security without causing large changes in the price of that security. For instance, markets with low bid-ask spreads are more transactionally efficient than markets characterized by high bid-ask spreads, and so are more liquid and deeper.

- *Functional or social efficiency* relates to the value added of the financial industry from a social point of view. This boils down to the financial sector's contribution to consumption smoothing and long-run economic growth. Financial markets can be characterized by low transaction costs, they can provide many different products, and they can do a decent job of evaluating all available information. However, if they do not contribute to long-term economic growth or stability, they will not provide any social return.

From a regulator's point of view, social efficiency should be the only relevant definition of financial efficiency. The other definitions of efficiency should be of concern to regulators only to the extent that they contribute to functional efficiency. In some cases, high transactional efficiency may even encourage speculative movements and eventually conflict with social or functional efficiency.

In discussing the status of the United States financial system in the early 1980s, Tobin (1984) concluded that markets were becoming more transactionally efficient but less functionally efficient. In his view, the United States financial market was increasingly resembling a casino, where gambling dominated activities with true social returns:

> [T]he process of deregulation should be viewed neither as a routine application of free market philosophy nor as a treaty among conflicting sectoral interests. Rather it should be guided by sober pragmatic consideration of what we can reasonably expect the financial system to achieve and at what social cost ... [W]e are throwing more and more of our resources, including the cream of our youth, into financial activities remote from the production of goods and services, into activities that generate high private rewards disproportionate to their social productivity.
>
> Tobin, 1984: 294.

Tobin's early assessment is corroborated by the fact that the United States financial system managed to completely decapitalize itself and had to be bailed out three times in three decades. In the light of the ongoing financial crisis, the notion of transactional efficiency also deserves to be re-examined. Financial expansion was based largely on huge amounts of unnecessary financial transactions, and on the creation of opaque financial instruments and a shadow financial system. However, on each transaction, even if economically redundant, financial institutions earned a commission.

Thus, financial expansion must be prevented from becoming an end in itself, through public regulation to ensure social efficiency. However, there is very little agreement on this view. Some observers even maintain that the present crisis has resulted from excessive regulation, not from a lack of it. They argue that with less stringent rules for commercial banks, the incentive for regulatory arbitrage would have been weaker. Moreover, several influential economists and policymakers maintain that the deregulated and super-sophisticated United States financial system succeeded in delivering the goods in terms of high GDP growth. According to this view, crises – and the associated public bailouts – are a necessary price to pay for having a financial system that promotes entrepreneurship and leads to high growth (Rancière, Tornell and Westermann, 2008).

Therefore, the ultimate test of social efficiency has to do with the relationship between financial development and long-term economic growth. There is a large body of empirical literature which shows that finance (measured by the size of the financial system) does indeed play a positive role in promoting economic development (Levine, 2005). The idea that financial development may cause decreasing social returns is hardly new (Kindleberger, 1996; Minsky, 1982; Tobin, 1984; Van Horne, 1985; Rajan, 2005), and Panizza (2009) has conducted a test to examine whether there can even be such a thing as too much finance. His analysis corroborates the standard result that the size of the financial sector has a positive impact on economic growth, but it also shows that there are decreasing returns to expanding the financial sector beyond a certain point, and that such returns can become negative for countries with a large financial sector. Econometric estimations suggest that returns become negative when credit to the private sector reaches 70–80 per cent of GDP (chart 3.1).[4] Another question, which has important implications for recommendations on how to manage financial systems, relates to the activities that are actually financed. "More" finance does not always mean more investment or faster growth and development. Many financial reforms aimed at "financial deepening" in developing and transition economies did not deliver on their promise of sustainable credit expansion to the private sector, greater availability of investment credit for firms and smaller interest spreads (*TDR 2008,* chap. IV). This points to the importance of considering not only the amount but also the quality of finance in the design and management of a financial system.

> Social return should be the only relevant criterion for efficiency of the financial system.

2. *Avoiding gambling*

A standard assumption behind most regulatory systems is that all financial products can potentially increase social welfare. The only problem is that some products may increase risk and reduce transparency. If these issues could be addressed, the argument goes, more financial innovation would always be beneficial from the social point of view. This assumption is wrong. Some financial instruments can generate high private returns but have no social utility whatsoever. They are purely gambling instruments that increase risk without providing any real benefit to society. They may be transactionally and informationally efficient, but they are not functionally efficient.

Policymakers should not prevent or hinder financial innovation as a matter of principle. However, they should be aware that some types of financial instruments are created with the sole objective of eluding regulation or increasing leverage. Financial regulation should therefore aim at avoiding the proliferation of such instruments. A positive step in this direction could be achieved with the creation of a financial products safety commission which would evaluate whether new financial products could be traded or held by regulated financial institutions (Stiglitz, 2009). Such an agency might also provide incentives to create standardized financial products that are more easily understood by market participants, thus increasing the overall transparency of the financial market.

In some cases it will be easy to identify products which provide no real service besides the ability to gamble and increase leverage. For instance, credit default swaps (CDSs) are supposed to provide hedging services. But when the issuance of CDSs reaches 10 times the risk to be hedged (see section C.4), it becomes clear that 90 per cent of those CDSs do not provide any hedging service; they are used for gambling, not insurance, purposes.[5] This is why there is need for regulations that limit the issuance of CDSs to the amount of the underlying risk and prohibit other types of financial instruments that are conducive to gambling. Such regulation is consistent with the notion that purchasers of insurance contracts have an

Chart 3.1

CORRELATION BETWEEN FINANCIAL DEVELOPMENT AND GDP GROWTH

(Per cent)

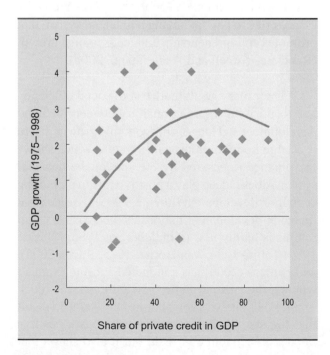

Source: Panizza, 2009.

insurable interest in the event for which they buy the insurance. Accordingly, there are laws, for example, against homeowners overinsuring their houses and laws against individuals buying life insurance contracts for unrelated persons.

Deciding on the legitimacy of the financial instruments will not always be easy. For financial instruments that provide both real and gambling services, regulators will need to evaluate the costs and benefits of each product and only allow instruments for which the benefits outweigh the costs. Other instruments may have high potential social returns but may also increase risk and opaqueness.[6] Therefore, they should be properly regulated and monitored. Of course, tighter regulations will have a negative effect on financial innovation (regulations would not be effective if they did not), and in some cases may prevent the adoption of useful financial instruments. But there is almost no evidence that financial innovation has a positive impact on economic development, and there is substantial evidence that financial innovation is often motivated by the desire to evade taxes or elude regulation (Crotty and Epstein, 2009).

In general, choices will not be easy. They will require value judgments and could easily backfire. However, this applies to all policy decisions. The way out may be to follow the "precautionary" principle and examine the usefulness and potential risks of any product before it is allowed to be offered to consumers: what applies to potentially toxic drugs and food should also be applied to "toxic financial products". The decision not to take any action is a regulatory action in itself, and uncertainty cannot be used as an excuse for not introducing regulation.

3. Avoiding regulatory arbitrage

Poorly designed regulation can backfire and lead to regulatory arbitrage. This is what happened with banking regulation.

Usually, banks take more risk by increasing their leverage, and modern prudential regulation revolves around the Basel Accords which require banks with

> Some financial instruments have no social utility whatsoever.

an international presence to hold a first-tier capital amount equal to 8 per cent of risk-weighted assets. Regulation has been effective in increasing the measured capital ratio of commercial banks. Over the past 25 years, the 10 largest United States banks have substantially decreased their leverage (chart 3.2), going from a non-risk-adjusted first-tier capital ratio of approximately 4.5 per cent (which corresponds to a leverage of 22), to a non-risk-adjusted first-tier capital ratio of approximately 8 per cent (which corresponds to a leverage of 12.5).[7]

Since capital is costly, bank managers have tried to circumvent regulation by either hiding risk or moving some leverage outside their bank. Indeed, the decrease in the leverage ratio of commercial banks

Chart 3.2

LEVERAGE OF TOP 10 UNITED STATES FINANCIAL FIRMS, BY TYPE OF ACTIVITY, 1981–2008

(Per cent)

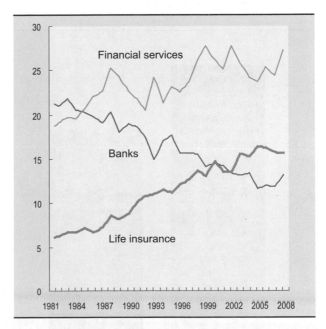

Source: UNCTAD secretariat calculations, based on balance sheet data from Thomson Datastream.
Note: Leverage ratio measured as a share of shareholders' equity in total assets. Data refer to four-quarter-moving averages.

has been accompanied by an increase in leverage ratios of non-bank financial institutions (chart 3.2). Thus bank regulation has pushed leverage to other parts of the financial sector – a classic case of regulatory arbitrage (Furlong and Keeley, 1989; Rochet, 1992; Jones, 2000).

This shifting of leverage has created a "shadow banking system" (a term coined by Paul McCulley of Pacific Investment Management Company). It consists of over-the-counter (OTC) derivatives, off-balance-sheet entities, and other non-bank financial institutions such as insurance companies, hedge funds and private equity funds. These new players can replicate the maturity transformation role of banks while escaping normal bank regulation. At its peak, the United States shadow banking system held assets of approximately $16.15 trillion, about $4 trillion more than regulated deposit-taking banks (chart 3.3).

Chart 3.3

SIZE OF THE BANKING SYSTEM AND THE SHADOW BANKING SYSTEM IN THE UNITED STATES, 2007 (2nd QUARTER)

(Trillions of dollars of assets)

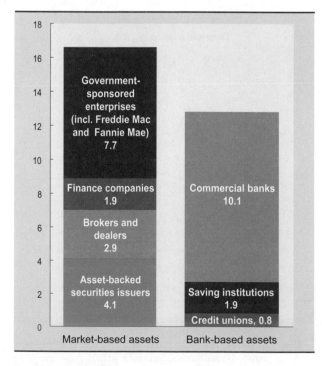

Source: Shin, 2009.

Regulators did not seem too worried by this shift in leverage because they assumed that, unlike deposit taking banks, the collapse of large non-bank institutions would not have systemic effects.[8] The working hypothesis was that securitization had contributed to both diversifying and allocating risk to sophisticated economic agents who could bear such risk. Consequently, they believed that the system could now take a higher level of total risk. The experience with structured investment vehicles (SIVs) shows the flaws in this line of reasoning (UNCTAD, 2007). While regulation focused on banks, it was the collapse of the shadow banking system which kick-started the current crisis and eventually hit the banking system as well.

In order to avoid regulatory arbitrage, banks and the capital market need to be regulated jointly, and financial institutions should be supervised on the basis of fully consolidated balance sheets (Issing et al., 2008). All markets and providers of financial products should be overseen on the basis of the risk they produce. If an investment bank issues insurance contracts like CDSs, this activity should be subject to the same regulation that applies to insurance companies. If an insurance company is involved in maturity transformation, it should be regulated like a bank (Congressional Oversight Panel, 2009).

4. Can securitization reduce risk?

The originate and distribute model – a process in which banks originate loans then sell them, packaged into different types of securities, to a wide range of investors – was supposed to increase the resilience of the financial system and isolate banks from costly defaults. It was also endorsed by the IMF:

> There is growing recognition that the dispersion of credit risk by banks to a broader and more diverse group of investors … has helped make the banking and overall financial system more resilient … commercial banks may be less vulnerable today to credit or economic shocks.
>
> IMF, 2006: 51.

The Bank for International Settlements (BIS) was more sceptical about the merits of the new model:

Assuming that the big banks have managed to distribute more widely the risks inherent in the loans they have made, who now holds these risks, and can they manage them adequately? The honest answer is that we do not know.

BIS, 2007: 145.

Indeed, securitization did not deliver as expected for several reasons (for a detailed discussion, see UNCTAD, 2007). First, banks entered the game because a regulatory loophole allowed them to buy structured products and increase leverage through lightly regulated conduits. Second, as banks are likely to be more careful in evaluating risk when they plan to keep a loan on their books, securitization led to the deterioration of credit quality.[9] Third, securitization increased the opaqueness of the financial system, leading to a situation characterized by "Knightian uncertainty" (i.e. where risk is unknown and cannot be modelled with standard probability distributions) in which nobody is willing to lend because nobody knows who holds the risk. Fourth, most investors in the collateralized debt obligations (CDOs) market were of the "buy-and-hold" type. This resulted in low market turnover and no price discovery. Instruments were valued based on theoretical models rather than on market prices. Securitization offered the law of large numbers as a compensation mechanism for the loss of soft information built into traditional lending.[10] However, the assumptions underlying these models were often flawed. Some assumptions were plainly wrong: for example, some rating agencies had models which assumed that real estate prices could only increase (Coval, Jurek and Stafford 2008). Others were more subtly incorrect, but even more dangerous.

Among the latter was the assumption that the risk associated with each debt contract packaged in a CDO was either *uncorrelated* or had a simple correlation structure (the so-called Gaussian cupola), with the risks of the other debt contracts included in the same CDO (box 3.1). These assumptions tend to work well in normal times. However, in bad times things work differently, because asset prices tend to collapse at the same time, and small mistakes in measuring the joint distribution of asset returns may lead to large errors in evaluating the risk of a CDO.[11] These problems are compounded by the fact that all models used in the financial industry use historical data to assess risk. But, by definition, historical data do not contain information on the behaviour of new financial instruments.

Another problem with standard models of risk is that they do not control for *counterparty risk* (i.e. the risk that one of the counterparties will not deliver on its contractual obligations), which is especially important for insurance and futures contracts. Several financial institutions are both buyers and sellers of risk, and gross exposure to risk is often much higher than the actual underlying risk. Even in a situation in which all parties are fully hedged, the presence of counterparty risk amplifies uncertainty, leading to a situation in which instruments that are supposed to diffuse risk end up increasing systemic fragility (Brunnermeier, 2008). For instance, the gross exposure from CDS in the United States market is about 10 times the net exposure (chart 3.4), and counterparty risk played a key role in the panic that followed Lehman Brothers' bankruptcy in September 2008. Moreover, this was the main reason for the bailout of giant insurer – American International Group (AIG) (Crotty and Epstein, 2009).

Transparency could be increased by creating a clearing house that can net the various positions (Segoviano and Singh, 2008) or by moving from OTC trading to organized exchanges.[12] The United States Administration seems to favour this latter line of action. In mid-May 2009, the United States Treasury unveiled a proposal aimed at encouraging regulated institutions to make greater use of exchange-traded derivatives. While this proposal goes in the right direction, it may end up being too timid because, by only "encouraging" the use of organized exchanges (or by limiting the requirement to operate on organized exchanges to standardized derivatives), it may lead to a substantial amount of trading remaining in opaque OTC markets. Indeed, the proposal may even end up being counterproductive, as research indicates that if only some derivatives are traded in organized markets, the risk of derivatives traded in OTC markets could increase, and so could total systemic risk (Duffie and Zhu, 2009).[13] Alternatively, it would be possible to prohibit the excessive use of CDSs by preventing the gross notional value of a CDS contract from exceeding its net notional value. This would still allow hedging, but limit gambling.

Box 3.1

COLLATERALIZED DEBT OBLIGATIONS AND CREDIT DEFAULT SWAPS

Two instruments at the centre of the current crisis are collateralized debt obligations (CDOs) and credit defaults swaps (CDSs).

COLLATERALIZED DEBT OBLIGATIONS[a]

A CDO is a structured financial product which is supposedly able to take risky financial instruments and transform them into less risky instruments. This transformation of risk is achieved through a two-step procedure involving pooling and tranching.

In the first step – pooling – a large number of assets (e.g. mortgages) are assembled into a debt instrument. Such a debt instrument can achieve risk diversification if the payoffs from the underlying securities are negatively correlated with each other. However, the new debt instrument cannot reduce risk to any great extent because the expected payoff of the whole portfolio is the same as the expected payoff of the underlying securities. Thus the credit rating of this new instrument would be similar to the average credit rating of the underlying securities. Therefore, there is no credit enhancement with pooling.

It is the second step – tranching – that produces credit enhancement. With tranching, the original debt instrument is divided into segments (tranches), which are prioritized according to the way they absorb losses from the original portfolio. For instance, CDOs are usually divided into three tranches. The bottom tranche (often referred to as "equity" or toxic waste) takes the first losses, the middle tranche starts absorbing losses after the bottom tranche is completely exhausted, and the top tranche starts taking losses only after the middle tranche is exhausted.

With this mechanism, it is possible to start with a pool of assets that are not investment grade and transform part of them into investment grade tranches of CDOs. The process does not necessarily stop here. By tranching the equity tranche of a regular CDO, asset managers can generate CDO-squared, which extracts AAA assets from the toxic waste component of the original CDO. In 2007, about 60 per cent of structured products were AAA-rated, while only about 1 per cent of corporate bonds received that rating (Coval, Jurek and Stafford, 2008).

This transformation of risk has several advantages for the issuer because sub-investment grade assets have a high capital charge for regulated commercial banks and cannot be held by institutional investors. It is not surprising that the market for CDOs grew exponentially, from issuances of $25 billion per quarter at the beginning of 2005 to issuances of $100 billion per quarter at the beginning of 2007 (Coval, Jurek and Stafford, 2008).

However, investors and regulators alike did not seem to understand that risk enhancement came at the price of transforming diversifiable risk into concentrated risk, which is strongly correlated with overall economic performance. Moreover, rating a CDO is more complex than rating a single name debt instrument because it requires knowledge of both the average probability of default of the various instruments included in the pool and the correlation between these probabilities of default. In other words, it requires knowledge of the joint distribution of the payoffs of the various instruments included in the CDO. Small mistakes in estimating such distribution (which are almost irrelevant in the rating of single debt instruments) can lead to large rating errors, which are compounded in CDO-squared.

Even if agencies improve their rating process, investors should be aware that the type of risk associated with a CDO is different from that of a single debt instrument and thus the same rating may mean completely different things. It may thus be appropriate to create a rating category that only concentrates on structured financial products.

CREDIT DEFAULT SWAPS

Most debt securities have two types of risks: interest rate risk and default risk. A CDS allows swapping the second type of risk to the insurer (this is why CDSs are also called swaps). In a typical CDS contract, those who buy insurance pay a premium, which should be equal to the probability of default times the notional amount of the CDS. This seems an efficient way of hedging one type of risk, which is why CDSs became very popular in 2006–2007: at their peak, they reached a notional amount of almost $60 trillion.

Box 3.1 (concluded)

However, there are two problems with CDSs. First, in order to buy a CDS on a given security, investors do not need to hold the security. Most CDSs were bought by people who were betting on the fortune of a given security, and not by investors who needed to hedge a certain exposure to risk. In fact, there seemed to be betting over betting, with gross exposure of a CDS being about 10 times its net exposure. As a result, nobody knew who was insured against or exposed to any type of risk. Second, while the insurance industry is regulated, CDSs are not. In the United States, regulation of these instruments is blocked by a measure inserted into an appropriations bill of December 2000. While insurance companies have rules limiting how much insurance they can sell, there is no limit on a financial institution's issuing of CDSs. Thus investment banks moved to the insurance business, which soon started looking more and more like a gambling business (Stiglitz, 2009).

When some insured securities started defaulting, sellers of CDSs realized that they could incur large losses which they had not provisioned against. This increased the risk that sellers of insurance would not be able to deliver on their obligations, and investors that felt hedged suddenly realized that they were exposed to risk. Rather than reducing uncertainty, CDSs ended up increasing uncertainty.

---

[a] The discussion of CDOs draws on Coval, Jurek and Stafford (2008).

Chart 3.4

OUTSTANDING CREDIT DEFAULT SWAPS, GROSS AND NET NOTIONAL AMOUNTS, OCTOBER 2008–MAY 2009

(Trillions of dollars)

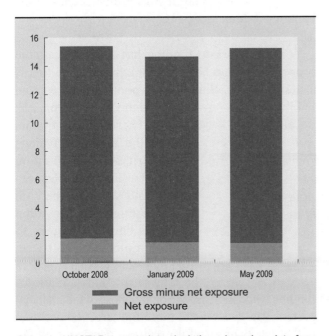

Source: UNCTAD secretariat calculations, based on data from the Depository Trust and Clearing Corporation.

5. Strengthening regulation

The current regulatory framework assumes that policies aimed at guaranteeing the soundness of individual banks can also guarantee the soundness of the whole banking system (Nugée and Persaud, 2006). This is problematic, because there are instances where actions that are prudent for an individual institution have negative systemic implications. Consider the case of a bank that suffers large losses on some of its loans. The prudent choice for this bank is to reduce its lending activities and cut its assets to a level in line with its smaller capital base. If the bank in question is small, the system will be able to absorb this reduction in lending. On the other hand, if the bank in question is large, or the losses affect several banks at the same time, the individual bank's attempt to rebuild its capital base will drain liquidity from the system. Less lending by some banks will translate into less funding to other banks, which, if other sources of liquidity are not found, might be forced to cut lending and thus amplify the deleveraging process. As a consequence, a bank's attempt to do what is prudent from its own point of view (i.e. maintain an adequate capital ratio) may end up causing problems for other banks, with negative effects on the banking system as a whole.

Another channel through which the current regulatory system may have a negative systemic impact relates to mark-to-market accounting, according to which banks need to value some assets by using their current market price. Consider again the example of a large bank that realizes losses and needs to reduce its risk exposure. Presumably, this bank will sell some of its assets and thus depress their price. This will lead to mark-to-market losses for banks that hold the same types of assets. If these losses are large enough to make capital requirements binding, the affected banks will also need to reduce their exposure. If they start selling assets, they will amplify the deleveraging process. As the opposite happens in boom periods, this mechanism leads to leverage cycles.

From this, it becomes clear that some of the assumptions that form the basis of the Basel Accords are questionable. Risk-weighted capital ratios impose high capital charges on high-risk assets and low capital charges on low-risk assets. This can increase systemic risk and amplify the leverage cycle, because during good times some assets will be deemed to be less risky than they actually are, and during bad times the same assets might be considered more risky than they are. Required capital ratios will end up being too low in good times and too high in bad times.

Moreover, relatively safe assets have the highest systemic risk. This argument, which may seem paradoxical, can be illustrated by thinking about a continuum of debt securities, going from super-safe assets (e.g. AAA government bonds) to high-risk junk bonds, and then imagining which assets are more likely to be downgraded if a systemic crisis were to happen. These are most likely to be the relatively safe assets, such as AAA-rated tranches of CDOs, rather than either the super-safe ones (because of flight to quality) or the high-risk ones (because they cannot be downgraded by much). But these are the assets that had low regulatory capital during the boom period, and, because of the downgrade, need larger regulatory capital in the crisis period (Brunnermeier et al., 2009).

> What may be prudent for one bank may cause problems for other banks.

> Risk-weighted capital ratios can amplify the leverage cycle.

As mark-to-market accounting plays a role in amplifying the leverage cycle (Plantin, Sapra and Shin, 2005), representatives of the financial industry have suggested that this form of accounting should be suspended during periods of crisis (Dallara, 2008).

This seems contradictory: on the one hand, the financial industry praises the market-discovery role of securitization and asks for light regulation; on the other hand, it argues that the "discovered" price may sometimes be too low.

An interesting proposal that would contribute to enhancing systemic stability without giving the financial industry a free lunch is "mark-to-funding" (Persaud, 2008). The basic idea is that assets should be valued on the basis of a bank's need to roll over the funding of its assets, and not on the basis of the bank's own idea of how long the assets will be held in its books. If the purchase of an asset is funded with a six-month loan, the financial institution should value the asset by concentrating on the expected price of the asset in six months' time. After all, it is then that the bank will either be able to roll over its debt or will have to sell the asset. If a bank funds its activities with overnight loans, mark-to-funding will be identical to mark-to-market. According to Persaud (2008), besides having the potential for reducing procyclicality, mark-to-funding could also provide incentives for reducing maturity mismatches in the banking system.

While mark-to-funding has several desirable properties, it also has some drawbacks. The first is a practical one. Since banks pool their assets and liabilities, mark-to-funding cannot be implemented on an asset-by-asset basis. Therefore, regulators need to find a way to average the maturity of both funding and assets. This complex exercise could stimulate the viral nature of financial innovation and lead bank managers to adopt complicated short-term funding strategies that appear to be long-term. Hence, mark-to-funding could increase the opaqueness of the financial system. The second and more fundamental problem is that banks are useful precisely because they are involved in a process of maturity transformation.

This is why the idea of narrow banks (Simons, 1948) never gained much traction: it would be dangerous if a mark-to-funding system were to eliminate the maturity transformation role of banks.

6. Implementing macro-prudential regulation

> The time for economy and for accumulation is before [the crisis]. A good banker will have accumulated in ordinary times the reserve he is to make use of in extraordinary times.
>
> Bagehot, 1873.

Most crises occur because financial institutions have similar vulnerabilities and are exposed to similar types of shocks. It is thus necessary to understand how these vulnerabilities grow over time, and to complement micro-prudential regulation with macro-prudential policies aimed at building up cushions during good times, rather than reducing liquidity during periods of crisis.

Borio (2003) provides a lucid discussion of the differences between micro- and macro-prudential regulation. The ultimate objective of micro-prudential regulation is to protect depositors, whereas the ultimate objective of macro-prudential regulation is to guarantee the stability of the system and avoid large output losses. Micro-prudential regulation is based on a model of exogenous risk, while macro-prudential regulation assumes that the risk is endogenous with respect to the behaviour of the financial system. Moreover, the correlation and common exposure across financial institutions, which is irrelevant for micro-prudential regulation, is fundamental for macro-prudential regulation.

Macro-prudential regulation should focus on both the *cross-sectional* and the *time* dimension of risk (Borio, 2003). For the former, regulators should internalize regulatory arbitrage and be aware that both banks and non-bank financial institutions can be a source of systemic risk. The key consideration for macro-prudential regulation is each institution's

contribution to systemic risk. Other things being equal, larger institutions should be subject to a heavier regulatory burden than smaller institutions: if institutions are "too big to fail", they are also too big to be saved, and are probably too big to exist (Subramanian and Williamson, 2009). However, size is not a sufficient indicator, because many small institutions which are subject to correlated risk may have the same systemic importance as large institutions. Regulators should also be concerned about leverage, maturity transformation, provision of essential services (such as payment or market-making) and interconnectedness.[14]

The time dimension of risk can be assessed by establishing early warning systems, and recognizing that booms (and the subsequent crashes) are fuelled by imprudent lending and high leverage stemming from the perception that risk has permanently lowered. Vulnerabilities can be attenuated by building buffers of capital in good times and reducing them in periods of crisis. Such countercyclical provisioning would also smoothen the leverage cycle (Goodhart and Persaud, 2008).

Some policymakers have argued against such "leaning against the wind" policies. They suggest that, rather than second-guessing the market, it is better to wait for the crisis and clean up the mess later. This view appears wrong for at least two reasons. First, the current crisis shows that cleaning up the mess is neither easy nor cheap. Second, anticipating vulnerabilities (or second-guessing the market) is not so difficult if one has a medium-term horizon. Borio and Drehmann (2008) and Borio and Lowe (2002) show that three simple early warning indicators based on real-time data (i.e. information that is available at the time the predictions need to be made) perform well in forecasting episodes of financial distress with a lead of up to four years. These indicators are: credit growth that is 6 per cent above its long-run trend, equity prices that are 60 per cent above their long-run trend, and real estate prices that are between 15 and 25 per cent above their long-run trend.

Another advantage of a system of countercyclical provisioning (or dynamic provisioning) is that it could be implemented as an automatic stabilizer.

> Anticipating vulnerabilities in the medium-term is not so difficult.

There are important political economy considerations that support the idea of a non-discretionary regulatory system. The seeds of a financial crisis are planted during boom periods, but it is precisely during booms that political support for regulation reaches its lowest point. Regulators endowed with large discretionary power may thus face pressure to adopt lax standards during periods of rapid credit expansion. A simple rule that relates capital standards to growth in credit or asset prices would protect regulators from such pressure (Brunnermeier et al., 2009).

7. Enhancing international coordination

Regulatory arbitrage not only applies to institutions within a jurisdiction, but also extends across jurisdictions.[15] It is therefore necessary to add an international dimension to financial regulation.

As a minimum, regulators based in different countries should communicate and share information. At this stage, it is impossible to implement a global early warning system because there are no data for either cross-border exposures among banks or derivative products (Issing and Krahnen, 2009). Regulators should work together towards developing joint systems for the evaluation of cross-border systemic risk, and share information on liquidity and currency mismatches in the various national markets. But international cooperation needs to go beyond sharing information. It needs to focus on regulatory standards, and ensuring that financial regulation by countries avoids a race to the bottom. Without international coordination, authorities in some countries may believe that they can turn their countries into international financial centres by deregulating their markets. Indeed, some authorities are even reluctant to share data on cross-border exposure because they think that greater transparency may have a negative effect on the competitiveness of their domestic financial sector (Issing and Krahnen, 2009). This position is wrong: investors want transparency and proper regulation. A race to the bottom may end up being a negative sum game and reduce the efficiency and the size of the world's financial system (Stiglitz, 2009).

Cooperation among regulators should work towards a uniform application and enforcement of regulatory standards (Group of 30, 2009) and should focus on closing regulatory gaps.

Regulators should also coordinate oversight of large international banking organizations and add clarity to the responsibilities of home and host countries (Group of 30, 2009; Issing et al., 2008). Formal agreements are especially important at times of crisis, because in normal times regulators tend to cooperate and share information on an informal basis. However, crises often lead to jurisdictional conflicts which make cooperation more difficult.

Subramanian and Williamson (2009) suggest that the host country should focus on macro-prudential regulation and the home country on micro-prudential regulation. Such division of responsibilities makes sense, because macro-shocks are often country-specific and micro-prudential rules tend to be more homogeneous. But again, whereas such allocation of responsibilities can be optimal in normal times, it can generate tensions at times of crisis, especially if the home country experiences large macroeconomic shocks. There is evidence that foreign affiliates play a stabilizing role for shocks that originate in the host country, but may propagate shocks that originate in the home country (Galindo, Micco and Powell, 2005).

While international coordination is certainly called for, it would not be wise to impose a single, common regulatory standard on all countries. There is no "one-size fits-all" model for the financial system, nor can there be any single regulatory system that is right for all economies. Countries at different levels of development, and with varying regulatory capacity and history need to adopt regulatory approaches that are in line with their specific needs and circumstances. International coordination could help prevent regulatory arbitrage across countries from remaining a source of instability in international financial relations. Competition among countries for – in most cases wrongly perceived – advantages from regulatory arbitrage tends to lead to a "race to the bottom", with negative consequences for financial and economic stability in all countries. The scope for regulatory arbitrage could also be significantly

> International coordination is important for minimizing the risk of regulatory arbitrage, but ...

reduced through reforms in international monetary and financial governance, as discussed in chapter IV of this *Report*. On the other hand, allowing countries to experiment with alternative regulatory approaches can provide regulators with a better understanding of the trade-offs of different regulatory models (Pistor, 2009). A better appreciation of these different needs and approaches could be achieved by increasing the participation of developing countries in the various standard setting bodies and international agencies responsible for guaranteeing international financial stability.

> ... there is no single regulatory system which is right for all countries.

At present, the responsibility for guaranteeing international financial stability rests with the IMF, the Basel Committee on Banking Supervision (BCBS), and the Financial Stability Forum (FSF, recently renamed Financial Stability Board). However, the problem is that these institutions not only have similar views but they also lack representation. The IMF has nearly universal membership, but its governance structure gives disproportionate power to developed countries. The BCBS (which is in charge of designing and implementing the Basel Capital Accords) comprises 20 countries, of which only 6 are developing countries or transition economies (Brazil, China, India, Mexico, the Republic of Korea, and the Russian Federation).[16] The full membership of the FSF consists of 12 high-income countries or territories (including Hong Kong, Special Administrative Region of China; and Singapore).

The G-20 summit in April 2009 enumerated several steps for making these institutions and forums more inclusive and representative. For instance, it supported reforms of the IMF's governance structure and procedures for electing its Managing Director, and it replaced the FSF with the Financial Stability Board (FSB) which will now comprise all G-20 countries (including 10 developing and transition economies).

While these are important steps in the right direction, the fact remains that most developing countries are still excluded from these agenda-setting bodies. Moreover, even after the reforms agreed by the G-20, the IMF and other agencies are still dominated by mainstream economic thinking which failed

miserably in predicting the current crisis.[17] These bodies and institutions need to be made more representative, not only in terms of membership but also in terms of the views of their various members. These deficiencies need to be addressed first, before the international community worries about procedures aimed at ensuring that the analyses and recommendations of these supervisory bodies are translated into action.

8. Financial regulation and incentives

In many countries, financial regulation (and deregulation) rests on the idea that bank managers would not do anything that would prejudice the long-term value of their firms (see, for example, Greenspan, 2003). With the benefit of hindsight, it is now clear that this idea is fundamentally flawed. Economists and policymakers have always been aware that managers' incentives are not aligned with those of shareholders, but they have operated on the assumption that, because of their reputation capital, long-lived institutions could be trusted to monitor themselves. However, large corporations are composed of individuals who always respond to their own private incentives, and those who are in charge of risk control are subject to the same types of incentives that dictate the behaviour of investment officers (Acemoglu, 2008). In most cases, risk officers who are too persistent in ringing bells and blowing whistles are either isolated or fired (Lo, 2008; Devine, 1997).

In fact, even self-interested individuals who spot potential profit opportunities driven by an episode of collective market irrationality may find it difficult to swim against the tide. If an episode of "irrational exuberance" lasts too long, investment managers who buck the trend will underperform and be likely to lose their clients and jobs. Lamont and Thaler (2003) have shown that long-lasting deviations from fundamental asset values are made possible by the fact that very few investors try to fight the trend. It is not surprising that one of the mottos of the financial industry is: "the trend is your friend".

Box 3.2

REALIGNING INCENTIVES IN THE CREDIT RATING INDUSTRY

The misalignment of incentives in the credit rating industry has generated two types of reactions. Some economists and policymakers take a radical view, suggesting that the regulatory use of ratings should be eliminated (Portes, 2008), and that market-based discipline is sufficient to guarantee the stability of the financial system (Calomiris, 2009). Others argue that eliminating the regulatory role of credit rating agencies is equivalent to throwing the baby out with the bath water. Those who share this view acknowledge the potentially useful role of credit rating agencies for regulatory purposes (Group of 30, 2009), and recognize that market-based discipline does not always work well, especially if the ultimate risk is not borne by those (e.g. asset managers) who choose the composition of a given portfolio of assets.

According to those who support the second view, problems linked to unjustified high ratings could be allayed by developing payment models which provide better incentives for truthful ratings. One possibility would be to return to investor-paid ratings financed through a transaction tax. A more radical proposal is to transform the agencies into public institutions since they provide a public good (Aglietta and Rigot, 2009). These institutions would need to be fully independent (as are many central banks) in order to avoid conflicts of interests in the rating of sovereign and quasi-sovereign entities. A less radical form of intervention is to subject rating agencies to regulatory oversight and regularly publish their rating performance (Issing et al., 2008).

A feasible and market-friendly way to provide the rating industry with the right incentives would be to require issuers who want to have their instruments listed in a given exchange to pay a listing fee (possibly based on the complexity of the instrument), which would then be used to hire a credit rating agency. If the securities are not traded, the same mechanism could be applied by clearing houses or central depositaries (Mathis, McAndrews and Rochet, 2008). Such a procedure would break the commercial link between the issuer and the rating agency, and eliminate the conflict of interest that leads to rating inflation. The issuer would still have to provide information to the rating agency, but would not be allowed to remunerate it. As this procedure may not provide incentives to put effort into the rating exercise for yielding unbiased but inaccurate rating, it would be possible to design incentive schemes by matching ratings with observable ex-post outcomes. One remaining issue concerning such a scheme relates to the optimal number of agencies and to the mechanism needed for including agencies in the roster of potential raters.

The list of distorted incentives at the root of the current crisis is long, but executive remuneration in the financial industry and the regulatory role of credit rating agencies are paramount.

(a) Executive pay

Remuneration in the financial industry depends on beating some benchmark while not taking additional risk. This risk-adjusted excess return is usually referred to as Jensen's alpha. In principle, rewarding alpha returns may seem a correct way to assign bonuses. In practice, though, it is very difficult to evaluate an asset manager's ability to generate alpha returns. Since such returns are difficult to obtain (not everybody can be above average), asset managers may try to generate fake alpha returns by adopting a strategy that leads to excessive returns in most states of the world but hides an enormous tail risk, that is, a very small probability of extremely large negative returns (Rajan, 2005; Foster and Young, 2008). An asset manager's ability to generate alpha returns can only be evaluated by observing his or her activity for many years.

While there is no regulatory framework that can assure a 100 per cent success in limiting incentives to take excessive tail risk, greater transparency, including full disclosure of compensation schemes that may then be used to measure incentive alignment (Issing et al., 2008), and the design of remuneration structures that focus on longer term performance – and not just on the returns of a single year – may be a step in the right direction.[18]

(b) Credit rating agencies

Credit rating agencies should improve information flows in financial markets and increase the overall efficiency of those markets. There are, however, problems arising from their peculiar role in modern finance. On the one hand, they are private profit-seeking companies (the "agency" part of their name is misleading). On the other hand, their decisions and activities are at the centre of the prudential regulatory system.[19]

Credit rating agencies do not take legal responsibility for their rating decisions on the ground that their activities are similar to those of financial journalists and are thus protected by freedom of speech legislation. This seems a paradoxical argument because their regulatory role gives them a virtual monopoly, which was officially sanctioned by according them the status of nationally recognized statistical rating organizations in the United States in the mid-1970s and by the Basel Accords. As a consequence, there are only three rating agencies with a worldwide presence (Elkhoury, 2008). Moreover, rating agencies are much more profitable than the financial newspapers with which they compare themselves in support of their freedom of speech arguments (Portes, 2008).

In the early 1970s the industry switched from investor- to issuer-paid fees. Since issuers may shop around for good ratings, credit rating agencies have an incentive to provide good ratings.[20] Incentives are further distorted by the fact that securitization would not be possible without credit rating agencies' assurance of the quality of these complex and opaque financial products, and credit rating agencies have an incentive to provide such an assurance because they earn large fees from rating complex instruments. For example, in 2006, 44 per cent of Moody's revenues came from activities related to structured finance.[21]

Problems related to unjustified high ratings could be addressed by either developing payment models which provide better incentives for honest and accurate ratings, or by subjecting rating agencies to regulatory oversight and by regularly publishing rating performance (box 3.2).

D. Lessons for developing countries

The present financial crisis is a developed-country crisis. But, although developing countries have been mostly innocent bystanders, they can derive several lessons from the current crisis for their own financial policies. Developing countries are paying a heavy economic price for a crisis that originated at the centre of the world's financial system, and they need to consider how they can protect themselves from similar external financial shocks in the future. Moreover, most developing countries are trying to build deeper and more efficient financial systems, and, although they are right to do so (as long as efficiency is defined as functional efficiency), they should be aware of the hidden risks of financial development. The current crisis shows that more sophisticated financial systems require more, and not less, regulation.

1. Increasing resilience to external shocks

In the absence of a complete overhaul of the global financial architecture (see chapter IV for a more detailed discussion), developing countries can limit external vulnerabilities by maintaining a competitive exchange rate. This would reduce vulnerabilities through at least three channels (UNCTAD, 2007): (i) when a real currency appreciation is prevented, a speculative attack that would cause currency crisis is less likely (Goldfajn and Valdes, 1999); (ii) a competitive currency tends to lead to current-account balance and reduces the vulnerability to a sudden stop of capital inflows; and (iii) avoiding real currency appreciation goes hand in hand with the accumulation of international reserves which can provide a first line of defence if a currency attack or sudden stop were to happen. Such a policy orientation, which may be reasonable from the point of view of an individual country, would, however, be problematic at the international level, because if several countries pursue the same strategy it would lead to competitive devaluations and endanger the stability of the entire system. This is why a truly multilateral exchange-rate system, as discussed in chapter IV, is called for. As an alternative or complementary measure, a well-designed capital-account management regime can also help to protect a fragile domestic financial system from undesirable swings in external financial transactions.

Developing countries should also try to avoid (or limit) currency and maturity mismatches in both private and public balance sheets. Debt management policies aimed at substituting foreign-currency-denominated public debt with domestic-currency-denominated public debt can help. Also useful is regulation limiting the ability of households and corporations that have domestic currency income to incur debt denominated in foreign currency.

Finally, developing countries should have contingency plans to be implemented if all else fails. Moderately intrusive capital controls can help during crisis periods (Kaplan and Rodrik, 2001), and market-friendly capital controls can limit risk accumulation in good times. There is much to be said for the sequencing of reforms, including a well-regulated financial sector, which is a necessary (but not sufficient) condition for benefiting from financial globalization. However, the standard policy prescription of regulating and then opening up (Kose et al., 2006) is more problematic in its assumption that a good regulatory system can be easily implemented in a relatively short period. The massive failure of financial regulation in the world's most sophisticated financial system suggests that it may take a long time before developing countries will be able to benefit

from an open capital account. Therefore, they should proceed with extreme caution along this path. It is probable that by the time a developing country is able to meet all the conditions for successfully opening up its capital account, it would no longer be a "developing" country.

2. More financial development requires more and better regulation

The financial systems of developing countries tend to be less functionally efficient than those of developed countries. Given the importance of finance for modern economic growth, several developing countries adopted ambitious structural reform programmes aimed at modernizing and improving their financial systems. There are now doubts as to whether these pro-market policies were successful in achieving their objective of increasing the size and efficiency of their financial sectors (*TDR 2008*, chap. IV). While deregulation generally led to an expansion of credit to the private sector, in many cases this expansion proved short-lived as it resulted in financial crises and a subsequent credit crunch, and most of the additional credit did not finance business investments. Neither did it achieve a narrowing of interest margins or a durable credit expansion. However, even more successful outcomes may be accompanied by an increase in risk-taking, and therefore require a better regulatory system.

> Policymakers should not aim for a sophisticated financial system ...

Consider a country characterized by a non-competitive financial system in which banks make good profits by paying low interest on deposits and charging high interest rates on loans, which they only extend to super-safe borrowers (or, in some cases, to their managers' friends). Shareholders and bank managers are content with rents arising from limited competition, but such a system is hardly conducive to economic development. Credit will be limited and unlikely to flow to high-return investment projects. High transaction costs will lead to small bond and stock markets.

Assume now that the country's policymakers decide on the need to reform the financial system and that they realize the reform process should target functional efficiency. They also know that financial instruments that may have high social returns in a more developed country may not be appropriate for their relatively underdeveloped economy. Thus, rather than aiming for excessive sophistication, they target the reform process to the real needs of their country. Further, assume that the reform process is successful and increases the competitiveness of the financial sector, it increases the availability of credit to the productive sector and, in general, improves overall access to credit.

... instead, they should target reforms to the real needs of their country.

Even with these rosy (and unrealistic) assumptions, financial regulators will soon start facing new problems, because, by reducing margins, the reform process leads to a whole new set of incentive-related problems. In the old system, bank managers were generally paid fixed salaries as there was no need to offer performance incentives (Rajan, 2005). Thus they had limited incentives for seeking higher profitability and acted conservatively, thereby facilitating the job of supervisors. The system was inefficient, but it was relatively easy to control.

A more competitive environment alters the incentive structure of bank managers in two ways. First, as their compensation now depends on returns on investment, they might be tempted to take more risks than they are able to evaluate. Along similar lines, regulators accustomed to an inefficient but stable banking system may not understand the new risks and vulnerabilities. Second, since bank managers know that they are evaluated against their peers, they have incentives to herd and take hidden risks (Rajan, 2005). Detecting this behaviour, which has the potential for generating large systemic shocks, requires sophisticated regulators.

On the investment bank side, the loss of a stable income from brokerage activities may provide incentives for increasing leverage and entering into activities that involve maturity transformation; in other words, for the creation of a shadow banking system. But, again, regulators may not be ready for this new structure of the financial system and may still work under the assumption that only commercial banks are of systemic importance.

This example shows that one danger of financial reforms that are successful in reducing margins is that in doing so they may induce bankers to take more risk than they are prepared to absorb or regulators are able to understand. This does not mean that developing countries should not try to improve the functional efficiency of their financial system. However, the process needs to be gradual and should be accompanied by a stronger and more comprehensive regulatory apparatus.[22]

3. There is no one-size-fits-all financial system

Developing countries face a difficult trade-off in the design and regulation of their financial systems. On the one hand, access to finance is necessary for economic development, and financial deepening may increase the ability of a country's financial system to absorb risk. On the other hand, greater financial sophistication does not equate with greater social efficiency of the financial system: a more sophisticated financial sector is also likely to lead to an increase in total risk (even if regulators are successful in regulating away socially inefficient financial instruments). If the second effect dominates, financial development may lead to an increase in systemic risk.

Until recently it was believed that good financial regulation could be a solution to this trade-off, and that most countries could build both sophisticated and stable financial systems. The current crisis suggests that this objective may not be within the reach of most developing countries, at least not in the near future. In choosing where to position themselves in the continuum between financial sophistication and stability, developing countries should recognize that there is no single model that is right for all countries or at all times. Each country needs to find the model which is most appropriate for its current level of development, needs and institutional capacity. This requires a cautious, exploratory process similar to the one that was the basis of the successful pro-market reforms in China, reflecting Deng Xiaoping's famous phrase: "crossing the river by feeling the stones".

Countries that have a stronger regulatory and institutional capacity and are better prepared to absorb shocks may decide to adopt a more aggressive process of financial liberalization and move towards a stronger market-based financial system. Other countries may want to be more cautious by relying on traditional banking. Some countries may find that their regulatory capacities do not even enable the proper working of private banks and may decide to rely more on State-owned banks. If they decide to do so, they should not be discouraged by the World Bank's (2001) claim that "state ownership tends to stunt financial sector development, thereby contributing to slower growth".

> Each country needs to find a model which is the most appropriate for its current level of development.

Recent research has shown that the previous evidence against State-owned banks is not as strong as originally believed, and that there are instances where such banks can play a useful role, especially during crises or in low- income countries (Levy Yeyati, Micco and Panizza, 2007; Detragiache, Tressel and Gupta, 2008). After all, the recent crisis has shown that, ultimately, all banks are public to a certain extent.

The rationale for public ownership of banks is not only based on limited regulatory capacities, but also on the fact that private banks seek, often short-term, private benefits and are not concerned with long-term development objectives.

E. Conclusions

It is often argued that financial regulators should not fight the last crisis. And yet this is exactly what agencies in charge of air traffic safety do with considerable success. Some may argue that things are different for finance. The principles of physics that keep aeroplanes in the air do not respond to regulatory changes, but financial markets do. It has been argued that the viral nature of financial innovation causes the system to react to regulation by producing more complex and opaque financial instruments, making each financial crisis different from the previous one, and therefore unpredictable. According to this view, nothing can be learned and nothing can be done, and new regulation can only do more harm.

This line of reasoning is certainly true for the particular instruments which are the proximate cause of any financial crisis. In 1637 it was tulip bulbs, in 1720 it was stocks of the South Sea Company, and in the current crisis it is mortgage-backed securities.

Nobody knows which financial instrument will be the root cause of the next crisis, most likely not mortgage-backed securities. Probably the instrument has not yet been invented.

However, the mechanism that leads to a crisis is always the same: a positive shock generates a wave of optimism which feeds into lower risk aversion, greater leverage and higher asset prices, which then feed back into even more optimism, leverage and higher asset prices. At the beginning, sceptical observers will claim that asset prices cannot grow forever at such a high rate – they never did. The enthusiasts will answer that this time it is different. If the boom lasts long enough, some of the sceptics will end up believing that this time it is indeed different. Those who remain sceptical will be marginalized and sometimes even ridiculed. Of course, things are never different. At some point the asset bubble will burst, triggering a deleveraging process and an economic crisis. A regulatory framework based on a clear understanding of this mechanism could have prevented some of the excesses that led to the current crisis.

The problem is that in the developed world financial crises are fairly rare events, and this leads to a regulatory cycle, with overshooting in both directions. After a crisis there is widespread political support for regulation, which may lead to overregulation. After a long period of stability, characterized by small, non-systemic crises, policymakers start forgetting the lessons of the previous major crisis (especially if it happened before they were born), and they no longer understand the rationale for the existing regulatory apparatus. This is when the deregulatory process starts. To the extent that the crisis led to too much regulation, this may be good. However, as there was overregulation in reaction to the crisis, there is likely to be excessive deregulation later. This is problematic because the costs of excessive regulation and excessive deregulation are unlikely to be symmetrical.

> An appropriate regulatory framework could have prevented some of the excesses that led to the current crisis.

A possible solution to this regulatory cycle is to follow the example of air safety regulators who, besides learning from relatively rare aeroplane crashes, also give considerable attention to near misses. For instance, there was much to be learned from the LTCM collapse of 1998. A proper regulatory response then may have played a positive role in limiting the consequences of the current crisis.

Seven practical lessons for regulators

The first and most important lesson is that financial efficiency should be defined as the sector's ability to stimulate long-term economic growth and provide consumption-smoothing services. Transaction costs, the number of available instruments, or the overall size of the financial system should not be the objectives per se; they are only relevant if they contribute to increasing social welfare.

Financial markets in many developed countries have come to resemble giant casinos, which almost always win, and when they lose they get bailed out, while everybody else loses. Many financial instruments generate large private returns, but, rather than contributing to economic development, they reduce transparency and misallocate resources. Consequently, their contribution to social welfare is negative. Tobin (1984) argued 25 years ago that there may be something wrong with an incentive structure which leads the brightest and most talented graduates to engage in financial activities "remote from the production of goods and services" and that the private rewards of financial intermediation might be much higher than its social rewards. More recently, Rodrik (2008) asked, without finding a convincing answer, "What are some of the ways in which financial innovation has made our lives measurably and unambiguously better?" National level measures are the first line of attack to significantly reduce, the "casino" element in financial markets. A key objective of regulatory reform should be the weeding out of financial instruments with no social returns and providing incentives to channel resources towards investment projects with high social returns.

The second lesson relates to regulatory arbitrage. The unregulated shadow banking system at the centre of the current crisis was a natural response to a regulatory apparatus that imposed tight controls on commercial banks and much laxer standards on the rest of the financial system. Regulatory arbitrage can only be avoided if regulators are able to cover the whole financial system and ensure that all financial transactions are overseen on the basis of the risks they produce.

The third lesson is that market-based risk indicators often send the wrong signals, and systemic stability cannot be achieved if regulators use the same models of risk adopted by the financial industry.[23] Regulation is necessary because markets sometimes do not work. But how can one prevent market failures by using the same evaluation instruments used by market participants? It is therefore necessary to complement micro-prudential regulation with macro-prudential policies aimed at smoothing the leverage cycle.

The fourth lesson relates to the incentive structure within the financial industry. Compensation schemes within the financial industry promote excessive risk-taking and the incentives of credit rating agencies are misaligned and lead to rating inflation. The first problem can be attenuated by designing remuneration structures that do not focus on annual returns but on returns over a long term: managers must not only care about gains but also about losses. The incentives of credit rating agencies could be improved by establishing a regulatory authority that supervises the operations of the agencies, or by breaking the commercial link between the issuers of financial instruments and the rating agencies.

The fifth lesson specifically relates to developing countries which today are paying a heavy economic price for a crisis that originated at the centre of the world's financial system. In the absence of a truly cooperative international financial system, developing countries can increase their resilience to external shocks by maintaining a competitive exchange rate, limiting currency and maturity mismatches in both private and public balance sheets, and having contingency plans to be implemented when all else fails.

The sixth lesson has to do with the trade-off between the size of the financial sector and financial stability. The majority of developing countries are far from the point where the size of the financial system starts yielding negative returns. Therefore, for them, a larger financial system tends to be growth-inducing. However, larger financial systems have a greater need for financial regulation. Almost every episode of financial deregulation and rapid credit growth has been followed by a banking crisis (Reinhart and Rogoff, 2008; *TDR 2008*). Developing countries should therefore develop their financial sector gradually and avoid this boom and bust cycle.

The seventh lesson relates to the need for international coordination. Regulators based in different countries should share information, aim at setting similar standards, and avoid a race to the bottom in financial regulation. However, it would be a mistake to impose a common regulatory standard. There is no single regulatory system that is right for all countries. Countries with different levels of development, regulatory capacity and history need to adopt different regulatory approaches. By increasing the participation of developing countries in the various agencies responsible for guaranteeing international financial stability, those agencies may develop a better understanding of their different regulatory requirements. ∎

> Regulation needs to weed out financial instruments with no social returns and channel resources towards investment projects with high social returns.

Notes

1　Prior to the bailouts in the current crisis, the United States banking system had to be bailed out after the Latin American debt crisis of the early 1980s and after the savings and loans crisis of the late 1980s.

2　One of the most lucid and detailed discussions of this hidden build-up of risk and the associated emerging problems came from an economist who was (and is) working for the Board of Governors of the United States Federal Reserve (Jones, 2000). It is thus unfortunate that the crisis caught United States regulators almost by surprise.

3　http://www.sec.gov/news/press/2008/2008-230.htm.

4　While the case against too much finance is often built on focusing on financial innovation, the statistical analysis discussed above follows the tradition of the empirical literature on finance and growth, and focuses on the size of the financial sector (measured as total credit to the private sector). Although there are problems with this variable (see Levine, 2005, for a detailed discussion), at this stage, size remains the best measure of financial development which is available for a large sample of countries. In fact, there is almost no research aimed at measuring the social welfare implications of financial innovation (Frame and White, 2002). The finding that even the simplest form of finance creates negative social returns suggests that this might be even truer for more sophisticated and complex forms of financial intermediation.

5　Such gambling instruments should be permitted only if one assumes that they are welfare-improving. However, the conditions under which "financial lotteries" can increase social welfare are rarely met (Buiter, 2009). See also United States Planning Commission (2009) and Crotty and Epstein (2009) for different views of this type of instrument.

6　For instance, a tighter risk assessment regulation which forces banks to evaluate credit risk by only considering a borrowers' capacity to service their debt out of their current income (without making any assumption on potential capital gains on the underlying assets) would greatly increase the soundness of the banking system and reduce "predatory lending". However, such a regulation would also have the negative effect of limiting access to credit for the most disadvantaged social groups.

7　The capital ratio plotted in the chart is not risk-adjusted. United States banks try to maintain risk-adjusted capital ratios of approximately 10 per cent, as United States regulators consider this a safe level of capital.

8　Indeed, in 2000 the United States Congress ruled out the possibility of regulating credit default swaps, and in 2004, the United States Securities and Exchange Commission allowed large investment banks to increase their leverage (Congleton, 2009).

9　Moreover, securitization severs the relationship between lenders and borrowers, and prevents borrowers who are unable to service their debt from reaching a rescheduling agreement with the lender.

10　With traditional banking, lenders acquire soft private information about the borrower. Since soft information is useless for "packaging" purposes, loan officers no longer care about it.

11　The presence of correlated risk may explain why the last 10 years witnessed the occurrence of several events that, according to the statistical models used by the financial industry, should be extremely rare (often referred to as "black swans"). In mid-2007, Goldman Sachs stated that large losses by some of its hedge funds were due to a "25 standard deviation event" (i.e. something that should happen once every 100,000 years), and Long Term Capital Management (LTCM) issued a similar statement after its collapse in 1998. Either an almost impossible event had happened (again and again), or the assumptions behind their risk models were wrong.

12　Subramanian and Williamson (2009) suggest that a tax on OTC contracts would provide the appropriate incentives in this direction. Crotty and Epstein (2009) favour a more drastic approach and suggest that financial products that are too complex to be sold on exchanges should be prohibited.

13   Moreover, without international coordination, a new policy in the United States may simply move OTC derivatives trading offshore.

14   New research aimed at developing CoVaR models – models that measure the value at risk of financial institutions, which is conditional on other financial institutions being under distress (Adrian and Brunnermeier, 2008) – can help regulators measure risk spillovers and thus assess the systemic importance of individual institutions.

15   Consider the case of Swiss banks that could not take too much real estate risk in Switzerland where mortgage lending is strictly regulated, but ended up taking enormous real estate risk by buying mortgage-backed instruments issued in the United States.

16   The Basel Capital Accords (Basel I and Basel II) set rules for the allocation of capital to banks' exposures to risks through its lending and other operations. These accords have two objectives. One is prudential, namely to help ensure the strength and soundness of banking systems. The other is to help equalize cross-border competition between banks by eliminating competitive advantages due to differences among countries in their regimes for capital adequacy. Basel I was originally designed for the internationally active banks of the Group of Ten. But by the second half of the 1990s it had become a global standard and had been incorporated into the prudential regimes of more than 100 countries (Cornford, 2008).

17   For example, in January 2007, when signs of financial turmoil were growing, participants at the FSF's European regional meeting referred to the "current benign global financial conditions", which they attributed to robust global growth, rising corporate profitability, financial innovation and structural reforms ("Financial Stability Forum concludes its European regional meeting". FSF Press Release 3/2007E, Basel, 31 January 2007). They noted that markets were characterized by low risk premiums, which, they claimed, were due to "healthy fundamentals and innovation in the management of risk exposure". Only as the crisis deepened, did the FSF's assessment became more sober. This is highlighted, for example, by a comparison between the preliminary draft (15 October 2007) and the final draft (7 April 2008) of the report of the FSF's Working Group on Market and Institutional Resilience to the G-7 finance ministers and central bank governors. The preliminary report fundamentally misjudged the depth of the financial crisis. The final report acknowledged the importance of stronger public oversight over financial markets, but still failed to recognize that there may be problems with complex structured financial products, which could result in a recurrence of such a crisis.

18   Rajan (2008) suggests that this could be achieved by holding compensation for alpha returns in escrow and releasing it only when there is a reasonable certainty that a particular return was indeed of the alpha type. Of course, this can reduce, but not solve, all problems of distorted incentives. After all, hedge funds and bank managers often have a substantial fraction of their wealth invested in the company or in the assets they manage (James Cayen, the former CEO of Bear Stearns, reportedly lost $900 million when that investment bank went bankrupt).

19   For instance, the Basel Accords build on the notion of risk-adjusted capital ratios, and credit ratings play an important role in determining risk weights. AAA rated instruments have capital charges that range between 0 and 20 per cent and non-investment grade debt instruments have capital charges that range between 100 and 150 per cent. In theory, a bank that holds only AAA rated sovereign bonds can operate with no capital, but a bank that holds only BB+ rated corporate bonds needs to have a capital equal to 12 per cent of its assets. A bank that holds only BBB- government bonds can operate with a 4 per cent capital ratio (because these bonds have a 50 per cent capital charge), but if these bonds are downgraded by one notch to BB+, the required capital ratio immediately doubles to 8 per cent (for a detailed discussion of Basel II and its implication for developing countries see Cornford, 2008). Moreover, ratings influence the type of instruments that can be held by institutional investors (e.g. in most countries, pension funds cannot hold non-investment grade securities).

20   While investor-paid ratings would provide better incentives for honest ratings, few private investors are willing to pay for what is effectively a public good (it is hard to hide a credit rating).

21   Credit rating agencies also offer advisory services, which issuers can use to improve the credit rating of their instruments. These types of services are particularly useful for issuers of CDOs who want to maximize the size of the AAA-rated tranche of the instrument. In fact, credit rating agencies even sold variants of their rating models which allowed issuers to "pre-test" their securities before applying for a credit rating (Issing et al., 2008). However, when these complex instruments (which are already difficult to rate) are "built to rating," the probability distributions used to rate them, which assume independently drawn observations, are no longer valid, making the rating process meaningless. Another issue relates to the fact that credit rating agencies use the same measure of the probability of default to evaluate sovereigns, corporates and complex instruments, ignoring the fact that these instruments face different liquidity risks.

22   Another channel through which financial development can increase risk has to do with the fact that such development often goes hand in hand with a process of disintermediation, whereby arm's length transactions take the place of traditional banking activities. Banks have an advantage in taking risks that require certain specific knowledge and that cannot be easily "standardized". However, deregulation, technical innovation and the development of deeper markets continually increase (or appear to increase) the types of "standardizable" risks. These risks are then taken by other parts of the financial sector which have lower funding costs than banks (Myers and Rajan, 1998), and banks have to search for new, possibly larger and more opaque forms of non-standard risks. Another potential source of instability relates to the fact that arm's length transactions are more institutionally demanding than regular banking. They require good corporate governance, good

dissemination of public information and well-defined shareholders and creditors' rights (Rajan, 2005). The current crisis shows that these institutional features are far from being perfect, even in the most sophisticated financial systems, and may be seriously lacking in countries with incipient financial markets.

23   Value at risk (VaR) models used by the financial industry only work if a small proportion of market participants use the same model, or if market participants are exposed to completely different sources of risk. These were good assumptions when financial systems were small and segmented, but they are unrealistic in today's world in which investors adopt correlated trading strategies in both the good and bad periods of the business cycle (Persaud, 2008). Regulation is necessary because markets sometimes do not work, but market failures cannot be prevented by using the same evaluation instruments as those used by market participants.

References

Acemoglu D (2008). The crisis of 2008: Structural lessons for and from economics (unpublished) Cambridge, MA, Massachusetts Institute of Technology.

Adrian T and Brunnermeier M (2008). CoVar. Staff Report No. 348, Federal Reserve Bank of New York, New York.

Aglietta M and Rigot S (2009). Crise et renovation de la finance. Paris, Odile Jacob.

Bagehot W (1873). Lombard Street: A Description of the Money Market. London, Henry S. King & Co.

Bank for International Settlements (2007). *77th Annual Report*. Basel, BIS.

Borio C (2003). Towards a macroprudential framework for financial supervision and regulation? *CESifo Economic Studies*, 49(2): 181–215. Also Bank for International Settlements Working Paper No. 128. Basel, BIS.

Borio C (2008). The financial turmoil of 2007-?: a preliminary assessment and some policy considerations. Bank for International Settlements Working Paper No. 251. Basel, BIS.

Borio C and Lowe P (2002). Assessing the risk of banking crises. *BIS Quarterly Review*, December: 43–54.

Borio C and Drehmann M (2008). Towards an operational framework for financial stability: "Fuzzy" measurement and its consequences. BIS Working Paper, November. Basel, BIS.

Brunnermeier MK (2008). Deciphering the liquidity and credit crunch 2007-08, NBER Working Papers 14612, National Bureau of Economic Research, Cambridge, MA.

Brunnermeier MK et al. (2009). The fundamental principles of financial regulation. *Geneva Reports on the World Economy,* 11. London, Centre for Economic Policy Research, and Princeton, NJ, Princeton University.

Buiter W (2009). Useless finance, harmful finance and useful finance, http://blogs.ft.com/maverecon/2009/04/useless-finance-harmful-finance-and-useful-finance/.

Calomiris CW (2009). Financial innovation, regulation, and reform (unpublished). New York, NY, Columbia University.

Congleton RD (2009). On the political economy of the financial crisis and bailout of 2008 (unpublished), Fairfax, VA, George Mason University, Center for Study of Public Choice.

Congressional Oversight Panel (2009). Special report on regulatory reform. Washington, DC. Available at: http://cop.senate.gov/documents/cop-012909-report-regulatoryreform.pdf

Cornford A (2008). Basel 2 at a time of financial peril. Paper prepared for the G-24 Technical Group Meeting, Geneva, UNCTAD, 8–9 September.

Coval JD, Jurek JW and Stafford E (2008). The economics of structured finance. Harvard Business School Finance Working Paper No. 09-060. Cambridge, MA, Harvard University.

Crotty J and Epstein G (2009). Regulating the US financial system to avoid another meltdown. *Economic and Political Weekly*, 44(20): 87–93, 28 March.

Dallara C (2008). Letter to IMFC Chair Hon. Tommaso Padoa Schioppa. Available at: http://www.sustainable-financialmarkets.net/wp-content/uploads/2008/05/policyletter_04082.pdf.

Detragiache E, Tressel T and Gupta P (2008). Foreign banks in poor countries: theory and evidence. *Journal of Finance*, 63(5): 2123–2160.

Devine T (1997). *The Whistleblower's Survival Guide: Courage Without Martyrdom*. Government Accountability Project, Washington, DC, Fund for Constitutional Government.

Duffie D and Zhu H (2009). Does a central clearing counterparty reduce counterparty risk? Rock Center for Corporate Governance at Stanford University Working Paper No. 46; Stanford University Graduate School of Business Research Paper No. 2022, May. Stanford, CA.

Eichengreen B (2009). The last temptation of risk. *The National Interest*, May/June.

Elkhoury M (2008). Credit rating agencies and their potential impact on developing countries. UNCTAD Discussion Papers 186. Geneva, UNCTAD.

Foster DP and Young HP (2008). Hedge fund wizards. *The Economists' Voice*, 5(2), Art. 1. Available at: http://www.bepress.com/ev/vol5/iss2/art1/

Frame WS and White LJ (2002). Empirical studies of financial innovation: Lots of talk, little action?. NYU Working Paper No. EC-02-18. New York, NY, New York University, Leonard N. Stern School of Business.

Furlong FT and Keeley MC (1989). Capital regulation and bank risk-taking: a note. *Journal of Banking & Finance,* 13(6): 883–891. Elsevier, December.

Galindo A, Micco A and Powell A (2005). Loyal lenders or fickle financiers: Foreign banks in Latin America. RES Working Papers 4403, Inter-American Development Bank, Washington, DC.

Goldfajn I and Valdes RO (1999). The aftermath of appreciations. *Quarterly Journal of Economics*, 114: 229–262.

Goodhart C and Persaud A (2008). How to avoid the next crash. *Financial Times*, 30 January.

Greenspan A (2003). Remarks at the 2003 Conference on Bank Structure and Competition, Chicago, Illinois,

8 May. Available at: http://www.federalreserve.gov/boarddocs/speeches/2003/20030508/default.htm

Group of 30 (2009). Financial reform: A framework for financial stability. Special report. Washington, DC, Group of 30, Consultative Group on International Economic and Monetary Affairs, Inc.

Hutton W (2009). A grand bargain for global capital. In: *Responses to the Global Crisis: Charting a Progressive Path*. London, Policy Network: 16–18. Available at: http://www.policy-network.net/events/events.aspx?year=2009&id=2882.

IMF (2006). *Global Financial Stability Report*. Washington, DC, International Monetary Fund.

IMF (2009). Initial lessons of the crisis for the global architecture and the IMF. Washington, DC, International Monetary Fund.

Issing O and Krahnen JP (2009). Why the regulators must have a global 'risk map'. *Financial Times*, 19 February.

Issing O et al. (2008). New financial order. Recommendations by the Issing Committee, Preparing G-20 Washington. 15 November. Available at: http://www.ifk-cfs.de/index.php?id=1570.

Johnson S (2009). The quiet coup, *The Atlantic,* May. Available at: www.theatlantic.com/doc/200905/imf-advice.

Jones D (2000). Emerging problems with the Basel Capital Accord: Regulatory capital arbitrage and related issue. *Journal of Banking & Finance*, 24(1–2): 35–58, Elsevier, January.

Kaplan ED and Rodrik D (2001). Did the Malaysian capital controls work? CEPR Discussion Paper No. 2754. London, Centre for Economic Policy Research.

Kashyap A et al. (2008). Rethinking capital regulation (unpublished). Chicago, IL, University of Chicago.

Kindleberger CP (1996). *Manias, Panics, and Crashes: A History of Financial Crises*. Wiley Investment Classics. New York, John Wiley & Sons.

Kose MA et al. (2006). Financial Globalization: A Reappraisal. NBER Working Paper No. W12484. Cambridge, MA, National Bureau of Economic Research.

Lamont OA and Thaler RH (2003). Can the market add and subtract? Mispricing in tech stock carve-outs. *Journal of Political Economy*, 111(2): 227–268.

Levine R (2005). Finance and growth: Theory and evidence. In: Aghion P and Durlauf S, eds. *Handbook of Economic Growth*, vol. 1. Amsterdam, Elsevier Science.

Levy Yeyati E, Micco A and Panizza U (2007). A reappraisal of state-owned banks. *Economia*, 7(2): 209–247.

Lo A (2008). Hedge funds, systemic risk, and the financial crisis of 2007-2008: Written Testimony for the United States House of Representatives Committee on Oversight and Government Reform Hearing on Hedge Funds, 13 November. Available at: http://oversight.house.gov/documents/20081113101922.pdf.

Mathis J, McAndrews J and Rochet J-C (2008). Rating the raters: Are reputation concerns enough to discipline rating agencies? *Journal of Monetary Economics* (forthcoming).

Minsky H (1982). Can "It" Happen Again?: Essays on Instability and Finance. Armonk, NY, M.E. Sharpe Inc.

Myers SC and Rajan RG (1998). The paradox of liquidity. *Quarterly Journal of Economics*, 113(3): 733–771, August. Cambridge, MA, MIT Press.

Nugée J and Persaud AD (2006). Redesigning regulation of pensions and other financial products. *Oxford Review of Economic Policy*, 22(1): 66–77.

Panizza U (2009). Can there be too much finance? (Unpublished). Geneva, UNCTAD.

Persaud A (2008). Reason with the messenger; don't shoot him: value accounting, risk management and financial system resilience. Presentation at the annual IMF/World Bank meetings hosted by the Banque de France on 12 October in Washington, DC. Summary available at: VoxEU.org: http://www.voxeu.org/index.php?q=node/2407

Pistor K (2009). Reforming the financial system: beyond standardization on "best practice" models. VoxEU.org, 2 February. Available at: www.voxeu.org/index.php?q=node/2969.

Planning Commission (2009). A hundred small steps. Report of the Committee on Financial Sector Reforms. Available at: http://planningcommission.nic.in/reports/genrep/report_fr.htm.

Plantin G, Sapra H and Shin Hyun-Song (2005). Marking to market, liquidity, and financial stability. *Monetary and Economic Studies*, 23(S1): 133–55. Institute for Monetary and Economic Studies, Bank of Japan, Tokyo, October.

Portes R (2008). Ratings agency reform, VoxEU, 22 January 2008. Available at: www.voxeu.org/index.php?q=node/887.

Rajan RG (2005). Has financial development made the world riskier? Kansas City, MO, Federal Reserve Bank of Kansas City.

Rajan RG (2008). Bankers' pay is deeply flawed. *Financial Times*, 8 January.

Rancière R, Tornell A and Westermann F (2008). Systemic crises and growth. *Quarterly Journal of Economics*, 123(1): 359–406.

Reinhart C and Rogoff KS (2008). This time is different: a panoramic view of eight centuries of financial crises. NBER Working Papers 13882. Cambridge, MA, National Bureau of Economic Research.

Rochet JC (1992). Capital requirements and the behaviour of commercial banks. *European Economic Review*, 36: 1137–1178.

Rodrik D (2008). Now's the time to sing the praises of financial innovation. Available at: http://rodrik.typepad.com/dani_rodriks_weblog/2008/09/nows-the-time-to-sing-the-praises-of-financial-innovation.html.

Segoviano MA and Singh M (2008). Counterparty risk in the over-the-counter derivatives market. IMF Working Paper WP/08/258. Washington, DC, IMF.

Shin HS (2009). Nature of systemic risk: Where should regulation be aimed? Presentation at the 11th Geneva Conference on the World Economy – The Fundamental Principles of Financial Regulations, 24 January. Geneva, The International Center for Monetary and Banking Studies.

Simons H (1948). *Economic Policy for a Free Society*. University of Chicago Press, Chicago, IL.

Stiglitz J (2009). Testimony before the Congressional Oversight Panel, Regulatory Reform Hearing, 14 January. Available at: cop.senate.gov/documents/testimony-011409-stiglitz.pdf.

Subramanian A and Williamson J (2009). The world crisis: reforms to prevent a recurrence. *Economic and Political Weekly,* XLIV (134): 55–58, March.

Tobin J (1984). On the efficiency of the financial system. *Lloyds Bank Review*, no. 153: 14–15.

UNCTAD (2007). Recent developments on global financial markets. Note by the UNCTAD secretariat for the 54th session of the Trade and Development Board, 1–11 October 2007, TD/B/54/CRP.2, Geneva, 28 September.

UNCTAD (various issues). *Trade and Development Report*. United Nations publication, New York and Geneva.

Van Horne J (1985). Of financial innovations and excesses. *The Journal of Finance,* 40(3): 621–631, July.

World Bank (2001). *Finance for Growth*. Washington, DC, World Bank.

Chapter IV

REFORM OF THE INTERNATIONAL MONETARY AND FINANCIAL SYSTEM

A. Introduction

The debate about the policy implications of the current financial and economic crisis has focused on emergency measures to overcome the crisis, and on the need to improve supervision and regulation of national financial markets (issues discussed in chapters I and III of this *Report*).[1] However, the lessons to be drawn for reform of the international monetary and financial system have received relatively little attention in the debate so far.

A massive influx of international capital contributed to the financial bubble in the United States in the build-up to the current financial crisis. Unrestrained capital flows led to huge imbalances in many other countries, too, and the reversal of those flows during the crises caused very serious payments difficulties and problems with exchange-rate management. This was quite similar to what had happened in previous crises in emerging-market economies, such as the debt crisis of the early 1980s and the 1997–1998 crises.

This illustrates the strong links between international financial transactions, on the one hand, and trade and macroeconomic performance of interdependent economies on the other. This chapter discusses some elements in the reform of the international monetary and financial architecture which

could, in combination with strengthened financial regulation at the national level, reduce the likelihood of similar crises in the future and help create a stable macroeconomic environment conducive to growth and smooth structural change in developing countries.

The lopsided distribution of domestic demand among major economies, along with a pattern of exchange rates that did not reflect the diverging fundamentals, led to imbalances in the external accounts of many countries. These factors contributed to the rapid spread of the financial crisis from the United States to other deficit countries that had been the destination of speculative carry trade flows, typically in combination with speculative bubbles in their domestic financial and real estate markets. These countries were affected by a sudden halt in capital inflows and reversals of carry trade positions. But the financial crisis also affected, with particular vigour, some of the major surplus economies, which, after many years of current-account surpluses, had accumulated large external asset positions vis-à-vis the deficit countries. These were often high-risk assets, as foreign investors were attracted to the market for dollar assets not only because the dollar is a reserve currency, but also because financial regulation in the United States has been less stringent than in their home countries, which allowed risk-taking that would not have been possible at home. Thus, losses from financial activities in the deficit countries had a strong contagion effect on the financial system in some of the surplus countries.

The absence of an appropriate system of governance in international monetary and financial relations is the main reason for the increasing prevalence of current-account imbalances in the global economy. It has allowed a dramatic increase in debtor-creditor relations between countries, and efforts by many developing countries, notably in Asia, to maintain stable, and slightly undervalued exchange rates vis-à-vis the dollar (*TDR 2006*, chap. IV).[2] This requires massive intervention in the foreign exchange market, leading to an accumulation of reserves and official capital outflows as a result of which asset claims on the reserve currency are built up. The reserves also serve as a cushion against the risk of attacks on the national currency from highly volatile international financial markets.

Another reason for the build-up of current-account disequilibria, and the resulting international asset-liability positions, is the large movements of relative prices of tradable goods across countries. These movements are often driven by speculation on currency markets that leads to distortions in the pattern of real exchange rates (RERs). The outbreak of the global financial crisis triggered the unwinding of these speculative positions, depreciated the former target currencies of carry trade, and forced companies and private households in the affected countries to deleverage their foreign currency positions or to default, which endangered the (mainly foreign) banks in these countries.

All these developments hint at major shortcomings in a global monetary and financial system, where financial markets can exercise enormous influence in determining the competitive position of entire economies in international trade. A large share of private capital flows is speculative in nature, and depends on the expectations of actors in international capital markets that are very often unrelated to macroeconomic fundamentals or medium- to long-term considerations.

> Financial markets can exercise enormous influence in determining the competitive position of entire economies in international trade.

This chapter seeks to highlight some elements of reform of the international financial architecture, which is long overdue. Section D discusses the problems associated with the behaviour of financial markets, which is increasingly determining macroeconomic performance and policies in the rapidly integrating world economy. Their behaviour is not based on a sound interpretation of data on income growth and employment at the macro level or on a proper assessment of the long-term performance potential of corporate firms in the real sector of the economy; instead it is motivated by financial returns and capital gains generated in the financial sector itself. In the resulting "confidence game" governments are tempted to cater to financial market participants, which, in the current financial crisis, have shown more clearly than ever their ineptitude at assessing risk and the sustainability of asset and liability positions. Against this background, section C discusses the need for more pragmatism in the management of international capital flows, in light of experience that it is not the quantity but the quality of such flows that matters. Short-term flows typically do more harm than good by distorting the pattern of exchange rates and destabilizing the financial systems of the destination countries.

Section D addresses the issue of the reform of the current international reserve system, which has received greater attention in the context of the crisis. The role of the dollar as the main reserve currency has been called into question, partly because it is believed to require a current-account deficit in the United States, and also because the dollar has significantly lost value. Reflections about an alternative reserve system are often linked to the question of how to provide more adequate international liquidity to developing and emerging-market economies. But equally if not more important for solving the problem of instability in international financial relations, is the need for appropriate reform of the multilateral system of exchange-rate determination. Section E discusses how a multilaterally organized system aimed at stabilizing RERs would not only provide a framework for greater financial stability, but would also foster stability and efficiency of the international trading system.

B. The problem of the predominance of financial markets over fundamentals

As in earlier episodes of financial crisis in developing countries, the surge in private capital flows towards developing and transition economies in the years preceding the current crisis was viewed by many observers as a sign of the growing strength of the receiving economies and as beneficial for development. However, as the financial crisis evolved and financial investors began moving out of risk, boom soon turned into bust, like many previous episodes in emerging-market economies.

The events of recent months have revealed a huge misallocation of resources and the creation and subsequent destruction of enormous book values, which have been driven by financial markets. This experience has shattered the belief that unfettered financial liberalization will maximize welfare. It would therefore seem appropriate to reassess the principles that have determined the attitude of many governments to financial markets over the past 25 years or so. These principles were based on the assumption that free financial markets always lead to optimal social outcomes, or at least to outcomes that are preferable to those that can be achieved with State intervention, and that the effects of market failure, should it occur, are less serious than those resulting from government failure.

Accordingly, privatization, deregulation and liberalization of trade and finance were promoted. These aimed not only at achieving more efficient resource allocation, but also at reducing the scope for State discretion. Equally important for developing

and transition economies was the shift from a national perspective on development towards an outward orientation, including price determination by global markets and a greater reliance on foreign capital inflows. Efficiency enhancement in resource allocation was sought to be achieved through opening up to global competition, both for market shares in goods markets and for foreign capital. As a result, orthodox macroeconomic and structural policies came to be conducted in such a way that they were judged to be "sound" by financial market participants who were assumed to have the appropriate knowledge to make such judgements.

With their growing size, financial markets today have acquired an enormous power not only to influence macroeconomic outcomes, but also to impose the orthodox approach to economic policy-making in line with their aim to reduce government interference in their businesses. The perceptions of financial market participants, rating agencies and financial journalists have been influenced to a large extent by the IMF, which has also propagated this approach since the early 1980s.

Thus, when financially fragile positions built up in emerging markets, they were typically interpreted as the consequence of deviations from orthodox policies, such as the absence of an inflation targeting framework or of an austere government budget rule. Budget deficits beyond a certain point, or inflation rates higher than 2 per cent, have typically been blamed on wrong national policies without

> The crisis proves that free financial markets do not lead to optimal social and macroeconomic outcomes.

any consideration given to, for example, the employment situation or the origin of price increases. Similarly, soft currency pegs, "too many" controls on the financial system, underdeveloped markets for securities, or the dominance of a relation-based banking system were also viewed as causes of financial vulnerability.

The traditional strategy of the IMF in providing assistance to countries in situations of external payments difficulties has been not only to help debtor countries keep up with their repayment obligations vis-à-vis foreign creditors, but also to restore the confidence of financial markets through the policy conditionality attached to its lending. In this approach, restoring investor confidence is considered to be a precondition for halting the flight of short-term capital and alleviating the pressure on the exchange rate to depreciate. Eventually, with the right policy reforms in place, the concerned economies would once again "deserve" new private capital inflows.

The financial crisis has shown that the basic assumption underlying this approach to economic policymaking is wrong: financial markets do not make correct judgments on economic performance and on the quality of economic policies. They are not concerned with the proper interpretation of macroeconomic fundamentals; otherwise a number of economies with excessive private debts – including those that were destinations of carry trade operations, but also the United States – would not have attracted excessive amounts of capital. Moreover, actors in financial markets are not concerned with properly assessing the performance of corporate firms or with the long-term valuation of real estate; otherwise large bubbles would not have occurred in stock and real estate markets. And they are not concerned with a correct interpretation of real demand-supply relations in primary commodity markets; otherwise there would not have been excessive commodity price fluctuations. Rather, they are concerned with guessing how certain "news" will influence the behaviour of other financial market participants, so as to derive maximum benefits from asset price movements

> Speculation based on uniform expectations cannot be sustained ...

> ... because speculative investments do not generate increases in real income.

triggered by "herd behaviour", no matter whether this is justified by fundamental economic performance indicators.

As the present crisis evolved, the vulnerability of different economies to the shocks varied, as did their capacity to cope with them. In some developing and transition economies, past fundamentals suddenly appeared to be unsustainable even when the financial markets had shown their "confidence" by moving funds to those economies and sharply revaluating their currencies before the crisis broke out (box 4.1). The same is true for countries that, prior to the financial shock, had fixed exchange-rate regimes in the form of pegging or a currency board system, but which were overvalued due to relatively high inflation rates and rapid wage growth measured in international currency. This was the case, for example, for the three Baltic States, Pakistan and Ukraine. In most cases, the IMF urged them to abandon the peg and to return to floating combined with its usual restrictive conditionality to restore the "confidence of the markets". Policies to restore "market confidence" have usually been sharply contractionary, at considerable economic and social costs. They have typically involved higher interest rates to prevent further currency devaluation in a floating regime, cuts in government spending to reduce budget deficits, and pressure on wages to counter inflationary effects of rising import prices as a result of depreciation and to boost the profitability of capital.

The deficiencies of the current system have never been better exposed than by the current crisis. Financial deregulation, driven by the belief in the efficiency of financial markets, has bred a spate of "innovative" financial instruments in the most sophisticated financial markets that are completely disconnected from productive activities in the real sector of the economy. Such instruments favour purely speculative activities based on apparently convincing information, which in reality is nothing but an extrapolation of existing price trends into the future. In this way, speculation on excessively high returns can support itself for a while, much like the

Box 4.1

PLAYING THE CONFIDENCE GAME: THE CASE OF HUNGARY

Hungary is among the countries that have been the hardest hit by the global financial crisis. It is also an outstanding example of boom-and-bust cycles generated by the belief that financial markets are always right.

Between 2000 and 2006 Hungary's economy performed fairly well, with annual GDP growth averaging 4.4 per cent and inflation falling from 10 per cent in 1999 to less than 4 per cent in 2005 and 2006. Exports expanded rapidly, but imports increased even faster, causing a deficit in the current account of 7.3 per cent of GDP, on average, from 2005 to 2008. In 2007, monetary and fiscal policies were tightened in an attempt to counter inflation that had re-accelerated to about 8 per cent, and to lower the budget deficit that was approaching 10 per cent of GDP (IMF, 2009).

In spite of the growing current-account deficit, the Hungarian currency, the forint, appreciated strongly from 2000 onwards. This was because the short-term interest rate was persistently higher than in many other European and Asian countries, and this differential attracted inflows of short-term capital. Even when domestic demand growth slowed down considerably in 2007 and 2008, the current account did not shrink due to a dramatic loss of international competitiveness of domestic producers. By 2005, the RER – the most comprehensive measure of overall competitiveness – had risen by more than 30 per cent, and by 2008 it had risen by almost 50 per cent compared to its 2000 level. During all these years, monetary policy aimed at checking inflation had been considered "sound", and financial markets had maintained their confidence in the Hungarian economy, despite its growing current-account deficits and its worsening competitive position. When the crisis hit in 2008, and investors suddenly stopped speculating on further gains from interest arbitrage and currency appreciation, turning instead to less risky assets, the forint depreciated sharply. This led to a sharp downward adjustment of the RER; however, by March 2009 the RER was still about 25 per cent above the level of 2000 (IMF, 2009).

The sharp devaluation had been necessary to regain some of the competitiveness lost and to reduce the current-account deficit. With the negative demand shock from the global crisis already looming and a budget deficit that had been brought down to 3.4 per cent in 2008, it would have been appropriate to support the expansionary effect of currency depreciation by reducing interest rates to stabilize domestic demand, while at the same time discouraging a new wave of speculation of the carry-trade type.

In November 2008, Hungary had to resort to IMF assistance to cope with the currency crisis, which meant that it had to accept the Fund's traditional conditionality package, including quick budget consolidation and interest-rate hikes. However, with the return of "appetite for risk" in the financial markets in early 2009, the return of Swiss-franc-based carry trade and a revaluation of the forint the interest rate was cut back in July 2009. Overall, the strategy of restoring the confidence of financial markets in the Hungarian economy, instead of strengthening real demand and improving the expectations of entrepreneurs willing to invest in real productive capacity and job creation, has led to a dramatic deterioration of the economic situation. Moreover, it has reduced the possibility of returning to sustained growth and balanced external accounts in the medium term.

It is indispensable to stabilize exchange rates through direct and coordinated government intervention, instead of letting the market find the bottom line, and trying to "convince" financial markets about the credibility of the government of the depreciating currency through procyclical policies such as public expenditure cuts or interest rate hikes.

Ponzi schemes of the 1920s. As long as new agents with large amounts of (frequently borrowed) money bet on the same "plausible" outcome (such as steadily rising prices of real estate, oil, stocks or currencies), and the expectations of market participants are "confirmed" and repeated by the media, so-called analysts and policymakers every day, betting on ever-rising prices appears to be a rather risk-free and high-return business.

However, as independent and non-partisan information is missing, this type of speculation, contrary to the mainstream view in the theoretical literature in economics, destabilizes, instead of stabilizing, the prices of the targeted assets. Sooner or later speculation based on uniform expectations of this kind cannot be sustained by the real economy, because the funds have not been invested in the capacity to produce goods and services that could have generated increases in real income. When the enthusiasm of the financial markets eventually fades, the adjustment of exaggerated expectations to real-life conditions becomes extremely painful: the more economic agents have been directly involved in speculative activities leveraged with borrowed funds, the greater becomes the pain of deleveraging (i.e. adjusting the level of borrowing to significantly diminished revenues).

As financial markets do not operate efficiently, the orthodox notion of "sound economic policies" and the rationale for restoring the "confidence" of the financial markets collapses. Giving financial markets the power to exercise the same strong influence on economic policy decisions and reforms, as in the past, would sow the seeds of a future crisis. It is therefore problematic that the current IMF policy response in developing and transition economies (see also chapter I, section D), instead of mitigating the results of misallocation driven by speculative financial markets, is again tending to aggravate the outcome, which will invite new rounds of speculation.

C. Stemming destabilizing capital flows

Financial globalization implies a de facto loss of national policy autonomy for developing countries and emerging-market economies. External financial conditions largely determine the scope for development strategies and domestic macroeconomic policies. These conditions are influenced mainly by monetary policy decisions taken in the economies that carry the largest weight in the world economy. But increasingly they are also influenced by the behaviour of participants in international financial markets. These participants are motivated by risk-return considerations aimed at optimizing returns on their portfolios which contain a large variety of assets in different currencies. Since these external factors themselves are unstable, and private capital flows can suddenly reverse direction entirely unrelated to domestic fundamentals, this pattern has led to boom-bust cycles in many developing and transition economies in the past, and again in connection with the present global financial crisis.

In the context of the present crisis, several authors (Rodrik and Subramanian, 2008; Reinhart and Rogoff, 2008; Wolf, 2008) have again suggested reconsidering the use of restrictions on international capital mobility, such as international

> Financial globalization implies a de facto loss of national policy autonomy.

taxes or national capital controls, as a means of reducing the risk of recurrent international financial crises. This option may be all the more relevant as efforts to strengthen international prudential regulation may not keep up with financial innovation. Thus, in citing advice by Keynes, Rodrik and Subramanian (2008) state: "If the risk-taking behaviour of financial intermediaries cannot be regulated perfectly, we need to find ways of reducing the volume of transactions. ... What this means is that financial capital should be flowing across borders in smaller quantities, so that finance is 'primarily national'".

> The financial crisis challenges the conventional wisdom ...

1. Taxing international financial transactions

The introduction of a tax on financial transactions has recently received renewed attention (Helleiner, 2009; Rodrik, 2009; Schmidt, 2007). Such a tax was first suggested in Keynes' *General Theory*, "to mitigate the dominance of speculation over enterprise", and advocated again in the 1970s by Nobel laureate James Tobin (1978), "to throw some sand in the wheels" of international financial markets. It was further discussed in the 1990s (*TDR 1996*; Dornbusch, 1997). Such a tax would serve to raise the cost of cross-border financial movements. It could be levied each time a unit of capital crossed borders, so that the effective tax burden would be greater, the shorter the time horizon of a financial transaction. This could discourage, in particular, short-term speculative flows that are the most volatile element in international financial markets, and that distort trade patterns through their cumulative impact on exchange rates, thereby reducing the policy autonomy of governments. The tax would not interfere with desirable long-term financial transactions in support of productive investment, since the tax burden for such long-term transactions would be insignificant as a cost item.

> ... that dismantling all obstacles to cross-border private capital flows is the best recipe for countries to advance their economic development.

This kind of tax has often been dismissed in the past on the grounds of difficulties in implementing it in an effective manner, since it would require the co-operation of all countries. However, foreign exchange trading relies on dense networks of information, accounting and legal services that exist only in a relatively small number of financial centres where the vast bulk of such trading is concentrated. If the tax were to be imposed in those centres, it is highly unlikely that the foreign exchange trading business would flee en masse to lightly regulated offshore financial centres (Cooper, 1994; Schmidt, 2007).

A tax on international financial transactions would not prevent imbalances in the external accounts, but by reducing the possible gains that can be had from interest arbitrage and exchange-rate movements, it would help to reduce the amount of potentially destabilizing speculative capital flows among countries that apply the tax (and in the system as a whole if a sufficiently large number of countries applied it).

2. Capital-account management

Another approach to crisis prevention is to put in place measures that hinder the free inflow and outflow of private capital in individual countries. For a long time, the idea of capital controls was taboo in mainstream discussions of appropriate financial policies, as market forces were considered the only reliable guide for the allocation of capital. This was despite the fact that the IMF Articles of Agreement provide for the possibility that "members may exercise such controls as are necessary to regulate international capital movements ..."[3] Some rethinking began in the aftermath of the Asian crisis, when the standard policy advice was for a "sequencing" of liberalization of international financial transactions, along with setting up domestic prudential regulatory and supervisory regimes. Experience with the current financial crisis also challenges the conventional wisdom that dismantling all obstacles to cross-border private capital flows is the best recipe for countries to advance their economic development.

When introduced in a period of crisis, capital-account management mainly takes the form of restrictions on capital outflows. On the other hand, when it is conceived as an instrument to prevent the build-up of speculative bubbles and currency misalignment and to preserve domestic macroeconomic policy space, it primarily implies certain restrictions on capital inflows. A regulatory regime of comprehensive capital-account management can target both the level and the composition of capital flows. A rich menu of both price-based and quantity-based types of instruments can be combined and flexibly handled to match specific local requirements (Stiglitz et al., 2006; Ocampo et al., 2008). In principle, barring or limiting certain types of inflows can be achieved in more ways than one, ranging from outright bans or minimum-stay requirements, to tax-based instruments like mandatory reserve requirements or taxes on foreign loans designed to offset interest rate differentials.[4] In many cases, instruments directly targeting private capital flows may also be appropriately combined with, and complemented by, prudential domestic financial regulations. The experiences of numerous emerging-market economies such as Chile, China, Colombia, India, Malaysia, Singapore and Taiwan Province of China (Epstein, Grabel and Jomo, 2004) belie the assertion that capital controls are ineffective or harmful.

> The experiences of numerous economies belie the assertion that capital controls are ineffective or harmful.

It has been suggested that capital-account management could be applied in a counter-cylical manner by restricting excessive foreign borrowing in good times and controlling capital flight during crises (Rodrik, 2009), although capital flows unrelated to investment and trade are undesirable at all times. In any case, it would certainly be a step forward if surging capital inflows were no longer perceived as a sign of a strong receiving economy, but as a potential for disequilibria, with negative repercussions on monetary

> The IMF should more actively encourage the use of capital controls and advise on their national implementation.

management and trade. The IMF should therefore change its stance by more actively encouraging countries to use the possibility of introducing capital controls as provided for in its Articles of Agreement, and advising them on their national implementation (Rodrik, 2009; South Centre, 2008). Since introducing flexible management of capital inflows requires certain administrative capabilities, it would also be appropriate for the Bretton Woods institutions to provide advice to policymakers in developing and transition economies and help them create and strengthen their administrative capacities to run a capital-account management regime that suits their country-specific requirements.

3. Dealing with debt and payments crises

In view of the potential impact of the global financial and economic crisis on developing countries, a multilaterally agreed mechanism for a temporary standstill on debt repayments would greatly help orderly debt workouts (*TDR 2001*, chap. VI, section D). Since it would involve the private sector in the resolution of financial crises in emerging markets, it would influence investor and creditor behaviour and portfolio decisions. This could also help reduce potentially destabilizing capital flows.

Once crises have broken out, the resolution of sovereign debt has also often been a messy and time-consuming affair that has been damaging to the interests of both private creditors and sovereign debtors. Given these experiences a clear set of international rules and procedures could be of benefit to all: they could force holdout creditors to accept the terms of debt restructuring, impose stays on litigation during restructuring negotiations, and provide for the extension of new credits during restructuring exercises. Proposals for the introduction of an orderly international debt workout mechanism for sovereign debt, modelled on national insolvency procedures, have been made by UNCTAD since the 1980s (*TDR 1986*, annex to chapter VI; *TDR 1998*, chapter IV; *TDR 2001*, chapter VI, section D). And after the experience with the Asian financial crisis, a "sovereign debt restructuring mechanism" was discussed in the IMF (Krueger, 2002). This proposal failed to gain sufficient support, but it helped generate momentum for the inclusion of collective action clauses (CACs) in new international bond issues. These clauses allow for such provisions as altering repayment terms by a super majority of bondholders and restrictions on individual creditors from disrupting restructuring processes. However, the effectiveness of CACs is limited because most of them do not cover all categories of bonds, nor do they endorse standstill provisions. They are designed primarily to facilitate the restructuring of sovereign debts *after* a crisis has broken out. In addition, CACs leave many of the key decisions concerning debt restructuring to private creditors, rather than allocating them to an independent arbiter, or sharing decision-making more equally with sovereign debtors in a formal institutional setting (Helleiner, 2009).

D. International reserves and the role of SDRs

1. Disadvantages of the current system

Another issue that has received renewed attention in the discussion about necessary reforms of the international monetary and financial system is the role of the United States dollar as the main international reserve currency. The current international monetary system, with flexible exchange rates between the major currencies, the dollar as the main international reserve currency, and free international capital flows, has failed to achieve the smooth adjustment of payments imbalances. This is the conclusion reached by the Commission of Experts of the President of the United Nations General Assembly on Reforms of the International Monetary and Financial System (also known as the Stiglitz Commission) (UNPGA, 2009). The main reason for this failure is that the system has not provided for any disciplines on surplus countries and on deficit countries whose currencies are used as an international means of payment or store of value, such as the United States. As a result, the international monetary system cannot influence the behaviour of the major players that have been responsible for the current global imbalances. Moreover, it allows other deficit countries to avoid adjustment as long as they can continue to borrow abroad. But when their ability to continue to borrow abroad is cut off, for whatever reason, their adjustment takes the form of a contractionary crisis, which may have knock-on effects on other economies with which they have trade and credit-debt relations.

> The current international reserve system does not provide for any disciplines on surplus countries and on deficit countries that issue reserve currencies.

No country is obliged to hold reserves in dollars; indeed, central banks have been increasingly diversifying their reserve holdings in other currencies, in particular the euro, in order to reduce the exchange-rate risk in a world of financial and currency instability. Nevertheless, since the dollar serves as the main currency for settling international transactions, it has continued to be the preferred choice. However, an international reserve system in which a national currency is used as a reserve asset and as an international means of payment has the disadvantage that monetary policy in other countries cannot be designed independently from the monetary policy decisions of the issuing central bank. These decisions are not taken in consideration of the needs of the international payments system and the world economy, but in response to domestic policy needs and preferences in the country of the reserve currency. This problem also exists in a multiple reserve currency system. Moreover, an economy whose currency is used as a reserve currency is not under the same compulsion as others to undertake the necessary macroeconomic or exchange-rate adjustments to avoid continuing current-account deficits. Thus, the role of the dollar as the main means of international payments has also played an important role in the build-up of the global imbalances in the run-up to the financial crisis.

> In the absence of symmetric interventions in currency markets, the system has a deflationary bias.

Another disadvantage of the current international reserve system is that it imposes the burden of adjustment exclusively on deficit countries (except if it is the country issuing the reserve currency). Yet, to the extent that one or several countries run surpluses, one or several others must run deficits. The asymmetry in the adjustment burden introduces a deflationary bias into the system, because deficit countries are compelled to reduce imports when their ability to obtain external financing reaches its limits, whereas surplus countries are under no systemic obligation to raise their imports in order to balance their payments. By the same token, central banks can easily counter pressure on their currency to appreciate by buying foreign currency against their own; but they only have limited possibilities to do so when there is pressure for currency depreciation, because their foreign exchange reserves are limited. IMF policies support this bias by imposing conditions of restrictive policies on deficit countries in connection with its lending activities, rather than pressing surplus countries for more expansionary policies in connection with its surveillance activities. Thus, as long as there is no multilaterally agreed rule for countries to support each others' economies through coordinated demand management and through symmetric interventions in the foreign exchange market, the system has a deflationary bias.

> The economic costs and benefits of reserve holdings cannot be seen in isolation from a broader macroeconomic strategy.

2. The cost of holding foreign exchange reserves

The experience with financial crises in the 1990s led developing and transition economies to believe they could not rely on adequate assistance from the international financial institutions in times of need. It also made them reluctant to abide by the procyclical conditionality typically attached to such support. As a result, many of them tried to avoid current-account deficits and, indeed, accumulated large amounts of international reserves as a form of self-insurance. This has led to discussions about the cost of holding foreign exchange reserves. However, defining these costs is not straightforward (box 4.2).

One way to look at the cost of reserve holdings is to compare the financial returns on the reserve holdings of a country – typically the interest on United States Treasury bills – with the generally higher interest which would have to be paid by that country on borrowing on international capital markets. In this case, the costs would imply an outward income transfer for the country holding the reserves. Such a calculation is valid when reserves are "borrowed", in the sense of being associated with capital inflows (i.e. increased liabilities vis-à-vis foreign lenders or non-residents who purchase domestic financial assets (Akyüz, 2009)). This applies to about half of the total reserves of developing and emerging economies. However, the capital inflow is rarely initiated by the receiving countries for the purpose of creating a cushion of foreign exchange reserves. Rather, they are often the outcome of portfolio investment decisions of foreign agents. In this case, the purchase of the reserve currency by the central bank is likely to be motivated primarily by the desire to counter pressure on the domestic currency to appreciate. This has often been the case not only in situations where central banks have wanted to fend off the effects of rising capital inflows on their currency, but also in situations where large current-account surpluses have exerted pressure for currency appreciation, such as in China and in fuel-exporting countries in recent years.

The link between exchange-rate management and changes in foreign exchange reserves suggests that the economic costs and benefits of reserve holdings cannot be seen in isolation from a broader macroeconomic strategy. In the absence of intervention in the foreign exchange market, and the associated reserve accumulation, currency appreciation would lead to a loss of international competitiveness of domestic producers, and lower exports, output and employment. At the same time, the unchecked net inflow of private capital could destabilize the domestic financial system, resulting in an increased risk of a banking crisis. The underlying problem is that in the current monetary system, effective multilateral agreements for exchange-rate management and the provision of adequate international liquidity in times of need are missing. Reform that aims at addressing the causes rather than the symptoms of the current crisis must therefore focus on these two latter aspects.

3. Reform of the reserve system and the role of SDRs

The question of the reserve currency in the current international monetary system has been reviewed at considerable length in the report of the Stiglitz Commission: it takes up the issue of reform involving Special Drawing Rights (SDRs) as the main form of international liquidity. One proposal discussed by the Commission, which has also been reiterated by other authors (see, for example, Bergsten, 2007), was first discussed in the late 1970s to facilitate reserve diversification away from dollars without creating the risk of a major dollar crisis. This proposal envisaged giving central banks the possibility to deposit dollar reserves in a special "substitution account" at the IMF, to be denominated in SDRs. The SDRs could also be used to settle international payments. Since the SDR is valued as the weighted average of the major currencies,[5] its value

is more stable than that of each of the constituent currencies. This does not mean that the exchange rate risk would disappear; it would simply be shifted to the IMF. The risk would have to be covered either through the generation of higher revenues by the IMF or by guarantees from member States. Moreover, the reserve currency country could still delay adjustment in case of external imbalances if the IMF invested the dollar reserves deposited by central banks in United States Treasury bonds. But then there would remain the problem of exchange-rate determination of the currencies of the member States.

A step that would go much further than the introduction of a substitution account would be to enable a new "Global Reserve Bank" or a reformed IMF to issue an "artificial" reserve currency, such as the "bancor" suggested by Keynes in his Bretton Woods proposals for an International Clearing Union.[6] The new global reserve system could be built on the existing system of SDRs (Akyüz, 2009). One possibility is for countries to agree to exchange their own currencies for the new currency, so that the global currency would be backed by a basket of currencies of all the members. But other variants are also discussed in the Commission's report. The new system could contain penalties against countries that maintain deficits, and equally against countries that maintain surpluses. A variable charge would be levied depending on the size of the surpluses or deficits.

Recognizing the need for increasing international liquidity in the current financial and economic crisis, the G-20, at its London Summit in April 2009, announced its support for a new general SDR allocation, which would inject $250 billion into the world economy and increase global liquidity. However, a major problem with the G-20 proposal is that the new SDRs are allocated among the IMF's various members in line with the existing pattern of quotas, so that the G-7 countries, which do not need liquidity support from the IMF, would get over 45 per cent of the newly allocated SDRs, while less than 37 per cent would be allocated to developing and transition economies, and less than 8 per cent to low-income countries. Countries most in need of international liquidity would thus receive the smallest shares.

> Any reform of the international monetary and financial system has to address the issue of SDR allocation.

Box 4.2

ON THE COST OF INTERNATIONAL RESERVES

The reasons for a central bank to build up foreign exchange reserves are manifold. One important reason appears to be disenchantment with international financial institutions in general, and a loss of faith in the IMF in particular. After the painful experiences of the financial crises of the 1990s, many developing and emerging-market economies were no longer willing to rely on the global monetary institutions as lenders of last resort. Consequently, they accumulated large reserves as an instrument of self-insurance.

While most observers agree that reserve accumulation can help reduce the probability of a financial crisis in developing and transition economies, it is often argued that this kind of self-insurance has high opportunity costs, because the money tied in reserves could be used for other purposes in support of economic development and poverty alleviation (see, for example, McKinley, 2006; and Stiglitz and Charlton, 2005). According to the Chairman of the United States Federal Reserve, Ben Bernanke (2005: 6), by accumulating reserves, "governments have acted as financial intermediaries, channelling domestic saving away from local uses and into international capital markets." Reserves are seen as part of a country's "savings", and very high reserves are interpreted as a kind of "surplus savings". However, the view that reserve holdings have opportunity costs in terms of foregone domestic consumption or investment is questionable.

A build-up of reserves in international currency implies an intervention of a country's central bank in currency markets, through the purchase of foreign currency with its own currency. The largest proportion of these reserves is denominated in United States dollars, which are not held in cash but invested in dollar-denominated interest-bearing assets, mostly United States Treasury bonds. However, the domestic currency that the central bank uses for the purchase of dollar reserves is not withdrawn from domestic income. It is not financed from tax revenues or by additional government borrowing, but results from a process of money creation. The purchase of foreign currency increases the amount of domestic currency in circulation in the same way as the central bank's purchase of domestic bonds in open market operations or that bank's credit to domestic commercial banks. This is reflected in the central bank's balance sheet as an addition both on the assets side (foreign bonds) and the liabilities side (currency in circulation). Whether the central bank increases the amount of currency in circulation by acquiring domestic government bonds or foreign government bonds has no impact on the amount of domestic consumption or investment. However, it has an impact on the exchange rate of the domestic currency vis-à-vis the dollar, which is what is intended by the intervention, namely to prevent an appreciation of the domestic currency.

Similarly, accumulated reserves cannot be turned into higher domestic consumption or investment by a decision of the central bank. Assume that in order to make reserves "available" for public infrastructure investment, the central bank decides to sell the United States Treasury bonds against its own currency. This will lead to an appreciation of the domestic currency against the dollar, while the domestic currency in circulation falls by an amount equal to that of the reduction in the stock of reserves. This implies the elimination of the money that was created at the time of the initial intervention in the currency market. In other words, whenever the central bank converts foreign currency reserves back into its own currency the money disappears.

This happens because a central bank does not function in the same way as a private firm or household. For them depositing money in a bank account has the opportunity cost of not being used for consumption or investment purposes. Those "reserves", if reactivated, indeed represent an increase in purchasing power. If invested wisely, the household or firm gains from the activation of its saved "reserves". Reserves of the central bank are of a completely different nature. As the central bank is able to create money out of nothing, the activation of reserves (through the bond or currency market) simply amounts to a destruction of currency in circulation: for the overall economy the money just disappears. This is so because the central bank is a unique institution with the monopoly of creating base money (if reserves are increased) and destroying base money (if reserves are reduced). On the other hand, if the central bank wants to

Box 4.2 *(concluded)*

stimulate investment in general, and is willing to finance public investment directly, it can do so at any time – independently of its level of international reserves.

However, reserve holdings may imply financial costs for the public accounts. When the increase in the amount of domestic currency in circulation resulting from the intervention is not desired for reasons of domestic monetary policy, the central bank sterilizes this effect by reducing its liquidity provision to the domestic banking system through other channels. In the case of full sterilization, the liabilities of the central bank remain unchanged, while on the assets side of its balance sheet the increase in the holdings of foreign bonds is compensated by a reduction of its holdings of domestic currency assets. In this case, the cost of the reserve holding for the central bank would be the difference between the interest earned on United States Treasury bonds and the foregone interest that would have been earned from domestic currency assets if – as is likely – the interest earned on the Treasuries had been lower. Similarly, if the sterilization is achieved through the central bank's issuing of domestic sterilization bonds, the cost will be the difference between the interest to be paid on these bonds and that earned on the Treasuries. These would represent financial costs for the central bank – or the public budget – but not for the economy as a whole, as no outward transfer of real income would take place.

The creation of reserves takes real resources away from the economy as a whole only if the intervention occurs in response to an inflow of foreign capital, rather than to an increase in demand for the domestic currency due to a rise in net exports. The additional reserves resulting from the intervention would then be accompanied by an increase of external liabilities on which interest has to be paid. If the interest to be paid to the foreign investor or creditor is higher than the interest rate on United States Treasury bonds, the reserve holding entails a net cost for the economy. This is generally, though not always, the case, because it is rare for low interest rates to be associated with an appreciation pressure for the domestic economy. The latter may occur in situations such as that of China, where a low valuation of its currency, stemming from a financial crisis in 1993, has led to a huge current-account surplus and where, additionally, a large inflow of foreign investment occurred. In this case, it is the current-account surplus that has caused the piling up of reserves, and not the other way around, as implicit in mainstream theory (see Bernanke, 2005).

In any case, an evaluation of the costs and benefits of reserve holdings needs to take into account the fact that the accumulation of foreign exchange reserves not only reduces the risk of a financial crisis, but also influences a country's exchange rate in a way that increases the international competitiveness of its domestic producers.

Thus any reform of the international monetary and financial system aimed at making the SDR the main form of international liquidity, with all the features of a global reserve medium, would have to address the issue of SDR allocation more generally. A fundamental question to be resolved at the outset would be what purpose the SDR as the main medium of international liquidity should fulfil. For example, would it be used for clearing among central banks or could it also be used by the private sector? Issuing SDRs then has a geographical and a time dimension.[7]

With regard to the geographical dimension, the Stiglitz Commission proposed that SDRs should be allocated to member States on the basis of some estimation of their demand for reserves, or, more generally, on some judgement of "need". Appropriate criteria for determining the need of countries would need to be worked out, but clearly an allocation according to the current structure of IMF quotas would be entirely out of line with needs. One approach would be to distribute new SDRs in relation to the size of the demand for reserves in recent years. Another approach would be to link the issuance of

SDRs with development financing by allowing the IMF to invest some of the funds made available through issuance of SDRs in the bonds of multilateral development banks. As highlighted by the Stiglitz Commission, such a proposal had been made by an UNCTAD panel of experts in the 1960s, before the international liberalization of financial markets began and when access to capital market financing by developing-country borrowers was very limited.

> A proposal to link the issuance of SDRs with development financing was made by UNCTAD as early as the 1960s.

With regard to the time dimension, the question of frequency and cyclicality arises. Over time, the need for international liquidity grows, in principle with the growth of the world economy and the expansion of international trade and financial transactions. Yet an annual increase of SDRs in line with global GDP would mean that additional SDRs would be issued in periods of high growth, while they are needed most in periods of slow growth or recession. The G-20 finance ministers meeting in April 2009 endorsed the proposal for a countercyclical issuance of SDRs. If the purpose of SDR allocation is to stabilize global output growth, it would indeed be appropriate to issue more SDRs when global growth is below potential or during crisis periods, and to issue smaller amounts or retire SDRs in periods of fast global output growth.

An international financial system that does not primarily aim at catering to financial market participants – whose decisions are more often than not guided by misconceived notions of "sound" macroeconomic fundamentals and policies – but at preventing crises and ensuring a favourable global economic environment for development, should provide emergency financing without the sort of conditions attached that exacerbate recessions and disequilibria.

> Unconditional countercyclical access to IMF resources would help prevent excessive currency depreciations.

The rationale for the unconditional provision of international liquidity in times of crisis is that, in order to balance the external payments, deficit countries need to restore the competitiveness of their domestic producers. Therefore countries in danger of a downward "overshooting" of the exchange rate need international assistance, rather than belt-tightening and procyclical policies. Without such assistance, they would have to lower the overall cost level, which mainly involves cutting wages. However, contrary to predictions by orthodox economic theory, wage cuts have an immediate dampening effect on domestic demand and further destabilize the economy. Moreover, wage cuts of the size needed to restore competitiveness are deflationary and add to the general depression of production and investment. In such situations, even countries with current-account deficits and weak currencies need expansionary fiscal and monetary policies to compensate for the fall in domestic demand, because the potential expansionary effects of currency devaluation are unlikely to materialize quickly in a sharply contracting global economy.

One of the advantages of using SDRs in such a countercyclical fashion is that it would, in principle, facilitate the task of preventing excessive currency depreciations in countries in crisis. This could best be achieved by allowing all countries unconditional access to IMF resources by an amount that is needed to stabilize their exchange rate at a multilaterally agreed level. However, the rules and conditions for access would need to be elaborated carefully, including determining the level at which exchange rates should be stabilized. Another important issue would be the extent to which SDRs should be made available in crisis situations, to cover not only current-account transactions but also capital-account liabilities. This is because, a priori, the purpose of giving countries unconditional access to international liquidity should be to ensure that the level of imports can be maintained, and not to bail out foreign investors.

Whatever form an enhanced scheme of SDR allocation takes, it will only be acceptable to all countries of the system if the terms at which SDRs can be used as international liquidity are absolutely clear-cut, particularly SDR parity vis-à-vis all national currencies.

E. A global monetary system with stable real exchange rates and symmetric intervention obligations

The most important lesson of the recent global crisis is that financial markets do not "get the prices right"; they systematically overshoot or undershoot due to centralized information handling, which is quite different from the information collection of normal goods markets. In financial markets, nearly all participants react in a more or less uniform manner to the same set of "information" or "news", so that they wind or unwind their exposure to risk almost in unison.[8]

The currency market, in particular, causes results quite different from those envisaged by theory, such as an appreciation of the nominal exchange rate in countries that have high inflation rates over considerable periods of time. In fact, high-inflation countries are the main targets for short-term capital flows, because they usually offer high interest rates. In so doing, they attract "investors" that use interest rate arbitrage by carrying money from countries with low interest rates to those with high interest rates, thereby putting pressure on the currency of the latter to appreciate. This is just the opposite of what is required by macroeconomic fundamentals: countries with relatively high inflation need nominal devaluation to restore their competitiveness in goods markets, and those with low inflation need appreciation.

A viable solution to the exchange-rate problem, preferable to any "corner solution", would be a system of managed flexible exchange rates which aims for a rate that is consistent with a sustainable current-account position. But since the exchange rate is a variable that involves more than one currency, there is a much better chance of achieving a stable pattern of exchange rates in a multilaterally agreed framework for exchange-rate management.

The Bretton Woods system and the European Monetary System provide precedents for what could be an appropriate solution to determine exchange rates within a multilateral framework. In these systems, the implicit rule was that the exchange rate of the national currencies with the international currency would be determined by the purchasing power of the currency expressed in all other currencies. This rule may be difficult to introduce at the time the system starts, because of the problem of determining the initial purchasing power parities of each currency. However, it would be straightforward and simple once the system is on track. It may also be necessary to apply some additional criteria that reflect structural features related to the level of development of different countries.

Once a set of sustainable exchange rates is found and accepted by the countries, inflation differentials may be the main guide for managing nominal exchange rates in order to maintain the real exchange rates (RERs) at sustainable levels. However, for some countries, at certain times additional factors may need to be taken into account. For instance, countries'

> Achieving a stable pattern of exchange rates stands a better chance within a multilaterally agreed framework for exchange-rate management.

falling export incomes resulting from factors that are beyond the control of an individual country may warrant an exchange-rate adjustment, even though it may have no impact on the general domestic price level. Sustainable levels of RERs can also change with countries' development, and the body in charge of exchange-rate management would need to take that evolution into account.

Management of the nominal exchange rate is therefore required to maintain stability in the RER, but the scope for an individual monetary authority to do so is limited. It can always check an unwanted appreciation of its exchange rate by purchasing foreign currencies against its own currency, thus accumulating foreign exchange reserves (with the need for sterilization of the domestic monetary effect); however, its capacity to counter a potentially overshooting devaluation is circumscribed by the amount of the foreign exchange reserves that it can sell in exchange for its own currency. The situation would be quite different if exchange-rate management became a multilateral task in which countries whose currencies were under pressure to devalue were joined in their fight against speculation by the monetary authorities of those countries whose currencies were under pressure to appreciate.[9]

An internationally agreed exchange-rate system based on the principle of constant and sustainable RERs of all countries would go a long way towards reducing the scope for speculative capital flows, which generate volatility in the international financial system and distort the pattern of exchange rates. Since the RER is defined as the nominal exchange rate adjusted by the inflation differentials between countries, a constant RER results from nominal exchange rates strictly following inflation differentials. A constant RER at a competitive level would achieve the following:

> An exchange-rate system based on the principle of constant real exchange rates would tackle the problem of destabilizing capital flows at its source.

- Curb speculation, because the main trigger for currency speculation is the inflation and interest rate differential. Higher inflation and higher interest rates would be compensated by the devaluation of nominal exchange rates, thereby reducing the scope for gains from carry trade.

- Prevent currency crises, because the main incentive for speculating in currencies of high-inflation countries would disappear, and overvaluation, one of the main destabilizing factors for developing countries in the past 20 years, would not occur.

- Prevent fundamental and long-lasting global imbalances, because all countries with relatively diversified production structures would maintain their level of competitiveness in global trade relations.

- Avoid debt traps for developing countries, because unsustainable current-account deficits triggered by a loss in international competitiveness would not build up.

- Avoid procyclical conditionality in case of crisis, because, if the system were to have symmetric intervention obligations, the assistance needed for countries under pressure to depreciate their currencies would come automatically from the partners in the system whose currencies would appreciate correspondingly.

- Reduce the need to hold international reserves, because with symmetric intervention obligations under the "constant RER" rule, reserves would only be needed to compensate for volatility of export earnings but no longer to defend the exchange rate.

Such a multilateral system based on the "constant RER" rule would tackle the problem of destabilizing capital flows at its source. It would remove the major incentive for currency speculation and ensure that monetary factors do not stand in the way of achieving a level playing field for international trade. It would also get rid of debt traps and counterproductive conditionality. The last point is perhaps the most important: countries facing strong depreciation pressure would automatically receive the required assistance once a sustainable level of the exchange rate had been reached in the form of swap agreements or direct intervention by the counterparty.

F. The role of regional cooperation and international policy coordination

Establishing an exchange-rate system such as outlined in the preceding section would take some time, not least because it requires international consensus and multilateral institution building. As long as an optimal multilateral exchange-rate system that minimizes the incentives for destabilizing capital flows is not in place, quantitative restrictions on capital mobility (as discussed in section C above) may be helpful in preventing speculative capital movements from exerting pressure on exchange rates and destabilizing the financial system in individual countries.

At the regional level, greater monetary and financial cooperation, including reserve pooling, regional payments clearance mechanisms that function without using the dollar, and regional exchange-rate systems could help countries in the region enlarge their macroeconomic policy space. They could also avert financial and currency crises, and reduce dependence on borrowing from the international financial institutions if such crises occurred.[10]

In this regard, considerable progress has been made among members of the Association of Southeast Asian Nations (ASEAN), plus China, Japan and the Republic of Korea (ASEAN+3): their Chiang Mai Initiative is evolving from a network of bilateral swap agreements into a collectively managed fund that will pool the foreign exchange reserves of these countries (Henning, 2009).[11] These exchange and credit facilities are intended to facilitate bilateral trade

> Greater monetary and financial cooperation would reduce dependence on borrowing from the IMF.

and investment, and to disconnect such exchanges from international trade credit shortages and possible disturbances in the international financial system. Other ongoing initiatives seek to create or revitalize regional payment mechanisms. In Latin America, for example, several countries have agreed to use their national currencies for payments in trading with each other.[12] Such agreements would be especially attractive if they were linked with easy access to trade credit, especially at times when such credit is more expensive and scarce. Furthermore, they could evolve towards a regional monetary system with a new regional currency. Currency swap agreements are also becoming more frequent among central banks of emerging-market economies in different regions.[13]

While a multilateral exchange-rate mechanism would minimize the risk of large current-account imbalances emerging, it may not necessarily be sufficient to correct large imbalances that are the result of diverging rates of domestic demand growth over several years, such as the United States deficit and the German, Japanese and Chinese surpluses that had built up since the early 1990s. Therefore, the global economic governance would gain greater coherence if multilateral trade rules and a multilateral exchange rate mechanism were complemented by an effective system of surveillance and macroeconomic policy coordination. So far, policy surveillance by the IMF has been effective only for countries borrowing from the Fund, and macroeconomic policy coordination has been provided only on an ad hoc basis during crises, but not for the purpose of preventing such crises.

The present global macroeconomic situation, in which the central economic policy concern in all countries is to overcome the recession, highlights the necessity of an internationally coordinated policy response that also takes into account the needs of developing countries. As discussed in chapter I, the United States Government was quick to introduce an impressive fiscal stabilization package as a complement to monetary easing with the aim of reviving the credit market. Governments of many other countries also acted with similar responses, in recognition of the need for countercyclical monetary and fiscal policies. But in many cases, especially in Europe, more expansionary fiscal action is required to support the global fight against recession. Unfortunately, this pattern of international demand stimulus is repeating the earlier pattern in the distribution of global demand growth that led to the build-up of the global current-account imbalances in the first place.

> A further accumulation of external debt obligations by the United States would make the world economy even more fragile.

Indeed, in the absence of a deep reform of the international exchange-rate system and appropriate rules and mechanisms for multilateral intervention in currency markets, there is a danger that, in responding to the present crisis, an increasing number of countries will aim at an undervalued exchange rate, bigger current-account surpluses and higher foreign exchange reserves. The question then is which country will run the necessary deficits. The experience of the years preceding the crisis suggests that the EU and Japan are quite reluctant to employ more expansionary policies. Thus, as long as the dollar is the main reserve asset in an unstable monetary system, the main deficit economy might again be the United States. However, a further accumulation of external debt obligations by that economy would make the world economy even more fragile. Therefore, developing countries may be well advised to turn to a more balanced growth strategy which gives greater emphasis than in the past to domestic and regional demand for increasing production and employment. ∎

Notes

1   See also UNCTAD (2009) for an analysis of the crisis and proposals for reform of the governance of the international monetary and financial system.

2   This has come to be called "Bretton Woods II" (Dooley, Folkerts-Landau and Garber, 2003).

3   IMF Articles of Agreement, Article VI, Section 3: Controls of capital transfers.

4   Like monetary policy itself, the use of tax-based instruments to offset interest rate differentials becomes complicated if expectations of significant exchange-rate changes come into play.

5   In July 2009, the SDR basket contained 0.632 dollars, 0.410 euros, 0.0903 pounds and 0.0543 yen.

6   Keynes first mooted the idea of a world unit of currency, together with proposals for an International Clearing Union, more than 50 years ago, at the Bretton Woods negotiations on post-war monetary arrangements. This set of proposals has been called the Keynes Plan. The Stiglitz Commission notes that the IMF, due to its current governance structure, may not be considered neutral enough by all countries or have the capacity to serve as the issuer of such a currency. It therefore proposes that a new Global Reserve Bank be created for the purpose.

7   A change in the allocation of SDRs would require an amendment of the IMF's Articles of Agreement. A precedent is the amendment that was made in 1997 in order to distribute SDRs to countries which had joined the IMF after 1981 and thus had never received any SDRs: mainly transition economies in

Eastern Europe and Central Asia. Because it was an amendment to the Fund's charter, it had to be approved by the legislatures of many IMF members, and specifically by the United States Congress, where it has languished for 12 years. However, the G-20 proposal for an increase in SDRs (see chapter I, section D.5 of this *Report*) has prompted the United States Government to call on Congress to finally take action.

8   The first quarter of 2009 shows this result: the parallel increase in stock and commodity prices, as well as the appreciation of previously devaluating currencies at the same time, shows once again a strong correlation between the unwinding of speculation in different markets that should be uncorrelated. Moreover, increases cannot be explained by any other factor than speculation. This yields the paradoxical result of rising prices of crude oil during the biggest global recession in decades.

9   This was practiced by the members of the European Monetary System before the introduction of the euro as a common currency

10 Options for, and experience and progress with, regional financial and monetary cooperation among developing countries were discussed in greater detail in *TDR 2007*, chap. V.

11 See also Shamin A and Seyoon K, Asia agrees on expanded $120 billion currency pool, Bloomberg, 23 February 2009.

12 The use of domestic currencies for regional payments is considered an option in the Latin American Integration Association (LAIA-ALADI), which has been managing a regional system of payments and clearing among 12 Latin American central banks since the 1960s (ALADI, 2009). In addition, countries that integrate the Bolivarian Alternative for the Americas (ALBA) are considering the establishment of a regional system for clearing and payments in local currencies. The Unified Regional System for Payments Clearing (Sistema Unitario de Compensación Regional de Pagos, SUCRE) would initially comprise Bolivia, the Bolivarian Republic of Venezuela, Cuba, Ecuador, Honduras and Nicaragua (Prensa Latina, "ALBA aprueba acuerdo macro de moneda virtual Sucre", 3 July 2009, at: http://www. alternativabolivariana.org/modules.php?name=New s&file=article&sid=4695).

13 For instance, between December 2008 and March 2009, China signed bilateral currency swap agreements with Indonesia, Hong Kong (China), Malaysia, the Republic of Korea, and, beyond the region, with Argentina and Belarus, for a total amount of 650 billion yuan ($95 billion). The agreements allow central banks to access to the partner's currency for a three-year (extendable) period. Such agreements may also enhance the yuan's role as an international currency and eventually favour the emergence of a multipolar exchange system.

References

Akyüz Y (2009). Policy Response to the Global Financial Crisis: Key Issues for Developing Countries. South Centre, Geneva, May.

ALADI (2009). Se celebró en la ALADI el Seminario para la Dinamización del Convenio de Pagos y Créditos Recíprocos y el uso de los Sistemas de Pagos en Monedas Locales, Press Release 23, 23 April 2009. Available at: http://www.aladi.org/nsfaladi/prensa. nsf/VComunicadosWebAnteriores?OpenView.

Bergsten C (2007). Toward a Free Trade Area of the Asia Pacific. Policy Briefs in International Economics 07–2. Washington, DC, Peterson Institute for International Economics, February.

Bernanke B (2005). The Global Saving Glut and the U.S. Current Account Deficit. Speech at the Sandridge Lecture, Virginia Association of Economics, Richmond, Virginia, 10 March. Available at: http://www.federalreserve.gov/boarddocs/speeches/2005/200503102/.

Cheng HS (1980). Substitution Account. Federal Reserve Bank of San Francisco Newsletter, 7 March: 1–3.

Cooper R (1994). What Future for the International Monetary System? In: Siklos P, ed. *Varieties of Monetary Reforms*. London, Kluwer Academic Publishers.

Dooley MP, Folkerts-Landau D and Garber P (2003). An Essay on the Revised Bretton Woods System. NBER Working Paper 9971. Cambridge, MA, National Bureau of Economic Research, September.

Dornbusch R (1997). Cross-border payment taxes and alternative capital-account regimes. UNCTAD, *International Monetary and Financial Issues for the*

1990s, Vol. VIII. United Nations publication, sales no. E.97.II.D.5, New York and Geneva.

Epstein G, Grabel I and Jomo K (2004). Capital Management Techniques in Developing Countries: Managing Capital Flows in Malaysia, India, and China. Revised version of the paper presented at the XVIth Technical Group Meeting (TGM) of the G-24 in Port of Spain, Trinidad and Tobago, 13–14 February 2003. Available at: http://www.jomoks.org/research/other/rp012.htm.

Helleiner E (2009). The Contemporary Reform of Global Financial Governance: Implications and Lessons from the Past. G-24 Discussion Paper No. 55. New York and Geneva, UNCTAD, April.

Henning C (2009). The Future of the Chiang Mai Initiative: An Asian Monetary Fund? Policy Brief 09–5. Washington, DC, Peterson Institute for International Economics, February.

IMF (2007). *World Economic Outlook,* Washington, DC, International Monetary Fund, October.

IMF (2009). *International Financial Statistics* database. International Monetary Fund.

Kaminsky GL, Reinhart CM and Vég CA (2004). When It Rains, It Pours: Procyclical Capital Flows and Macroeconomic Policies. NBER Working Paper No. 10780, September.

Kenen P (2001). The International Financial Architecture: What's New? What's Missing? Washington, DC, Institute for International Economics.

Keynes JM (1936). *The General Theory of Employment, Interest and Money.* New York, Harcourt, Brace and Company.

Krueger A (2002). A New Approach to Sovereign Debt Restructuring. Washington, DC, International Monetary Fund.

McKinley T (2006). The monopoly of global capital flows: who needs structural adjustment now? Working Paper, 12. International Poverty Centre, United Nations Development Programme, March.

Ocampo JA, Spiegel S and Stiglitz JE (2008). Capital Market Liberalization and Development. In: Ocampo JA and Stiglitz JE, eds. *Capital Market Liberalization and Development.* New York, Oxford University Press for the Initiative for Policy Dialogue, Columbia University.

Prasad ES et al. (2003). Effects of Financial Globalization on Developing Countries: Some Empirical Evidence. Occasional Paper 220, International Monetary Fund.

Reinhart C and Rogoff K (2008). Is the 2007 US Financial Crisis So Different? An International Historical Comparison. *American Economic Review,* 98 (2): 339–344.

Rodrik D (2009). Let Developing Nations Rule. VOX EU, 28 January. Available at: http://www.voxeu.org/index.php?q=node/2885.

Rodrik D and Subramanian A (2008). Why We Need to Curb Global Flows of Capital. *Financial Times,* 26 February.

Schmidt R (2007). The Currency Transaction Tax: Rate and Revenue Estimates. Ottawa, North-South Institute.

Shamin A and Seyoon K (2009). Asian Ministers Agree to Partly Pool Foreign Reserves. Bloomberg, 5 May.

Stiglitz JE and Charlton A (2005). The Strategic Role of the IMF: Risks for Emerging Market Economies amid Increasingly Globalized Financial Markets. Paper prepared for the G-24 Technical Group Meeting, 15–16 September, Washington, DC.

Stiglitz JE et al. (2006). Stability with Growth: Macroeconomics, Liberalization and Development. New York, Oxford University Press for the Initiative for Policy Dialogue, Columbia University.

South Centre (2008). Calls for Revamping the Global Financial Architecture. Statement by Board Members of the South Centre. Geneva, 29 October. Available at: http://www.southcentre.org/index.php?option=com_content&task=view&id=871&Itemid=1.

Tobin J (1978). A proposal for international monetary reform. *Eastern Economic Journal,* 4: 153–59.

Ul Haq M, Grunberg I and Kaul I, eds. (1996). *The Tobin Tax.* New York, Oxford University Press.

UNCTAD (2009). The Global Economic Crisis: Systemic Failures and Multilateral Remedies. United Nations publications, sales no. E.09.II.D.4. New York and Geneva, April.

UNCTAD (various issues). *Trade and Development Report.* United Nations publications, New York and Geneva.

UNPGA (2009). Report of the Commission of Experts of the President of the United Nations General Assembly on Reforms of the International Monetary and Financial System. Available at: http://www.un.org/ga/president/63/commission/financial_commission.shtml.

Wolf M (2008). Fixing Global Finance. Baltimore, Johns Hopkins University Press.

Chapter V

CLIMATE CHANGE MITIGATION AND DEVELOPMENT

A. Introduction

The warming of the global climate system as a result of increasing greenhouse gas (GHG) concentrations in the atmosphere has become a major concern worldwide. Climate change is manifest in higher average global temperatures, rising global mean sea levels, melting ice caps and an increased intensity and frequency of extreme weather events. Most scientific research suggests that the consequences of unabated climate change could be dramatic. And while doubts remain about some of the concrete impacts, it seems clear that global warming will significantly increase the risk of a severe deterioration of the natural environment, with attendant effects on human well-being. It is virtually impossible to reasonably quantify the impact of unabated climate change in economic terms, as this involves a very long time horizon and highly subjective judgments. But because of the large risks and uncertainties, and the potential for severe economic repercussions, strong and early action to mitigate climate change is advocated (Stern, 2006; Weitzman, 2007). Looking at long-term climate change mitigation from this risk-management perspective is not primarily an economic issue but an ethical imperative.

> Climate change mitigation has much in common with other processes of structural change in which new economic opportunities arise.

A certain degree of global warming and its related impacts have already become unavoidable and will require adequate adaptation measures. Adaptation is therefore an important issue, which is mainly related to addressing natural disasters in developing countries that suffer the most from the negative effects of climate change. This necessitates substantial financial and technical support for the poorer among the countries affected. A different, though related issue is that of mitigating further climate change by shifting global production and consumption patterns towards the use of more climate-friendly primary commodities, production equipment and consumer goods than the current GHG-intensive ones. This chapter focuses on some of the economic and development policy implications of climate change mitigation.

There is broad agreement that the scale of emission reductions needed to reduce global warming to more acceptable levels requires global action, and that developed countries have to make a major effort in this regard. They are mainly responsible for the current levels of GHG concentration, and they have greater financial and technological capabilities to take the necessary GHG abatement actions. However, developing countries, where GHG emissions are growing rapidly, cannot afford to remain as passive bystanders. Climate change mitigation is as much in their interests as in those of developed countries; it would considerably improve their prospects for development and poverty reduction. The possible linkages or trade-offs between developing-country policies for climate change mitigation and policies geared towards their development and poverty reduction objectives are therefore of central importance for their development path.

Historically, growth has been associated with increasing emissions, which gives the impression of an inevitable trade-off between growth and mitigation. In this chapter, it is argued that efforts directed at climate change mitigation can be compatible with faster growth. However, stronger political will is needed to make emissions regulation and control more stringent and to internalize the hitherto external costs of production and consumption. Furthermore, the wider dissemination of existing technologies and the development of new technologies and more climate-friendly modes of production and consumption cannot be left to market forces alone; they also require strong and internationally coordinated government action.

This chapter shows that developing countries have many options for contributing to climate change mitigation, which deserve to be pursued vigorously with the support of the international community. The economic approach to climate change mitigation has been dominated by calculating the costs of such mitigation and exploring mechanisms for attaining mitigation targets in the most cost-effective way. This chapter takes a different perspective: it argues that climate change mitigation should be associated with a process of global structural change, the parameters for which should be set politically by international agreements and national decisions on desirable reductions of GHG emissions. In the course of this process, demand will shift from GHG-intensive modes of production and consumption to more climate-friendly ones, causing losses and adjustment costs for many economic agents, but also generating new income for others. In this sense, climate change mitigation has much in common with other processes of structural change in which new economic opportunities arise in both developed and developing countries, especially as a result of the rapid growth of new markets.

From this perspective, the challenge for developing countries will be not only to adjust their modes of production and consumption to the requirement of reducing GHG emissions, but also to seize new growth opportunities created by new and fast growing markets. The process of structural change at the global level offers new opportunities for output growth because it may bring with it a revalorization of certain natural comparative advantages, and because the fast growth of domestic and international markets for what is sometimes called "environmental goods" is providing new possibilities for value-added creation.

Section B, which follows, summarizes findings on the economic implications of climate change for different groups of countries. Section C reviews policy measures that have already been introduced or are under discussion in the context of climate change mitigation. Section D elaborates on the notion of viewing climate change mitigation as a process of structural change, and consequently suggests a new interpretation of the economic costs of mitigation policies. In the subsequent section, the interaction between growth and development, on the one hand, and climate policies, on the other, is discussed. This is followed by an examination of specific options for GHG abatement in developing countries. The case is made for integrating GHG abatement policies with development policies. This not only offers considerable potential to generate synergies between climate change mitigation and development, it can also help developing countries gain from global efforts directed at GHG emission reductions, rather than losing out. Section F revisits, from a developing-country perspective, the emerging global framework for climate change mitigation, and the final section summarizes the conclusions of this chapter.

B. Greenhouse gas emissions and the global impact of climate change

Climate modellers expect that by the end of this century accumulated GHG emissions could cause a rise in the average global temperature of up to 6°C from the mean temperature of 1980–1999, if the current upward trend in GHG emissions is not reversed in the coming decades (IPCC, 2007a, table SPM-2). This global warming trend is a stock-pollutant problem. The emissions of carbon dioxide (CO_2) and other GHGs discharged into the atmosphere are causing relatively little harm by themselves; the main problem arises from the progressive accumulation of these gases over many decades.

There is a strong scientific consensus that most of the increase in the mean global temperature since the mid-twentieth century can be attributed to the progressive rise in atmospheric concentrations of GHGs resulting from human activities since the beginning of industrialization in the eighteenth century (IPCC, 2007b). The main determinants of GHG emissions are economic growth, population growth and technological progress. But there is no mechanical link between these factors and the levels of those emissions; rather, their current levels have been influenced largely by the behaviour of consumers and producers. There are very different levels of emissions for similar levels of development: for example, CO_2 emissions per capita in the United States are more than twice the level found in European countries or Japan, which are at similar levels of development (table 5.1). Efforts to reduce such emissions will therefore also need to focus on encouraging more environment-conscious behaviour among households, firms and public administrations. Accordingly, policies to mitigate climate change by reducing GHGs need to encourage not only the development of cleaner technologies, but also the wider adoption of existing and new, cleaner technologies by consumers and producers.

The rise in GHG concentrations is mainly due to CO_2 resulting from the use of fossil fuels, especially for power generation and transport in developed countries. Another important source of CO_2 emissions is change in land use, mainly deforestation (chart 5.1). Together with emissions of methane and nitrous oxides, which originate primarily in the agricultural sector, CO_2 accounts for nearly 99 per cent of global GHG emissions.

Developed countries account for most of the historical GHG emissions, especially the energy-related ones since 1900, and they are therefore largely responsible for the problem of global warming (IEA, 2008b). They also have much higher current per capita emissions than developing countries. On the other hand, most of the growth in total GHG emissions over the past four decades has taken place outside developed countries. Thus their share in total current GHG emissions fell considerably over the past 35 years. This tendency is expected to persist in the coming decades, primarily on account of the strong economic growth projected for developing countries, especially for the largest economies, China and India. This means that action in developed countries alone will not be sufficient to achieve a reduction in emissions by the amount necessary for obtaining a significant degree of climate change mitigation.

The impact of the accumulation of GHGs is felt not only in global warming, but also through related symptoms, such as changing rainfall patterns, receding glaciers, melting ice caps and rising sea levels. According to most scientific studies, climate change will also result in a higher frequency and intensity of extreme weather events (e.g. droughts, floods and storms), declining water resources, increased transmission of vector-borne diseases (e.g. malaria) and loss of biodiversity.

Table 5.1

CO_2 EMISSIONS RELATIVE TO POPULATION, GDP AND ENERGY CONSUMPTION, 1980–2006

(Tons of CO_2 equivalent)

	1980	*1990*	*2000*	*2006*	*Percentage change 1980–2006*
	Emissions per capita				
World	4.2	4.1	3.9	4.4	3.6
Developed countries	11.1	10.6	11.1	10.9	-1.2
Europe	8.7	7.9	7.6	7.6	-12.6
Japan	7.5	8.7	9.4	9.5	26.7
United States	20.5	15.6	16.0	15.2	-25.7
Transition economies	11.2	12.0	7.3	8.1	-28.3
Developing countries	1.1	1.4	1.7	2.3	105.3
Africa	0.9	1.0	0.9	1.0	17.6
Latin America	2.0	1.8	2.1	2.2	8.6
West Asia	3.8	4.4	5.9	6.8	78.9
Other Asia, excl. China	0.6	0.8	1.1	1.3	133.3
India	0.4	0.7	1.0	1.1	165.1
China	1.5	2.1	2.4	4.3	185.5
	Emissions per \$1 000 of GDP[a]				
World	0.7	0.6	0.5	0.5	-32.9
Developed countries	0.7	0.5	0.5	0.4	-39.7
Europe	0.6	0.4	0.4	0.3	-44.1
Japan	0.5	0.4	0.4	0.3	-24.4
United States	0.9	0.7	0.6	0.5	-44.0
Transition economies	1.4	1.7	1.8	1.3	-3.6
Developing countries	0.5	0.6	0.5	0.5	-9.3
Africa	0.4	0.4	0.4	0.4	2.6
Latin America	0.3	0.3	0.3	0.3	-6.7
West Asia	0.4	0.8	0.9	0.9	102.3
Other Asia, excl. China	0.4	0.4	0.4	0.4	-7.9
India	0.4	0.4	0.4	0.3	-8.1
China	1.7	1.2	0.6	0.6	-63.6
	Emissions per ton of oil equivalent[b]				
World	2.5	2.4	2.3	2.4	-4.4
Developed countries	2.6	2.5	2.4	2.3	-11.5
Europe	2.7	2.4	2.2	2.2	-20.4
Japan	2.6	2.4	2.3	2.3	-9.8
United States	2.6	2.5	2.5	2.5	-4.7
Transition economies	2.9	2.8	3.1	2.8	-3.1
Developing countries	1.9	2.1	2.1	2.4	21.1
Africa	1.5	1.4	1.4	1.4	-5.4
Latin America	1.9	1.7	1.9	1.8	-1.6
West Asia	2.6	2.6	2.5	2.5	-4.3
Other Asia, excl. China	1.5	1.8	1.8	2.0	32.5
India	1.4	1.8	2.1	2.2	57.9
China	2.4	2.6	2.7	3.0	26.8

Source: UNCTAD secretariat estimates, based on IPCC reference approach.
  Note: CO_2 emissions based on IPCC reference approach.
     a Calculations are based on constant 2000 dollars and purchasing power parities.
     b An oil equivalent is the common unit of account for energy commodities. It is defined as 10^7 kilocalories (41.868 gigajoules); this quantity of energy is approximately equal to the net heat content of 1 ton of crude oil.

The overall impact will depend on the extent to which the mean temperature rises, but this is non-linear. Thus, there is a risk that critical thresholds ("tipping points") will be exceeded, which could cause irreversible damage to ecosystems and the inability to prevent potentially catastrophic impacts. The latter makes the measurement of the economic impact of climate change very difficult. Estimates in this regard have a large margin of uncertainty because of the long time horizon involved, but they are also highly sensitive to subjective assumptions. Most of the effects are "priceless" in that they are not reflected in any private or national accounting systems (Ackerman and Finlayson, 2006). The impact is often estimated in terms of material wealth lost, for example as a result of the increased frequency and intensity of natural disasters and loss of land due to rising ocean levels, as well as GDP foregone, mainly due to lower agricultural output. According to some such estimates, the cost of inaction in the face of global warming could reach 8 per cent of GDP annually by 2100 (Ackerman and Stanton, 2006; Kemfert 2005; Watkiss et al., 2005).

The extent to which the consequences of global warming will affect human life in the future largely depends on the success of environmental and economic policies in limiting GHG emissions through their influence on the patterns of production, consumption, and research and development (R&D). A target that seems viable, both scientifically and politically, is to limit the temperature increase to 2–2.5°C by 2050 (Stern, 2006; IPCC, 2007b). If this target is reached, a large proportion of the potential damages from, and economic costs of, climate change may be avoided. But even a mean global temperature rise of this order is expected to have significant adverse impacts.

Even though climate change is a global phenomenon, there are large differences in the vulnerability of different geographical regions and individual countries to its symptoms. Climate models that gauge regional impacts of global warming show that developing countries are more vulnerable to climate change than developed countries (table 5.2). Assuming global warming is in the order of 2–2.5°C, such estimates suggest that Africa, South Asia and West Asia would likely be the worst affected. In developing countries, the costs of climate change reflect mainly their geographical location and their greater reliance on agriculture, forestry and fisheries, which are particularly climate-sensitive. Moreover, the impact of climate change on human health will

Chart 5.1

SOURCES OF CURRENT GHG EMISSIONS

(Per cent of total GHG emissions)

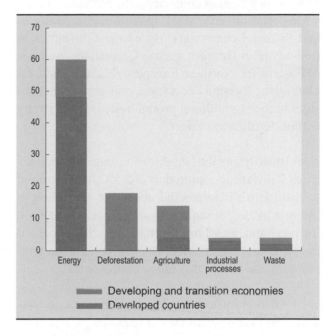

Source: von Braun, 2008.
Note: Agriculture excludes land use changes.

Table 5.2

ECONOMIC IMPACT OF A GLOBAL WARMING OF 2–2.5°C BY 2100, ESTIMATES BY REGION

(Percentage change of GDP)

	Mean	Lower bound	Upper bound
Developed countries			
North America	0	1	-2
Asia	-1	0	-3
Europe	-1	0	-3
Transition economies	1	0	2
Developing countries			
Africa	-4	-1	-9
Latin America	-2	0	-4
West Asia	-3	-2	-4
South and South-East Asia	-3	1	-9
China	-1	2	-5

Source: Burniaux et. al., 2008: figure 6.2.
Note: Mean temperature increase is measured against the pre-industrial level.

reduce the productivity of the workforce, and extreme weather events, with their attendant effects on physical infrastructure, are also likely to hamper economic growth. In addition, the adaptive capacity of most developing countries is limited due to their widespread poverty, weak institutional capabilities and financial constraints. By contrast, countries at mid- to higher latitudes, such as Canada, the countries of Eastern and Northern Europe and Central Asia, including the Russian Federation, may actually benefit from higher agricultural productivity due to a strong carbon fertilization effect.[1]

In analysing the tangible economic implications of global warming limited to 2–2.5°C, it is common to distinguish between the needs for adaptation to the inevitable consequences of climate change, on the one hand, and those for managing the process of the structural change necessary to contain the temperature rise within this range on the other.

Adaptation to the adverse effects on ecosystems, biodiversity, fresh water resources, agricultural output, human health and desertification, and to the increased risk of major natural disasters, poses a major challenge and a heavy financial burden for the countries concerned. Although dealing with this challenge requires adaptation programmes that have to be tailored to the specific needs and circumstances of each country, the financial burden should be borne by the international community as a whole. At the same time, developed countries need to acknowledge responsibility for the impact of their emissions that have accumulated over many decades, and provide the necessary support, primarily in the form of aid.

The issue of managing the process required to achieve mitigation targets is distinct from that of adaptation to inevitable climate change; it relates to the need for structural change to reduce emissions. The remainder of this chapter focuses on the economic and developmental dimensions of this process, and on the policies urgently needed at the national and international levels to support and accelerate the process of structural change.

C. Policies for climate change mitigation: some general considerations

1. Correcting market failure

The problem of climate change has arisen as a result of a global market failure: part of the costs of using factors of production is borne by society, rather than by the economic agents that control the underlying activity and profit from it. Thus, GHG emissions are an "external" effect of production and consumption. The absence of mechanisms to make the emitters of GHGs pay a sufficiently high price has led to an overuse of the atmosphere.

The correction of this market failure requires government intervention in the form of policies that will create adequate incentives to deter emitters from producing too many emissions. However, so far governments have been unwilling to impose a carbon price or to introduce regulations that are sufficiently stringent to lead to a substitution of carbon-intensive modes of production and consumption with more climate-friendly ones.

Generally, a distinction is made between two main types of instruments for correcting market failures related to environmental pollution: market-based instruments that establish an explicit price for emissions, and regulations and standards, which create an implicit price for emissions. There is wide agreement that a progressive increase in the price of GHG emissions is a necessary condition for their sizeable abatement to required levels.

Carbon prices are also essential for inducing research and development (R&D) and the diffusion of technologies that are less carbon-intensive. But manipulating markets and introducing a price for future carbon emissions is only a starting point; it is equally necessary for governments to take action to strengthen research in carbon capture and storage technology, support innovation and the diffusion of new, low-carbon technologies, tighten standards for vehicle fuel efficiency and facilitate the transfer of climate-friendly technologies to developing countries (UNDP, 2007: 20, 21). Government intervention in these areas is necessary because the current patterns of production and consumption and the existing technological frontier reflect the lack of appropriate incentives for research on more climate-friendly technologies in the past. "Autonomous" technical progress cannot be expected to advance fast enough to contribute sufficiently to climate change mitigation. For example, solar energy appears to be a promising alternative source of energy, but the capability to capture, store and transport this energy is still woefully underdeveloped.

> So far, governments have been unwilling to impose sufficiently stringent regulations that would encourage more climate-friendly modes of production and consumption.

The role of the price mechanism in stimulating R&D and technology diffusion is limited due to the positive externalities and other market failures associated with invention, innovation and technology diffusion. In many respects, the problem of introducing technologies that support climate change mitigation is similar to that of all innovation activities, which, in a dynamic economy, emerge from entrepreneurial spirit and the search for competitive gains. Such activities invariably take place within a system of incentives and disincentives, and within a framework of regulations that imposes or prohibits certain forms of production in line with public preferences. The introduction of more climate-friendly modes of production and consumption is increasingly becoming such a public preference, and therefore cannot be left to market forces alone. The public-good nature of low-carbon technologies and the urgency of reducing GHG emissions in light of the risks of unabated climate change for future generations calls for public support measures in the form of regulations, standard setting and financing. In any case, climate change mitigation will have to involve a mix of different instruments to guide a process of structural change, which depends also on country-specific circumstances. Some of these instruments are discussed next.

2. Carbon taxes, emissions trading and regulation

There are two main types of market-based policy instruments: price-based and quantity-based. A carbon tax is a price-based instrument, because it imposes a direct charge on the use of fossil fuels based on their carbon content. Given that the carbon content is proportional to emissions of these fuels, the carbon tax is equivalent to an emissions tax. In contrast, in a system of tradable permits, the regulator determines the maximum permissible aggregate emission level (the "cap"), and issues corresponding allowances for emission dischargers. Emission allowances can be auctioned, which generates government revenues, or freely distributed, for example in proportion to past emissions ("grandfathering"). Supply and demand for allowances in the emissions trading market then determine the carbon price. Emissions trading is therefore a quantity-based policy instrument.

Theoretically, a carbon tax can achieve the same result as a tradable permit system (Baumol and Oates, 1988), and both can lead to an equalization of the marginal costs of abatement among emitters (i.e. a given emission reduction is achieved overall at the lowest cost). However, in practice both systems have different sets of advantages and disadvantages. Price and quantity controls have different outcomes in the face of uncertainty about compliance costs (Weitzman, 1974).

The key feature of the tradable permit system is that the regulator establishes a target for emissions. The volume of emission reductions is therefore known ex ante, but the abatement cost is not. Carbon prices may be higher or lower than expected and they can also be quite volatile. Uncertainty about abatement costs of future GHG emissions results mainly from the difficulty in predicting the development of low-carbon technologies and baseline emissions. In contrast, an emissions tax, or carbon tax, determines the marginal abatement cost, but the resulting emissions reduction is uncertain: it could undershoot or overshoot the level implicitly targeted by the regulator.

A hybrid "cap-and-tax" system could combine the advantages of a tax (cost certainty) with the environmental advantages of a tradable permit system (emission certainty). Under such a scheme, the government would set an emissions limit, but at the same time would guarantee making additional allowances available at a certain maximum "trigger" price. This maximum price would act as a "safety valve" that would reduce firms' adjustment costs (e.g. in the presence of inelastic capital substitution). It is effectively a carbon tax that would allow emissions without permits. This would prevent companies from having to cut back on output, or even closing down or relocating to countries with less stringent policies. Besides a ceiling on the carbon price, the government could also fix a lower bound price level; if this were crossed, it would intervene by removing allowances from the market. The minimum price would effectively be a subsidy per unit of unused emission permits. The function of the minimum price is to prevent carbon prices from falling below a level that eliminates incentives for investments in low-carbon technologies by firms and households. In a more general way, such a hybrid scheme would be able to cope with unexpected shocks to economic growth and abatement costs. The safety valve function could also become operational in the event of a serious crisis in energy supply (Helm, 2008).

The regulator would need to make periodic adjustments to either carbon taxes or emission ceilings that have been set too high or too low. In any case, both tradable permit schemes and carbon tax schemes would have to be adapted over time to take into account new knowledge about required emission reduction needs and technological change. It is important to make these changes in a predictable way so as not to thwart incentives for R&D and technology diffusion. Given that stringent emission reductions

will require a progressive increase in carbon prices over the coming decades, the major question is whether it would be easier for policymakers to adjust tax rates or emission caps (Nordhaus, 2008).

The main reason why cap-and-trade schemes have been the preferred solution in some cases is that they remove uncertainty about the level of emission reductions. Cap-and trade programmes that cover CO_2 emissions (mainly from energy-intensive sectors) are operational in the EU Greenhouse Gas Emission Trading System (EU ETS) and in some other European countries (Norway, Switzerland), as well as in 10 northeastern and mid-Atlantic states of the United States that participate in the Regional Greenhouse Gas Initiative and in some of the more industrialized provinces of Canada. In the United States, a national market-driven system of tradable emission allowances is part of the new American Clean Energy and Security Act.[2]

> A progressive increase in carbon prices will be necessary to achieve strong emission reductions.

Viewed from an international climate policy perspective, quantity-based mitigation policies have the advantage that the commitments made by countries in terms of emission reductions over a given time period are widely known. The "targets and timetable" approach is in fact the major characteristic of the current international approach to climate change mitigation enshrined in the Kyoto Protocol (see box 5.1).

An international carbon tax would preclude the need to negotiate national emission target levels. However, it would not only be difficult to administer, but it also implies that the relative adjustment burden would be higher on developing countries that are trailing in energy efficiency. A global carbon market in the form of a cap-and-trade system, as called for in the Stern Review, appears to be a more viable solution (Stern, 2006, 2008a and b). Such a system could be designed in a way that would allow developing countries to sell emission rights that are not needed to cover domestically produced emissions. The amount of financing mobilized for developing countries through such a system would depend on the modalities of the initial allocation of permits.

The effectiveness of introducing a price for carbon, and its subsequent increases, depends on the price elasticity of demand for energy. Price incentives are quite effective in influencing changes in energy use and carbon emissions by industries, but not by households, because household demand for electricity is much less elastic. For both industrial energy use and electricity generation, there are alternative fuels that yield the same result with differing levels of carbon emissions. A higher carbon price would therefore cause a noticeable reduction in industrial energy demand and a relatively small reduction in household electricity consumption, but it would also lead to a shift towards the use of fuels with lower carbon content, such as replacing coal with natural gas.

Use of the price mechanism to influence demand for less carbon-intensive energy is central to market-based intervention ...

The picture is different in the transportation sector, where, so far, petroleum fuels have been practically the only choice.[3] The bulk of crude oil is used for transportation, and a portion of the remainder goes to non-fuel uses such as petrochemicals, where there are no close substitutes. The connection between petroleum and transportation is projected to grow even tighter: transportation is expected to account for about two thirds of the growth in oil demand to end-2030 (EIA, 2007; OPEC, 2007). Thus the oil/transport market is almost disconnected from the market for other fuels and end uses. The lack of alternatives to oil means that, in the short run, price elasticity will remain close to zero for many consumers, and an increase in oil prices is likely to lead to only a modest change in short-run oil demand while representing a heavy burden on consumers.[4] Its main effect will emerge over the longer term, as it will accelerate the transition to more fuel-efficient vehicles.

Use of the price mechanism to influence the demand is central to market-based intervention in favour of climate change mitigation, but it would have to be accompanied by intervention on the supply side of other sources of energy in order to avoid the move towards a low-carbon economy being stalled by unfavourable movements in relative prices. Managing supply adjustments and price formation for different sources of energy is necessary to prevent the prices for non-fossil, renewable sources from increasing in response

... but it has to be accompanied by intervention on the supply side of other sources of energy.

to fast growing demand for them, while at the same time the prices of the more carbon-intensive types of energy fall. For example, the replacement of coal with gas could be jeopardized if the increasing demand for gas leads to a sharp increase in its price. Gas supply would then need to increase with rising demand, or the price of coal would have to be raised artificially in spite of lower demand for this source of energy. Similarly, cutting down on the demand for oil could lower its price if supply is not adjusted to the lower demand. Therefore, producers of different fuels need to get involved in the formulation and implementation of an international climate change mitigation policy.

In addition to changes in the incentive structure through the market mechanism, direct government intervention through the introduction of emission performance standards and strict regulations that prescribe specific modes of GHG abatement appears to be indispensable for achieving ambitious targets within the envisaged time horizon. Regulatory standards have already been widely used, notably in developed countries, to address various forms of environmental pollution. They typically prescribe either a specific abatement technology – so-called best-available technology – for limiting the amount of emissions discharged, or they set performance standards (such as maximum emissions per unit of output) while leaving the choice of technology to the emitter. While technology standards are easier to implement than performance standards, they do not provide any incentives for firms to develop more efficient technologies than required by the regulation. They are appropriate when the polluter does not have many options for reducing emissions, or when emissions are difficult to monitor and measure systematically (such as fugitive emissions from pipelines and methane emissions from agriculture). Performance standards, on the other hand, provide emitters with more flexibility for reaching a mandatory emissions target: they can respond, for example, by changing their production technologies, their product mix and/ or the types of fuels they use.

Box 5.1

KEY FEATURES OF THE CURRENT MULTILATERAL FRAMEWORK FOR A GLOBAL CLIMATE CHANGE POLICY AND ITS FUTURE

The broad foundation for addressing climate change was established by the United Nations Framework Convention on Climate Change (UNFCCC), which was adopted in 1992 and ratified by 192 countries. The central objective of the Convention is embodied in its Article 2, which provides for the "stabilization of greenhouse gas concentrations in the atmosphere at a level that would prevent dangerous anthropogenic interference with the climate system". But the treaty does not define what that level is. It establishes that climate change is a common concern of mankind, but it recognizes important historical differences in the contributions of developed and developing countries to this global problem. It also recognizes that there are differences in their respective economic, institutional and technical capacities to tackle it. In accordance with the principle of "common but differentiated responsibilities", the treaty calls on developed countries to "take the lead in combating climate change and the effects thereof" (Article 3, para 1). Annex I of the treaty lists the countries (developed countries and countries with economies in transition) that agreed to take on GHG mitigation commitments.

The Kyoto Protocol to the UNFCCC, which was adopted in 1997 but entered into force only in 2005, established for the first time legally binding economy-wide GHG emission targets (excluding emissions from international aviation and maritime transport) for the Annex I countries to the Protocol. Targets are country-specific, but on average Annex I Parties agreed to a 5.2 per cent reduction of aggregate emissions during the period 2008–2012 (the so-called first commitment period) compared with emission levels in 1990 (baseline year).

The Kyoto Protocol abolishes free use of the atmosphere by assigning each Annex I country a certain quota of emission rights based on the emission targets. Since the Protocol does not prescribe how commitments are to be met, there is considerable flexibility in identifying opportunities for GHG emission reductions in different economic activities and in the design of country-specific approaches to climate change mitigation. The Protocol has established three "flexible mechanisms" through which Annex I Parties can attain their emission targets. These are: (i) emissions trading among Annex I countries, (ii) the Clean Development Mechanism (CDM), and (iii) joint implementation.

The economic rationale for emissions trading (cap-and-trade system) is to exploit the differences in marginal abatement costs among emitters within and across Annex I countries. The CDM allows Annex I countries to earn certified emission reductions (CERs), or carbon credits, by investing in GHG abatement projects in developing countries, which can be counted against the national emission targets or traded in the carbon market. In most cases, however, only a limited percentage of emission reductions can be achieved through CERs. This limits the use that can be made of CDM (see box 5.2 below). Joint implementation is similar to CDM, but it is designed to allow an Annex I country to earn emission reduction units by investing in a project in another Annex I country (de facto, mainly transition economies).

It should be pointed out that the Kyoto Protocol puts the mitigation burden of a country only on its production activities, but not on the consumption of carbon-intensive products. This gives producers in developed countries the option to shift carbon-intensive production to developing countries, and/or consumers in developed countries the option to rely increasingly – in the aggregate – on imports of carbon-intensive goods for domestic consumption.

It could be argued that the environmental effectiveness of the Kyoto Protocol will be limited, given the short-term focus and the small magnitude of emission reduction commitments. Besides, the United States, the major emitter of GHGs at the time the Kyoto Protocol was adopted, has not ratified the Protocol, and no formal mitigation commitments are demanded of developing countries. However, the Kyoto Protocol provides a clear signal that climate change mitigation is no longer a concern only for a minority of the population that is particularly sensitive to environmental issues; rather, it is becoming a central parameter

Box 5.1 (concluded)

for public and private decision-making at all levels. Negotiations on the second commitment period of the Kyoto Protocol are currently under way, and are expected to be concluded at the forthcoming United Nations Climate Change Conference, the 15th Conference of the Parties (COP-15), in Denmark in December 2009.

To meet the emission reduction targets set by the Intergovernmental Panel on Climate Change in 2007 (IPCC, 2007a), it will be necessary for a successor agreement to the current Kyoto Protocol to set considerably more ambitious targets and involve a larger number of countries, including all developed and emerging-market economies, which contribute to a rapidly increasing share of the world's GHG emissions. In order to avoid cumbersome negotiations in the forthcoming meetings over which countries should be included in Annex I, it would be desirable to agree on a formula for determining their inclusion. A formula approach would automatically require countries that pass certain thresholds – for example in terms of the size of the economy, per capita income and/or carbon-intensity – to make formal commitments for GHG emission reductions.

3. Technology and innovation policies

While the wider dissemination of existing technology could go a long way towards reducing GHG emissions, climate change mitigation is an imperative that also requires faster creation and application of new technology. Carbon prices may provide a stimulus for accelerating the creation and application of appropriate cutting-edge technologies for carbon reduction compared to past decades. However, there is a high risk that the stimulus may not be strong enough to generate sufficient technological progress to keep up with the speed required to lower emissions, given that, owing to market failures and government lethargy in the past, GHG concentration in the atmosphere has reached a dramatic level. Current modes of production and consumption are shaped by "carbon lock-in", meaning that carbon-intensive technologies gained an early lead at a time when there was little, if any, concern about global warming (Unruh and Carrillo-Hermosilla, 2006). Today, the economic benefits of standardization and the low costs of imitating and replicating existing technologies keep the world locked into that same undesirable path.

> There has been considerable underinvestment in research aimed at the development of alternative sources of energy and cleaner production methods.

In the past, there was considerable underinvestment in research aimed at the development of alternative sources of energy and cleaner production methods, as CO_2 emissions could be generated at no cost. Moreover, private R&D investment is often hampered by the existence of knowledge spillovers, whereby innovators are able to appropriate only a small proportion of the social benefits of their innovations. There are also market failures in the adoption and diffusion of new technologies resulting from learning-by-using, learning-by-doing, or network externalities. And incomplete information about the potential of new technologies frequently slows down their application in practice (Jaffe, Newell and Stavins, 2004; Fischer and Newell, 2004).

A carbon tax, a cap-and-trade system, and more stringent regulations and standard setting will all help to promote the diffusion of climate-friendly technology and advance the technological frontier, but new technologies have rarely evolved independently of public policies. They are created through a process of what is often described as "learning curves" or "experience curves" (Ackerman, 2008; Abernathy and Wayne, 1974). The process of technological change is path dependent, in the sense that the current options available depend on past policies and actions, just as the available technological options in the future will depend on our actions and policies today.

In all countries technological change typically advances faster when it benefits from public support, which can take the form of publicly financed R&D, such as in nuclear power and, more recently, in wind power and ethanol production. Wind power became commercially viable only as a result of decades of government support in the EU, the United States and other countries, in the form of subsidies and support for R&D. The same will be true of other low-carbon energy technologies that will be needed for a sustainable resolution of the climate problem.

It is not merely the financing of research, but also the initial investments in the application of the new technology that help to make it a competitive choice for private enterprises, as prices fall with growing demand and larger scale production. Therefore, in both developed and developing countries, government procurement can play an important role in advancing climate-friendly technological progress, as it has done in other areas in the past. As pointed out by Ackerman (2008: 7): "Computers got their start with military purchases; the Internet grew out of a network sponsored by the United States Defense Department that was set up in the 1960s to connect military researchers around the country ... if the world had waited for autonomous technical change or relied on getting the prices right, microelectronics might never have happened." Similarly, public sector initiatives are likely to be essential to ensure that the global economy moves along a climate-friendly path. Direct and indirect subsidies for the diffusion of new technologies and the use of alternative sources of energy can also be crucial. Examples are tax credits for energy-efficient equipment, and price support such as feed-in tariffs for solar- and wind-powered electricity.

As mentioned above, the level of carbon emissions is also determined by individual behaviour patterns at a given rate of growth and a given state of technology. These are influenced to a large extent by regulations and price incentives, but also by climate-related information and knowledge. With regard to energy efficiency, there is often a lack of information on the economic and environmental implications of using certain products, at both the firm and household level. Mandatory labelling pertaining to energy efficiency of consumer goods, including household appliances, cars and office equipment, could help promote more rational purchasing decisions by reducing transaction costs. There is also an important role for governments in raising environmental awareness through education and information campaigns, and demonstrating effective leadership in terms of application of stringent building and appliance standards.

> Climate-friendly technological change advances faster when it benefits from public support.

D. Structural change for curbing global warming

In order to curb GHG emissions sufficiently to prevent a mean temperature rise beyond 2–2.5°C, factors of production will partly have to be allocated to alternative economic activities, and capital accumulation will need to be geared, more than in the past, to the use of sources of energy and modes of production that generate fewer GHG emissions. This process may entail costs for producers and consumers, but efforts to measure the "costs of climate change mitigation" encounter serious conceptual and methodological problems. The economic implications of averting dangerous global warming cannot be adequately addressed within the framework of a traditional cost-benefit analysis, for various reasons. First, not enough is known about the resilience of the ecosystem to global warming, nor about the risks of discontinuous and irreversible changes caused by crossing "tipping points" that could have potentially catastrophic impacts with incalculable costs.

Second, there is little sense in adding up the costs that individual agents will incur in the coming decades by choosing climate-friendly modes of production or consumption instead of carbon-intensive ones. Effective mitigation policies imply structural change in response to the new public preferences. The whole process is comparable to the disappearance of telegraphs, telex machines and public fixed line telephones following the arrival of new communication technologies. More importantly, microeconomic costs on the demand side correspond to incomes generated on the supply side: the production of new technologies and equipment generates income and employment.

> Investment in activities that promote climate change mitigation can provide a stimulus for growth and employment creation.

Third, these costs are sometimes measured by the input of capital, labour and land to processes that are required to achieve a certain volume of emission reductions, based on the assumption that these resources have to be withdrawn from other uses of value to a firm or society at large. This is a highly theoretical rationale, which assumes full employment of all factors of production in a static sense. In reality, economic activities that are associated with high GHG emissions will indeed be discontinued. Other activities that can be conducted in a more climate-friendly manner are created. Moreover, in the real world there is no full employment of labour, and fixed capital formation in support of one economic activity is rarely crowded out by investment in another economic activity. Rather, increased investment is a driver of overall economic growth and innovation.

To some extent, climate change mitigation may be achieved by reducing certain forms of consumption. But primarily it entails switching to or increasing expenditure on alternative types of energy, technology, production equipment and final goods. From this perspective, investment in activities that promote climate change mitigation is likely to create new income in addition to existing output, and implies a potential stimulus for growth and employment creation

Official estimates of the economic costs of climate change mitigation do not reflect these macroeconomic dynamics of structural change, and should therefore be taken with cautions. These estimates are

Table 5.3

LOSS OF GDP FROM CLIMATE CHANGE MITIGATION: SELECTED ESTIMATES

	Stabilization of GHG concentrations		Loss of GDP	
	At CO_2 equivalent ppm[a]	Target year	Per cent	Target year
IPCC	445	2050	-5.5	2050
Burniaux et. al./ OECD	550	2050	-4.8	2050
IMF	535–590	2100	-2.6	2040
Stern Review	550	2050	-1.0	2050

Source: IPCC, 2007a; Burniaux et al., 2008; IMF, 2008; Stern, 2006.
   a Particles per million.

based on a comparison of two hypothetical future states of the economy: a baseline scenario, which projects economic developments and emissions in the absence of specific mitigation policies, and an alternative scenario that includes policies to achieve a certain volume of emission reductions. The results of such estimates depend on a host of assumptions concerning economic growth trends, future price levels of fossil fuels, substitution opportunities and the rate of technological progress.[5] They normally exclude the possibility of shifting preferences. The timing and location of mitigation measures influence the overall costs, because of the long-service life of energy-intensive capital stock and the costs of premature scrapping, as well as the fact that an equal reduction of emissions can be achieved at lower costs in countries that are relatively far from the existing technology frontier.

Official estimates along these lines suggest that accumulated global macroeconomic costs of mitigating climate change by limiting GHG concentrations to levels at which global warming can be expected not to exceed 2.5°C could be in the order of 5.5 per cent of global GDP in 2050 (table 5.3). This corresponds to a reduction in the average annual rate of global economic growth in the order of 0.15 percentage point between 2010 and 2050. To put this in perspective, the same models typically assume that in 2050, the world's real GDP will be more than twice its current level. In developing countries, aggregate GDP is projected to increase, on average, by a factor of four by 2050. Moreover, these costs of mitigation would have to be compared with the costs of unabated climate change, which are impossible to quantify reasonably in terms of economic accounting, but which, according to many experts, could be much larger.

Thus, the standard model estimates suggest that the net costs of mitigation for the world economy as a whole would be fairly small, even though they assume exogenous technological progress. Yet decisive policy action in support of climate change mitigation is likely to spur not only the wider application of existing climate-friendly technologies, but also to accelerate the development of new technologies that favour cleaner modes of production, consumption and energy generation. This aspect is partly captured in models that allow for induced technological change and consequently show even lower macroeconomic costs than models that assume exogenous technical progress, if not overall benefits (Barker, Qureshi and Köhler, 2006).

> The macroeconomic costs of mitigating climate change may be negligible for the world economy as a whole, but they may differ considerably across countries ...

However, while the macroeconomic costs of mitigating climate change may be negligible for the world economy as a whole, the net costs of adjusting production and consumption patterns to meet global mitigation target may differ considerably across regions and countries, depending on the extent to which climate-friendly technologies and environmental goods are available domestically or have to be imported from abroad. The latter aspect is of major importance for the international distribution of income generated by the production of more climate-friendly technologies, infrastructure, equipment and consumer goods. It is taken up in section E.4 of this chapter, which focuses on the design of development strategies that include climate change mitigation.

The potential economic opportunities arising from the transition to a low carbon economy may be illustrated by calculations of the International Energy Agency (IEA), based on a comparison of estimated future expenditures on low-carbon technologies for meeting a given projected increase in energy demand under specific emission constraints and hypothetical investment expenditures for traditional fossil-fuel-based technologies. These *incremental* expenditures during the period 2010–2030 will be within a range of $200 billion per annum for stabilizing GHG concentrations at a level that limits the increase in the mean global temperature to 3°C, and $450 billion per annum to limit global warming to 2°C (IEA, 2008a). This corresponds to 0.3–0.7 per cent of global GDP in 2008. About half of this additional capital expenditure will have to be made by developing countries, a large proportion by China and India. For individual economic agents, these investment costs will likely be offset to a large extent by fuel savings over time.

> ... depending on the extent to which climate-friendly technologies and products have to be imported from abroad.

The UNFCCC (2008a) has provided estimates of additional global financing needs, not only specifically for the energy sector but also for moving more generally to more climate-friendly products and processes. These estimates suggest that the worldwide annual additional expenditures involved in shifting towards more climate-friendly modes of production and consumption would amount to $440–$1,800 billion per annum up to 2030, equivalent to 0.7–2.1 per cent of world GDP in 2008. Between $180 and $500 billion of this world total would have to be borne by developing countries annually, corresponding to 1.1–2.9 per cent of their GDP in 2008 (and falling to 0.3–0.8 per cent of their GDP in 2030).

Against this background, major concerns have been raised that commitments of developing countries to GHG emissions reduction will jeopardize their development objectives. This issue is addressed in the next section.

E. Climate change mitigation and the development imperative

1. Emissions reduction, growth and development

There is a commonly held belief that significant reductions in GHG emissions inevitably imply a trade-off with economic development. This perception is based on the understanding that the key to progress in development and poverty eradication is sustained economic growth, and that, since the beginning of industrialization, economic growth has been accompanied by a greater use of natural resources (notably fossil fuels), environmental pollution and the accumulation of GHG emissions. However, since more recent industrialization has also been accompanied by a reduction in current emissions relative to GDP, it may not be necessary for future development to repeat the experience of the past.

The overall impacts of economic growth on emissions such as CO_2 can be decomposed into three effects (Copeland and Taylor, 2004):

- A scale effect (i.e. additional emissions due to increasing production and consumption);

- A composition effect (i.e. the change in emissions due to a shift in the structure of production and consumption towards activities and products with lower emissions intensity);

- A technology effect (which reflects the favourable impact of technological progress in terms of lowering emissions per unit of output).

Theoretically, an increase in emissions can be avoided if the scale effect of economic growth is offset by the composition and technology effects, but historically the technology effect has not kept pace with the scale effect. However, it should be noted that this has been the outcome of a major market failure: the use of the environment as a factor of production has not been included in cost and price calculations, resulting in its overuse. The relative importance of each of the three determinants for emissions, and the interactions between them, depend on how growth dynamics unfold over time in response to the pattern of relative prices and to legal and policy frameworks. They will be influenced by economic, environmental and technology policies, which can set appropriate incentives for economic behaviour that limits CO_2 emissions and appropriate disincentives for behaviour that continues to produce such emissions.

This means that, while slower economic growth based on given patterns of production and consumption could help reduce GHG emissions, it is not a precondition for climate change mitigation, nor is it a requirement for developing countries that are at relatively early stages of their industrialization. However, governments in both developed and developing countries need to influence the pattern of growth (i.e. the patterns of inputs and outputs) (Arrow and Bolin, 1995). This is not an entirely new challenge. Shaping structural change has been a key element in the design of successful development strategies that have focused on diversification away from a reliance on only a few export commodities and towards building comparative advantages in other areas of economic activity. Such strategies have given particular emphasis to industrialization in sectors that are expanding both nationally and internationally.

In many areas this structural change offers the possibility of synergies between the pursuit of mitigation and development objectives (Cosbey, 2009).

> Slower economic growth is not a precondition for climate change mitigation.

The first reason why climate change mitigation has a positive impact on development is that in its absence there would be an increased risk of a significant slowdown in development progress. But there is also a potentially positive link between policies that favour climate change mitigation, on the one hand, and policies that support growth and development on the other. Considerable reductions in GHG emissions have already been achieved in both developed and developing countries as a by-product of policies that are primarily aimed at other objectives, such as raising overall productivity, diversification or increasing energy security. Conversely, many national policy measures in support of climate-friendly structural changes may also help achieve development objectives, including providing new employment opportunities and reducing poverty (UNCTAD, 2009a).

Beyond these possible synergies, the imperative of climate change mitigation also sets new parameters for development strategies: it implies a worldwide move towards new sources of energy, the development of new technologies and the production of equipment that embeds such technologies, as well as the adoption of more climate-friendly consumption patterns. This opens up new opportunities for creating value added in the markets for more climate-friendly energy, equipment and consumer goods. For some countries it may offer new possibilities to exploit natural comparative advantages that so far have been of minor importance economically, and for many others it may offer opportunities to build new dynamic comparative advantages.

2. Options for climate change mitigation in developing countries

(a) Production and use of energy

Energy supply is the largest single global source of CO_2 emissions, and, with current technology and sources of energy, growing levels of per capita income will lead to greater energy consumption in all major regions of the world in the coming decades. Thus production and use of energy are the priority areas of action for climate change mitigation. In these areas, developing countries face three major challenges. They need to: (i) satisfy the energy needs of their large number of rural poor, most of whom are not connected to any grid, while also increasing the provision of energy in urban centres to boost overall production capacity and accommodate rising household demand; (ii) switch from traditional to cleaner sources of energy, enhancing, in particular, the use of renewable energy from solar, wind, hydro or geothermal sources; and (iii) combine the increased total energy supply with measures to raise efficiency of production, dissemination and end use of energy.

About 2.5 billion people, or 40 per cent of the world's population, most of them in South Asia and sub-Saharan Africa, still experience energy poverty. They rely on traditional biomass fuels for cooking and heating, with associated ambient air pollution and adverse effects on health. And about 1.6 billion people have no access to electricity. Nevertheless, energy demand in developing countries has been rising sharply in all major regions in recent decades. Energy consumption during the period 1990–2006 in developing countries rose at an average annual rate of 4.1 per cent, compared to a world average of 1.8 per cent, reflecting robust economic expansion and associated growth in real per capita incomes. As a result, the share of developing countries in global energy demand increased to some 42 per cent in 2006, up from 29 per cent in 1990. China and India alone accounted for 21 per cent of global energy demand in 2006, compared with 13.6 per cent in 1990. This trend is expected to continue. Thus, although developing and transition economies consume much less energy per capita than developed economies at present (table 5.4), they will account for the bulk of growth in global energy demand by 2030 (IEA, 2008a). Again, China and India alone are expected to account for half of this increase.

With regard to energy use per capita, there is considerable variation in regional levels and trends. In Africa, there has been only a moderate upward trend since 1980, with levels only about one third of the world average in 2006. The past few decades have seen very little growth in energy use per capita in Latin America. However, in India there has been a steady upward trend, although its overall energy

> Developing countries need to combine an increase in total energy supply with a greater use of renewable sources of energy and higher energy efficiency.

consumption per capita was less than one third of the world average in 2006 and about half of its population has no electricity supply. China's energy consumption per capita more than doubled between 1980 and 2006, but compared with consumption levels in developed countries it is still much lower (by nearly 70 per cent).

The strong growth in energy consumption has led to a sharp rise in CO_2 emissions. Developing countries accounted for 41 per cent of global energy-related CO_2 emissions in 2006, compared with some 26 per cent in 1990. By 2020, developing countries are expected to contribute to more than half of global energy-related CO_2 emissions and for an even larger share (56 per cent) by 2030. China's share in energy-related CO_2 emissions is projected to increase from about 20 per cent to nearly 30 per cent by 2030. China, India and West Asia combined are projected to account for more than 40 per cent of global CO_2 emissions in 2030, up from some 30 per cent in 2006. Similar to energy use, per capita CO_2 emissions in developing countries are on an upward trend, but have remained significantly lower than in developed countries (see table 5.1 above).

Although economic growth is generally associated with higher energy demand, the energy intensity of economic activity (i.e. energy use per unit of real GDP) can be expected to vary with the stage of development. In the process of industrialization, and with per capita incomes growing up to a certain level, developing countries' energy consumption intensity typically increases, but with greater affluence the structure of the economy tends to shift from heavy to light industry and services. This leads to a fall in the intensity of energy use (Hannesson 2002; *TDR 2005*, chap. II, sect. B). On average, the intensity of energy use has been on a slightly downward trend in developing countries over the past three decades. South, East and South-East Asia, where the intensity of energy use is quite similar to that in developed countries (table 5.4), have contributed strongly to this overall trend, even if China is excluded.[6]

A number of other developing countries have achieved considerable improvements in their intensity

Table 5.4

ENERGY USE RELATIVE TO POPULATION AND GDP, 1980–2006

(Tons of oil equivalent)

	1980	*1990*	*2000*	*2006*	*Percentage change 1980–2006*
Energy use per capita					
World	1.63	1.66	1.65	1.80	10.43
Developed countries	4.22	4.33	4.71	4.70	11.37
Europe	3.18	3.26	3.40	3.49	9.75
Japan	2.96	3.59	4.15	4.13	39.53
United States	7.95	7.70	8.15	7.74	-2.64
Transition economies	4.26	4.80	3.09	3.87	-9.15
Developing countries	0.56	0.66	0.79	0.97	73.21
Africa	0.58	0.62	0.62	0.66	13.79
Latin America	1.01	0.97	1.10	1.17	15.84
West Asia	1.44	1.74	2.34	2.76	91.67
Other Asia, excl. China	0.36	0.45	0.61	0.63	75.00
India	0.30	0.38	0.45	0.51	70.00
China	0.61	0.77	0.88	1.44	136.07
Energy use per \$1 000 of GDP[a]					
World	0.29	0.26	0.22	0.20	-31.03
Developed countries	0.26	0.22	0.20	0.18	-30.77
Europe	0.22	0.18	0.16	0.15	-31.82
Japan	0.18	0.15	0.16	0.15	-16.67
United States	0.35	0.27	0.24	0.21	-40.00
Transition economies	0.48	0.61	0.57	0.48	0.00
Developing countries	0.28	0.27	0.23	0.21	-25.00
Africa	0.26	0.29	0.30	0.28	7.69
Latin America	0.16	0.17	0.16	0.15	-6.25
West Asia	0.17	0.30	0.35	0.36	111.76
Other Asia, excl. China	0.25	0.22	0.22	0.17	-32.00
India	0.26	0.23	0.19	0.15	-42.31
China	0.74	0.45	0.22	0.21	-71.62

Source: UNCTAD secretariat estimates, based on IPCC reference approach.
  a Calculations are based on constant 2000 dollars and purchasing power parities.

of energy use as a result of policies to strengthen overall productivity, even without the explicit objective of contributing to reducing global warming. Brazil, China, India and Mexico have reduced their CO_2 emissions growth over the past three decades by some 500 million tonnes per annum – an amount that exceeds what the Kyoto Protocol requires of Annex I countries (IPCC, 2007b; Chandler et al., 2002).

There appears to be a huge potential for greater energy efficiency that could be exploited by wider dissemination of existing technologies in both developed and developing countries (UNCTAD, 2009a). The large difference in CO_2 emissions between the United States, Europe and Japan reflects, among other things, different degrees of application of existing technologies. For example, if Chinese coal power plants were to reach the average efficiency of Japanese plants, China would consume 20 per cent less coal (World Bank, 2007).

A large amount of GHG emissions could be prevented at the level of end users, through the introduction of efficiency standards and labelling, and by mandating the use of low-energy appliances and energy-efficient construction of new buildings. According to IEA estimates, a package of 25 energy efficiency measures could save up to one fifth of the global emissions projected for 2030 in a reference scenario (IEA, 2008b; Cosbey, 2009: 27). The timing of such efforts is important, not only from an environmental perspective, but also from an economic point of view: replacing or retrofitting an existing capital stock is much more difficult and generally more costly than mandating efficiency at an early stage. Power plants have a long service life, which can exceed 50 years. Therefore, the continued construction of relatively inefficient plants based on traditional fuels implies a risk of technology lock-in with associated high GHG emissions, even though in this case climate change mitigation could be achieved with the help of carbon capture and storage technologies (Gallagher, 2007).

A number of policies are already in place to encourage the development and deployment of low-carbon-emitting technologies in several developed countries, as well as in some developing countries, including Brazil, China, India and Mexico. Many developing countries have adopted targets for enhanced use of renewable sources of energy (table 5.5). Indeed, the share of developing countries in worldwide investments in energy efficiency and use of renewable sources of energy has risen steeply, from 13 per cent in 2004 to 23 per cent in 2007, partly as a result of improved policy and regulatory frameworks for clean energy investments, and partly in response to rising petroleum prices and concerns over supply constraints (UNEP, 2008). An outstanding example of these policies is Brazil's national ethanol programme for motor vehicles (PROALCOOL), which was launched in 1974 to reduce its dependence on oil imports. More recent policy measures in Brazil aim at the promotion of biodiesel and renewable energy technologies (PROINFA).

In energy-intensive industries, such as iron and steel, non-ferrous metals, chemicals, petroleum refining, cement, and pulp and paper, the main options for CO_2 abatement include improved energy efficiency and fuel switching. Many facilities in these sectors are relatively old and inefficient in terms of energy use, but there are also a number of others in developing countries that are new and already operate with the latest technology and use less energy. As these industries are expanding faster in developing countries

Table 5.5

SHARE OF RENEWABLES IN ENERGY CONSUMPTION IN 2006 AND TARGETS FOR 2020

(Per cent of total energy consumption)

	2006	2020 target
Developing countries		
Argentina	8.2	..
Brazil	43.0	..
China	8.0	15.0
Egypt	4.2	14.0
India	31.0	..
Indonesia	3.0	15.0[a]
Jordan	1.1	10.0
Kenya	81.0	..
Mali	..	15.0
Mexico	9.4	..
Morocco	4.3	10.0[b]
Republic of Korea	0.5	5.0[c]
Senegal	40.0	15.0[a]
South Africa	11.0	..
Thailand	4.0	8.0[c]
Developed countries		
Canada	16.0	..
European Union	6.5[d]	20.0
Japan	3.2	..
United States	4.8	..

Source: REN21, 2008, table R.7.
  a 2025.
  b 2010.
  c 2011.
  d 2005.

than in developed countries, there are also greater opportunities for CO_2 abatement when developing countries invest in additional production capacities. This points to the need for strengthening regulatory standards to accompany the development of these industries in developing and transition economies, not least to discourage the relocation of production associated with high GHG emissions from countries with stronger environmental regulations to countries where such regulations or their enforcement are lax or non-existent.

In the construction industry, CO_2 abatement can be achieved mainly by improving energy efficiency in new and existing buildings. Among the major instruments are building codes that establish stringent energy efficiency standards, and strict product standards for lighting and electrical appliances. CO_2 emissions can also be significantly reduced even with existing mature technologies for energy efficiency. To support the use of such low-cost abatement opportunities it is important to improve the dissemination of public information on the possible microeconomic gains from energy efficiency measures, alleviate financing constraints, and eliminate subsidies for energy use based on fossil fuels (McKinsey Global Institute, 2007).

In transport, the main mitigation options are energy switching, introduction of fuel-efficiency standards, a modal shift from road to rail transport, and greater use of public transport systems. Growing transportation activity is part of economic development, and an appropriate transport infrastructure is a prerequisite for many economic activities. Thus the share of developing countries in transport-related CO_2 emissions is projected to grow rapidly in the coming decades. With current technology, transport relies predominantly on petroleum, which accounts for 95 per cent of the total energy used for transport worldwide. Today, transport is responsible for 18 per cent of global CO_2 emissions and it is one of the most rapidly growing sources of such emissions in both developed and developing countries. Road transport accounts for 72 per cent of transport-related CO_2 emissions (Baumert and Winkler, 2005). Shipping, on the other hand, which is the predominant means of global freight transport, is already one of the least energy-intensive transport modes; nevertheless, there appear to be relatively large opportunities for improving energy efficiency even in this sector (IPCC, 2007a).

The limited scope for substitution of petroleum has been a major reason for the highly price-inelastic demand for vehicle fuels. With "business as usual", CO_2 emissions from road transport are expected to increase by almost 40 per cent until 2030 (IEA, 2008b; Cosbey, 2009: 31).[7] Under these circumstances, significant CO_2 abatement can only be achieved by large increases in fuel prices or taxes, or by introducing prohibitive measures. This can be a problem in rural areas with predominantly low-income populations, or

in areas where public transport is often lacking or is not a sufficiently attractive alternative to private cars. But in urban areas, well-designed public policies and urban planning can make an important contribution to reducing emissions by influencing transportation choices.

Stringent efficiency standards for vehicles may help lower CO_2 emissions, but integrated urban planning that seeks to reduce the need for transportation and encourages commuting by offering attractive means of public transport is equally important.[8] This would not only cut down on energy use and CO_2 emissions, but would also improve the quality of life of the population and productivity. Examples of the implementation of eco-efficient transport networks are the cities of Curitiba in Brazil and Bogota in Colombia. Curitiba pioneered the idea of an efficient all-bus transit network, which inspired a similar approach (TransMilenio) in Bogota (Cosbey, 2009).

> The development of energy-efficient industries should be accompanied by strengthened regulatory standards.

(b) Agriculture and forestry

Agriculture will likely be the worst-hit economic sector from global warming, particularly in developing countries. On the other hand, it is itself a major source of emissions, contributing 10–12 per cent of total global anthropogenic GHG emissions. Of the total agriculture-related emissions in 2005, 75 per cent originated in developing countries (UNFCCC, 2008b).[9] Moreover, projected population growth and changing diets with greater meat intake, associated with rising per capita incomes, particularly in developing countries, will lead to even larger increases in agriculture-related emissions.

In agriculture and forestry, rising current GHG emissions are mainly attributable to changes in land use. Adjustments in these sectors could contribute significantly to GHG abatement, without much technological innovation. They include, for example, improved crop and grazing land management, such as the restoration of organic soils that have been drained for crop production and restoration of degraded lands. In addition, soil carbon sequestration could contribute to 90 per cent of the mitigation potential of agriculture (representing between 11 and 17 per cent of the total mitigation potential). Improved water management and rice management,[10] as well as improved livestock and manure management, are other important options for developing countries. Indeed, 70 per cent of the mitigation potential of this sector could be achieved in developing countries (IPCC, 2007b). GHG emissions could also be reduced by substituting fossil fuels with agricultural feedstock for energy production.[11]

> Slowing down deforestation is a high-priority mitigation option in tropical regions.

Sustainable agricultural production methods, including organic agriculture, can contribute to climate change mitigation and other improvements in the environment through the reduction or elimination of chemical pollutants, and water and soil conservation practices. Organic agriculture improves soil fertility and structure, thus enhancing water retention and resilience to climatic stress. It also mitigates climate change by utilizing less energy than conventional agriculture and by sequestering carbon (UNCTAD, 2009a and b).

Forests serve as sinks of GHG emissions, so that deforestation implies the loss of these important environmental sinks. Deforestation and forest degradation in developing countries are estimated to account for some 18 per cent of global GHG emissions. Their main objective is to gain land, in Africa for subsistence farming and in Latin America for the extension of large-scale cattle ranching and soy plantations. In South-East Asia, deforestation occurs mainly for timber production and for palm oil and coffee plantations (Stern, 2006, chap. 25). Reducing and reversing deforestation is believed to offer the highest potential of any sector to contribute to low-cost mitigation between now and 2030 (Enqvist et al., 2007). It should therefore be considered a high-priority mitigation option in the tropical regions of Africa, Asia and Latin America.

> Developing countries should enhance their capabilities for effective participation in international climate policy negotiations.

Important instruments in this area are programmes at the national and international levels to reward the avoidance of deforestation. Several countries in Latin America are already making efforts in this direction.

Costa Rica and Mexico pay premiums to landowners for protecting forests, and Brazil has launched an international fund to attract financing for programmes that help preserve the Amazon rainforest, with an initial pledge of $100 million by Norway. While the principle of rewarding avoided deforestation is straightforward, several difficulties in verification and monitoring still have to be overcome. The terms "forest", and thus also "deforestation", are not easy to define, and there are problems arising from the possibility that one country's avoided deforestation might lead to accelerated deforestation elsewhere (Watson et al., 2000). Programmes that aim at avoiding deforestation have to be supported by strengthening national legal and regulatory systems as well as national capacity for resource management.

(c) Administrative and institutional capacity-building

Mitigation policies and strategies need reliable and comprehensive data for setting goals, monitoring policy implementation and elaborating plausible scenarios for future emissions. Designing effective mitigation strategies also requires reliable projections of future emissions. This not only depends on an accurate and comprehensive inventory of GHG emission sources and sinks, but also on a good understanding of the key economic drivers of emissions. The development of reliable GHG inventories is also necessary to enable firms to gain insights into their mitigation opportunities and GHG-related risks.

The UNFCCC requires developed countries to submit such inventories on an annual basis, whereas reporting obligations are much less stringent for developing countries. In a 2005 UNFCCC compilation of national communications from developing countries on GHG emissions, most of the countries reported data for 1994 only (UNFCCC, 2005a,b; 2008c). For more than half of the countries, some important activity data were either lacking or not accessible. Major problems are the lack of institutional capacity for the collection, storage and management of the data needed for preparing a GHG inventory. This is an area where developing countries could benefit considerably from technical assistance. The GHG Protocol Initiative, for example,[12] has been promoting common standards and tools for GHG measurement, as well as capacity-building.

In order to reap possible development benefits from global climate change mitigation efforts, developing countries also have to enhance public sector capabilities for designing, implementing and monitoring climate policy measures, for effective participation in international climate change negotiations, and for effective use of international instruments such as the Clean Development Mechanism (CDM) (Willems and Baumert, 2003; Gallagher, 2007; see also box 5.2 below).

Clearly, this approach would have to be tailored to country-specific circumstances, but it involves institutionalizing a close dialogue between all key actors and institutions, including the relevant ministries, industries and research institutions. Such a forum could play a key role in managing the integration of efforts in support of climate change mitigation with those in pursuit of development objectives. This would include identifying synergies between climate change mitigation and development, and increasing participation in the markets for innovative, climate-friendly products and services. These are discussed in the next section.

3. Development opportunities arising from climate change mitigation

(a) Synergies

The effects of GHG abatement will not only be felt globally in terms of better climatic conditions conducive to economic and social progress in the developing world, compared to non-action; many effects will also be felt at the local level in the countries, regions or cities where efforts to mitigate climate change are undertaken, in the form of improved air, water and land quality, with attendant benefits for health and labour productivity. There are also concrete synergies between strategies for climate

change mitigation and development (Cosbey, 2009; UNCTAD, 2009a). For example,

- There is broad agreement that the provision of energy to the poor constitutes developmental progress in its own right. In many cases, this objective can be pursued using energy from renewable sources at the micro level (e.g. biogas digesters, micro hydropower, solar cookers or photovoltaic panels can reduce the need for large energy infrastructure investments).

- In combination with measures for forest conservation, equipping poorer households with more climate-friendly energy sources will also lead to substantial benefits in terms of reduced indoor air pollution from inefficient biomass use and its attendant health problems.

- Increasing national energy efficiency generates considerable benefits for the national economy in terms of greater productivity and stronger international competitiveness of domestic producers.

- Efforts to achieve household energy efficiency will allow households, particularly the poorer ones, to switch their expenditures from heating and lighting to other purposes, including health and education.[13]

- Elimination of subsidies for traditionally produced energy can free substantial resources for use elsewhere, including public investment in more climate-friendly technologies and equipment.

- Efforts to restore forest cover or avoid deforestation or land degradation have important effects on development, as they help improve flood control in watersheds (Stern, 2006).

- Reducing the need for commuting through proper urban planning and providing attractive means of public transport would also improve the quality of life of the population and increase overall productivity.

- Switching to different sources of energy, in particular towards locally available renewable sources, would free foreign exchange for the purchase of capital goods, including equipment that uses climate-friendly technology. It would also contribute to local employment generation, and thus to poverty reduction. For example, Brazil's ethanol programme, which seeks to replace petroleum as automobile fuel, has not only avoided 26 million tons of CO_2 emissions annually, it has also reduced energy import costs by almost $100 billion compared to a baseline scenario, and created hundreds of thousands of jobs for the rural population (Bradley and Baumert, 2005).

- A greater share of renewable sources of energy in the overall energy mix also enhances energy diversification and energy security, which are pursued as objectives in their own right. It thus helps to ensure smooth and continuous access to energy at affordable rates, and shields countries from the balance of payments impacts of fluctuations in global prices of fossil fuels (IEA, 2008c; Bacon and Mattar, 2005).[14]

(b) New market opportunities

More stringent climate-related standards and policies, in conjunction with increased consumer preferences for "green products" have already led to a rapidly growing global market for environmental goods and services. Private investments in energy efficiency and renewables rose from $33.2 billion in 2004 to $148.4 billion in 2007. New fixed investments in clean energy in 2007 were equivalent to 9.6 per cent of global energy infrastructure investment and 1 per cent of fixed capital formation (UNEP, 2008). Since dynamic growth in many developing countries has put enormous pressures on their national environments, policymakers in these countries are increasingly realizing that environmental pollution and inefficient use of raw materials entail huge costs. As a result, there is considerable potential for further growth of the market for energy from renewable sources and for equipment to generate such energy, as well as for energy-efficient cars, buildings and appliances. The overall size of this market is difficult to gauge, given that many environmental goods can also be used

for purposes other than environmental protection. According to estimates by a leading private strategy consulting firm, the global market for environmental products and services may amount to as much as $1,400 billion (UNEP, 2008). Equipment that helps achieve climate change mitigation represents a significant share of this market.

Thus, there are considerable opportunities for income generation through increased participation in this market. Developing countries could seek such participation by integrating into international production chains, as many of them have successfully done in other fast-growing sectors. In addition, they themselves could contribute to innovation in climate protection processes and environmental goods based on specific local circumstances and comparative advantages. The development of "clean technologies" and early participation in the production of equipment embodying such technologies in the context of a rapidly expanding international market confers "first-mover advantages", given that other countries will eventually need to adopt these technologies as well. So far, the global export market for environmental goods is still clearly dominated by developed countries, which account for about 80 per cent of the total traded value of such goods. But developing economies such as Brazil, China, India, Indonesia, Malaysia and Taiwan Province of China already account for an increasing share of this market. China, for example, is already a major producer of equipment in the global wind power market, and it is among the world's largest producers of solar cells and lighting products. Brazil is the second largest global producer of biofuels, and India's photovoltaic production capacity has expanded rapidly in recent years (REN21, 2008; UNEP, 2009).

Developing countries should seek to participate in the rapidly growing global market for environmental goods and services.

As environmentally sound equipment, consumer goods and sources of energy can be considered "sunrise" industries, developing countries could improve their prospects for growth and employment creation by directing their industrial and agricultural development in this direction (UNCTAD, 2009a). Initially, many developing countries will be mainly engaged in adapting these new technologies to their specific national and local contexts. But if integrated into a broader development strategy, these efforts could ultimately lead to the development of domestic supply capacities for exporting these adapted technologies to other countries with similar needs. This represents a growing potential not only for exports to developed countries but also for enhanced South-South trade.

Promotion of these technologies will require an appropriate framework for technology transfer. It will also require the development of mechanisms to promote domestic knowledge accumulation, technological learning and innovation in order to increase technological absorptive capacity. The level of domestic technological capabilities will determine to what extent developing countries could, where possible, move directly ("leapfrog") to the frontier technologies developed in industrialized countries, rather than merely imitating and adapting second-best technologies with a strong emphasis on end-of-pipe solutions.[15]

4. Integrating climate change mitigation policies with development strategies

Although responsibility for the already high levels of GHG concentrations in the atmosphere rests primarily with developed countries, developing-country governments should not remain passive. There are growing opportunities for their economies resulting from increasingly stringent policies for GHG abatement around the world. The most effective way forward is to integrate climate change mitigation strategies with more proactive national industrialization strategies. As in other areas of industrial policy, in order to benefit from these opportunities a set of coherent policies and effective institutional arrangements is needed that supports the process of economic restructuring and technological change. It will also be necessary to integrate the development and diffusion of climate-friendly technology, equipment and consumer products with wider national R&D, innovation and investment promotion policies (Rodrik, 2008; *TDR 2006*, chap. V).

Climate policies will involve a revalorization of comparative advantages and open new options for agricultural and industrial development. Relying on market forces to trigger adequate responses to the new challenges and opportunities would be risky in light of both objectives: achieving the desired limit of global warming and successfully integrating developing countries in the markets for climate-friendly energy, technology and equipment. Experiences with economic catch-up in mature and late industrializers (*TDR 2006*: chap. V; Amsden, 2001; Chang, 2002; Rodrik, 2006) have shown that the dynamic forces of markets that underlie structural change and economic growth can be, and often have to be, stimulated by targeted government policies.

The main reason for such policy support is insufficient information and associated uncertainty about the viability of new modes of production or the success of new products. This is particularly the case in countries and sectors where industrial development is at a relatively early stage and the scope for imitation is relatively limited. This uncertainty may discourage investment in new, low-carbon modes of production and the integration into markets for innovative, climate-friendly technologies, equipment and consumer goods. Supportive policies could help improve the information base for decision-making and thereby encourage the necessary investment, which in turn could lead to economies of scale. Such support should take into account both national needs for climate-friendly technologies and products, as well as the structural move towards their use at the global level that offers opportunities for strategic integration into the global market for these products.

> The dynamic forces of markets that underlie structural change and economic growth often have to be stimulated by targeted government policies.

Many developing countries are likely to have natural comparative advantages – especially in the production of energy – that become more valuable in an era when the level of CO_2 emissions has to be sharply reduced. For example, solar, wind and hydro energy are likely to be highly valued substitutes for fossil fuels in domestic energy generation and consumption in a large number of developing countries. Their potential for exports may improve over time, once the problems of storage and transport of energy over long distances are solved through technological advances.

However, developing countries may also be well advised to evaluate to what extent they can acquire new comparative advantages in the growing market for environmental goods. These can be the result of an early establishment of an industry and the consequent acquisition of specialized knowledge or economies of scale or scope (Gomory and Baumol (2000: xiii). Such acquired comparative advantages play a particularly important role in medium- and high-technology-intensive industries such as those that contribute to climate change mitigation. Entry into such industries "is slow, expensive, and very much an uphill battle if left to free-market forces" (Gomory and Baumol, 2000: 5).

As in other industries, it may be possible for a developing country to start producing climate-friendly equipment by initially carrying out labour-intensive functions and thereafter progressively undertaking technological upgrading. Government support could serve to obtain dynamic scale economies, which requires both successive innovative investments and learning processes. Policy measures in support of industries that contribute to climate change mitigation may also include attracting FDI, particularly if it comes with a transfer of technology, organizational and managerial skills, and helps entry into international networks.

As with structural change policies more generally, specific policy measures depend on a country's particular initial conditions and its stage of economic development. However, there are several types of policy measures that may be relevant for different developing and transition economies in their efforts to combine global climate change mitigation with building domestic production capacity in the growing markets for environmental goods. Measures of relevance for industrial policy in a broader development context were discussed in greater detail in *TDR 2006* (chap.V). In the specific case of building domestic capacities for the provision of climate-friendly products and services, support could be provided, for example, by the following types of instruments:

- Fiscal incentives, apart from those that may be provided for innovative GHG abatement activities, could aim at encouraging investment in developing capacities to produce or participate in the production of climate-friendly equipment and appliances.

- Direct public credit, possibly in the form of loans by development banks at preferential interest rates and with favourable repayment schedules, could facilitate the financing of investments for the purpose of creating capacities to produce climate-friendly equipment and appliances and for acquisition of such goods produced locally.

- Subsidies could be allocated to those firms which show the greatest potential capacity to facilitate the use of locally available renewable sources of energy and to strengthen the country's position in the market for environmental goods.

- Venture capital institutions could play an important role in providing risk capital for firms engaging in the production of equipment and appliances that can substitute to more carbon-intensive ones. Since such organizations themselves often face financing constraints, development banks and other public actors that are motivated by social returns and externalities, rather than by private profit, could play a crucial role.

- Research and development (R&D) activities in support of technology upgrading and local adaptation of technology for the production of climate-friendly equipment and appliances could be carried out by public institutions, or private institutions and firms could be given public grants for this purpose. In this case, budgetary constraints could be alleviated through royalty payments by the private users of public research output commensurate with their profits, or by common-project-financing through regional cooperation agreements. Such measures may be complemented by according favourable treatment to FDI that is associated with spillovers of climate-friendly technologies and know-how.

> Industrial policy to promote the environmental goods sector is of particular relevance for forward-looking development strategies.

- The creation and expansion of firms involved in the development of climate-friendly technologies and the production of related equipment and appliances could be supported by public procurement schemes (see also section C.4 of this chapter). This could help the domestic firms reach the economies of scale necessary for making their environmental goods competitive relative to those of external suppliers. It could even help domestic firms take the lead in certain subsectors.

- Specific policy measures may also be relevant for the purpose of strategic integration into the global market for environmental goods, such as the creation of export processing zones that offer preferential tax and customs treatment. Measures such as selective liberalization through differentiated tariff and non-tariff barriers and granting duty drawbacks for imports of certain capital and intermediate goods have been successfully employed in the past for the development of specific industries in many countries. However, in recent years their use has become more difficult, and in many cases impossible, as a result of multilateral and bilateral regional trade agreements. While trade liberalization may help in the diffusion of climate-friendly technologies, it may render the exploitation of comparative advantages in markets for renewable energies more difficult. It may also hamper the development of domestic capacities for the production of climate-friendly technologies, equipment and appliances. While it is important, from a development perspective, to arrive at an appropriate balance between these two objectives in multilateral trade negotiations (see section F below), developing countries need to identify what policy space is still available to them in support of domestic climate-friendly industries. They should also avoid commitments in regional or bilateral agreements with developed countries that would circumscribe this policy space more narrowly than multilateral trade agreements have done.

Industrial policy with a special focus of using comparative advantages and creating new ones in environmental goods is of particular relevance in the context of forward-looking development strategies. This is not only because of the growing size of the market for such products, but also because the policy space for support measures in this area is less narrowly circumscribed by multilateral agreements than in other areas. According to Article 8 of the WTO Agreement on Subsidies and Countervailing Measures (SCM), specific subsidies for research or for the pursuit of environmental objectives are classified as non-actionable.[16] Subsidies are permitted for the "promotion of adapting existing facilities to new environmental regulations". They are also permitted for R&D, including the financing of venture capital funds and for the provision to the private sector of technologies and innovations developed in government research laboratories. Also included in this category is public procurement policy in support of the proliferation of domestically defined standards for particular technologies. Moreover, in order to support a shift in economic activity to new products or to the use of new technologies, activities can be subsidized as long as they are in the pre-competitive phase (i.e. before they result in the production of goods that are exported or subject to significant import competition).

> In the climate-friendly goods sector policy space for support measures is less narrowly circumscribed by multilateral agreements than in other areas.

The practical relevance of subsidies that fall under Article 8 of the SCM Agreement becomes very clear from the assistance measures that many developed countries have adopted in response to the current recession in support of their ailing automobile firms. Due to their subsidy elements, these measures could be challenged as violations of the subsidy rules under that Agreement. However, if assistance is tied to new fuel-efficiency and environmental standards, they are likely to fall under the exemptions from WTO subsidy discipline for environmental reasons. Another example concerns China's granting of about $1.5 billion in research subsidies to bolster its automobile industry by encouraging the development of more environmentally friendly cars. This move is designed to encourage Chinese auto-makers to focus on electric-vehicle technology (Shirouzu, 2009).

Several types of these support measures have an impact on the public budget. It may therefore be difficult for developing countries, particularly the poorest, to implement such measures. This constraint applies to domestic development policies in general, and has to be addressed in the broader context of strengthening public finances in developing countries. However, it may be easier to gain access to external financial support for the specific area of climate change mitigation than for other areas of industrial policy, given the possibilities arising from the emerging international framework for climate policies. For example, a strengthened CDM or a global carbon market in the form of a cap-and-trade system (Stern, 2008a and b) would allow developing countries to sell emission rights that they do not need to cover domestically produced emissions.

F. Towards an effective international climate policy framework

1. The broad agenda

Decisive action to reduce GHG emissions is required by national governments, especially those of developed and emerging-market economies that are responsible for the bulk of current GHG emissions. At the same time, because of the global nature of climate change and the risks involved, this action needs to be coordinated and organized within an international framework that includes all countries. International cooperation started with the establishment of the UNFCCC in 1992. Since the UNFCCC entered into force in 1994 there have been annual Conferences of the Parties (COPs) with the aim of strengthening the international climate policy framework. A further step in this direction was the adoption of the Kyoto Protocol on Climate Change at COP-3 in 1997, which entered into force in 2005 (see box 5.1 above).

Given that the Kyoto Protocol expires at the end of 2012, a new global agreement is needed to deal with climate change mitigation thereafter. A first step towards a post-Kyoto Protocol agreement was taken in December 2007 with the adoption of the Bali Action Plan adopted by COP-13. It defines four main building blocks of a new agreement, which will be presented for endorsement at COP-15 to be held in Copenhagen in December 2009. These are mitigation, adaptation, technology and financing. There was also agreement on the need to develop a shared vision for long-term cooperative action, including a long-term goal for global emission reductions.

The negotiations will have to address the need for "enhanced national/international action on mitigation of climate change" by both developed and developing countries. This primarily involves determining the extent of mitigation commitments to be made by Annex I Parties. But in addition, negotiations will also have to extend to "nationally appropriate mitigation actions" by developing countries. Without their effective participation, it will not be possible to ensure stabilization of GHG concentrations at relatively "safe" levels, in the light of past and projected future regional trends in economic growth and associated GHG emissions.

The negotiations will also have to agree on main policy approaches to achieve emission reductions, including the future role of the CDM, which so far has been the main vehicle for involving developing countries in the international framework for climate policy (box 5.2). An important issue to be resolved pertains to policy approaches and incentives for reducing emissions from deforestation and forest degradation in developing countries. Other key issues are how to support adaptation in developing

Box 5.2

THE CLEAN DEVELOPMENT MECHANISM: LARGE POTENTIAL BUT UNDERUTILIZED

The Clean Development Mechanism (CDM)[a] is based on the recognition that since GHG emissions are a problem at the global level, it does not matter where emission reductions are achieved. The same amount of additional emission reductions can be achieved more easily and at a lower cost in developing countries, which tend to operate at a greater distance from the world's technological frontier, than in developed countries. The CDM offers investors from Annex I countries (see box 5.1 above) the possibility of earning carbon credits – or CERs – if they undertake projects in developing countries that help these countries prevent or reduce GHG emissions.

Interest in CDM projects has grown rapidly in recent years. In July 2009, there were more than 4,400 projects in the "CDM pipeline", up from 534 at the end of 2005. Of these, 1,725 projects had been approved by that date. The UNFCCC expects the approved projects to reduce emissions by a cumulative 1.6 billion tons of CO_2 equivalent by the end of 2012, or by an annual average of 308 million tons. This indicates that CDM has considerable potential to contribute to a reduction in global GHG emissions, which totalled 41 billion tons in 2005.[b] The value of CDM projects by investors from Annex I countries amounted to $7.4 billion in 2007, up from $5.8 billion in 2006 (World Bank, 2008). This corresponds to about 1.3 per cent of total direct investment flows to developing and transition economies (UNCTAD, 2008).

So far, CDM projects have been concentrated in only a few activities, including hydro power, and in a small number of countries. In July 2009, China and India accounted for nearly two thirds of all CDM projects in the pipeline and for 70 per cent of all expected CERs by 2012, the end of the first commitment period of the Kyoto Protocol. China alone is expected to supply some 55 per cent of these carbon credits. Besides China and India, the two other major players in the CDM market are Brazil and Mexico, but the gap with China and India in terms of both the number of projects and CERs is considerable. By contrast, the share of the least developed countries (LDCs) is only about 1 per cent, which is even lower than their share in FDI to all developing and transition economies. This may reflect not only a limited number of potential projects that can generate GHG emission reductions relatively easily, but also the limited administrative capacity of these countries to participate in the mechanism.

Wider participation of developing countries in CDM has been encouraged through the Nairobi Framework launched in November 2006. This cooperation agreement, initially concluded among six multilateral agencies (UNDP, UNEP, UNFCCC, the World Bank, the Asian Development Bank and the United Nations Economic Commission for Africa), which UNCTAD joined in May 2009, aims at building capacity in developing countries, especially in sub-Saharan Africa, to develop CDM projects and benefit from access to carbon finance.

Although CDM can make a substantial contribution to climate change mitigation, its potential remains underutilized to date, for various reasons. The absolute amount of investment in CDM projects will be higher the more restrictive emission limitations become as cap-and-trade systems evolve. The role of the CDM is also circumscribed by the possibility of Annex I countries to limit the share of their domestic GHG emissions that can be offset through CERs. Just as it does not matter for global warming where GHGs are emitted, it does not matter for climate change mitigation as to where those gases are reduced. Considering the urgent need to reduce GHG emissions in the coming years, it is desirable that all "quick wins" possible in developing countries be utilized, and that low-cost abatement opportunities in those countries be exploited. On the other hand, the larger the scope for counting emission reductions achieved through the CDM in developing countries against commitments made by developed countries, the lower will be the incentive for clean technology innovations in developed countries. Therefore, a strengthening of the CDM should be accompanied by tighter emission restrictions, as well as greater government support for R&D and for wider application of innovative technologies in developed countries.

The effectiveness of the CDM also depends on the capacity of the CDM Executive Board to expedite approval and implementation of CDM projects. Judging by the backlog of projects, this capacity appears

Box 5.2 (concluded)

**DISTRIBUTION OF CDM PROJECTS, BY REGION
AND SELECTED COUNTRIES, 2009**

	CDM projects in the pipeline (as at 1 July 2009)		CERs expected by 2012	
	Number	Per cent	Million	Per cent
Africa	105	2.35	81	2.92
of which:				
Egypt	12	0.27	16	0.59
Nigeria	7	0.16	28	1.00
South Africa	29	0.65	20	0.72
Latin America	797	17.84	392	14.20
of which:				
Brazil	346	7.75	175	6.32
Mexico	154	3.45	65	2.36
Chile	69	1.54	40	1.44
West Asia	49	1.10	34	1.21
Other Asia and the Pacific	3 470	77.68	2 237	81.00
of which:				
China	1 754	39.27	1 534	55.52
India	1 127	25.23	424	15.34
Republic of Korea	63	1.41	103	3.72
Viet Nam	71	1.59	22	0.78
Europe and Central Asia	46	1.03	18	0.67
Total of 76 countries	4 467	100.00	2 762	100.00
Memo item:				
Least developed countries	45	1.01	26	0.94

Source: UNEP, Risø CDM Pipeline Analysis Database, at: http://www.cdmpipeline.org/overview.htm (accessed 1 June 2009).

to be low at present. The approval process could perhaps be accelerated by simplifying and streamlining the criteria for approval. At present, CDM projects submitted for approval have to pass a counterfactual test: the emission levels associated with a project have to be below those that would occur under a "business-as-usual" scenario. It has been observed that "the projects that have made it through the CDM project cycle have tended to be those that are the simplest to quantify [in terms of GHG-emissions reductions] and not necessarily those with the greatest benefits in terms of co-benefits or sustainable development" (Schmidt et al., 2008: 2; Cosbey et al., 2005). Promoting co-benefits of CDM projects is also an important objective in the ongoing negotiations on the future climate mitigation framework (Kinley, 2009). Depending on the project, co-benefits may include, for example, the elimination of a health hazard or the generation of local employment. Such co-benefits are highly desirable, but it is also important to avoid too much emphasis on such co-benefits in the evaluation of CDM project submissions so as not to further complicate and retard the approval process.

---

[a] For a more detailed review of the CDM, see UNCTAD, 2009c.

[b] UNFCCC, CDM statistics online, at: http://cdm.unfccc.int/Statistics/index.htm (accessed 10 June 2009). The European Commission Joint Research Centre shows worldwide GHG emissions growing faster (http://ec.europa.eu/dgs/jrc/index.cfm?id=2820&obj_id=341&dt_code=HLN&lang=en, accessed 25 May 2009).

countries as well as their transition to low-carbon economies through technology transfer and financing. The challenge is to carefully balance commitments and entitlements across the four proposed pillars between developed and developing countries, taking into account their diverse socio-economic conditions and vulnerabilities to climate change.

The widely varying socio-economic conditions across countries suggest that it will be necessary to adopt a multi-track framework involving different degrees of commitments and/or national policy measures for different groups of countries based on their level of development. In addition, new mechanisms for financial and technological support will need to be established, depending on the development stages of countries and their contributions to the climate change problem (Bodansky and Diringer, 2007). There is considerable GHG abatement potential in developing countries, which can be exploited at much lower costs than in industrialized countries. It is therefore in the interest of the developed countries to strengthen cooperation with developing countries in the pursuit of climate change mitigation. The CDM is a promising starting point for mutual action in that direction, even though it does not by itself lead to additional emissions abatement at the global level.

2. Involvement of developing countries

In order to reach a new climate agreement, it will be necessary that all parties view the distribution of responsibilities as sufficiently fair or equitable. The challenge is to secure a commitment to GHG reductions not only by developed countries, but also by emerging-market economies, which in recent years have drastically increased their GHG emissions.

The principle of common but differentiated responsibilities is a starting point for defining the type and scale of mitigation actions to be undertaken by developed and developing countries. In accordance with this principle, several studies have proposed that, since the GHG emissions of developed countries peak earlier than those of developing countries, the developed countries

> Commitments have to vary for different categories of countries and over time.

should reduce their emissions at a more rapid rate than developing countries (Stern, 2006: 495; UNDP, 2007. 7, IPCC, 2007b. 748).

A promising approach to reducing GHG emissions would be to extend the coverage of existing cap-and-trade systems and increase their effectiveness. Ideally, all developed and developing countries that have made reduction commitments would trade under the same system so as to discourage double standards and ensure fair competition. However, in order to ensure the participation of developing and transition economies in the same international cap-and-trade system, it will be indispensable to allow different levels of commitments and target dates for different categories of countries, and, accordingly, to find acceptable criteria for the distribution of emission permits amongst all participating countries.

Proposed criteria include, *inter alia,* per capita GDP, per capita emissions, emissions per unit of GDP, current emissions, historical emissions and population size.[17] One possibility would be to use a sequence of formulas for dynamic emission target setting within a cap-and-trade framework that would be determined by a combination of historical emissions, current emissions, population, income, and possibly some other country-specific indicators. This could also involve indexing emission targets to economic growth (Frankel, 2007). Similarly, a graduation index has been proposed that combines a country's per capita income and per capita emissions for determining emission thresholds, which would oblige developing countries to take on emission reduction commitments (Michaelowa, 2007).

For the time being, several developing countries, in particular low-income and least developed countries, may be exempted from formal reduction commitments. But in order to avoid larger adjustment burdens at later stages, these countries should nevertheless begin to work early on, and with the support of the international community, towards developing capabilities to introduce climate-friendly modes of production and consumption.

There are a number of proposals for progressively engaging developing countries in climate change mitigation. A major focus has been on the sectoral approach that targets emission reductions for a range of energy-intensive industries, such as power, iron and steel, and cement. The thrust of these approaches is to achieve large volumes of emission reductions, while also mobilizing, via carbon trading credits or other mechanisms such as CDM, sufficient funds for the deployment and diffusion of clean technologies. The sectoral approach could also serve as a stepping stone for developing countries towards adoption of economy-wide emission limitation goals in the medium term. The longer term goal would be to increasingly integrate developing countries into international cap-and-trade systems (Bodansky, 2007; Jackson et al., 2006).

This sectoral approach could be incorporated into a modified CDM, or organized outside the CDM. A sectoral CDM would involve the reduction of emissions below a specified baseline for a predetermined time period, with a corresponding supply of carbon credits. Incorporating a sectoral approach into the CDM would help counteract a growing trend towards fragmentation of mitigation efforts and thereby facilitate uniform standards and monitoring. However, establishing a sectoral mechanism outside the CDM appears to be simpler in many ways. First, it would preclude the need to demonstrate additionality and compliance with an increasing number of conditions, which at present make approval of projects extremely cumbersome, lengthy and costly. Second, it would enable the emission baseline to be negotiated directly between developing and developed countries within the framework of the UNFCCC. In both cases, emissions below baseline would generate carbon credits, but failure to reduce emissions below baseline would not lead to penalties that would require developing countries to purchase corresponding emission allowances. This approach is therefore known as the "sectoral no-lose target" (SNLT).

> Reducing deforestation has the highest potential to contribute to low-cost mitigation, but ...

> ... the present international climate policy framework does not address deforestation.

A variant of SNLT has the main objective of providing additional specific incentives – in the form of financial support and transfer of cutting-edge technology – to major emitting developing countries to enable them to reduce emissions in a given sector by a certain agreed amount below the initial no-lose target baseline. Given the additional support provided, only emissions below this more stringent target would be credited. The emission baseline established under SNLT would be based on a country's past emission trends, and would assume the implementation of policies and measures aimed at reducing emissions below the SNLT baseline. It has been proposed (Schmidt et al., 2008) that a more ambitious reference path for emissions than that of the SNLT approach could be achieved with additional external financial and technological support for domestic abatement measures.[18]

Sectoral agreements could require considerable financial transfers from developed countries to specific sectors. But such transfers may not be forthcoming for agreements that cover major competitors in internationally traded goods sectors. The sectoral approach may therefore be best suited for domestically oriented sectors that have only a few major emitters, such as electricity generation (Bradley et al., 2007). However, sectoral agreements need not be limited to carbon crediting schemes; they could also focus on technological standards similar to the vehicle emission standards of the EU, or they could mandate the use of specific technologies or alternative sources of energy, or proscribe heavily polluting equipment.

Reducing emissions from deforestation and forest degradation is an example of a sectoral approach that could make a significant contribution to climate change mitigation. Although reducing and reversing deforestation has the highest potential of any sector to contribute to low-cost mitigation between now and 2030 (Enqvist et al., 2007), emissions from this source are not addressed in the existing international climate policy framework. The Bali Plan of Action has therefore emphasized the strategic importance of slowing deforestation, which is a high-priority mitigation option in the tropical regions of Asia, Africa and Latin America. One option for international support in the prevention of deforestation could be to establish an explicit carbon crediting mechanism. But this would have to overcome considerable methodological challenges of establishing credible baselines, accurately measuring emissions, and ensuring that local emission reductions are permanent. There has also been a proposal to establish a dedicated fund under the UNFCCC to support voluntary engagement of countries in reducing emissions from deforestation. Some funds designed to support a slowdown in the rate of deforestation are already operational (UNFCCC, 2008a). Moreover, "positive incentives" could be provided by developed countries to build institutional capacities for reducing illegal logging and fire outbreaks, and banning imports of illegal timber.

Agriculture, particularly in developing countries, also has a significant potential to mitigate climate change at a relatively low cost. However, existing financing mechanisms under the Kyoto Protocol enable only a very small fraction of the mitigation potential of agriculture to be realized (Martino, 2009). For instance, soil carbon sequestration, which accounts for most of the mitigation potential in agriculture, is outside the scope of the CDM. It would therefore be desirable to include the issue of GHG emission reduction in agriculture on the agenda of the forthcoming climate change negotiations (see also FAO, 2009; IAASTD, 2009).

Developing countries have implemented a host of measures that focus primarily on promoting priority national development goals, but which also contribute to global GHG abatement as a "by-product". These policies and measures fall in the wider category of sustainable development policies and measures (SD-PAMs). It has been proposed that in the post-Kyoto climate regime, developing countries should have the possibility of unilaterally pledging implementation of specifically tailored policies with a development focus that have climate-friendly co-benefits as a major characteristic (Baumert and Winkler, 2005). This would allow them to gain formal recognition for their contribution to GHG abatement and help overcome the perception that countries without emission targets do not contribute to climate change mitigation. Implementation of SD-PAMs would allow developing countries to accumulate knowledge about the mitigation potential of the economy, and related economic, social and environmental costs and benefits. It could also contribute to increasing the capacity of domestic institutions for effective policy integration. To encourage SD-PAMs, developed countries could

offer to provide financial and technical assistance. But linking SD-PAMs with carbon crediting mechanisms is unlikely to be feasible given the difficulty in establishing "additionality" and credible emission baselines (Bradley et al., 2007).

3. External financing, trade and technology transfer

The effective participation of developing countries in global GHG abatement depends to a large extent on their utilization of climate-friendly technologies. The issue of technology development and transfer is therefore high on the agenda of the climate policy negotiations. The incremental investment costs of introducing clean energy technologies in developing countries are estimated at several hundred billion dollars per annum over the next few decades.[19] As discussed in the previous section, participating in the production of equipment and appliances that embed such technologies, and contributing to further technological progress in this sector, are important aspects of industrial development that should become major elements in the design of development strategies for the coming decades. The poorer developing countries may require additional foreign direct investment (FDI) and official development assistance (ODA) if they need to import the technology and equipment for helping GHG abatement.

The funds available through the UNFCCC (from the Global Environment Facility (GEF) Trust Fund, the LDC Fund and the Special Climate Change Fund) are very small compared to the size of resources required to cover the external financing needs of developing countries, particularly those that will not benefit from a revalorization of comparative advantages in the production of energy, or will not be able to build relevant new dynamic advantages. Various other multilateral financial mechanisms exist that rely on developed-country contributions for promoting GHG abatement in developing countries, such as the World Bank Climate Investment Fund and the Clean Technology Fund (CTF). In addition, a number of new financing options have been proposed, including a World Climate Change Fund, based on financial contributions by all countries, except the LDCs, to scale up financing for climate change mitigation and adaptation.

An international carbon market in the form of a cap-and-trade system could be a source of income for many developing countries. If designed in a manner that takes into account the responsibility of the industrialized countries for the existing GHG concentrations in the atmosphere, on the one hand, and the need for developing countries to contribute to global climate change mitigation, on the other, such a system might go a long way towards meeting their requirements for the financing of imports of the technology and equipment necessary for GHG abatement. For example, if population size were to be given an important weight in the initial allocation of permits across countries, many developing countries would be able to sell their emission rights because they would be allotted considerably more permits than they need to cover domestically produced emissions.

Access of developing countries to clean energy technologies could also be promoted through bilateral, regional and international cooperation agreements, such as the Asia-Pacific Partnership on Clean Development and Climate Change (APP). This agreement, launched in 2005, comprises Australia, Canada, China, India, Japan, the Republic of Korea and the United States. These countries have agreed to work together, along with private sector partners, to meet goals for energy security, national air pollution reduction and climate change mitigation by accelerating the development and deployment of clean energy technologies. In addition to renewable energy, the APP focuses on GHG emission reductions in industries such as steel and cement. Another example is the EU-China Partnership on Climate Change, formed in 2005. It aims to: promote the development and deployment of "zero emissions" and carbon capture and sequestration technologies; lower the costs of major clean energy technologies to enhance their diffusion and use; and support the mutual goal of improving energy efficiency.

In addressing climate change, it would be appropriate for the international community to consider support measures for developing countries that combine GHG abatement with the promotion of development objectives (Cosbey, 2009). From this perspective, it is regrettable that developed countries have been resisting liberalization of imports of agricultural products, including ethanol, while subsidizing their own biofuel production. Yet ethanol from sugar cane is currently considered by many experts as a very efficient biofuel in terms of cost, energy balance and GHG abatement. The reductions obtained from the use of biofuels based on feedstocks that are used in Europe and North America are much smaller than those from ethanol, and their supply and use are being supported by sizeable government subsidies. These subsidies, which are projected to rise from $11 billion in 2006 to $25 billion per year by 2015, correspond to $960 to $1,700 per ton of CO_2 equivalent saved (OECD, 2008). If the same fiscal expenditure were to be allocated for emission reduction projects in developing countries, a much larger abatement effect could be obtained, while respecting their comparative advantages in biofuel production.

Another potential obstacle for developing countries to contribute to climate change mitigation and at the same time grasp the opportunities provided by fast growth in the market for environmental goods is the protection of intellectual property rights. Typically, technology transfer is either associated with FDI or it is organized on the basis of licensing. The WTO Agreement on Trade-related Aspects of Intellectual Property Rights (TRIPS Agreement for short) severely restricts reverse engineering and other forms of imitative innovation, since it upholds the private rights of patent holders. As a result, it tends to limit the access of developing countries to proprietary knowledge. This implies an asymmetry that favours the producers and holders of protected intellectual property – mainly in developed countries – at the expense of those trying to gain access to protected intellectual property, mainly in developing countries (*TDR 2006*, chap.V). Exceptions are limited to very specific cases, such as access to medicines in developing countries. This exception is made for humanitarian reasons, but it can also have a positive impact on the development of pharmaceutical industries in developing countries.

Multilateral rules on proprietary knowledge aim at protecting the interests of the innovating firms in gaining an adequate profit. However, they also have to strike a balance between these interests and global

> An international cap-and-trade system could be a source of income for many developing countries.

public interests. The Doha Declaration explicitly recognized the flexibility within TRIPS to grant compulsory licences, and clarified the need to interpret TRIPS from a public health perspective. Given the global public good character of climate change mitigation, and that it is in the interest of developed countries to involve developing countries in global efforts to reduce GHG emissions, similar flexibility as that applied to medicines appears to be justified for proprietary rights in the field of climate-friendly technologies.

Another means for enabling developing countries to enhance their own production of equipment and appliances that help reduce global warming would be for developed countries and/or multilateral institutions to provide them with financial support for the acquisition of the appropriate licences. In this spirit, China and India have recently proposed the establishment of a Technology Acquisition Fund, to be financed by Annex I countries, to enable the purchase by developing countries of international property rights for low-carbon technologies.

G. Conclusions and policy recommendations

The impact of unabated global warming is the most severe in developing countries. Past and present GHG emissions, the bulk of which have been produced by developed countries, are commonly considered to be the main cause of global warming. But in developing and transition economies, especially in the largest and fastest growing among them, such emissions are now on a steeply rising trend. This trend will continue unless vigorous action is taken to change the energy mix and modes of production and consumption.

Developed countries need to lead global action to mitigate climate change by adopting strong policy measures, not only in their own interest, but also for ethical and economic reasons. They need to assume responsibility for the accumulation of emissions affecting the global climate, which have resulted from their past actions, particularly as they have greater economic, technological and administrative capacity to shift rapidly to a low-carbon economy. It is equally in the interests of developing and transition economies to contribute to global mitigation efforts in line with the principle of common but differentiated responsibilities, because current trends in their GHG emissions are not sustainable. And developed countries have an ethical obligation to support developing and transition economies in their efforts.

Climate change is the outcome of a gigantic market failure, and mitigation efforts now require strong government action at the national and international level. The international framework for a climate policy is still weak. If strengthened, many of its elements could contribute to more effective global GHG abatement efforts and to the greater participation of developing countries in those efforts. These elements include, *inter alia*, the promotion of carbon trading, and the two project-based mechanisms of the Kyoto Protocol – the Clean Development Mechanism and Joint Implementation – as well as the prevention of deforestation.

> Climate change is the outcome of a gigantic market failure, and mitigation efforts require strong government action at the national and international level.

Putting a price on emissions, in the form of taxes or tradable emission permits, and thereby changing the incentive structure for producers and consumers, could help set in motion a process towards establishing low-carbon economies. Measures that increase the demand for less carbon-intensive or carbon-free sources of energy are central to market-based intervention in favour of climate change mitigation, but these measures also need to be accompanied by intervention on the supply side of energy from other sources. Managing supply adjustments and price formation for different sources of energy is necessary in order to prevent prices of non-fossil, renewable energy from increasing – relative to the prices of the more carbon-intensive types of energy – as demand for them grows. Therefore, producers of different fuels need to be involved in the formulation and implementation of an international climate change mitigation policy.

In addition to changes in the incentive structure through the market mechanism, direct government intervention in the form of emission performance standards and strict regulations that prescribe specific modes of GHG abatement is indispensable in order to achieve ambitious targets within the envisaged time horizon. Also, more proactive policies to advance technological progress are required, because innovation towards low-carbon modes of production has become a necessity, unlike innovations in most other areas. Leaving this process to the market mechanism alone carries the risk that it may not provide a sufficiently strong stimulus for accelerating the development and application of appropriate cutting-edge technologies for carbon reduction to reach the required targets. This is partly because there has been considerable underinvestment in research aimed at the development of alternative sources of energy and cleaner production methods in the past, so that current modes of production and consumption are shaped by "carbon lock-in". In many cases, private firms may be reluctant to increase R&D investment sufficiently, because

> There is considerable scope for developing economies to gain from the structural change towards climate-friendly modes of production and consumption ...

> ... but they need sufficient space for proactive industrial policies to promote the domestic development of renewable sources of energy, climate-friendly technologies and the production of low-carbon equipment and appliances.

knowledge spillovers may prevent them from fully reaping the profits from their innovations. In the case of technology and know-how that advance more climate-friendly modes of production and consumption, such spillovers may even be desirable. Therefore, subsidies and public acquisition of patents could be ways to compensate private firms for possible losses resulting from such spillovers. Moreover, experience shows that technological change often advances faster when it also benefits from R&D in public institutions, and when the public sector takes the lead in applying new technologies in practice.

The engagement of developing countries in climate change mitigation efforts will largely depend on how a global climate policy is designed. Such a policy should facilitate their access to clean technologies, to financing for emission reducing investments, and to compensation for income losses that certain countries may face, for example as a result of energy-switching or forest conservation. International emissions trading within the framework of a global cap-and-trade system with a distribution of emission rights that favours developing countries could serve as a new financing mechanism. This could complement increased ODA for public GHG abatement projects and additional FDI in low-carbon activities.

Climate change mitigation does not have to be at the expense of growth and development. Experiences from both developed and developing countries show that many synergies are possible between GHG abatement, on the one hand, and development objectives on the other. Similarly, action undertaken primarily in the pursuit of other social and economic development objectives can often also lead to GHG abatement as a by-product. More generally, in order to implement successful programmes to reduce GHG emissions, developing countries need the strengthened administrative and institutional capacity that typically comes with development.

Climate change mitigation is best understood as a process of structural change. This process certainly implies adjustment costs for many economic agents but the time horizon for climate change mitigation is so long that it is difficult to estimate the total "costs of mitigation". Estimations of these costs may be misleading as they are subject to a considerable uncertainty and have to be based on highly subjective judgements. It is important to recognize that, as in other instances of structural change, this process also offers enormous new opportunities for product and process innovation, income growth and employment generation. From this macro-economic perspective, climate change mitigation is likely to involve only negligible net costs in terms of lower global GDP; it may even have a growth stimulating effect in many countries. Economic development always implies a process of structural change. What is important is to guide this change in the direction that is compatible with public preferences (in this case the need to reduce the risks arising from global warming), and to design development strategies that take account of the new opportunities offered by this process.

In the years and decades ahead there is considerable scope for developing economies to gain from the opportunities that will emerge from the structural change towards renewable sources of energy, climate-friendly technologies, low-carbon equipment and appliances, and more sustainable modes of consumption. Successful participation in the new markets is largely a matter of reassessing natural comparative advantages, especially in the production of clean energy, and creating new dynamic comparative advantages through a proactive industrial policy. Such a policy should aim at the early creation of capacities to produce or participate in the production of such goods, and their subsequent upgrading.

> It would be justified to allow compulsory licensing of patents for the production of climate-friendly equipment and goods that embed climate-friendly technologies.

Each developing and transition economy will need to define its own strategy for integrating into the emerging new markets for new products that help achieve GHG abatement objectives, taking into account both the local needs for specific "environmental goods" and the options for producing such goods for local, regional or global markets. Experience from developed countries and several emerging-market economies shows that a successful industrial policy may comprise, among other elements, public sector engagement in R&D, simplifying access to patents, fiscal and financial support for new production activities, information dissemination and FDI policies that favour integration into international production chains, government procurement and temporary protection of specific subsectors. A proactive industrial policy with a special focus on using existing comparative advantages and creating new ones in the environmental goods sector is of particular relevance in the context of forward-looking development strategies. This is because the policy space for support measures in this area is less narrowly circumscribed by multilateral agreements than in other areas.

The international community can support industrial development in this direction by allowing developing countries sufficient policy space in the context of relevant international agreements on climate change, trade, FDI and intellectual property rights. Given the global public good character of climate change mitigation, it would be justified to interpret the flexibilities of the TRIPS Agreement in a way that would allow compulsory licensing of patents for the production of climate-friendly equipment and goods that embed climate-friendly technologies, similar to the exemptions accorded for medicines in support of public health. ∎

Notes

1   In general, agricultural output and productivity are expected to decline given an adverse carbon fertilization effect. The carbon fertilization effect is the potentially beneficial effect of rising GHG concentrations in the atmosphere on crop growth by stimulating photosynthesis and lowering water requirements. But in tropical regions, crops are already close to critical temperature thresholds. However, some parts of China may benefit from this effect due to moderate temperature increases (Stern, 2006, chap. 3). A study by Cline (2007) finds that a global mean warming of 3°C will have a negative impact on global agricultural productivity in the longer run (by 2080), even in the presence of a carbon fertilization effect. The study suggests that the adverse impact on agricultural productivity will be felt first in developing countries, and they will suffer much more than developed countries.

2   The House of Representatives passed the American Clean Energy and Security Act on 26 June 2009 (for full text see: http://energycommerce.house.gov/Press_111/20090701/hr2454_house.pdf).

3   At the global level, the available supply of biofuels is too small to make a noticeable dent in the demand for oil.

4   Clearly, carbon pricing also has a distributional impact that is not negligible. An analysis of the distributional effect has to identify the social groups that finally have to bear the direct burden by paying higher prices for certain types of energy or goods, the production and consumption of which implies environmental costs that so far have not been accounted for in price calculations. This is relatively easy, but it is only part of the analysis, which also needs to take account of a number of other factors. It is true that the final consumers will have to pay the price, and consumption patterns across income groups are such that the share of energy in total consumption is higher among lower income groups. Thus, the direct effect of the introduction of instruments, such as carbon prices or taxes, on income distribution is regressive. However, the overall distributional effect of policies for climate change mitigation is also influenced by the use of revenues from carbon emission reduction policies and the distribution of income from production based on new technologies and more environment-friendly goods compared to that of production based on traditional technologies and goods. Since there are likely to be considerable differences in each of these variables, depending on the different policy instruments chosen, the actual impact on income distribution could only be assessed based on concrete policy choices. For this reason, the distribution and equity effects of climate change mitigation policies in general are not pursued further in this chapter.

5   Global integrated assessment models such as those used by the IMF (2008) or the OECD (2007) employ a least-cost approach, involving equalization of marginal abatement costs across sectors and countries based on internationally harmonized carbon taxes or global emissions trading. In these models, the shift to low-carbon technologies is driven by assumptions about exogenous technological change and endogenous substitution away from carbon-intensive inputs in response to higher carbon prices (see also Burniaux et al., 2008).

6   In China, there was an exceptionally large reduction in intensity of energy use as a result of the country's dramatic structural change after 1980 (see *TDR 2005*, chap. II). This decline bottomed out during the period 2000–2006, but the Government's 11th five-year plan for 2006–2010 specifies the objective of a reduction of energy consumption by 20 per cent in 2010 from its 2005 level. This reflects its concern about the sustainability of the rapid growth in energy demand in view of the potential adverse economic and environmental consequences (see People's Republic of China, State Council Information Office, 2008).

7   In many fast-growing developing countries, where private automobile transportation is expanding rapidly, estimates are much higher: based on data

from IEA (2004). Baumert and Winkler (2005) have estimated an increase in CO_2 emissions from road transport by 2020, in China of 143 per cent, in India of 67 per cent, in Indonesia of 122 per cent, in Mexico of 71 per cent and in West Asia of 68 per cent.

8   Locating residences close to places of work and other destinations is probably the most effective policy option. This option is of particular relevance for urban centres that are expected to expand in the future, but less so for urban areas that have already been built.

9   UNFCCC (2008c) presents an in-depth discussion of the challenges and opportunities emerging from climate change mitigation in agriculture, along with case studies.

10 As rice is the major crop grown in developing countries, improving water and rice management is considered an important option for methane abatement in developing countries, notably in South-East Asia.

11 In sectoral carbon reduction accounting, such substitution would be counted in favour of the sectors using the energy.

12 For details, see www.ghgprotocol.org.

13 Cosbey (2009) found that household energy efficiency projects scored higher than all other types of projects in terms of "development dividend", as calculated for the assessment of projects under the Clean Development Mechanism.

14 On the other hand, the search for energy diversification does not necessarily imply a move towards a more climate-friendly energy mix, since it can also imply the development of a conventional source of energy, such as domestic coal, at the expense of other fossil fuels, such as imported oil.

15 End-of-pipe systems are used for the treatment of emissions where these cannot be avoided in the first place. This traditional approach still plays an important role in many industries, and will continue to do so as long as carbon-intensive technologies remain in use. The sensible environmental and developmental option is to minimize the need for such treatment and to maximize the use of cleaner solutions upstream in the production process, especially when new productive capacities are built.

16 Formally, these subsidies became actionable following a review of the initial provision in 2000 and the failure to reach agreement over its extension. However, in practice no action has been taken in this regard. In order to qualify for the initial provision, subsidies for research must be for activities conducted by firms or research establishments on a contract basis with firms, on the condition that the assistance covers not more than 75 per cent of the cost of industrial research or 50 per cent of the cost of pre-competitive development activity. Regarding environmental objectives, subsidies are permitted for the "promotion of adapting existing facilities to new environmental regulations". The Doha Ministerial Conference took "note of the proposal to treat measures implemented by developing countries with a view to achieving legitimate development goals, such as regional growth, technology research and development funding, production diversification and development and implementation of environmentally sound methods of production as non-actionable subsidies, and agrees that this issue be addressed ... [as an outstanding implementation issue]. During the course of the negotiations, Members are urged to exercise due restraint with respect to challenging such measures" (WTO, 2001: 6). In the meantime, however, the issue of Article 8 subsidies seems to have been eclipsed by negotiations on other issues.

17 For an overview, see Bodansky, 2004.

18 This would imply that emission reductions below the initial baseline but above the more ambitious new reference path would not be credited any more. Instead, they would be permanently "retired from the atmosphere" as a mitigation contribution of developing countries.

19 According to UNDP estimates, developing countries will need to undertake investments of about $44 billion per annum by 2015 for "climate-proofing" existing infrastructure, in addition to investments for adaptation to climate change. A similar amount is considered necessary for adapting poverty reduction programmes to climate change (e.g. support for public health, rural development and community-based environmental protection). A further $2 billion per annum will be needed for strengthening disaster response measures (UNDP, 2007: table 4.3).

References

Abernathy WJ and Wayne K (1974). Limits of the learning curve. *Harvard Business Review*, 52(4): 109–119.

Ackerman F (2008). Carbon markets and beyond: The limited role of prices and taxes in climate and development policy. G-24 Discussion Paper No. 53, New York and Geneva, UNCTAD, December.

Ackerman F and Finlayson IJ (2006). The economics of inaction on climate change: a sensitivity analysis. Working paper no. 06-07, October, Global Development and Environment Institute, Tufts University, Medford, MA.

Ackerman F and Stanton E (2006). Climate change: the cost of inaction. Report to Friends of the Earth England, Wales and Northern Ireland. Global Development and Environment Institute, Tufts University, Medford, MA. Available at: http://ase.tufts.edu/gdae/Pubs/rp/Climate-CostsofInaction.pdf

Amsden AH (2001). The Rise of "the Rest": Challenges to the West from Late-Industrializing Economies. New York, Oxford University Press.

Arrow K and Bolin B (1995). Economic growth, carrying capacity, and the environment. *Ecological Economics* (15): 91–95.

Bacon R and Mattar A (2005). The vulnerability of African countries to oil price shocks: major factors and policy options. The case of oil importing countries. *Energy Sector Management Assistance Program Report,* 308 (5).

Baer P and Athanasiou T (2007). Frameworks & proposals: a brief, adequacy- and equity-based evaluation of some prominent climate policy frameworks and proposals. Global Issue Papers No. 30, Heinrich-Böll-Stiftung, Berlin, June.

Barker T, Qureshi M and Köhler J (2006). The costs of greenhouse gas mitigation with induced technological change: A meta-analysis of estimates in the literature. Tyndall Centre for Climate Change Research Working Paper 89, Norwich.

Baumert K and Winkler H (2005). Sustainable development policies and measures and international climate agreements. In: Bradley R and Baumert K, eds. *Growing in the Greenhouse: Protecting the Climate by Putting Development First,* chapter 2. Washington, DC, World Resources Institute. Available at: www.wri.org.

Baumol W and Oates W (1988). *The Theory of Environmental Policy.* Second edition, Cambridge, Cambridge University Press.

Bodansky D (2004). International climate efforts beyond 2012: a survey of approaches. Arlington, VA, Pew Center on International Climate Change. Available at: www.pewclimate.org.

Bodansky D (2007). International sectoral agreements in a post-2012 climate framework. Working Paper. Arlington, VA, Pew Center on Climate Change, May. Available at: www.pewclimate.org.

Bodansky D and Diringer E (2007). Towards an integrated multi-track climate framework. Arlington, VA, Pew Center on Global Climate Change, December. Available at: www.pewclimate.org.

Bradley R and Baumert K (eds.) (2005). *Growing in the Greenhouse: Protecting the Climate by Putting Development First.* Washington, DC, World Resources Institute.

Bradley R et al. (2007). Slicing the pie: Sector-based approaches to international climate agreements. Washington, DC, World Resources Institute, December.

Burniaux J-M et al. (2008). The economics of climate change mitigation: Policies and options for the future. OECD, Economics Department Working Paper No. 658. Paris, OECD.

Chandler W et al. (2002). Climate change mitigation in developing countries: Brazil, China, India, Mexico, South Africa, and Turkey. Arlington, VA, Pew Center on Global Climate Change, October. Available at: www.pewclimate.org.

Chang HJ (2002). Kicking Away the Ladder: Development Strategy in Historical Perspective. London, Anthem.

Cline W (2007). Global warming and agriculture. *Finance and Development*, March 2008. Washington, DC, International Monetary Fund.

Copeland B and Taylor M (2004). Trade, growth and the environment. *Journal of Economic Literature* (XLII): 1.

Cosbey A et al. (2005). Realizing the development dividend: Making the CDM work for developing countries. Phase 1 Report, Executive Summary. Available at: www.iisd.org.

Cosbey A (2009). Developing Country Interest in Climate Change Action and the Implications for a Post-2012 Climate Change Regime. New York and Geneva, UNCTAD.

Daviet F (2009). The role of sustainable development policies and measures in REDD. Climate and Forests Policy Series, March 2009, Washington, DC, World Resource Institute. Available at: www.wri.org.

EIA (United States Energy Information Administration) (2007). International Energy Outlook. Washington, DC, United States Department of Energy.

Enqvist PA et al. (2007). A cost curve for greenhouse gas reduction. *The McKinsey Quarterly*, 1.

FAO (2009). Climate change talks should include farmers. Agriculture in developing countries could play crucial role in mitigating greenhouse gas emissions. Press release at: http://www.fao.org/news/story/en/item/11356/icode/.

Fischer C and Newell R (2004). Environmental technology policies for climate change and renewable energy. Discussion Paper 04–05, Resources for the Future, Washington, DC, April.

Frankel J (2007). Formulas for quantitative emission targets. In: Aldy J and Stavins R, eds. *Architecture for Agreement: Addressing Global Climate Change in the Post-Kyoto World*. Cambridge, Cambridge University Press: 31–56.

Gallagher KS (2007). China needs help with climate change. *Current History*, 106 (703): 389–394, November. Available at: www.belfercenter.ksg.harvard.edu.

Gomory RE and Baumol WJ (2000). *Global Trade and Conflicting Interests*. Cambridge, MA, and Landon, MIT Press.

Hannesson R (2002). Energy use and GDP growth, 1950–1997. *OPEC Review*, 26(3): 215–233, September.

Helm D (2008). Caps and floors for the EU ETS: A practical carbon price, October. Oxford, Oxford University. Available at: www.dieterhelm.co.uk.

IAASTD (International Assessment of Agricultural Knowledge, Science and Technology for Development) (2009). (http://www.agassessment.org/)

ICTSD (International Centre for Trade and Sustainable Development) (2008). Liberalization of trade in environmental goods for climate change mitigation: The sustainable development context. Available at: www.ictsd.org.

IEA (2004). *World Energy Outlook 2004*. Paris, International Energy Agency.

IEA (2008a). *World Energy Outlook*. Paris, International Energy Agency.

IEA (2008b). *CO2 Emissions from Fuel Combustion*, 2008 edition. Paris, International Energy Agency.

IEA (2008c). *Energy Technology Perspectives 2008*. Paris: International Energy Agency.

IMF (2008). Climate change and the global economy, in *World Economic Outlook: Housing and the Business Cycle*. Washington, DC, April.

IPCC (2007a). Climate Change 2007: Mitigation. Contribution of Working Group III to the Fourth Assessment Report of the International Panel on Climate Change: Mitigation of Climate Change. Cambridge and New York, Cambridge University Press.

IPCC (2007b). Climate Change 2007: The Physical Science Basis. Summary for Policymakers. Contribution of Working Group I to the Fourth Assessment Report of the Intergovernmental Panel on Climate Change. Available at: www.ipcc.ch.

IPCC (2007c). Climate Change 2007: Impacts, adaptation and vulnerability. Summary for Policymakers. Contribution of Working Group II to the Fourth Assessment Report of the Intergovernmental Panel on Climate Change. Available at: www.ipcc.ch.

Jackson M et al. (2006). Greenhouse gas implications in large scale infrastructure investments in developing countries: Examples from China and India. Working Paper No. 54, Program on Energy and Sustainable Development. *Stanford, Stanford University*. Center for Environmental Science and Policy. Available at: http://pesd.stanford.edu.

Jaffe A, Newell R and Stavins R (2004). A tale of two market failures: Technology and environmental policy. Discussion Paper 04–38. Washington, DC, Resources for the Future, October.

Kemfert C (2005). Global climate change protection: Immediate action will avert high costs. *DIW Weekly Report,* 1(12): 135–141.

Kinley R (2009). Trade and investment opportunities and challenges under the Clean Development Mechanism. Address by Deputy Executive Secretary of UNFCCC, delivered at UNCTAD Expert Meeting on Trade and Climate Change, 27 April 2009, Geneva.

Martino D (2009). Main Findings of IPCC AR4 on Agriculture. Available at: http://www.agritrade.org/documents/martino20090406.pdf.

McKinsey Global Institute (2007). Global energy demand growth: The energy productivity opportunity. Available at: www.mckinsey.com/mgi.

Michaelowa A (2007). Graduation and deepening. In: Aldy J and Stavins R, eds. *Architecture for Agreement: Addressing Global Climate Change in the Post-Kyoto World*. Cambridge, Cambridge University Press: 81–104.

Nordhaus W (2008). A Question of Balance: Weighing the Options on Global Warming Policies. New Haven and London, Yale University Press.

OECD (2007). Environmental Outlook to 2030. Paris, OECD.

OECD (2008). Biofuel support policies: An economic assessment. Paris, OECD.

OPEC (2007). *World Oil Outlook 2007*. Vienna, Organization of the Petroleum Exporting Countries.

People's Republic of China, State Council Information Office (2008). White Paper: China's policies and actions on climate change, October. Available at: www.china.org.cn/government/news.

REN21 (2008). Renewables 2007 Global Status Report. Paris, REN21 Secretariat and Washington, DC.

Rodrik D (2006). Goodbye Washington Consensus, Hello Washington Confusion? A Review of the World Banks's *Growth in the 1990s: Learning from a Decade of Reform. Journal of Economic Literature* 44 (4): 973–987, December.

Rodrik D (2008). Normalizing Industrial Policy. Working Paper No. 3, Commission on Growth and Development. World Bank, Washington, DC.

Schmidt J et al. (2008). Sector-based approach to the post-2012 climate change architecture. *Climate Policy* (8): 494–515. London, Earthscan.

Sheehan P (2007). The new global growth path: Implications for climate change analysis and policy. CSES Climate Change Working Paper No. 14, Centre for Strategic Economic Studies, Victoria University, Melbourne.

Shirouzu N (2009). China uses green cars to bolster auto sector. *Wall Street Journal*, 23 March. Available at: http://online.wsj.com/article/SB123773108089706101.html.

Stern N (2006). *Stern Review: The Economics of Climate Change*. Cambridge, Cambridge University Press.

Stern N (2008a). The economics of climate change. *American Economic Review: Papers and Proceedings* 98(2): 1–37, May.

Stern N (2008b). Key elements of a global deal on climate change. London, The London School of Economics and Political Science. Available at: www.lse.ac.uk.

UNCTAD (2005). *Trade and Development Report, 2005: New Features of Global Interdependence*. United Nations publications, Sales No. E.05.II.D.13, New York and Geneva.

UNCTAD (2006). *Trade and Development Report, 2006: Global Partnership and National Policies for Development*. United Nations publications, Sales No. E.06.II.D.6, New York and Geneva.

UNCTAD (2008). *World Investment Report 2008: Transnational Corporations and the Infrastructure Challenge*. United Nations publications, Sales No. E.08.II.D.23, New York and Geneva.

UNCTAD (2009a). *Trade and Environment Review 2009: The World at Crossroads: Utilising Green Growth Poles in Developing Countries to Foster Low-carbon Development*. United Nations publication, New York and Geneva.

UNCTAD (2009b). Sustaining African agriculture: Organic production. UNCTAD Policy Brief 6, Geneva, UNCTAD. Available at: http://www.unctad.org/en/docs/presspb20091rev1_en.pdf.

UNCTAD (2009c).Trade and investment opportunities and challenges under the Clean Development Mechanism (CDM). Note by the UNCTAD secretariat for UNCTAD Trade and Development Board, Expert Meeting on Trade and Climate Change: Trade and Investment Opportunities Under the Clean Development Mechanism (CDM), Geneva, 1–3 April 2009.

UNDP (2007). Human Development Report 2007/2008: Fighting Climate Change – Human Solidarity in a Divided World. New York, Palgrave Macmillan.

UNEP (2008). Green jobs: Towards decent work in a sustainable, low-carbon world. Produced for the UNEP/ILO/IEO/ITUC Green Jobs Initiative. Washington, DC.

UNEP (2009). Risø CDM Pipeline Analysis Database, June.

UNFCCC (2005a). Sixth compilation and synthesis of initial communications from Parties not included in Annex I to the Convention, Addendum: Sustainable development and integration of climate change concerns into medium- and long-term planning, FCCC/SBI/2005/18/Add. 1, 25 October. Bonn.

UNFCCC (2005b). Sixth compilation and synthesis of initial communications from Parties not included in Annex I to the Convention, Addendum: Measures contributing to addressing climate change, FCCC/SBI/2005/18/Add. 3, 25 October. Bonn.

UNFCCC (2008a). Investment and financial flows to address climate change: An update. Technical Paper, (FCCC/TP/2008/7), 26 November. Bonn.

UNFCCC (2008b). Challenges and opportunities for mitigation in the agricultural sector. Technical Paper FCCC TP/2008/8, 21 November 2008. Bonn, UNFCCC. Available at: http://unfccc.int/resource/docs/2008/tp/08.pdf.

UNFCCC (2008c). National greenhouse gas inventory data for the period 1990–2006, FCCC/SBI/2008/12, 17 November. Bonn.

Unruh GC and Carrillo-Hermosilla J (2006). Globalizing carbon lock-in. *Energy Policy*, 34 (14): 1185–1197.

von Braun J (2008). *Food prices, Biofuels, and Climate Change*. International Food Policy Research Institute, Washington, DC, February. Available at: http://www.ifpri.org/presentations/200802jvbbiofuels.pdf.

Watkiss P et al. (2005). The social costs of carbon review: Methodological approaches for using SCC estimates in policy assessment. London, Department for Environment, Food and Rural Affairs.

Watson R et al. (eds.) (2000). *Land Use, Land Use Change and Forestry*. Special Report of the IPCC. Cambridge, Cambridge University Press.

Weitzman M (1974). Prices vs. quantities. *Review of Economic Studies*, 41(4): 477–491, October.

Weitzman M (2007). A review of the Stern Review of the Economics of Climate Change. *Journal of Economic Literature* (45): 703–724, September.

Willems S and Baumert K (2003). Institutional capacity and climate change. OECD/IEA, COM/ENV/EPOC/IEA/SLT(2003)5. Paris, OECD/IEA.

World Bank (2007). Global Economic Prospects 2007: Managing the Next Wave of Globalization. Washington, DC.

World Bank (2008). State and trends of the carbon market 2008. Washington, DC, May.

WTO (2001). Implementation-related issues and concerns. Decision of 14 November 2001. Document WT/MIN(01)/17, World Trade Organization, Geneva.

**UNITED NATIONS CONFERENCE
ON TRADE AND DEVELOPMENT**

Palais des Nations
CH-1211 GENEVA 10
Switzerland
(www.unctad.org)

Selected UNCTAD Publications

Trade and Development Report, 2008   United Nations publication, sales no. E.08.II.D.21
Commodity prices, capital flows and the financing of investment   ISBN 978-92-1-112752-2

Trade and Development Report, 2007   United Nations publication, sales no. E.07.II.D.11
Regional cooperation for development   ISBN 978-92-1-112721-8

Trade and Development Report, 2006   United Nations publication, sales no. E.06.II.D.6
Global partnership and national policies for development   ISBN 92-1-112698-3

Chapter	I	Global Imbalances as a Systemic Problem
		Annex 1: Commodity Prices and Terms of Trade
		Annex 2: The Theoretical Background to the Saving/Investment Debate
Chapter	II	Evolving Development Strategies – Beyond the Monterrey Consensus
Chapter	III	Changes and Trends in the External Environment for Development
		Annex tables to chapter III
Chapter	IV	Macroeconomic Policy under Globalization
Chapter	V	National Policies in Support of Productive Dynamism
Chapter	VI	Institutional and Governance Arrangements Supportive of Economic Development

Trade and Development Report, 2005   United Nations publication, sales no. E.05.II.D.13
New features of global interdependence   ISBN 92-1-112673-8

Chapter	I	Current Issues in the World Economy
Chapter	II	Income Growth and Shifting Trade Patterns in Asia
Chapter	III	Evolution in the Terms of Trade and its Impact on Developing Countries
		Annex: Distribution of Oil and Mining Rent: Some Evidence from Latin America, 1999–2004
Chapter	IV	Towards a New Form of Global Interdependence

Trade and Development Report, 2004   United Nations publication, sales no. E.04.II.D.29
Policy coherence, development strategies   ISBN 92-1-112635-5
and integration into the world economy

Part One		Global Trends and Prospects
	I	The World Economy: Performance and Prospects
	II	International Trade and Finance
Part Two		Policy Coherence, Development Strategies and Integration into the World Economy Introduction
	III	Openness, Integration and National Policy Space
	IV	Fostering Coherence Between the International Trading, Monetary and Financial Systems
		Annex 1: The Concept of Competitiveness
		Annex 2: The Set-up of Econometric Estimates of the Impact of Exchange Rate Changes on Trade Performance
		Conclusions and Policy Challenges

Trade and Development Report, 2003   United Nations publication, sales no. E.03.II.D.7
Capital accumulation, growth and structural change   ISBN 92-1-112579-0

Part One		Global Trends and Prospects
	I	The World Economy: Performance and Prospects
	II	Financial Flows to Developing Countries and Transition Economies
	III	Trade Flows and Balances
		Annex: Commodity prices
Part Two		Capital Accumulation, Economic Growth and Structural Change
	IV	Economic Growth and Capital Accumulation
	V	Industrialization, Trade and Structural Change
	VI	Policy Reforms and Economic Performance: The Latin American Experience

Trade and Development Report, 2002
Developing countries in world trade

United Nations publication, sales no. E.02.II.D.2
ISBN 92-1-112549-9

Trade and Development Report, 2001
Global trends and prospects
Financial architecture

United Nations publication, sales no. E.01.II.D.10
ISBN 92-1-112520-0

* * * * * *

The Global Economic Crisis:
Systemic Failures and Multilateral Remedies
Report by the UNCTAD Secretariat Task Force
on Systemic Issues and Economic Cooperation

United Nations publication, sales no. E.09.II.D.4
ISBN 978-92-1-112765-2

* * * * * *

These publications may be obtained from bookstores and distributors throughout the world. Consult your bookstore or write to United Nations Publications/Sales Office and Bookshop, Bureau E4, Palais des Nations, CH-1211 Geneva 10, Switzerland (tel.: +41-22-917-2613 / +41-22-917-2614; fax: +41-22-917.0027; e-mail: unpubli@unog.ch; Internet: https://unp.un.org); or United Nations Publications, Two UN Plaza, Room DC2-853, New York, NY 10017, USA (tel.: +1-212-963.8302 or +1-800-253.9646; fax: +1-212-963.3489; e-mail: publications@un.org).

G-24 Discussion Paper Series

*Research papers for the Intergovernmental Group of Twenty-Four
on International Monetary Affairs and Development*

No. 56	June 2009	Anuradha MITTAL	The 2008 Food Price Crisis: Rethinking Food Security Policies
No. 55	April 2009	Eric HELLEINER	The Contemporary Reform of Global Financial Governance: Implications of and Lessons from the Past
No. 54	February 2009	Gerald EPSTEIN	Post-war Experiences with Developmental Central Banks: The Good, the Bad and the Hopeful
No. 53	December 2008	Frank ACKERMAN	Carbon Markets and Beyond: The Limited Role of Prices and Taxes in Climate and Development Policy
No. 52	November 2008	C.P. CHANDRASEKHAR	Global Liquidity and Financial Flows to Developing Countries: New Trends in Emerging Markets and their Implications
No. 51	September 2008	Ugo PANIZZA	The External Debt Contentious Six Years after the Monterrey Consensus
No. 50	July 2008	Stephany GRIFFITH-JONES with David GRIFFITH-JONES and Dagmar HERTOVA	Enhancing the Role of Regional Development Banks
No. 49	December 2007	David WOODWARD	IMF Voting Reform: Need, Opportunity and Options
No. 48	November 2007	Sam LAIRD	Aid for Trade: Cool Aid or Kool-Aid
No. 47	October 2007	Jan KREGEL	IMF Contingency Financing for Middle-Income Countries with Access to Private Capital Markets: An Assessment of the Proposal to Create a Reserve Augmentation Line
No. 46	September 2007	José María FANELLI	Regional Arrangements to Support Growth and Macro-Policy Coordination in MERCOSUR
No. 45	April 2007	Sheila PAGE	The Potential Impact of the Aid for Trade Initiative
No. 44	March 2007	Injoo SOHN	East Asia's Counterweight Strategy: Asian Financial Cooperation and Evolving International Monetary Order
No. 43	February 2007	Devesh KAPUR and Richard WEBB	Beyond the IMF
No. 42	November 2006	Mushtaq H. KHAN	Governance and Anti-Corruption Reforms in Developing Countries: Policies, Evidence and Ways Forward
No. 41	October 2006	Fernando LORENZO and Nelson NOYA	IMF Policies for Financial Crises Prevention in Emerging Markets
No. 40	May 2006	Lucio SIMPSON	The Role of the IMF in Debt Restructurings: Lending Into Arrears, Moral Hazard and Sustainability Concerns
No. 39	February 2006	Ricardo GOTTSCHALK and Daniela PRATES	East Asia's Growing Demand for Primary Commodities – Macroeconomic Challenges for Latin America
No. 38	November 2005	Yilmaz AKYÜZ	Reforming the IMF: Back to the Drawing Board
No. 37	April 2005	Colin I. BRADFORD, Jr.	Prioritizing Economic Growth: Enhancing Macroeconomic Policy Choice
No. 36	March 2005	JOMO K.S.	Malaysia's September 1998 Controls: Background, Context, Impacts, Comparisons, Implications, Lessons
No. 35	January 2005	Omotunde E.G. JOHNSON	Country Ownership of Reform Programmes and the Implications for Conditionality
No. 34	January 2005	Randall DODD and Shari SPIEGEL	Up From Sin: A Portfolio Approach to Financial Salvation

G-24 Discussion Paper Series

Research papers for the Intergovernmental Group of Twenty-Four
on International Monetary Affairs and Development

No. 33	November 2004	Ilene GRABEL	Trip Wires and Speed Bumps: Managing Financial Risks and Reducing the Potential for Financial Crises in Developing Economies
No. 32	October 2004	Jan KREGEL	External Financing for Development and International Financial Instability
No. 31	October 2004	Tim KESSLER and Nancy ALEXANDER	Assessing the Risks in the Private Provision of Essential Services
No. 30	June 2004	Andrew CORNFORD	Enron and Internationally Agreed Principles for Corporate Governance and the Financial Sector
No. 29	April 2004	Devesh KAPUR	Remittances: The New Development Mantra?
No. 28	April 2004	Sanjaya LALL	Reinventing Industrial Strategy: The Role of Government Policy in Building Industrial Competitiveness
No. 27	March 2004	Gerald EPSTEIN, Ilene GRABEL and JOMO, K.S.	Capital Management Techniques in Developing Countries: An Assessment of Experiences from the 1990s and Lessons for the Future
No. 26	March 2004	Claudio M. LOSER	External Debt Sustainability: Guidelines for Low- and Middle-income Countries
No. 25	January 2004	Irfan ul HAQUE	Commodities under Neoliberalism: The Case of Cocoa
No. 24	December 2003	Aziz Ali MOHAMMED	Burden Sharing at the IMF
No. 23	November 2003	Mari PANGESTU	The Indonesian Bank Crisis and Restructuring: Lessons and Implications for other Developing Countries
No. 22	August 2003	Ariel BUIRA	An Analysis of IMF Conditionality
No. 21	April 2003	Jim LEVINSOHN	The World Bank's Poverty Reduction Strategy Paper Approach: Good Marketing or Good Policy?
No. 20	February 2003	Devesh KAPUR	Do As I Say Not As I Do: A Critique of G-7 Proposals on Reforming the Multilateral Development Banks
No. 19	December 2002	Ravi KANBUR	International Financial Institutions and International Public Goods: Operational Implications for the World Bank
No. 18	September 2002	Ajit SINGH	Competition and Competition Policy in Emerging Markets: International and Developmental Dimensions
No. 17	April 2002	F. LÓPEZ-DE-SILANES	The Politics of Legal Reform
No. 16	January 2002	Gerardo ESQUIVEL and Felipe LARRAÍN B.	The Impact of G-3 Exchange Rate Volatility on Developing Countries

* * * * * *

G-24 Discussion Paper Series are available on the website at: **www.unctad.org**. Copies of *G-24 Discussion Paper Series* may be obtained from the Publications Assistant, Macroeconomic and Development Policies Branch, Division on Globalization and Development Strategies, United Nations Conference on Trade and Development (UNCTAD), Palais des Nations, CH-1211 Geneva 10, Switzerland; fax +41-22-917-0274.

UNCTAD Discussion Papers

No. 194	June 2009	Andrew CORNFORD	Statistics for international trade in banking services: requirements, availability and prospects
No. 193	Jan. 2009	Sebastian DULLIEN	Central banking, financial institutions and credit creation in developing countries
No. 192	Nov. 2008	Enrique COSIO-PASCAL	The emerging of a multilateral forum for debt restructuring: The Paris Club
No. 191	Oct. 2008	Jörg MAYER	Policy space: What, for what, and where?
No. 190	Oct. 2008	Martin KNOLL	Budget support: A reformed approach or old wine in new skins?
No. 189	Sep. 2008	Martina METZGER	Regional cooperation and integration in sub-Saharan Africa
No. 188	March 2008	Ugo PANIZZA	Domestic and external public debt in developing countries
No. 187	Feb. 2008	Michael GEIGER	Instruments of monetary policy in China and their effectiveness: 1994–2006
No. 186	Jan. 2008	Marwan ELKHOURY	Credit rating agencies and their potential impact on developing countries
No. 185	July 2007	Robert HOWSE	The concept of odious debt in public international law
No. 184	May 2007	André NASSIF	National innovation system and macroeconomic policies: Brazil and India in comparative perspective
No. 183	April 2007	Irfan ul HAQUE	Rethinking industrial policy
No. 182	Oct. 2006	Robert ROWTHORN	The renaissance of China and India: implications for the advanced economies
No. 181	Oct. 2005	Michael SAKBANI	A re-examination of the architecture of the international economic system in a global setting: issues and proposals
No. 180	Oct. 2005	Jörg MAYER and Pilar FAJARNES	Tripling Africa's primary exports: What? How? Where?
No. 179	April 2005	S.M. SHAFAEDDIN	Trade liberalization and economic reform in developing countries: structural change or de-industrialization
No. 178	April 2005	Andrew CORNFORD	Basel II: the revised framework of June 2004
No. 177	April 2005	Benu SCHNEIDER	Do global standards and codes prevent financial crises? Some proposals on modifying the standards-based approach
No. 176	Dec. 2004	Jörg MAYER	Not totally naked: textiles and clothing trade in a quota free environment
No. 175	Aug. 2004	S.M. SHAFAEDDIN	Who is the master? Who is the servant? Market or Government?
No. 174	Aug. 2004	Jörg MAYER	Industrialization in developing countries: some evidence from a new economic geography perspective
No. 173	June 2004	Irfan ul HAQUE	Globalization, neoliberalism and labour
No. 172	June 2004	Andrew CORNFORD	The WTO negotiations on financial services: current issues and future directions
No. 171	May 2004	Andrew CORNFORD	Variable geometry for the WTO: concepts and precedents

UNCTAD Discussion Papers

No. 170	May 2004	Robert ROWTHORN and Ken COUTTS	De-industrialization and the balance of payments in advanced economies
No. 169	April 2004	Shigehisa KASAHARA	The flying geese paradigm: a critical study of its application to East Asian regional development
No. 168	Feb. 2004	Alberto GABRIELE	Policy alternatives in reforming power utilities in developing countries: a critical survey
No. 167	Jan. 2004	R. KOZUL-WRIGHT and P. RAYMENT	Globalization reloaded: an UNCTAD perspective
No. 166	Feb. 2003	Jörg MAYER	The fallacy of composition: a review of the literature
No. 165	Nov. 2002	Yuefen LI	China's accession to WTO: exaggerated fears?
No. 164	Nov. 2002	Lucas ASSUNCAO and ZhongXiang ZHANG	Domestic climate change policies and the WTO
No. 163	Nov. 2002	A.S. BHALLA and S. QIU	China's WTO accession. Its impact on Chinese employment
No. 162	July 2002	P. NOLAN and J. ZHANG	The challenge of globalization for large Chinese firms
No. 161	June 2002	Zheng ZHIHAI and Zhao YUMIN	China's terms of trade in manufactures, 1993–2000
No. 160	June 2002	S.M. SHAFAEDDIN	The impact of China's accession to WTO on exports of developing countries
No. 159	May 2002	J. MAYER, A. BUTKEVICIUS and A. KADRI	Dynamic products in world exports
No. 158	April 2002	Yilmaz AKYÜZ and Korkut BORATAV	The making of the Turkish financial crisis
No. 157	Nov. 2001	Heiner FLASSBECK	The exchange rate: Economic policy tool or market price?
No. 156	Aug. 2001	Andrew CORNFORD	The Basel Committee's proposals for revised capital standards: Mark 2 and the state of play
No. 155	Aug. 2001	Alberto GABRIELE	Science and technology policies, industrial reform and technical progress in China: Can socialist property rights be compatible with technological catching up?
No. 154	June 2001	Jörg MAYER	Technology diffusion, human capital and economic growth in developing countries

* * * * * *

UNCTAD Discussion Papers are available on the website at: www.unctad.org. Copies of *UNCTAD Discussion Papers* may be obtained from the Publications Assistant, Macroeconomic and Development Policies Branch, Division on Globalization and Development Strategies, United Nations Conference on Trade and Development (UNCTAD), Palais des Nations, CH-1211 Geneva 10, Switzerland; fax +41-22-917-0274.

QUESTIONNAIRE

Trade and Development Report, 2009

In order to improve the quality and relevance of the Trade and Development Report, the UNCTAD secretariat would greatly appreciate your views on this publication. Please complete the following questionnaire and return it to:

Readership Survey
Division on Globalization and Development Strategies
UNCTAD
Palais des Nations, Room E.10009
CH-1211 Geneva 10, Switzerland
Fax: (+41) (0)22 917 0274
E-mail: tdr@unctad.org

Thank you very much for your kind cooperation.

1. What is your assessment of this publication?　　*Excellent*　　*Good*　　*Adequate*　　*Poor*

	Excellent	Good	Adequate	Poor
Overall	☐	☐	☐	☐
Relevance of issues	☐	☐	☐	☐
Analytical quality	☐	☐	☐	☐
Policy conclusions	☐	☐	☐	☐
Presentation	☐	☐	☐	☐

2. What do you consider the strong points of this publication?

    _____
    _____
    _____

3. What do you consider the weak points of this publication?

    _____
    _____
    _____

4. For what main purposes do you use this publication?

    Analysis and research ☐　　　　Education and training ☐
    Policy formulation and management ☐　　　　Other (*specify*) _____

5. Which of the following best describes your area of work?

    Government ☐　　　　Public enterprise ☐
    Non-governmental organization ☐　　　　Academic or research ☐
    International organization ☐　　　　Media ☐
    Private enterprise institution ☐　　　　Other (*specify*) _____

6. Name and address of respondent (*optional*):

    _____
    _____
    _____

7. Do you have any further comments?

    _____
    _____
    _____